MODELS
OF
BUYER
BEHAVIOR

Harper & Row's
Series in Marketing Management
Jagdish N. Sheth, Editor

Concepts of Marketing Management
Joseph C. Seibert

Marketing Research: Management and Methods
Walter B. Wentz

Society and Marketing: An Unconventional View
Norman Kangun

MODELS OF BUYER BEHAVIOR

CONCEPTUAL, QUANTITATIVE, AND EMPIRICAL

JAGDISH N. SHETH

University of Illinois
at Urbana

HARPER & ROW, PUBLISHERS
NEW YORK, EVANSTON, SAN FRANCISCO, LONDON

Sponsoring Editor: John Greenman
Project Editor: William B. Monroe
Designer: Michel Craig
Production Supervisor: Stefania J. Taflinska

Models of Buyer Behavior: Conceptual, Quantitative, and Empirical

Library of Congress Cataloging in Publication Data

Sheth, Jagdish N
    Models of buyer behavior: conceptual, quantitative,
and empirical.

    (Series in marketing management)
    Bibliography: p.
    1. Consumers—Addresses, essays, lectures.
2. Consumers—Mathematical models—Addresses, essays,
lectures. 3. Market segmentation—Addresses, essays,
lectures. I. Title.
HF5415.3.S52   658.8′34   74-6119
ISBN 0-06-046092-X

CONTENTS

PREFACE

This book represents efforts by several well-known scholars in marketing to extend our knowledge in consumer psychology toward the development of comprehensive models and theories related to specific aspects of buyer behavior. It therefore goes beyond the popular textbooks such as Engel, Blackwell, and Kollat's *Consumer Behavior* (1968) and the well-known specific theories such as Howard and Sheth's *The Theory of Buyer Behavior* (1969). In fact, it is my hope that this book will become a good supplement to other books both in advanced undergraduate and in graduate courses.

WHY THIS BOOK?

Several factors have led me to put time and effort into preparing this book:

1. Very few journals in marketing now find space to print articles that are primarily conceptual and theoretical. Perhaps this is because the current stage of maturity of marketing as a discipline dictates that greater emphasis be placed on strategy of marketing research, methodological issues, and empirical evidence. On the other hand, theoretical writings have their place in any discipline, irrespective of its stage of maturity.

2. Often scholars prefer the freedom of writing what they think rather than being constrained by the editorial policies of scholarly journals or the biases of the referees. This is especially

true when one is attempting to synthesize existing knowledge and to develop a comprehensive model of buyer behavior specific to one aspect. It seems that a book or monograph is the only viable medium for the expression of such constraint-free thinking.

3. Any textbook normally lags behind research and thinking by about three to five years. Hence it does not become a viable medium. In a discipline that is mature and stagnant, this lag may not be serious. However, consumer behavior is in such rapid transition that this lag necessitates supplemental volumes such as the present book.

4. Several years ago, I suggested that we have probably behaved like the seven proverbial blind men and the elephant long enough to consciously attempt complex and comprehensive theories of buyer behavior (Sheth, 1967). It is gratifying to see that a number of scholars in the discipline are making a concerted effort to integrate existing knowledge and develop models that envision the world of buyer behavior as the complex mechanism that it really is. This book contains a representative sample of this effort.

The foregoing factors also led to the arranging of two annual conferences at Columbia University under the leadership of John A. Howard. Most of the papers in this book were prepared explicitly for these conferences.

A TEASER

I have deliberately neglected to include abstracts or lengthy summaries of the various parts of the book, hoping that the interested reader will go through the authors' papers and not rely on summaries. As a teaser, I describe below the format and structure of the book, allowing the reader to go directly to any particular paper.

The book consists of 21 papers, mostly written individually by well-known scholars in buyer behavior and marketing. The papers are divided into five parts.

Part I contains Armstrong's views on the philosophical and pragmatic strategy of conducting research to validate constructs and a network of constructs that constitutes a theory.

Part II consists of 12 articles dealing with comprehensive models of buyer behavior. Section A contains three papers that present conceptual models. It includes Sheth's theory of family buying decisions, Lunn's evaluation of decision process as central to modeling buyer behavior, and Carman's inductive effort to generate and synthesize constructs related to buying behavior from studies on grocery stores.

Section B includes three papers representing quantitative modeling of buyer behavior. Sexton describes simulation of consumers at a micro level to incorporate individual psychological processes and constructs. Haines examines the information-processing viewpoint and attempts to quantify the sequential decision rules to produce a measure of attitude. Finally, Kernan, in a unique mixture of decision making under uncertainty and information theory, presents a stochastic approach to buyer behavior.

Section C contains six papers, all dealing with empirical verification of comprehensive models of buyer behavior. Some of these papers have been published in edited forms in scholarly journals. The first paper by Farley and Ring is an ingenious attempt to translate the Howard-Sheth theory of buyer behavior in terms of a simultaneous-equations model. However, its validation with a data bank generated by the Columbia Buyer Behavior Project raises a number of problems related to establishing rules of correspondence between the hypothetical constructs of the theory and the reality of the marketplace. Howard's paper is an attempt to examine in depth and to validate with data the hypothetical construct called Confidence in the Howard-Sheth theory of buyer behavior. Those familiar with that theory will remember that the two authors disagree on the role of Confidence in their own theory. The paper by O'Shaughnessy represents a unique effort to theorize and develop a model of personal communication in a dyadic situation based on research findings in experimental mass communication. The model is explicitly utilized to study the interaction between a prospective car buyer and the automobile dealer.

In his paper, Day presents a model of the relative contribution of word-of-mouth sources, in contrast to mass media, in buyers' decisions. Although the paradigm is not original, its validation with the use of data collected at Columbia University, based on the Howard-Sheth theory, is indeed innovative in design and in results. The paper by Alexis summarizes long-term joint research on inner-city buyers conducted at University of Rochester. Although the paper does not provide a comprehensive theory of inner-city buyer behavior, it supplies rich evidence on the mediating influence of income and physical mobility on buying behavior. Finally, Sheth describes a model of the attitude-behavior

relationship and tests it on data collected at Columbia University
with the use of canonical correlation analysis. The study
demonstrates the critical influence of situational factors on
attitude and purchase behavior.

Part III puts together comprehensive models of innovative
behavior and adoption process. Section A contains Robertson's
review paper, which critically examines numerous paradigms
presented in rural sociology, mass communication, and marketing.
He concludes that the adoption process cannot be put into a
straitjacket consisting of specific stages of the decision-making
process. Section B contains a paper on quantitative models of new
product adoption and diffusion. Charnes et al. describe the
planning and application of the famous DEMON model developed
at BBD&O. This paper focuses on the recursive regression
approach to measuring the effect of advertising. Section C
includes three papers dealing with empirical testing of adoption
process models. Robertson's paper describes a study of group
influence on the innovative behavior of members of the group
based on theories of Homans and Festinger in social psychology.
Arndt examines the interplay of individual buyers' innovativeness,
opinion leadership, prior learning, and perceived risk in the
adoption of soft margarine, electric toothbrushes and electric
dishwashers. Finally, Ehrenberg and Goodhardt examine the history
of repeat buying of new brands and provide a number of
intervening variables useful in bettering prediction of new
production adoption.

Part IV includes papers that furnish models of consumer
typology and market segmentation. The paper by Ramond
and Assael is an effort to provide product typology based on the
interaction of consumer behavior and physical distribution. The
paper is unique inasmuch as it takes an aggregate view of
customers instead of investigating individual customer's behavior
or psychological process. The second paper, written by Myers,
attempts to provide customer typology based on the author's
I/E paradigm, which is designed to give a typology based on
interaction of the individual consumer with his social environment.

Part V contains a speculative analysis of the changes that
are likely to emerge in buyer behavior theory and research.
It is concluded that just as marketing divorced itself from economics,
we are likely to see buyer behavior divorcing itself from
marketing, to establish its own identity as a social science
discipline.

In addition to the 21 papers, the book contains an extensive reference bibliography related to comprehensive models of buyer behavior. The bibliography is both heterogeneous and comprehensive. I hope the reader will find it useful.

ACKNOWLEDGMENTS, DEDICATION, AND ALL THAT

There are no specific individuals or entities who deserve separate acknowledgments because no one has contributed extraordinarily or in a special way toward preparing this volume. Needless to say, this book would not have come into existence without the participation and contribution of scholars who have written or coauthored various papers contained in the book.

I similarly find no one to whom this volume should be dedicated. Nor do I think it is necessary to dedicate everything that is published in marketing. Who started that practice anyway? I have often wondered how the person to whom the book was dedicated reacts if the book turns out to be a bomb!

JAGDISH N. SHETH

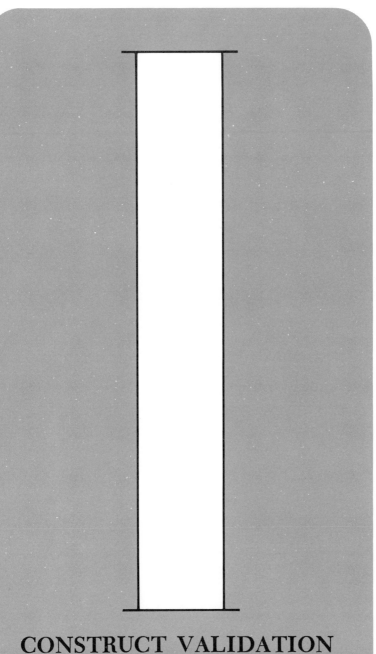

CONSTRUCT VALIDATION
IN MODEL
DEVELOPMENT

*Far better an approximate answer to the right
question which is often vague than an exact
answer to the wrong question which can always
be made precise (Tukey, 1962).*

1

ECLECTIC RESEARCH AND
CONSTRUCT VALIDATION

J. SCOTT ARMSTRONG
*Associate Professor of Marketing
Wharton School
University of Pennsylvania*

Consider the following situation: You have a fixed budget and would
like to measure causal relationships in a study involving buyer behavior. How would you go about allocating the budget for this
study?

This paper outlines two possible research strategies—*intensive
research* and *eclectic research*. Each strategy utilizes the budget in
a different manner. The intensive approach involves allocating the
budget to a single study, and the eclectic approach divides the
budget among a series of smaller-scale studies that differ markedly
from one another.

Intensive research is called for when problems of *reliability*
are of utmost concern; eclectic research is called for when problems
of *construct validity* are paramount. Since we believe that problems
of construct validity deserve more attention than they currently
receive for problems in nonexperimental research, we advocate
stronger emphasis on eclectic research.

RELIABILITY AND VALIDITY:
SOME WORKING DEFINITIONS

It is important to differentiate the concept of construct validity
from that of reliability. Construct validity asks essentially whether·

the operational measure of a relationship measures what it purports to measure. Reliability, on the other hand, asks whether the operational measure produces similar results when the measurement is replicated.[1] In practice, the distinction is not always easy to make. One way of making this distinction is adapted from D. T. Campbell and Fiske (1959).[2] They expanded on a definition that apparently drew from Thurstone (1937). Thus *reliability* is seen as the agreement among two or more operational measures of a relationship through *approaches that are as similar as possible*. In other words, reliability asks for replication when no relevant factors are altered. *Construct validity* is seen as the agreement between two or more operational measures of a relationship through approaches that are *as different as possible*.

These concepts are illustrated in Figure 1.1. Approaches x_1 and x_2 are similar. Agreement between these approaches would be termed as evidence of reliability. The same is true for the agreement between approaches x_3 and x_4. Approaches x_1 and x_3 are rather different, however, as are x_2 and x_4 or x_2 and x_3. The agreement among these "different" approaches is termed evidence of construct validity.

"Shotguns Versus Rifles"

In the social sciences, it is usually difficult to devise realistic experiments. As a result, there is a heavy dependence on the use of nonexperimental data. Results from nonexperimental data are, however, subject to interpretation by any one of a large number of hypotheses. In terms of Figure 1.1, there is only a weak correspondence between any one estimate (e.g., x_1) and X, the true relationship. If the correspondence between x_1 and X is weak, a highly reliable estimate of x_1 may be of little value. This could yield a highly reliable estimate of the *wrong* value.

A familiar analogy may help to clarify the above. Assume that a hunter is about to shoot a bird, but he cannot see his target. However, he does know the general location of the target because he saw the bird go into a bush, can hear the bird, and can see branches moving. Since it is getting late, he decides to try to shoot the bird. The question he now faces is whether to use his rifle or his shotgun.

If he uses the rifle, there appears to be a very strong likelihood that he will miss his target altogether and the bird will fly away. If

---

[1] See, for example, Selltiz, Jahoda, Deutsch, and Cook (1959) for a more complete discussion of reliability and construct validity.

[2] This paper is concerned with the measurement of *relationships* between variables, rather than the measurement of variables.

| Construct or conceptual relationship (not directly observable) | Typical observable data (from which estimates of the construct may be obtained) |

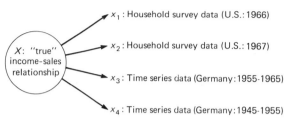

x_1 : Household survey data (U.S.: 1966)

x_2 : Household survey data (U.S.: 1967)

X: "true" income-sales relationship

x_3 : Time series data (Germany: 1955-1965)

x_4 : Time series data (Germany: 1945-1955)

Figure 1.1 Measurement of a Hypothetical Construct

he were to hit the bird, of course, it is very likely that the shot would be fatal. If he loads the shotgun with buckshot, he is more likely to hit the bird, but the blast may not kill the prey. By wounding the bird, however, he will get further information on its location and can then move in to capture it.

The rifle is analogous to the use of intensive research. When aimed precisely, it does the job and with little waste. Poorly aimed, however, it does little good at all. The shotgun, like eclectic research, is likely to do some good if aimed in the *general* direction of the target. It may down the bird or at least slow it and allow for a second shot.

THE NEED FOR ECLECTIC
RESEARCH IN THE SOCIAL SCIENCES

Social scientists often use the physical sciences as an ideal in considerations of research methodology, but this approach has shortcomings. In realistic experiments performed in the physical sciences, the correspondence between the operational measure and the construct can be rather close. The "target" is easier to see than it is in the social sciences. In this situation, the intensive approach (the rifle) is useful.

Seldom is the correspondence between operational measure and construct so clear-cut in the social sciences. The social sciences must utilize nonexperimental data, which are subject to a substantial amount of measurement error. Even economics, one of the more highly developed of the social sciences, must draw heavily on nonexperimental data of low reliability (e.g., see Morganstern, 1963).

The lack of correspondence between a construct and its measure implies that construct validation should receive much at-what is now considered to be a classic on construct validity in psychological tests. In a somewhat different context, Payne (1951) pointed out that problems with (construct) validity seem to be far more important than problems with reliability in the wording of survey questions. More recently, Webb et al. (1966) based their arguments for the selection of "unobtrusive measures" on the notion of construct validity. Mayer and Brown (1965) attempt to direct attention toward "non-sampling errors" (related to our use of construct validity) in sample surveys. S. W. Cook and Selltiz (1964) and Curtis and Jackson (1962) discuss the assessment of construct validation in attitude measurement.

Problems with construct validation, then, have been noted in tention in the social sciences. Cronbach and Meehl (1955) presented various ways by numerous social scientists. If we view eclectic research at one end of a continuum and intensive research at the other, this concern argues for an increased emphasis on eclectic research in the social sciences.[3] The same concern seems to be less evident in the physical sciences; in fact, the opposite approach was advocated by Bridgman (1927): "If we have more than one set of operations, we have more than one concept, and strictly there should be a separate name to correspond to each different set of operations."

The State of the Art

Despite the concern of numerous writers about the importance of assessing construct validity, most published studies today are intensive rather than eclectic. My impression is that the reward structure in our research institutions is strongly oriented toward intensive research.

Intensive research calls for the specialist, who typically has expensive equipment, elaborate experiments, or large samples. His team is composed of specialists in the same field. The specialist is the man who understands and can argue for expensive equipment or large-scale surveys. He finds it easier to publish his results, since journals are usually organized by rather narrow technical areas, and editors appear to judge the reliability rather than the validity of a finding.

Eclectic research calls for the generalist, who has an interdisciplinary staff and spreads his budget to get by with makeshift equipment, crude experiments, or small samples.

[3] D. T. Campbell and Fiske (1959) make a strong argument for an eclectic approach. They refer to this strategy as "multiple operationalism," "methodological triangulation," "convergent operationalism," "operational delineation," or "convergent validation."

Although the individual scientist may be motivated to emphasize the reliability of a relationship rather than its construct validity, the history of science depends quite heavily on the use of construct validity. A researcher will start with a relationship and demonstrate its applicability in a very limited context. Later researchers may show that the relationship has more generality by finding evidence for it in other situations. Alternatively, the additional research may serve to define the limits to which the relationship may be generalized; for example, Newtonian concepts of time and space are useful on earth but alternative theories prove more valuable elsewhere. Or perhaps the additional studies show that the original relationship was spurious.

Thus, while the demonstration of construct validity is regarded as something that is good for *science*, it does not seem to be regarded as a good strategy for the individual *scientist*. The emphasis among individual scientists is on demonstrating reliability rather than construct validity.

VELIKOVSKY: A CRITICAL
CASE FOR ECLECTIC RESEARCH

To demonstrate the value of eclectic research when nonexperimental data are involved, a critical case is presented. The case is "critical" in that the theories generated by the eclectic research *differ drastically from those generated by intensive research*. In addition, this case is well documented, and more recent evidence allows us to compare the predictive validity of the theories generated by each approach.

The eclectic research was carried out by Immanuel Velikovsky (1950), whose theories demonstrated high construct validity but not high reliability. The existing theories, on the other hand, demonstrated high reliability and low construct validity. Velikovsky used historical papers and cultural artifacts to develop theories about the history of the earth. These documents, such as the Bible, are regarded by most scientists as being so unreliable that they are unworthy of use in the development of scientific theory. For example, any passage in the Bible is subject to almost as many interpretations as there are interpreters. Since somewhat different explanations are given by each interpreter, the source itself may be said to have low reliability.

Velikovsky's theories about the history of the earth are supported by evidence from the Bible, Greek mythology, ancient calendars, and geological findings. His approach uses unreliable data and encompasses many different scientific disciplines.

Velikovsky proposes that there were some catastrophic events in the history of the world. These events, such as the near-collision of Venus and Earth about 1500 B.C., had such a great effect on our planet that there was no need for highly reliable instruments to record the events. Everyone on earth was aware of what was happening. Velikovsky (1950) summarizes his argument:

> If a phenomena has been similarly described by many peoples,
> we might suspect that a tale, originating with one people
> had spread around the world, and consequently there is
> no proof of the authenticity of the event related. But just
> because one and the same event is embodied in traditions
> that are very different indeed, its authenticity becomes highly
> probable, especially if the records of history, ancient charts,
> sundials, and the physical evidence of natural history
> testify to the same effect [p. 308].[4]

Velikovsky's use of extremely different approaches, or eclectic research, to test his theory did not impress the scientific community. In fact, prominent scientists mounted an active and somewhat successful campaign to suppress the publication of Velikovsky's theories. The stated reasons for this attack involved primarily the theoretician's "lack of scientific method" and his failure to be an "expert" in each of the fields affected by his theories. The history of this case is summarized in *The Velikovsky Affair* (de Grazia et al., 1967).

The power of Velikovsky's approach, which we call eclectic research, has been demonstrated over the past two decades. Velikovsky made a series of very different predictions based on his theory. Most of these predictions were labeled impossible in the light of existing theories. Recent evidence from space probes and other sources has confirmed many of the predictions, however, and no prediction has yet been proved incorrect. A summary of the cases that support the predictive validity of Velikovsky's theories is presented in de Grazia et al. (1967). The predictions that have received support include the high temperature of Venus, the existence of electromagnetic fields in the solar system, the possibility that the length of the day (on Earth) may change, the likelihood of radio noises from Jupiter, the presence of hydrocarbons in the atmosphere of Venus, the rather recent age of oil deposits in the Gulf of Mexico, the likelihood that signs of advanced human culture would be found

---

[4] See also the last three paragraphs of Chapter 12 in Velikovsky (1955) for a similar argument.

in uninhabited areas of northeastern Siberia, and the age of the ancient civilization of Mexico.

In summary, Velikovsky made dramatic use of "different approaches" or eclectic research. That eclectic research led to accurate predictions of phenomena that had not been previously obvious testifies to the power of this strategy (as well as to the usefulness of nonexperimental data and, of course, to Velikovsky himself). The history of this case also demonstrates that eclectic research is not a well-accepted research strategy.

ECLECTIC RESEARCH IN
A STUDY OF BUYER BEHAVIOR

Most of what we know about buyer behavior comes from studies of nonexperimental data, and the vast majority of these studies are based on a single approach; in short, eclectic research seems to receive little use.

In this study, two simple but specific relationships were examined. The first was the relationship between buying power and the purchase of cameras, which is referred to as the *income-sales relationship*. The second considers the relationship between the price of cameras and the purchase of cameras, which is referred to as the *price-sales relationship*. These two studies are presented to indicate an operational procedure for interpreting the results of eclectic research and to examine the importance of eclectic research in the study of buyer behavior.

The Income-Sales Relationship

Four different approaches were used to measure the income elasticity for camera sales. The approaches differed because each used a different type of data:

Subjective Data. Previous studies of other durable goods (e.g., automobiles and refrigerators) were used to provide a subjective estimate of the income elasticity of camera sales. This estimate was made prior to the analysis of the camera sales data gathered for this study. The subjective analysis serves to force the researcher to specify what he thinks he knows about the relationships that he will study. The subjective estimates vary from one researcher to another, but the researcher must start with a well-defined hypothesis.

Cross-Sectional Data (Differences Among 12,000 Households in the United States, 1960–1961). Data on income and dollar purchases of cameras were analyzed for households, which were grouped into

TABLE 1.1
ALTERNATIVE MEASURES OF CONFIDENCE FOR THE
INCOME-SALES RELATIONSHIP

SOURCE OF ESTIMATE	TYPE OF MEASURE	STANDARD ERROR
Subjective analysis	Reliability	0.2
Household survey data	Reliability	0.2
International cross section	Reliability	0.1
Longitudinal data over countries	Reliability	1.0
Comparisons among all the above	Construct validity	0.4[a]

[a] Represents the standard deviation among the expected values from each of the four estimates.

six income categories. In these data, the camera supply factors were relatively constant for all households; that is, the price at which cameras were offered for sale did not vary across households. The model that was used to explain differences among households accounted for age and education as well as the income of the household head.

Cross-Sectional Data (Differences Among Countries). Data from 19 countries were examined. The model for explaining differences among countries used not only a measure of buying power but also eight other variables, including the price of cameras, the population, and the climate. These data were based on averages from the period 1960–1965.

Longitudinal Data Across Countries. Data on the *changes* in sales rates from 1961 to 1965 were obtained for 21 countries. Differences among the various countries on the amount of change were explained by a model that incorporated measures of income, price, and population.

Each of the above types of data has its own advantages; for example, cross-sectional data over households are useful for assessing the income elasticity, since their incomes vary greatly. Rather than select the "best data," however, the emphasis was on using many types of data in studying the same parameter.

Figure 1.2 presents the results of the four different approaches, as well as a measure of the confidence interval for each estimate. All estimates except the subjective estimate were obtained from

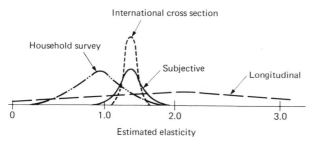

Figure 1.2 Confidence Intervals for Estimates of Relationship Between Income and Sales

multiple regression analyses.[5] As indicated previously, an attempt was made to include all important variables in each regression model to measure the effect on sales due to income alone.[6]

Each confidence interval was derived from the standard error of the estimate for the income coefficient, except of course for the subjective data. These standard errors correspond to measures of reliability.

Figure 1.2 shows a fair amount of agreement among the various estimates. For example, a "true" income elasticity of 1.3 would not be inconsistent with any of the estimated confidence intervals. Another way to examine the same data is presented in Table 1.1, which summarizes the measures of the confidence that one might have in each estimate of the income-sales relationship. The reliability estimates are again the standard errors around the income coefficients from each model. The construct validity estimate was obtained in a crude and simple fashion by taking the expected value (i.e., the regression coefficient for income) from each approach and estimating the standard deviation among these four values.

The rather common practice of using the standard error (a reliability estimate) as *the* measure of confidence in a research report can be misleading if there is a high likelihood that the estimate lacks construct validity (i.e., is biased). The measure used for construct validity in Table 1.1 represents an attempt to assess the amount of bias in the estimates. Therefore, we suggest that the

[5] The details of these analyses, which are not important to the argument, can be found in Armstrong (1968). One defect of the eclectic approach, however, is that it would be rather difficult to describe a number of approaches in a single journal article.

[6] See J. R. Meyer and Kuh (1957) for a discussion of the factors that may lead to differences between estimates obtained from time series and from cross-sectional data.

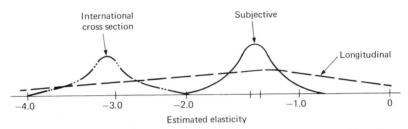

Figure 1.3 Confidence Intervals for Estimates of Relationship Between Price and Sales

research report contain *both* measures of reliability and measures of construct validity, the latter being of special importance.[7]

The results on the income-sales relationship provide evidence for high reliability and high construct validity. Further research in this area, if deemed necessary, might follow an intensive strategy (especially regarding the longitudinal data) or an eclectic strategy (to find still other types of data).

The Price-Sales Relationship

A similar analysis was used to examine the relationship between the price of cameras (an industry index) and the purchase rate of cameras. With one exception, which involved household survey data, the approaches used for the income-sales relationship were also useful for the price-sales relationship. (Since the price at which cameras were sold did not vary according to household, there was no way to obtain an estimate of price elasticity from these data.)

The three different estimates for the price-sales relationship are presented in Figure 1.3. In contrast to the income-sales study, it is difficult to find a single estimate that would be consistent with each of the confidence intervals. Thus we would say that the estimates do not show evidence of high construct validity. The measures of confidence are also summarized in Table 1.2.

Eclectic research led to conclusions quite different from those that would have been reached if intensive research had been used. The estimate of construct validity of the price-sales relationship indicates *much more* uncertainty about the true value than does any one of the reliability estimates. We are not confident about our ability to use the price elasticity estimate in generalizing to other

---

[7] One may also desire an overall index of confidence, such as the mean square error. The *mean square error* makes an explicit attempt to include problems of both reliability (variance about the sample mean) and construct validity (bias).

TABLE 1.2
ALTERNATIVE MEASURES OF CONFIDENCE FOR
THE PRICE-SALES RELATIONSHIP

SOURCE OF ESTIMATE	TYPE OF MEASURE	STANDARD ERROR
Subjective analysis	Reliability	0.2
International cross section	Reliability	0.3
Longitudinal data over countries	Reliability	1.0
Comparisons among all the above	Construct validity	1.7

situations (e.g., for forecasting changes in sales over time). Since the estimates themselves are biased, it is unlikely that the problems with the estimates of price elasticity could be resolved by improving the *reliability* of the existing estimates.

Since we are unable to *control* the sources of bias in nonexperimental data, we must find ways to compensate for their effects. Although a strategy of using more intensive research has some merit (e.g., to ensure that all relevant variables have been included in the international cross section), the most obvious course of action would be to employ more eclectic research. We should find still different approaches, which might include time series data from the United States, household expenditure data from Europe, consumer panel data from the United States, shopping experiments, or consumer intentions surveys.

Conclusions

The studies on income-sales and the price-sales relationships demonstrated the use of eclectic research. In particular, the agreement among the expected values of a given parameter as measured by different approaches was used to assess construct validity. The standard deviation among these values served as a summary statistic for construct validity.

These investigations, especially the study of the price-sales relationship, supported the notion that problems with construct validity are serious. Measures of reliability did not adequately reflect the uncertainty in the estimates. It is especially useful, then, if some measure of construct validity is provided in published studies on buyer behavior.

SUMMARY

Intensive research is a strategy used to demonstrate that the findings from a study are reliable. *Eclectic research* is a strategy that tries to demonstrate that the findings from a study have construct validity. These strategies represent extreme points on a continuum, with the intensive side advocating that the research budget be spent on a single study and the eclectic side favoring a large variety of small-scale studies.

This paper argued that research in the social sciences, which must depend heavily on nonexperimental data, should place more emphasis on eclectic research than on intensive research.

The research of Velikovsky was mentioned to illustrate the power of eclectic research. This example provided a critical test for the eclectic approach, since the predictions generated by this approach differed greatly from those obtained by intensive research. Recent evidence suggests that the superiority of the eclectic approach was proved dramatically in this case.

Finally, eclectic research was applied to a study of buyer behavior. A simple operational procedure was suggested for using the results to assess construct validity. The results supported (1) the idea that problems with construct validity are of great importance, and (2) the argument that greater use should be made of eclectic research when nonexperimental data are involved. It was also suggested that published studies of relationships involving buyer behavior should present evidence of construct validity.

COMPREHENSIVE MODELS
OF
BUYER BEHAVIOR

A
CONCEPTUAL MODELS

2

A THEORY OF FAMILY BUYING DECISIONS

JAGDISH N. SHETH
Professor of Business
Department of Business Administration
University of Illinois at Urbana-Champaign

Family decision making is probably unique among research areas of the social sciences in that several disciplines have contributed to its development—rural sociology, social anthropology, social psychology, clinical psychology, home economics, consumer psychology, marketing, and economics. Diverse disciplines are interested in family decision making largely because the entire social structure in the Western world rests on the composition, maintenance, and survival of the family unit. In addition, from birth until death most decisions and consequent behaviors of individuals are anchored to the family. Consequently, family decision making enjoys a long tradition of research.

This paper presents a comprehensive theory of family decision making in consumer behavior. A theory in general serves any of the following functions: (1) the *descriptive function*, in which it describes and narrates a phenomenon with the use of a set of constructs or categories; (2) the *delimiting function*, by which it explicitly states the purpose of the theory, hence specifies what it does not include; (3) the *generative function*, which indicates the extent of speculation, inventiveness, and creativity a theory provides; and (4) the *integrative function*, in which the theory attempts to reconcile a variety of findings and thoughts by a network of constructs (Howard and Sheth, 1969, chap. 1). Since family decision making is a well-researched area, the first and the third functions are already being performed by others. However, the second and the fourth functions warrant some attention because little has been done in the area of consumer behavior to specify the purpose and nature of family decision making and to integrate existing thinking. Accordingly, this theory is an attempt to specify the perimeters of family decision making in consumer behavior and to integrate diverse findings by means of a nomological network of constructs. It appears to me that no other area of consumer behavior is as well prepared for such an integrative effort as family decision making.

REVIEW OF FAMILY DECISION MAKING

In developing the theory of family decision making, one is struck with the variety of perspectives that researchers have taken and the variety of findings that have emerged. This section briefly reviews the current thinking and knowledge.

Approaches to Family Decision Making

Most of the approaches to family decision making can be summarized in the following categories:

Macro Versus Micro Approach. Economics, social anthropology, and marketing have tended to take a macro approach in which households, rather than members of the household, are the primary units of observation and investigation (Alexander, 1947; W. Bell, 1958; David, 1962; Ferber, 1962; Foote, 1961; H. D. Meyer, 1957; Oeser and Emery, 1954; Shaffer, 1963; Wolgast, 1957; Young, 1952; Young and Willmott, 1957; Zimmerman, 1947; Zober, 1964). On the other hand, rural sociology, consumer psychology, and clinical psychology have generally adopted a micro approach, in which the major thrust was observing and investigating the interaction processes among members of the family (Alderson, 1957a; Blood and Wolfe, 1960; Bott, 1957; Bortel and Gross, 1954; Foote and Cottrell, 1955; Gilbert, 1957; Kenkel, 1966; Kirkpatrick, 1963; Nicosia, 1966; Olsen, 1956–1957; Parsons and Bales, 1955). These two approaches have polarized thinking and findings that are otherwise interrelated.

Descriptive Versus Determinative Approach. Some researchers have been interested primarily in observing and empirically describing the phenomenon of family decision making (Alderson, 1957a; Berry and Pollay, 1968; Bortel and Gross, 1954; Ferreira and Winter, 1965;

Glick, 1947; Kirkpatrick, 1963; O'Rourke, 1963; Shaffer, 1963; Wolgast, 1958). No attempt is made to examine the determinants of observed phenomenon. Others have hypothesized a variety of determinants, including personality, family orientations, and childhood upbringing and background, to explain the interactive processes and the development of roles among family members (Blood, 1958; Blood and Wolfe, 1960; Bott, 1957; Foote, 1961; Foote and Cottrell, 1955; Heer, 1958; Hoffman, 1960; Ingersoll, 1948; Kenkel, 1961; Kenkel and Hoffman, 1956; K. King, 1967; Komarovsky, 1946, 1961; *Life*, 1965; Lu, 1952; Motz, 1950; Oeser and Emery, 1954; Parsons and Bales, 1955; Strodtbeck, 1954; Weller, 1968; Wilkening and Bharadwaj, 1967; Zimmerman, 1947).

Attitudinal Versus Behavioral Orientation. Most of the research seems to be attitudinal; that is, the verbal responses of the family members have been the basic source of information. The attitudinal approach has generally produced more information that has been useful in examining the causal factors of family decision making. The behavioral orientation has tended to concentrate on the terminal aspects of family decision making that culminate in actual behaviors. Several basic characteristics of terminal behavior are observed and analyzed. For example, the Market Research Corporation of America panel reports weekly on such characteristics as price, brand, store, and quantities of purchases of numerous grocery and personal care products for the family. Attitudinal approaches have also remained largely cross sectional, and behavioral approaches have tended to be continuous observations. There are some recent exceptions, however—notably the General Electric panel and the Berkeley-Illinois panel on household decision making, where both types of information are gathered continuously over time.

Classification of Findings
on Family Decision Making
Research findings on family decision making exist by the hundred in disciplines such as sociology and social psychology. I have attempted to summarize most of the findings in terms of the following categories:

Types of Family Decisions. Most of the research in this area deals with the distinction between buying decisions and comsumption (Alderson, 1957a; Converse and Crawford, 1950; Coulson, 1966; Ferber, 1954; Foote, 1961; Fry, 1967; Gilbert, 1957; Herbst, 1954; Hill, 1958; Howard and Sheth, 1969; *Life*, 1964; Morgan, 1961;

Nicosia, 1966; Shaffer, 1963; Wells, 1966). It is pointed out that one
member, particularly the housewife, may be the buyer, but the
products and services may be consumed either by all the members,
or only by some other member. Specific attention has been paid to
the role of the housewife as a purchasing agent and to the question
of whether some decisions are truly joint among all members of the
family.

In general, the consumption of goods and services is classified
into three types: (1) consumption by individual members themselves, (2) consumption by the whole family jointly, and (3) consumption by the household unit. The third category includes the
accumulation and maintenance of assets, such as a house, a boat,
or household furnishings (Shaffer, 1963).

Process of Family Decision Making. Three distinct aspects of the
process of decision making have received considerable research attention. The first relates to the role structure in decision making
among members of the family. Perhaps the single most consistent
finding is that the husband plays the instrumental (idea man) role
and the wife plays the expressive (emotional) role in family decision
making (Blood and Wolfe, 1960; Burchinal and Bauder, 1965;
Ferreira and Winter, 1965; Hill, 1954; Kenkel, 1961; Komarovsky,
1946; *Life*, 1965; Lu, 1952; Parsons and Bales, 1955; Strodtbeck,
1954). Wolgast (1957, 1958) found that in the joint decision making
of buying automobiles, the husband usually initiated the thought of
buying a new car and the make of the vehicle to be purchased,
while the wife concentrated on the interior features of the car.
Specialization brought about by differential decision making roles
among family members is considered to be significant in minimizing
conflict in this function.

The second aspect involves the pattern of interaction and the
exchange of information among family members (Alderson, 1957a;
Berry and Pollay, 1968; Bott, 1957; G. H. Brown, 1961; Converse
and Crawford, 1950; Coulson, 1966; Foote, 1961; Fry, 1967; Gilbert,
1957; Gisler, 1948; Glock and Nicosia, 1964; Granbois, 1964; Herbst,
1952; Hill, 1958; Kenkel, 1961; *Life*, 1964; Morgan, 1961; Murphy,
1960; Nicosia, 1966; Olsen, 1956–1957; Pollay, 1968; Sharp and Mott,
1956; Strodtbeck, 1954; Wells, 1966; Wilkening, 1958; Wolgast,
1958). Probably the most salient aspect was brought out by Carter
(1954), who suggested that three patterns called individual predominance, group goal facilitation, and sociability are manifested by
small groups, including the family.

The last aspect encompasses the individual differences in

motives, preferences, and even values among family members and their effects on the process of family decision making (Bott, 1957; Clawson, 1961; Coulson, 1966; Fry, 1967; Gilbert, 1957; Morgan, 1961).

Determinants of Family Decision Making. The bulk of the research in the field explores the determinants of family decision making. This exploration has covered a wide territory, ranging from basic personality traits of the spouses to specific life styles of the members (Alexander, 1947; W. Bell, 1958; Bott, 1957; Foote and Cottrell, 1955; Heer, 1958, 1963; Ingersoll, 1948; Komarovsky, 1946, 1961; Lu, 1952; Oeser and Emery, 1954; Parsons and Bales, 1955; Zimmerman, 1947). Kenkel (1957), for example, examined the reinforcing or counteracting effects of dominance, persistence, and self-confidence. The latter characteristic has been treated further by other researchers in terms of specific self-confidence and general self-confidence (see Howard, chap. 9, of this volume). Lu (1952) constructed a scale on which a spouse can be rated dominant, equalitarian, or submissive vis-à-vis the other spouse, and he investigated as many as 11 background factors, such as attachment or conflict with parents and home involvement prior to marriage.

Several studies have, directly or indirectly, examined the status of the wife in a family. Both Converse and Crawford (1950) and Zober (1964) find greater autonomy of the wife among the upper and lower social classes, and less in the middle class. This agrees with Komarovsky's (1961) exhaustive work in this area.

Perhaps the determinant that has attracted the biggest attention is the family's life style. W. Bell (1958), for example, presents a typology of families based on whether familism, career, or consumership are the dominant themes of living. White (1966) names five types of family values: flexible versus rigid, nonevaluative versus evaluative, objective versus family role, emancipated versus limited, and appreciated versus unappreciated. Based on combinations of these values, one family's life style may be quite distinct and different from that of another family. Wilkening (1958, 1964) has investigated familism, integration, and father-centered orientations as manifestations of life style.

In addition, a number of studies have specifically examined factors such as sex (Alexander, 1947; Komarovsky, 1946) social class (W. Bell, 1958; Bortel and Gross, 1954; Glock and Nicosia, 1964; Komarovsky, 1961; Motz, 1950; Oeser and Emery, 1954; Olsen, 1956–1957; Zimmerman, 1947), peer group influences (Neiman, 1954), ethnic background (K. King, 1967), and prior family orienta-

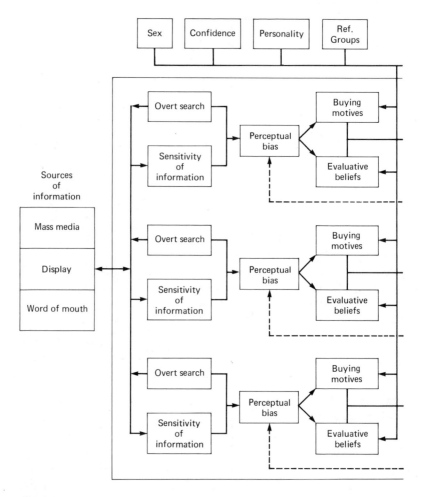

Figure 2.1 A Theory of Family Buying Decisions

tions (Lu, 1952; Wilkening, 1958) as determinants of variety in family decision making.

A THEORY OF
FAMILY DECISION MAKING

After reviewing the existing knowledge on family decision making, I attempted to integrate the findings and thoughts that seem to be intimately related to buying decisions of the family. This integration

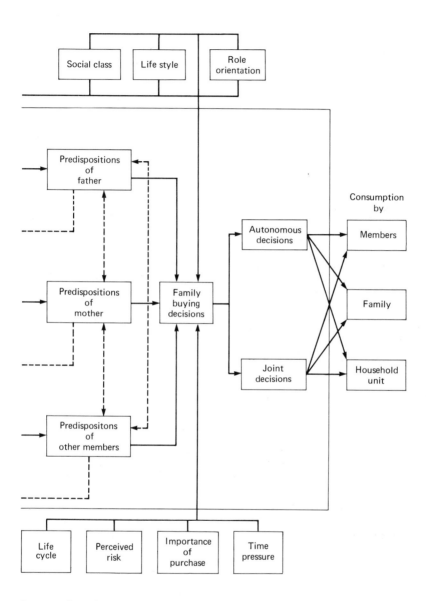

has produced a theory of family buying decisions that is not yet tested in its totality; several parts, however, have substantial empirical evidence. Furthermore, the theory is "static" in that it does not deal yet with *repetitive* family decisions over a period of time. It does, however, examine the process of a specific decision that extends over time.

The theory of family buying decisions is summarized in Figure 2.1. It looks quite similar to the Howard-Sheth (1969) theory of buyer behavior because in fact it is very similar with respect to format; but it is only partly similar with respect to the type of constructs and to their network of relationships. Clearly, the theory is a complex set of interactions among a large number of constructs and also among several individuals. But family decision making is a complex process itself, and to describe it (map it, if you will) mandates the complexity inherent in comprehensiveness. I am, indeed, tempted to repeat my viewpoint on buyer behavior (Sheth, 1967); namely, that if we do not remain farsighted enough to comprehend the totality of a research area, we are liable to resemble the seven proverbial blind men and the elephant. Yet the theory can be somewhat simplified in at least two ways. First, not all the constructs are likely to be active at a point in time, because a number of them are temporally related to one another. Also, several of them can be considered as antecedent conditions for holding constant some of the differences either among families for a specific decision or among decisions of a family. Second, several constructs, particularly the exogenous constructs that surround the rectangular box in Figure 2.1, can be abstracted further into a much smaller set. For example, we may want to lump social class, reference groups, role orientation, and so on, into a grosser construct called "societal values." This would be especially useful for a decision situation in which there are no large differences in the effects of each of the specific exogenous constructs.

Brief Summary of the Theory

Before describing parts of the theory, it may be useful to provide a brief overview, starting with the consumption behavior of the family and working backward toward the buying decisions that determine it.

The total consumption of a family is classified by (1) the individual members, (2) the family as a whole, and (3) the household unit. For example, beer may be used exclusively by the father, hair spray by the mother, and cereals or baby food by the child. On the other hand, vegetables and cake mix may be consumed, after suitable transformation, by everyone. Finally, several items (e.g., paints, wallpaper, lawn mowers) are used by the family indirectly in the process of living in the household shelter unit. This classification of consumption behavior has the advantage of pointing out whether the demand for goods and services is collective and indirect, or otherwise.

The family consumption behavior is considered to be largely the derivative of family buying decisions. Accordingly, consumption of gifts, rentals, and acquisitions by means other than buying are not explicitly taken into account. Family buying decisions are considered to be of two types: autonomous (by a single member) or joint (by several or all members of the family).

If a particular member consumes a product one might think that it would be his autonomous decision to choose a specific brand; however, this is not always true. For quite a number of products, particularly those consumed by children, the buying decisions are made strictly by the mother. In addition, many products are actually bought by the housewife acting as a purchasing agent for all members; thus the consumer member exerts his preferences but does not himself do the buying (Alderson, 1957a; Berry and Pollay, 1968; Coulson, 1966; Gilbert, 1957; Hill, 1958).

On the other hand, the buying decision may be the completely autonomous act of one member, although the consumption is joint by the whole family. It has been found that in grocery and personal care products, where the brand is not visible at the time of consumption (e.g., spaghetti) and where the product has been transformed considerably by the time it is consumed (e.g., cake mix), the housewife is an autonomous buyer for the joint consumption of the family. However, many buying decisions are likely to be joint if the products' consumption is also joint.

Since there is no one-to-one correspondence between the type of consumption and the type of family decision making, it is critical to examine the determinants of joint versus autonomous decision making. According to the theory, determinants of whether a buying decision will be joint or antonomous include the family's social class, role orientation, and life cycle, as well as the relative importance of the purchase, the perceived risk, and the time factor contributing to a buying decision. The first three determinants are not product-specific (although they are family-specific), whereas the last three are product-specific.

An autonomous decision is largely a function of the particular member's predispositions toward specific brands, and these are based on his buying motives and evaluative beliefs about salient alternatives. All the three constructs—predispositions, buying motives, and evaluative beliefs—are aggregately called his cognitive world, relevant to the autonomous buying decision. This concept is based on three factors: (1) the availability of information at the time of decision from a variety of sources, including mass media and word of mouth, and the processing of such information by the individual member to make it congruent with his previously stored knowledge; (2) internal family influence from other members that attempts to revise his buying motives or his evaluative beliefs about alternatives; and (3) a set of antecedent factors, including personality, life style, social class, role orientation, and reference groups, that have exerted considerable influence in the past to mould the individual's cognitive world in a certain biased way.

A member making an autonomous buying decision is likely to take into consideration specific requests and preferences of other members, especially when the latter are likely to participate in the consumption of the products and services to be decided on. Even when he is the only consumer member, he may consider preferences and biases of other members, so that his choice and consumption is consistent with the family's general behavior pattern.

By definition, joint buying decisions are more complex, and perhaps they require more time between initiation and completion. Not only do they result in greater communication among family members, it is probable that they also evoke intermember conflict and its resolution. The theory states that conflict is likely to be caused by the presence in joint decisions of both the necessary condition (of felt need for joint decision making) and sufficient conditions (of differences in goals and perceptions among members). How this conflict is resolved and what benefits or hardships resolution entails are described later.

Description of Parts of the Theory

The theory of family decision making consists of the following meaningful subparts.

1. Individual members of the family, their predispositions, and the underlying cognitive world of buying motives and evaluative beliefs about products and brands.
2. Determinants of the cognitive world of individual members, which are both external and internal.
3. Determinants of autonomous versus joint family decision making.
4. The process of joint decision making, with consequent intermember conflict and its resolution.

A brief description of each of these parts follows.

Cognitive Aspects of Individual Members. The theory classifies family members as husband, wife, and all other members. "All others" usually means children, but the category includes other relatives, such as in-laws. It assumes that two married persons have formed a family unit if and only if they live away from their parents and are not totally dependent on someone else. Accordingly, it excludes a young married couple living with parents in the initial stages of forming a family unit. In such a case, the parents form a family unit in which the young couple are other members.

At a point in time, each member of the family has a set of predispositions, both positive and negative, toward products and specific brands involved in a buying decision. These predispositions are presumed to differ frequently because of differences in motives and perceptions of individual members. For example, in the buying of an automobile, the husband may prefer a medium-priced, full-size sedan; the wife may prefer a low-priced, full-size station wagon, and the teen-age children may prefer a small high-priced, imported sports car. Within each of these types, the members may perceive the benefit of specific cars differently.

A member's predisposition is a function of his buying motives and evaluative perceptions (beliefs) of specific brands in attaining or blocking his buying motives. Motives are the biogenic or psychogenic needs, wants, or desires of the person in purchasing and consuming a product or service. By using the plural, I imply that a person has a *set* of motives in a specific buying situation, and generally these are ordered by him to provide a real motive structure. Buying motives not only impel or arouse behavior, they also direct behavior toward specific alternatives because most buying motives are learned from past experiences and acculturation. For an excellent treatise on motivation, see Cofer and Appley (1964).

Evaluative beliefs about specific brand alternatives (i.e., whether they block or facilitate achievement of buying motives) comprise another determinant of a family member's predisposition. As I have pointed out elsewhere, the evaluative beliefs are a small part of the total cognitive awareness and knowledge about relevant products and brands (Sheth, 1969a, 1971). They consist solely of the person's evaluation of an alternative as a perceived instrument to satisfy a set of motives. Thus evaluative beliefs of an alternative may vary from one member to another, not only because buying motives differ but because members assess the same alternative differently as a perceived instrument to satisfy those motives.

It is easy to see that compared with an individual's buying decisions, family buying decisions tend to be more complex because of the variety of predispositions and the underlying cognitive worlds of family members.

Determinants of Differences in Predispositions. Three factors govern a family member's buying motives, evaluative beliefs, and the consequent predispositions. The first is a series of exogenous constructs (top of rectangular box in Figure 2.1). These consist of the individual member's personality, life style, perception of his social class, and role orientation within the family and reference groups. It would be repetitive to demonstrate how these exogenous conditions determine a person's cognitive world because considerable thinking has been provided in Nicosia (1966) and Howard and Sheth (1969). However, two things should be pointed out. First, the same exogenous constructs are considered to affect members of the family differently. This partly explains the conflicts and incompatibilities existing in most families, even about some fundamental values (Alderson, 1957a). Second, some exogenous constructs are likely to be more homogeneous determinants than others among family members, particularly between spouses. These include life style, social class, and role orientation. By contrast, personality and reference groups are very specific to individual members, hence more heterogeneous in their effects among family members.

A second factor determining the cognitive world of an individual member is the availability during family decision making of information from a variety of sources, including mass media, displays, and word of mouth. However, the sources are seldom equally accessible to all members, who in turn are likely to differ in their sensitivity toward information and in the extent of their overt search for information. Compared with other family members, for example, the husband may easily secure information on a given buying decision from sources near his place of work; he may be more sensitive to printed media and may indulge in greater search prior to making the buying decision. The wife, on the other hand, may readily use displays and broadcast media and may be more sensitive to them than other members. In particular, the family members are likely to be heterogeneous in their sources of word-of-mouth communication.

In addition, each member is likely to process actively sought or passively received information differently from other members because each has different predispositions. The cognitive consistency theorists (S. Feldman,. 1966) tell us that the perceptual distortion of received information is a clear function of existing attitudes and predispositions. This is indicated by the dashed lines from predisposition to the perceptual bias construct in Figure 2.1.

The third factor determining the cognitive world of each member is the family itself. Members of the family interact and influence one another over the life cycle of the family. This, therefore, is an internal determinant in the theory, and it is represented by the dashed lines among the members' predisposition constructs.

Determinants of Autonomous Versus Joint Decision Making. As discussed earlier, all family buying decisions can be classified as autonomous (by any one member) or joint (by all or some members of the family). Many buying decisions are made autonomously by the wife. In quite a few instances, however, the housewife acts merely as a purchasing agent who carries out family members' desires and sometimes their independent decisions (Coulson, 1966). The process of autonomous decision making by any one member is tantamount to individual buyer behavior, which has been extensively examined by others. Accordingly, I have attempted to focus here on joint decision making.

The identification of factors that determine joint decision making among family members is critical. In Figure 2.1 I have isolated these determinants from a variety of sources: social class, role orientation, family life cycle, perceived risk of a decision, importance of the purchase decision, and time pressure felt by family members. Let us briefly discuss the manner in which each determinant enhances or curtails joint decision making in a family.

Social class. A number of studies have clearly indicated that there is greater autonomy of buying decisions among all the members in both the upper and the lower social classes. This, in turn, suggests that the incidence of joint decision making is likely to be greater among middle-class families. Knowing that middle-class families have the least discretionary income and the highest perceived risk (Bauer, 1960), it seems plausible to suppose that there will be greater planning, deliberation, and participation by all members in decision making.

Role orientation. Specific roles are implicitly or explicitly allotted to family members in the process of continuous interaction. The more distinct the allocation of the roles, the greater is the specialization and division of labor in the family. Hence role orientation tends to bring about greater autonomy and less joint decision making. Even in joint decisions among families in which the roles are clearly marked, the participation of each member in the joint decisions may only partly depend on his expertise and specific role. For example, the husband may perform only the function of gathering information on decisions related to home furnishings, thus enabling the wife to decide more rationally.

Life cycle of family. In general, we should expect that the extent of joint decision making will vary inversely with the age of the family. Hence joint decision making is likely to be less prevalent among newly marrieds than among families with children.

Perceived risk in buying decisions. The greater the perceived risk of making a wrong decision for the family, the greater the amount of joint decision making among members of the family. This results primarily because adverse consequences affect the whole family directly or indirectly; hence the members tend to seek support and guidance from one another.

Importance of purchase to family. The greater the importance of a specific buying decision to the family, the more likely it is to be jointly made by all members of the family. Decisions to buy most of the "big ticket" items (major durable appliances, automobiles, and houses) are arrived at jointly by all members of the family, including the children.

Time pressure. The more a family is pressed for time, for whatever reason, the less will be the incidence of joint decision making. One major factor in increased time pressure on the family today is the increase in the number of working wives (*Media/Scope,* 1968). Even children seem to be heavily engaged in part-time work. A second factor is related to the ever increasing achievement motivation that the society seems to encourage. Time is a scarce resource, along with monetary resources, and the importance of any activity that uses up time more than it can return to the family is reduced.

Process of Joint Decision Making. The heart of the theory of family buying decisions is the process of joint decision making. As discussed earlier, considerable attention has been paid to the specific roles that spouses take in joint decisions: the husband performs the instrumental function and the wife performs the expressive function. In consumer behavior we need to investigate several other aspects of joint decision making.

First, who initiates the joint decision? This ought to be important from the marketer's viewpoint, since he could selectively direct advertising appeals to intensify the initiator's buying motives. The theory suggests that the identity of the one who will initiate a buying decision depends on the life style and the role orientation of family. If a member is dominant, he is likely to be the initiator of buying decisions. On the other hand, if all members are equal, the initiation of a purchase decision will not be centralized in any one member. In broad terms, the father seems to be predominant in initiating joint buying decisions.

Second, who provides information related to joint buying decision? Several studies have indicated that all the members share this task proportional to their expertise in various aspects of a specific decision. For example, the father is reputed to concentrate on technical and economic aspects, the mother on decorative and ornamental matters, and the children on socially related elements of the buying decision. It is, however, increasingly felt that children, particularly teenage children, have become the primary source of information for numerous joint decisions, including those on automobiles, appliances, homes, and vacations (Gilbert, 1957).

Third, who actually does the shopping and buying? In the grocery stores, contrary to common belief, both the father and the children shop for the family, either alone or together with the mother. However, it seems that children are generally less involved here. Furthermore, even between parents, the majority of shopping and buying rests with the mother because the time that she spends will not cut into the leisure activity of the whole family, and she is generally the budget manager in a family.

Finally, and probably most important, there is the question of *conflict* that may exist in joint buying decisions. March and Simon (1958) have presented a conceptual framework of interperson conflict that seems to be extremely relevant to the family decision making. The necessary condition for interperson conflict is a felt need for joint decision making. The theory of family buying decisions elaborated on a number of factors that mandate joint decision making among family members, hence the necessary condition is certainly present. The sufficient conditions for intergroup conflict are (1) differences in goals and (2) differences in perceptions about relevant alternatives or goal-objects. Both these conditions are considered to be present in family decision making in that each member has a specifically defined cognitive world in buying behavior. We pointed out how family members are likely to differ with respect to their buying motives (goals) and evaluative beliefs (perceptions about alternatives). In fact, some studies have explicitly examined the husband-wife conflict in joint decision making about buying automobiles and other major items (Alderson, 1957a; Hill, 1958; *Life*, 1965). Other unpublished studies have indicated that a good deal of conflict arises between parents and children in buying homes and choosing vacations.

The presence of intermember conflict in joint buying decisions means that there will be attempts to resolve it prior to choosing specific brands. These attempts are tactically different, and a particular type is more appropriate if the conflict has arisen primarily because of differences in evaluative beliefs as opposed to differences in buying motives. Resolution of conflict is presumed to take one of the following forms:

Problem solving. If the intermember conflict is the consequence of disagreement on evaluative beliefs rather than buying motives (i.e., if the family members agree on the need of a product or service but argue on the type or brand that seems most appropriate), problem solving is the most common approach. For example, all members may agree that the family needs a new car, but they may differ on whether it should be a sedan, a station wagon, or a personal car. A large number of the family's joint buying decisions seem to involve this type of conflict.

The immediate consequence of this situation is that members actively seek more information or deliberate more on available information. The next step is to look for support from credible personal sources outside the family, and finally to cast about for alternatives previously not considered in joint decision making.

Persuasion. Sometimes family members disagree about specific criteria by which alternatives are evaluated. In other words, there is agreement at a fundamental level, but there is conflict on specific subgoals. This type of conflict is resolved by persuasion; that is, an attempt is made to test for consistency in the motive hierarchy of the members and to avoid any suboptimization that may be found. For example, if the husband initiates the thought of replacing the car when the family is already quite heavily in debt, other members may persuade him to change his mind by pointing out the economic inconsistency.

Persuasion involves no attempt to gather more information on any of the alternatives. There is greater interaction among the members in conflict, and sometimes an outsider is brought in to reconcile the differences.

Bargaining. If the disagreement over buying motives is taken as fixed by the family members, the conflict is resolved by the process of bargaining. In resorting to bargaining, the concept of distributive justice or fairness is quite likely to be invoked, and members explicitly acknowledged that conflict exists. One common way of resolving conflict through bargaining is to turn the joint decision into an autonomous one by a member *in return for* some favor granted to all other members. For example, the father may be allowed to buy a new car for his business activities in return for an agreement to provide other things desirable to members of the family.

Bargaining seems to be quite common in family buying decisions, since the economic resources of a family are scarce and since some spouses hold incompatible viewpoints because of differential premarital backgrounds.

Politics. When the members of a family disagree not only about specific buying motives but, more fundamentally, about the whole style of life, the constant conflict is likely to be resolved either by dissolution of the family or by politics. Choice of the latter alternative usually results in formation of coalitions and subgroups of some of the family members in an attempt to isolate the member with whom there is conflict. Although this type of conflict resolution in buying decisions is not likely to be widespread, neither is it uncommon. In particular, children are likely to be used as coalition members with one parent against the other. Also, today we seem to witness coalitions of teenage children against parents.

All conflicts within a family are undesirable from the social-value viewpoint. They do occur, however, and it appears that conflict resolution by the processes of problem solving and persuasion is much less harmful than ironing out difficulties by bargaining and politics.

I hope this presentation of a theory of family buying decisions motivates researchers to test it, modify it, or comment on it.

3

CONSUMER DECISION-PROCESS MODELS

J. A. LUNN
Research Bureau
(Research International) Ltd.
London

Market research is an essentially pragmatic discipline. Its chief objective is to gather information relevant to short-, medium-, or long-term marketing and advertising decisions. Researchers have borrowed heavily from a variety of sources, especially the behavioral sciences, but they have been concerned mainly with methodology.

During recent years there has been a growing awareness of the need to introduce a more theoretical element into market research. This is by no means universally accepted, however, and to some people, especially businessmen, the very term "theory" sounds academic and impractical. Others, on the contrary, have realized that the saying "There is nothing as practical as a good theory" is just as relevant to marketing as to other applied fields: that marketing is indeed in urgent need of a more scientific and systematic approach (Sheth, 1967).

This paper reviews the current position in buyer behavior theory, with particular reference to an approach, which is gaining increasing popularity, that places major emphasis on consumer decision processes. The paper is in three parts. The first briefly sketches reasons for the growing interest in theory; the second describes three main approaches to theory building prevalent in market research; the third indicates the practical value of theory both for day-to-day problem solving and for basic marketing research. The attitude-behavior issue has been selected as the chief illustration.

THEORIES AND MODELS

A distinction is often drawn between theories and models, but the terms are used interchangeably here. As Lawrence (1966) has pointed out, the term "model" has a more practical ring to it, and it has been more widely adopted in marketing. However, both theories and models are concerned with providing a coherent and systematic structure for a field of study. Both involve (1) postulating a number of key variables (e.g., market forces such as advertising and price, or consumer characteristics such as motives and attitudes); (2) specifying causal relationships among these variables (e.g., the effect of advertising on attitudes); and (3) indicating the extent to which changes occur over time, either within the variables themselves or in their interrelationships. Both theories and models can differ in their objectives and in their level of generality: for instance, distinctions are made between macro and micro models and between descriptive and analytical models (Averink, 1970; de Jong, 1970; Fontela, 1970; Lambin, 1971). Again, Hendrickson (1967) presents his St. James's Model on two levels—at one he provides a conceptual framework of how advertising might work, at the other he presents a mathematical basis for calculating the relative importance of brand attributes.

Much activity to date—both published and unpublished—has involved building large-scale descriptive models of particular markets, using approaches heavily influenced by developments in operations research. See, for instance, the papers by Averink (1970), de Jong (1970) and Fontela (1970). These models are concerned mainly with the relative effects of different market forces on sales. Consumer characteristics tend not to be specified. Rather, they are lumped together into an undifferentiated "black box." Such models are valuable both for forecasting purposes and, especially when simulation procedures are used, for testing the likely results of future policy decisions (Lambin, 1971). But they provide relatively little explanation of how marketing activity can influence consumer behavior, hence only restricted guidance for the kind of action that may be called for in a particular market. By contrast, the models described in this paper specify key elements within the "black box" and are primarily aimed at providing diagnostic information to guide management decisions. The two approaches are, of course, complementary rather than contradictory, and it has been argued (e.g., Nicosia, 1969) that true progress in marketing theory will arise only when they are applied simultaneously.

MODELS FOR PRACTICAL PROBLEM
SOLVING AND FOR BASIC RESEARCH

The impetus behind theory development has arisen partly within the context of practical problem solving for marketing companies. This has occurred when marketing men, researchers, or both, have appreciated the need to conduct strategies and projects within a coherent framework rather than on a piecemeal basis. Even more important, however, has been the influence of "business academics" —that is, the growing number of researchers in business schools and the business departments of universities. "Business academics" in particular have been concerned with basic research in marketing. For them, the establishment of a coherent framework has been almost an end in itself or a means of guiding basic research. Practical problem solvers and basic researchers often have different perspectives, but their activities can be mutually beneficial. The issues outlined below concerning the need for and function of theory apply to both groups of people, if from different standpoints.

NEED FOR AND FUNCTION
OF BUYER BEHAVIOR THEORY

It has often been claimed that marketing theory fulfills two main functions: description and prediction. An amplification has been suggested by Howard and Sheth (1969), whose schematic has been adopted, in modified form, in this section.

Description and Explanation

A major purpose of buyer behavior theory is to increase our understanding of the consumer. This is especially important because throughout their activities, both marketing men and researchers make *assumptions* about how the consumer ticks—about how he arrives at purchasing and usage decisions and about how these decisions can be influenced by marketing action. Marketing men make these assumptions when planning product strategies, when commissioning research, and when acting on its findings; so do researchers when designing, carrying out, and interpreting research projects and when developing new techniques. We all have a personal model of man. The problem is that most of these assumptions are implicit, few have any empirical foundation, and many are contradictory. A well-constructed body of consumer theory would at least help to make these assumptions explicit and would also enable some of the key ones to be tested. At the same time, it would provide a foundation for technique development; for instance, the development of advertising pretesting systems presupposes that we understand how advertising works. On a more day-to-day level, a good consumer theory would also increase the probability of relevant variables being included in specific market projects.

Explanation and description are closely related. A major part of theory building consists of identifying certain key variables and describing their interrelationships. As our *descriptions* became increasingly more detailed and sophisticated, we come to provide *explanations* of the phenomenon of interest—in this case, consumer behavior. During this process, we may generate hypotheses to account for the nature of the variables and their interrelationships and to specify the conditions under which these interrelationships may be expected to hold.

Delimitation

Description—and explanation—must operate selectively; they cannot include everything. To attempt to account for too many phenomena may lead to confusion. A primary function of a theory is to delimit the area being embraced—to clarify what aspects are being covered and what are not. One means of achieving this is to specify the key variables.

Integration

Buyer behavior may lack theory, but there is no shortage of data. Individual companies often have vast amounts of information available to them about particular markets gathered from their own past research and other sources. At the more general level, the published literature in marketing abounds with reports of studies dealing with a wide variety of issues, ranging from market segmentation to the influence of reference groups. Similarly, there is a great diversity in the concepts used to describe consumer behavior. To quote from Sheth's (1967) review of buyer behavior:

> What we really have, then, are a set of insular hypothetical concepts and a set of peninsular intervening variables

reflecting a lack of formal science. What is more, they have lived an independent existence. Indeed, this reviewer has more than once felt that the situation resembles the seven blind men touching different parts of an elephant and making inferences about the animal which differ and occasionally contradict one another.

At all levels, there is a strong need for an agreed conceptual framework to integrate the plethora of disparate concepts and findings. This can be regarded as another prime function of buyer behavior theory. An example of this integrative role is given later in the paper in the discussion of Howard and Sheth's theory (1969).

A further benefit of integration should be better communication. Within the company setting, marketing men and researchers all too often mean different things by the same terms, and vice versa. The same is also true for researchers within the published literature: consider, for instance, the ambiguity generated by different definitions of the term "attitude" (Lunn, 1969b). Hopefully, an integrative framework will lead to clear and agreed definitions of central concepts.

Generation

The integrative function of buyer behavior theory is related to its role in generating ideas for future research. The act of drawing a variety of concepts and findings into a coherent system at once clarifies what we do know—or feel able to make firm assumptions about—and indicates where we are uncertain. This is especially true when a theory contains sets of fairly general hypothetical constructs and numerous combinations of relationships between these constructs. "A theory must stimulate hypotheses, or it must provide essential notions, hunches, ideas, and so on from which someone can create hypotheses which can then be tested" (Howard and Sheth, 1969). Marketing men should, as a result, obtain clearer guidance about the kind and amount of research needed for specific policy decisions; researchers should obtain guidance about priorities for future basic research.

APPROACHES TO
BUYER BEHAVIOR THEORY

Attempts at developing buyer behavior theory have taken various forms. The writer has found it useful in previous papers (Lunn,

1969a, 1969b, 1971a) to categorize these under three headings, namely, a priori, empirical, and eclectic. These categories are a bit arbitrary, but they provide a useful schematic for discussing the various theoretical approaches.

The A Priori Approach

Researchers using the a priori approach have introduced concepts and theories from other disciplines, mainly the behavioral sciences, and have explored their value for understanding the consumer. Well-known instances include the various manifestations of motivational research and such attitude theories as those of Festinger and Fishbein. This has sometimes involved giving the consumer an all-embracing label, such as "Economic Man," "Problem-Solver," "Learner" (Oxenfeldt, 1966), and, more recently, "Existentialist" (Christopher, 1970). For an overview of these contributions, see Sheth (1967) and Nicosia (1966).

Consumer behavior is, of course, a specific aspect of general human behavior, and the a priori approach is appropriate here because it attempts to harness existing knowledge and insights from behavioral science. But as traditionally applied, it has severe limitations. Many of the concepts adopted are still somewhat speculative. They have often been developed in contexts remote from consumer behavior—for instance, in laboratory situations with students as experimental subjects. Moreover, they have usually been developed to account for restricted aspects of human behavior (e.g., learning and perception). Nevertheless, protagonists of different theoretical positions have been all too ready to represent them as rival rather than complementary explanatory systems (McGuire, 1969b) and to overgeneralize their areas of application. Narrowness of perspective may help the advancement of academic knowledge, but it can be destructively limiting in a problem-oriented field such as marketing.

The Empirical Approach

A priori researchers have attempted to fit consumer behavior to previously developed theoretical frameworks. Researchers in the empirical category have adopted the opposite approach. Consumer behavior itself has been their prime focus of study. They have attempted to derive laws from observations of patterns and regularities in this behavior, often though not invariably using consumer panel data. Both general laws of buyer behavior and deviations from these laws have stimulated interest.

A key exponent of this approach is Ehrenberg (1969), who has recently extended it to an examination of the attitude-behavior issue (Bird and Ehrenberg, 1970). By and large, however, empirical theoreticians have been chary of working with other than "hard" behavior data and also of venturing too far into the realm of interpretation.

The strength of the a priori position lies in the firm and systematic basis of knowledge provided about certain aspects of the consumer. Its weaknesses lie in the virtual disregard of potentially illuminating theories from the behavioral sciences, and consequently, the relative lack of explanatory power.

The Eclectic Approach

The previous two approaches broadly encompass the major attempts at consumer theorizing up to about 1964. More recently, however, a third, more eclectic approach has become increasingly popular. Basically, it attempts to incorporate the strengths of the a priori and empirical approaches but to avoid their weaknesses. Its distinguishing feature is the attempted synthesis of two sets of information: on the one hand, the theories, concepts, and findings in the various behavioral sciences that appear relevant to consumer behavior; on the other hand, the rapidly escalating findings from market research studies, whether commissioned in the marketing context for specific problem-solving situations or in the more generalized context of the business school.

The strength of this approach is the comprehensiveness of its perspective. But this comprehensiveness is also a potential source of weakness, for it imposes a herculean task on researchers. It is hard enough to establish an agreed outlook among specialists within a discipline (e.g., learning theorists within psychology). It is harder still to achieve among representatives of different aspects of a major discipline (e.g., learning theorists and psycholinguisticians), and even harder among representatives of quite different disciplines such as psychology, sociology, and economics. There is, moreover, a danger of undue complexity, of having too many variables and interrelationships.

Nevertheless, the eclectic approach offers considerable promise. Only by attempting to integrate the major influences on consumer behavior within a single framework—or series of related frameworks—are we likely to provide really illuminating guidelines for marketing action and for basic research. The challenge is to strike a balance between, on the one hand, the relatively narrow focus of the theory (i.e., market place and consumption behavior) and, on the other hand, the wide range of findings, concepts, and theories that may help to illuminate this behavior.

The next sections of this paper delineate some of the major features of the eclectic approach. This is done in two ways: first, by briefly summarizing some prominent published contributions; second, by drawing together some of their more important aspects. It should be emphasized that it is impossible to do justice to any of these contributions in the space of a short review paper: there has been space for only a few facets in each case. Consequently, the reader interested in the detail of any particular model is advised to read the original.

THE NICOSIA MODEL

Nicosia must be regarded as one of the leading figures in the eclectic approach. In a major work (1966), he produced one of the first large-scale reviews of findings and theories in the behavioral sciences relevant to consumer behavior. In his book, he also evolves a conceptual framework, specifying the major elements and their interactions; the book concludes with an attempt to express the framework in mathematical terms, making particular use of differential equations.

A distinctive feature of Nicosia's approach is the shift of emphasis away from the purchasing act itself and toward the decision processes that both precede and follow this act. As he points out, "the act of purchasing is only one component of a complex, ongoing process of decision making—a process of many interactions among many variables over time." This emphasis on decision processes has become a hallmark of the eclectic approach: hence the title of this review paper.

In a subsequent paper Nicosia (1968), argues the case for computer simulation and attempts to translate his model into simulation terms. Most recently (Nicosia, 1969), he has urged the synthesis of what he describes as behavioral and behavioristic models:

> In behavioral approaches the stress is on *behavioral*
> constructs (predispositions, opinions, images, attitudes,
> motivations, and social influences, and so on) which may
> intervene, in different ways, between environmental stimuli
> and the act of purchase, and/or may be affected by
> this act. In the other research approach, the stress is on

behavioristic constructs; that is, on the object of choice
(a store, a product, a brand) and related indicators of the
choice-object (e.g., how much was spent, the package size,
the deal, the time, the kind of store).

He has also speculated further on the thought and decision
processes. In both recent works, he emphasizes the importance of
combining conceptual elaboration with formal attempts at quantification of these concepts, by mathematical formulas and by simulation; that is Nicosia expresses the need to combine the richness
of (often speculative) insights with the relative power and precision provided by mathematical formulation.

Nicosia's model (1966)—like those of the other two contributions summarized below—can be represented in terms of flow
charts. These are presented together in Figure 3.1 in the appendix
to this paper. The model can be expressed in terms of a series of
fields, each one serving as both output from a preceding field and
input to a succeeding one. Let us summarize a few major features.

First, like other eclectic theoreticians, Nicosia represents the
consumer as purposive, seeking to fulfill certain goals through
purchasing behavior and going through various decision processes
that help him to at least approximate an optimum solution.

Second, there is the notion of the "funnel." Nicosia places
much store in the idea of consumer predispositions moving from
generality (very broad intentions) through the search and evaluation of alternative products and culminating in the selection of
one particular brand.

Third, there is the crucial concept of feedback. Too many
representations of the consumer have assumed a one-way process
leading from marketing action to purchase and usage. In practice,
the process continues with a feedback from consumer behavior.
This feedback will affect marketing action itself, which may be
adjusted in the light of reactions in the marketplace. It will also
affect consumer predispositions that may be reinforced or modified
in the light of experience with the product and also of the buying
act itself.

Consumer predispositions are influenced by a variety of factors, some of them external to the consumer. External influences
may be both commercial (e.g., media, point-of-sale factors) and
noncommercial (e.g., word of mouth). For a full account, see
Nicosia (1966).

It is possible to level a number of criticisms at Nicosia's work, and he himself would be the last to regard it as definitive. For instance, the search and evaluation process as represented is over-rational, and although applicable to infrequently purchased high-cost products, it has less relevance for frequently purchased low-cost goods. Moreover, the definitions of attitude and motivation seem to be unsatisfactory, and the attempt to formalize the model mathematically (Nicosia, 1966, chap. 7) appears as prematurely ambitious. An especially harsh criticism given by Ehrenberg (1968) is worth reading as an illustration of how a researcher with strongly empirical orientations finds it difficult to accept the eclectic approach.

However, for all the possible objections, Nicosia has provided an invaluable pioneering contribution.

THE ENGEL MODEL

A second major work is that of Engel, Kollat, and Blackwell (1968). The authors' thorough documentation of research in the behavioral sciences relevant to marketing is worth reading in its own right. At the same time, they have elaborated a decision-process model that resembles Nicosia's in many respects and is explicitly linked to the various facets of behavioral science covered in the book. A flow chart of the model is given in Figure 3.2 in the Appendix. Some of the distinctive features can be summarized as follows:

1. Like Nicosia, Engel et al. portray an ongoing series of processes whereby products are sought and evaluated in terms of the consumer's goals and future purchases are influenced by previous experience.

2. They discuss the interaction of past experience and stored information with general predispositions such as personality variables. This interaction leads to the formulation of values and attitudes that are defined as "organizations of concepts, beliefs, habits and motives associated with a particular object." All these variables are contained within a central control unit. This unit produces response sets that play a key monitoring role throughout the decision process.

3. A distinction is made between the system itself, which consists essentially of a series of predispositions, and the arousal of the system on a specific occasion. Arousal can be triggered both by internal states, such as feeling hungry, or by external factors, such as advertising messages or point-of-sale displays.

4. Even when the system is active, the individual does not necessarily perceive all the stimuli to which he is exposed. He

will filter out information that is relevant to his current motives
and is consistent with his stored knowledge and expectations. Moreover, even when information is allowed into the system, it may
be structured and distorted to make it consistent with existing
predispositions.

5. Engel et al. suggest a series of processes that may follow
the act of purchase. For instance, perceived doubt about the wis-
dom of the action can lead to a search for information to justify
the decision.

Although the literature reviewed by Engel et al. is more thorough than Nicosia's, their model is less detailed and has not, to
the writer's knowledge, been put in mathematical or simulation
form. It does, however, have heuristic value in pointing out some
of the major factors bearing on consumer decision making. One
specific criticism is that, as with Nicosia, the search and evaluation
process is portrayed as highly rational. For an elaboration of decision strategies see the "Other Contributions" section of this paper.

THE HOWARD-SHETH THEORY

By far the most thorough, comprehensive, and well-articulated
model of the consumer published to date is that of Howard and
Sheth. It is distinguished by a richer specification of variables and
their interrelationships, and it attempts a much deeper and more
detailed integration of theoretical positions from several behavioral sciences. Seven instances of integration are listed by Howard
and Sheth (1969, chap. 10). To quote just one (p. 396):

> Conflict arising from an ambiguous stimulus is one of the
> regulators of buyer attention and overt search behavior
> (Berlyne, 1966), as we saw in Chapter 5. Also, there we saw
> how it shapes the nature of how the buyer perceives what-
> ever information he admits into his nervous system (Osgood,
> 1957b). Conflict in overt buying behavior—incompatible
> responses—also influences his attention and overt search
> behavior (N. E. Miller, 1959), as indicated in Chapter 8.
> Given that a buyer has well-formed Choice Criteria for a
> specified product class, the certainty (Confidence) with which
> he judges a brand in that class leads to a decrease in
> cognitive conflict. The cognitive conflict that occurs with
> low Confidence is manifested by search for information,
> for example, as postulated by one version of the consistency
> principle, namely, dissonance theory (Brehm and Cohen,

1962). "Inconsistency" is also used to describe cognitive conflict when it is manifested in attitude change. Furthermore, expectancy, as used by Lewin and others roughly to mean probability of payoff (J. W. Atkinson, 1964), implies conflict as a consequence of being unable to choose when certainty is low. "Inconsistency in the mind threatens to paralyze action" (R. W. Brown, 1965, p. 606). The behavioral manifestation of low "expectancy" (low Confidence) is vacillation (N. E. Miller, 1959). Thus by postulating the construct of Confidence we bring together (1) the processes by which the buyer obtains his *informational inputs*, (2) their *cognitive* consequences that will affect future purchases, and (3) their *behavioral* consequences for the current purchases. In using the concept of conflict to explain search effort we have developed a specific mechanism to explain what was postulated in an earlier version of the theory (Howard, 1963, p. 58), namely, that buyers further along the learning curve with respect to a brand are less inclined to seek information.

A flow chart of the theory is given in Figure 3.3 in the Appendix. A few of its main characteristics are outlined below:

1. As in the previously described models, the focal point is the individual consumer, whose "internal" states are treated as a system. In the tradition of econometric models, a distinction is made between *endogenous* variables (i.e., those that the theory is designed to explain) and *exogenous* variables (i.e., additional variables, largely, but not entirely, "outside" the consumer, which have a key influence on the system). In Figure 3.3, the seven exogenous variables—importance of purchase, culture, social class, and so on —are listed at the top. Within the book their respective influences are described and charted in detail.

2. Again, the core of the decision process is seen as the matching of products to the consumer's motives. However, there is a more detailed account of the nature and development of the "choice criteria" (e.g., attributes such as nourishment value and economy) whereby this matching occurs.

3. Choice criteria can be viewed from two standpoints: the extent to which the product or brand is believed by the consumer to possess the attribute in question, and the value of this attribute to the consumer—that is, the extent to which it represents a requirement sought from the product. This balance of perception

and value characterizes the "means-end" approach to attitudes that has played a leading part in the theoretical developments of Rosenberg and Fishbein, among others.[1] It also figures prominently in the thinking of other decision-process theoreticians such as Hansen (1970b), who advances the case for relating value importance to the anticipated situation in which purchasing or consumption will take place. Hansen (1963) also makes some useful points about the various ways in which particular decisions originate, the extent to which they are reversible, and the extent to which they form chains along with other interrelated decisions.

4. Two crucial and related concepts are those of "product class concept" and "evoked set of brands." The former indicates that consumers do not necessarily perceive markets in the same way as manufacturers and that for the consumer, a product class is the set of brands or products that are broadly substitutable for a given set of motives (see also Lunn, 1969b, 1970). Product classes can be described at various levels (see Howard and Sheth, 1969, chap. 8). The evoked set concept postulates that the consumer does not necessarily choose, on any particular occasion, from all the alternatives that fall within his definition of the product class. Under some circumstances (e.g., when he is buying in an unfamiliar product field), the consumer may undertake a wide search for information about products and may select from among many possibilities. Under other circumstances, he may consider one or at the most two alternatives.

5. Perceptual processes are dealt with extensively. Key concepts here are the arousal (e.g., consumer hunger) as well as the directive (e.g., kind of food that is appropriate) value of the individual's motives, the ambiguity of the commercial stimulus (e.g., product display, advertisement), and the effects of these concepts on both the attention that will be paid to the stimulus and any distortion (perceptual bias) of the information to which he is exposed.

6. Like Nicosia and Engel et al., Howard and Sheth emphasize the importance of feedback, that is, the effects of the purchase act and usage experience on consumer predispositions toward particular products; here they incorporate the concept of satisfaction. However, they also explore the dynamics of the buying process in terms of a distinction adopted in Howard's previous

[1] See the collection of papers edited by Fishbein (1967), and a review article by McGuire (1969b), which puts this approach into perspective.

work (1963) between (*a*) extensive, (*b*) limited, and (*c*) routinized problem solving.

Extensive problem solving is called for when the buyer is confronted by an unfamiliar brand in an unfamiliar product class. The choice criteria by which alternatives are assessed will be weak or nonexistent, and the buyer will search diligently for information, with both commercial (e.g., advertising) and noncommercial (e.g., consumer reports, discussions with friends) sources playing a part. Chapter 9 of Howard and Sheth (1969) provides an elaboration of the respective effects of these sources.

Limited problem solving applies to the situation of a buyer confronted with a new, unfamiliar brand in a familiar product class, usually where existing brands do not provide an adequate level of satisfaction. Choice criteria will be better formed, but there will still be a certain amount of search and evaluation prior to purchase.

These first two situations accord with the somewhat rational accounts of the decision process propounded by Nicosia and Engel et al., although these authors would admit, along with Howard and Sheth, that decision processes may occur at the unconscious as well as the conscious level and may not always appear rational to the outside observer. Quite different is the *routinized problem solving* of the buyer who is purchasing familiar brands within a familiar product field and requires relatively little information. Under this situation, considerable brand loyalty would be expected.

No single model or theory can be fully comprehensive at this state of our knowledge. Nevertheless, the Howard-Seth approach is a clearly admirable attempt. It has already guided research in a variety of product fields, and some of its propositions have been rigorously tested under the Columbia Buyer Behavior panel projects (Arndt, 1968a; see also Farley and Ring, 1970 and chap. 8 of this volume).

On the whole, the tests have provided favorable support for the theory. However, as Farley and Ring point out, they have also indicated certain weaknesses in the measuring instruments used in the Columbia Buyer Behavior project. This underlines an important issue: namely, the necessity of combining conceptual sophistication with methodological precision. Nicosia (1969) refers to "the problems of translating a construct (e.g., intelligence, attitude, etc.) into a measurable entity: this translation implies a number of methodological decisions: (*a*) choice of the construct dimension(s); (*b*) choice of indicator(s) for each dimension; and (*c*) choice of measuring instrument(s) for each indicator." As mentioned earlier in this paper, better theory is needed to guide technique development. Equally, to put theoretical developments to the test, we need adequate techniques of data collection and analysis.

OTHER CONTRIBUTIONS

So far we have been concerned largely with three representations of the eclectic approach. There are several other published contributions based on similar lines that should be referred to. These include the works of Arndt (1968a) and Hansen (1970a). In addition, the author, along with a number of colleagues in the Research International group, has evolved a conceptual framework of consumer decision processes that has helped to guide a program of basic research carried out for a multinational group of manufacturing companies (Lunn, 1969a).

There is no space to review any of the other approaches, even in outline. However, two more specific discussions of consumer decision making will be mentioned. The first is that of Cooper (1969), whose discussion of decision strategies provides valuable enrichment in this area. Cooper postulates two major dimensions underlying these strategies: rational–irrational and routine–dramatic. He then suggests eight different strategies based on the recognition that all decisions involve uncertainty and that, consequently, people making decisions face risk. Risk may involve wider considerations than money, including loss of self-esteem. "The decision-maker is, therefore, under considerable pressure to reduce risk and its accompanying anxiety, or otherwise to devise strategies for resolving risk." The eight strategies suggested by Cooper are the following:

> (a) *Scrutinize alternatives.* This is the solution of rational decision-making. The decision-maker assembles impartial information by using his or her own skills or through "expert" sources, in order to optimize the decision.
>
> (b) *Use related cues.* For example, Price, Company Images, etc., are traditionally associated with value. This is a working solution where full information is not available.
>
> (c) *Avoid hazardous decisions.* The decision-maker can rely upon past experience—"brand loyalty."
>
> (d) *Wait.* Planning to spend, for example, on consumer durables, can pass through a lengthy "incubation period." To wait (saving) or to engage in "diversionary" activity (buying in a completely different product field),

permits the consumer to resolve risk of when and
what to buy.

(e) *Imitation*. Following other people's choices externalizes
the risk. Mass media aid this solution by confirming
widespread preferences.

(f) *Flirt with risk as in gambling*. That is, deliberately
choosing an alternative with a high pay-off value, but
which has little chance of success (bargains).

(g) *Ignore the risk*. Choose alternatives at random, irrespective of cost, pay-off, or value. Lack of time, other
work, are often put forward as reasons for opting for
this alternative.

(h) *Satisficing*. "Satisficing" refers to choosing that solution
first encountered which meets minimal requirements.

The effects of risk on consumer decision making are also dealt
with from a number of standpoints in the book of papers edited by
Cox (1967). Here interrelationships are traced among variables
such as consumer involvement in the product field, consumer self-
confidence, methods of handling information, and persuasibility.
However, neither Cooper nor the contributors to the Cox volume
attempt to incorporate decision-making strategies into a broader
framework of the total buying process.

SOME GENERAL FEATURES
OF THE ECLECTIC APPROACH

Decision-process models can be discussed at many levels. At one
extreme is the complex integration of theories from the various
contributory disciplines (e.g., the study of learning, motivation,
perception, cognitive structures, and attitude change). But the discussion can also be carried on at the level of systematized common
sense, with a fairly general description of the main concepts and
their interrelationships from the standpoint of the individual consumer. The latter approach has been adopted here. But it should
be borne in mind that much of the value of eclecticism lies in the
former, more complex account.

Decision-process models too, may have different purposes and
referents. For instance, we may be primarily interested in the perceptual and communication processes as the background to de-
vising an advertising pretesting system, in product innovation
processes, in modeling the effects of promotions, and in illuminating the attitude-behavior controversy. Some of these specific

issues are taken up later in this paper. For the moment, however, we are concerned with a global picture of the consumer, a picture that in any case is necessary as a context setter for more specific models. See, for example, the way in which Sheth has evolved models of attitude-behavior relationships (Sheth, 1971) and family decision processes (Sheth, chap. 2 of this volume) from the broader Howard and Sheth theory.

We now outline a series of propositions derived from the eclectic approach. It should be pointed out that these are hypotheses rather than proven facts. For a detailed discussion, and for an evaluation of the nature and status of supporting evidence from market research and the behavioral sciences generally, see Howard and Sheth (1969), Nicosia (1966), and Engel et al. (1968).

1. The consumer is not the defenseless or recalcitrant creature portrayed by many theoreticians. Rather, he is purposive and goal oriented. The needs and motives he seeks to satisfy through purchasing are of many kinds and exist at several levels of generality. They range from specific product field requirements (e.g., a margarine with a creamy texture) to such general values as experimentation and economy-mindedness; from basic drives such as hunger to general aspects of personality such as extroversion (Lunn, 1971b).

2. Nor is the consumer a passive being, waiting to be influenced and manipulated by marketing men. He actively seeks information to satisfy his various motives, and he structures information coming from the environment as a guide to need satisfaction.

3. Nor is the individual's role as consumer pursued in isolation from the remainder of his life. Purchasing and consumption are carried out within the wider context of day-to-day living. Here the notion of plans, incorporated by Twyman (1969) into a model of the advertising process, is a useful one.

> They [i.e., G. A. Miller et al., 1960] suggest that an individual's behavior can be represented by a hierarchy of plans analogous to a computer program for living. The essence of these plans is that they are goal directed and the goals or objectives can be progressively broken down into a series of subgoals and plans to achieve them. The plans are arranged hierarchically in the sense that any single plan has been generated by a higher order plan and itself generates lower order plans which form part of it. For example, one could postulate a housewife having a general plan or program to "look after the family" which would

lead to various subplans to cover shopping and the preparation of meals and so on down to small subroutines for laying the table, cooking and serving the meal and washing-up after a meal and asking people if they had enjoyed it.

Twyman uses the concept of plan to hypothesize some of the different levels at which an advertisement for food might operate, for instance: ·

(a) by suggesting something about the status of purchasers of a product

(b) by appeal to plans concerned with care of self and family, e.g., health

(c) suggesting new approaches to the form of meals, e.g., that convenience foods could be quickly prepared and served while watching television

(d) by suggesting plans for ensuring that particular products are always kept in adequate supply in the home

(e) by suggesting ideas for when and where to shop

(f) by showing ways of using the product in meals at either the preparation or the serving stage

(g) by suggesting advantages which might accrue from a more careful assessment of product qualities

(h) by trying to create greater feedback of product qualities to the housewife from other members of the household.

4. As described in the section on the Howard-Sheth theory, the individual establishes over time sets of choice criteria in terms of which he identifies and evaluates products. Choice criteria develop through learning and may be based on actual experience with the product, generalization from related experiences, and information derived from advertising, and so on, or from word of mouth. Choice criteria lead to the development of favorable or unfavorable attitudes toward products and of varying levels of buying intention. They also determine which products are perceived as substitutable for certain needs and which products will remain in the evoked set from which decisions are made on particular occasions.

5. In today's complex, highly developed society, the consumer is assailed daily by vast quantities of information. Only some of this is relevant to his purchasing goals. Even this, however, may be too much for any single person to pay serious attention to. The individual, therefore, in his role as consumer as well

as in his other roles, develops strategies for dealing with information overload. These are often referred to as defense mechanisms. All involve the concept of selectivity.

Thus under some circumstances (e.g., extensive problem solving) the individual will deliberately seek out information and will selectively expose himself to advertisements. Under other circumstances he may adopt essentially negative strategies; that is, he may deliberately avoid certain advertisements or experiences. Similarly, he will pay selective attention to information about certain products in two senses: vigilance to those aspects he finds valuable or acceptable, and rejection of those that are unacceptable or of low value. Selectivity does not stop here. Even when exposed to and paying attention to product information (e.g., an advertisement), the individual's defense mechanisms may lead him to restructure information in terms of already existing needs, attitudes, and expectancies: the advertiser may say one thing, the consumer perceive another. Selectivity also extends to the retention of information, with value and acceptability again determining whether particular messages are remembered or forgotten.

6. It was pointed out earlier that the decision-making situation itself is not invariably—if at all—a matter of consciously and rationally evaluating alternatives and settling for the product that provides the best all-round prospect. Sometimes (e.g., routinized problem solving) decisions may not, strictly speaking, be made at all. When they are, concepts such as confidence (in distinguishing between different brands and in the probability of the product performing as expected), involvement in the product field, and the extent of perceived risk may all play a part in the search and evaluation process. Moreover, in his day-to-day shopping, the consumer may adopt one or more of a variety of decision rules or strategies.

7. The ongoing nature of decision processes has also been discussed. The consumer's choice criteria are modified through past experiences with the product as well as by information and impressions from advertising. Search will continue when products are unsatisfactory. Search may also continue with the aim of providing reassurance that a good purchase has been made, particularly in ambiguous situations and when the consumer is highly involved but lacks confidence.

8. The above propositions have been stated in terms of a hypothetical individual. There are two fundamental qualifications here. First, individuals differ in respect to many of the characteristics listed, including decision rules as well as needs and motives.

These differences have increasingly been recognized by marketing men and researchers and have been incorporated into market segmentation policies (Lunn, 1971b). Second, the individual makes and implements purchasing decisions within a social environment. Hence a variety of social influences bear on these decisions. Some of these are personal (e.g., other family members, neighbors, friends, workmates). Others are more impersonal—(e.g., people observed in the street or on television, reference groups and prevalent cultural values, such as the quest for youthfulness or the decline in authority).

To recognize the importance of social influences is not to devalue "internal" processes. The cornerstone of the eclectic approach is, of course, that sociological and psychological concepts should be brought together into a common framework.

Social influences have two distinctive functions. They help to formulate product awareness, choice criteria, attitudes, and buying intentions. They also help to mediate or modify the translation of these predispositions into actual behavior. For instance, a housewife who is highly predisposed toward certain exotic foods may buy other foods instead because of her husband's traditional tastes.

THE PRACTICAL VALUE
OF DECISION-PROCESS MODELS

Earlier we outlined several functions of consumer models, including explanation, integration, and the generation of guidelines for research priorities. It was also pointed out that theory building can have a broad, long-term role in marketing by placing our knowledge and assumptions on a more scientific footing and enabling the latter to be tested. At the same time, theory can have a more specific function in day-to-day research projects by improving our interpretation of particular research findings and by suggesting which variables should be included, manipulated, and controlled. It is suggested that the eclectic approach, because it is poblem focused but comprehensive, is more valuable for these objectives than either the empirical or the a priori approach in their respective extreme forms—although either of the latter might be equally suitable for particular problems and situations.

Four instances of the value of the eclectic approach are now outlined.

Market Segmentation

The explosive popularity of market segmentation studies has been reviewed elsewhere (e.g., Lunn, 1971a, 1971b). These studies have been increasingly useful in describing market structures and in guiding marketing policies concerned both with the maintenance of existing brands and products and with the identification of market opportunities. But a segmentation study can only provide a snapshot of a market at one period of time. For a complete perspective, these studies should be incorporated into a dynamic picture both of the market in question and of consumers in general. In addition, there is the crucial issue of which variables to include in segmentation projects, whether as "active" variables to help in the formation of target groups or as "passive" variables for cross-tabulation against these groups in an attempt to elucidate consumer behavior in the product field in question. In the writer's experience, the increasing insights into consumer decision processes gained in recent years can have immense benefits in these respects. For instance, "new" variables are suggested, such as the degree of involvement with product fields and the degree of problem solving (extended, limited, or routinized).

The Influence of In-Store Factors

Research Bureau Ltd. has recently carried out a major investigation into the influence of in-store factors upon purchasing intentions and actual behavior. An earlier project not based on a theoretical framework found few systematic results, despite the use of a large sample of shoppers and clear specification and recording of the in-store factors. Following this project, a consumer decision framework was developed within the Research International group (see "Other Contributions" section), which included a series of concepts of apparent relevance to the purchasing situation (e.g., the concepts of product class and evoked set, and different decision strategies). A second project was then carried out incorporating these variables: it has provided valuable evidence of in-store influence for a variety of product fields.

In addition, the project itself has contributed to the Research International conceptual framework—for example, through results that have extended the definition of purchases from the oversimplified dichotomy of planned and unplanned, postulated at the outset of the project. Moreover, through the use of factor and cluster analysis it has led to the development of six basic shopper types defined in terms of responses to basic attitudes salient to the shopping situation (e.g., the "happy, impulsive shopper," and the "reluctant, organized shopper").

An Advertisement Pretesting System

Advertisement pretesting is a major field of market research that has been the center of innumerable controversies and disputes between rival methodologists. This is not only because of deficiencies in particular techniques but because few pretesting systems have been based on a systematic conceptualization of how advertising might work. All too often when an underlying model has been adopted, it has been oversimplistic, such as the now-notorious hierarchy of effects schemata (Palda, 1966).[2] Lately this area has been examined more systematically. At an Esomar Workshop, Joyce (1967) attempted one of the first main syntheses of our knowledge about how advertising works. In the United States, Sheth (1969b) has applied the Howard-Sheth theory to a specific examination of the advertising process. Also in the United States, McGuire (1969a) has evolved an eclectic theory of the advertising process based on a variety of standpoints in the attitude change, persuasion, and communication fields. Both Sheth and McGuire point out that provided the hierarchy of effects paradigm is not regarded as irreversible or the sole form in which persuasion can take place, it can supply a valuable structure for assessing advertisements. But they also emphasize that different advertisements will probably have different effects at each point of the hierarchy (e.g., an ad with high attention value may have little persuasive power). However, quite different measuring instruments will be necessary at each stage.

Similar points have been made by Twyman (1969, 1970). Along with Juchen and colleagues from the Research International group, he has provided a review of the advertising field having two main foundations: an empirical review of existing advertising pretesting systems and an elaboration of consumer decision process theory. An integration of these two bases has led to a revised form of pretesting approach.

The Attitude-Behavior Controversy

The relationship between attitudes and behavior is an area that has recently undergone critical scrutiny in market research (e.g., Fishbein, 1972; Fothergill, 1968; Lunn, 1970; Wicker, 1969) and in the social sciences generally (e.g., Festinger, 1964; A. Cohen, 1964; Insko, 1967). "Attitude" has been a central concept in market research for many years and in psychology for even longer. Attitudes

[2] For example, Attention–comprehension–attitude change–retention of change–behavior.

generally structure the way in which an individual perceives his environment, and they guide the ways in which he responds to it. Moreover, attitude data have a variety of practical applications in market research, including fulfilling the following functions:

1. An essentially predictive function; that is, consumer attitudes are often treated as a kind of early warning system whereby changes of attitude are expected to anticipate changes in purchasing.

2. A derived predictive function; that is, attitudes are often included in product, advertisement, and similar tests; here the relative performance of different products, advertisements, and so on, are judged in terms of attitude measures on the assumption that attitude change in the test will be followed by corresponding attitude and behavioral change in the marketplace. In a sense, attitudes in the test situation are being used as surrogates for behavior.

3. An essentially diagnostic function; that is, attitude data are often used to indicate the kind of supportive or corrective action necessary for existing products and to provide guidance for new product development. For this function, attitude data may be gathered in several different kinds of projects (e.g., qualitative motivation research studies, quantitative market segmentation studies, and product and advertising tests). Here again it is assumed—often implicitly—that when marketing action succeeds in changing consumer attitudes, there will be subsequent changes in purchasing.

Unfortunately, there is, allegedly, little or no evidence that changes in people's attitudes toward an object (or person or situation) are in fact followed by corresponding changes in behavior in relation to that object (person or situation). This applies to social psychology as well as to market research. Indeed, it has been claimed that where relationships are to be expected they will be in the direction of attitude change following rather than preceding behavioral change (e.g., Festinger, 1964). As a result, some researchers have begun to despair of the value of consumer attitude data.

This is preeminently an area that demands a sound theoretical underpinning. Yet it is also one that has been characterized by naïve and oversimplistic conceptualization. The remainder of this section is largely devoted to an outline of some of the potential values of better theory.[3]

[3] A thorough review of the attitude-behavior issue goes beyond the scope of this paper; and the topic has been covered by Sampson (1971) and by the writer at a recent Esomar Seminar (Lunn, 1970).

As a prelude to theory, a few points are made about research findings, definitions, and measurements.

Research Findings

Assertions about the low relationships between attitudes and behavior are somewhat misleading. The literature contains positive as well as negative findings. This applies to research in social psychology (e.g., Fishbein, 1972; Wicker, 1969) and in market research (e.g., Assael and Day, 1968; Day, 1970b; Sheth, 1971). Moreover, the studies purporting to show negative findings have been criticized on a number of counts, including research design measurement, and interpretation (Fishbein, 1972; Rokeach, 1968). As Fothergill (1968) pointed out—in a paper highly critical of certain market research studies that had reported positive relationships—it is hard to credit the notion that attitude will never precede behavioral change. The challenge for researchers is to identify the circumstances and conditions under which such change should or should not be expected, and both measurement and theory have a part to play.

Definitions of Attitude

Some of the problems in the attitude-behavior controversy have arisen because different researchers have used the term *attitude* to refer to quite different concepts. The writer has found it valuable to categorize the major uses in market research under two main headings: (1) perceptual and (2) motivational. The former refer to the consumer's reactions to a specific object, person, or situation; the latter to characteristics of the consumer that indicate the satisfaction sought through purchasing and usage behavior.

1. Perceptual
   a. Overall evaluation
   b. Buying intention
   c. Specific evaluative beliefs
2. Motivational
   a. Specific product field requirements
   b. Consumer values
   c. General personality

These distinctions have been discussed at length elsewhere (e.g., Lunn, 1969b, 1970), and just four points are made here:

1. There is a growing tendency in both psychology (Fishbein, 1972) and market research (Howard and Sheth, 1969), to restrict the term "attitude" to overall evaluation. The writer supports this but would argue that the crucial point is less one of terminology as such than of the need to preserve clear distinctions between different constructs.

2. Specific evaluative beliefs are a subset of the total collection of beliefs that a consumer holds about a particular object (person, or situation). As such they can be distinguished from descriptive beliefs—the latter have no motivational properties (unlike evaluative beliefs, which possess such properties by definition).

3. Evaluative beliefs and product field requirements represent the two facets of choice criteria (see above). That is, a consumer will hold certain beliefs about the attributes of particular products and will regard these attributes as more or less important.

4. When evaluating attitude-behavior relationships, it is important to ensure that the attitudes (or intentions, beliefs, etc.) being assessed are appropriate to the behavior in question. We return to this issue later.

Measurement

It was pointed out earlier that good theory is inadequate without good measurement. Recent years have seen considerable advances in attitude measurement, and these have been described elsewhere (e.g., Lunn, 1968, 1969a). Two particularly important stages are:

1. Identification of the variables that are relevant to or determinative of (J. H. Myers and Alpert, 1968) the behavior that one wishes to predict or understand. Commonly used techniques are group discussions, extended interviews, and the Kelly Repertory Grid.

2. Development of measuring instruments for these variables that are at once sound (i.e., valid and reliable) and feasible to use in market research conditions. A commonly used technique is factor analysis, applied either to sets of bipolar phrases or "Likert" type agree–disagree scales.

These stages are especially important for the measurement of attitudes in the motivational category and for evaluative beliefs. Overall evaluation and buying intention are usually measured on single, quantitative scales, probably with five or seven categories. Especially for predictive purposes, however, more attention should be paid to their measurement; in particular, for buying intention, care should be taken over the phraseology—the more precise and specific the wording, the greater the probability of obtaining relationships with subsequent behavior—and the choice situation with which the consumer is likely to be faced.

Attitude Theory

Attempts by market researchers to introduce a more theoretical element into the attitude-behavior controversy fall neatly into the empirical–a priori–eclectic categorization outlined here. The *empirical* approach is illustrated by the work of Ehrenberg (1969) and a number of coauthors (e.g., Bird and Ehrenberg, 1970). This work has indicated some interesting relationships between attitude and behavior but has operated in too limited a manner to warrant detailed comment at this stage. Perhaps its major use for the moment is to warn researchers against interpreting too literally and superficially data involving general measures (whether of attitudes or of behavior) and against working with unsegmented samples of respondents.

The a priori approach has been the most popular to date. Many researchers have examined the explanatory power of psychological theories such as cognitive dissonance. Probably the most promising single theory adopted is that of Fishbein (1967, 1971), and it is still being developed. Particular strengths of Fishbein's approach include the following:

1. A precise definition of attitude (i.e., as overall evaluation) and the distinction of this concept from other related concepts such as beliefs and behavioral intentions (see above).

2. A recognition that when prediction is the main research aim, it is best achieved through precise measures of behavioral intention (rather than overall evaluation: an individual may have a high regard for an object but be in no position to purchase it), and also precise measures of behavior.

3. The incorporation of Rosenberg's value–instrumentality formulation (see above).

4. Recognition of the importance of social and situational factors.

In the writer's opinion, it is a mistake to treat Fishbein's theory (1967) as a ready-made model for consumer attitude data, excluding other approaches. Like other academic work, the model has been developed apart from the context of consumer behavior, and, in consequence, disregards certain key concepts relevant to this behavior (Lunn, 1970; see also below). It does, however, represent a useful foundation on which to build a consumer attitude model.

Nevertheless it appears that the eclectic approach to consumer theory holds most promise for illuminating the attitude-behavior controversy. It is not that any single theory is rejected; rather, several possibly relevant theories are allowed to contribute to our understanding of consumer attitudes. In passing, it is worth noting that a more eclectic tradition is also developing among certain academic attitude researchers, especially in the United States. McGuire (1969b, 1970) is a protagonist of the approach. In the American Marketing Association paper, McGuire gives a fivefold classification of what he calls the guiding theories behind attitude change research, and he indicates some of their applications for the marketing area. The five theoretical paradigms are labeled Perceptual, Consistency, Learning, Functional, and Information Processing. In both papers McGuire insists that the various so-called rival theories are supplementary rather than conflicting. "Their assumptions about man and persuasion are quite different, but the difference resides in the tendency for each of the approaches to stress aspects of man and the social influence process which are neglected by other approaches." All the more reason, it might be argued, to incorporate a variety of these approaches into the study of consumer attitudes.

Sheth (1971) has presented a comprehensive conceptual model of attitude-behavior relationships, based on the work of several researchers including Dulany, Fishbein, Howard and Sheth, Rokeach, and Rosenberg. One of the aims has been to sort out the various dimensions of "attitudes" (see above), hypothesizing about their interrelationships and linking them to subsequent behavior.

A major contribution of Sheth's work has been to test this theory in a naturalistic setting, involving the choice behavior of a representative sample of 954 American housewives. The respondents formed a panel and recorded their purchases of several convenience foods, including instant breakfast (the object of the research), over five months. In addition, panel members were interviewed four times, with a questionnaire that included, in addition to relevant background data, a variety of attitudinal measures. The project monitored the launch of two new brands and the effects of these on sales of an existing brand. Since the study was longitudinal, time-lag analyses could be carried out on the same respondents.

Sheth's results, based on analysis carried out to date, include the following:

1. Evaluative beliefs are good predictors of overall evaluation and, to a lower extent, of buying intention.

2. Buying intention predicts subsequent behavior, although at a lower level.

3. Changes in behavior also predict changes in the various dimensions of attitude; that is, people appear to adjust their attitudes in the light of experience with the product. (It will be recalled that the interdependence between attitudes and behavior is a central tenet of consumer decision-process theory.)

4. Situational factors unanticipated by respondents at the time of stating buying intentions (e.g., competitive promotional efforts from two new brands with different appeals, the frequent unavailability of the new brands when the housewife went shopping) appeared to exert a significant effect on the predictive power of buying intentions.

To quote Sheth (1971, p. 121):

> All of this indicates that what is found to be a very high correlation between behavioral intention and behavior in the laboratory type experimental studies (Dulany, 1968; Fishbein, 1967) may be due to two factors, both of which are likely to be nonexistent in naturalistic situations. They are (1) contiguity of expressing behavioral intention and actual behavior and (2) lack of situational variations from one individual to the other and from one time period to the other because these are controlled in the experiment.

This ties in with the findings of the R.B.L. In-Store Influence project quoted above. Here a high relationship was observed between actual purchase and buying intention in relation to specific brands and products, established shortly prior to the shopping visit.

Sheth also raises problems surrounding the definition and measurement of consumer behavior. His project used panel data, which should in general provide a relatively high level of accuracy and precision. However, the time interval problem can arise here. For instance, in the Columbia Buyer Behavior study that provided Sheth's data, many consumers did not buy even once between interviews, particularly in the case of the two new brands.

This leads in to a more general issue raised by the writer elsewhere (Lunn, 1970): namely, that in attitude-behavior projects, it has usually been assumed—if implicitly—that any weakness lay in the attitudinal rather than in the behavioral component. However, the behavioral questions used in market research field projects take various forms and often leave much to be desired. Not only do they lack precision (e.g., "brand usually bought"), they also fail to recognize that consumers are by no means always single-brand buyers. Here the consumer decision-process concept of a repertoire of brands, all of which the housewife may regard as sufficiently satisfactory for her purpose, might provide more precise behavioral data. R.B.L. is currently experimenting with a technique that may contribute to a solution: the housewife is asked to estimate how many times she expects to buy each of a list of brands during her next ten purchases.

A further valuable theoretical consideration is that of attitude stability. Building on the work of Sherif, Sherif, and Nebergall, (1965), Day (1970a, 1970b) has developed measures of stability in terms of consumers' involvement in the product field and their confidence in brand purchase. He claims to have found higher relationships between attitude change and subsequent behavioral change where attitudes are stable than where they are unstable, as defined above.[4] This theoretical position could be related to that of Rokeach and others who have distinguished between central and peripheral attitudes. The former are more deeply held and have more relationships with other attitudes and cognitions. As a result they will be harder to change; but once changed, they might be expected to exhibit greater stability and closer relationships with behavior.

Day quotes his findings as an argument for analyzing attitude-behavior data within consumer segments (i.e., contrasting consumers with stable and unstable attitudes) rather than on aggregate samples. The writer would argue for extending the principle of segmentation to include additional variables. Market segmentation studies have firmly established the value of defining target groups of consumers in terms of needs and values relevant to the product field (e.g., Lunn, 1971b). It is probable that different levels of attitude-behavior relationships would be found within such target groups.

To conclude this section on the attitude-behavior controversy, we note that it has been argued that the published findings in this area are by no means as negative as is sometimes implied. Nevertheless, there is considerable scope for improvement if confidence in the value of consumer attitude data is to be maintained. Part of this improvement must occur in the area of methodology. Many published studies have used crude and inadequate measures of both attitudes and behavior.

---

[4] Day used the same Columbia panel data as Sheth.

There have also been conceptual weaknesses. For instance, general evaluations of particular objects have been related to specific future behavior in relation to these objects, regardless of the variety of additional variables that might be expected to determine behavior, including the situations in which it takes place. It is valuable here to distinguish the purposes for which attitude information is required. For prediction, buying intention would seem to be the most appropriate concept; but care should be taken over the phraseology of the measuring instrument and over the definition and measurement of behavior. For many consumer research problems, we should attempt to represent the brand choice situation in our behavioral measure. For diagnostic purposes, specific evaluative beliefs and attitudes of a motivational kind (as defined above) will be most relevant.

A greater interest in theory has already led to the clearer conceptualization described in this section. But theory is, of course, playing a wider part by indicating some of the personal and social variables that intervene between consumers' attitudes—however defined and measured—and their behavior and in guiding the interpretation of attitude-behavior data—for instance, in recognizing the interdependence of these two variables. The promise of Fishbein's theoretical work has been referred to, but in the writer's opinion, it would be a mistake to restrict theoretical development to any single approach, especially one evolved outside the consumer context.

Finally, a distinction should be made between the requirements of basic research designed to advance our general understanding of the consumer and research for day-to-day practical problems. Basic research tends to be complex, and one project may involve the inclusion of a large number of variables (e.g., the Columbia Buyer Project). However, the point of such projects is to add to knowledge and to test our assumptions. This degree of detail and complexity would normally be inappropriate and unfeasible for day-to-day projects. At the same time, the inclusion of more rather than fewer variables is likely to "remove the noise from the channel" and to increase the precision of the results. It is a matter of deciding the optimum balance in each case.

CONCLUSION

This paper has reviewed the current position of decision-process models and has argued that they hold considerable promise for market research, on both a day-to-day level and a more basic level

—not least because they help us to clarify our assumptions about how marketing action can influence consumer behavior. They have, moreover, an important part to play in identifying variables for inclusion in specific research projects. Here it is important to strike a balance between what may be gained in precision and what may be lost in complexity. Such models also draw attention to the needs for greater clarification of the concepts and measures we use in market research and for a greater use of longitudinal research designs and studies designed to replicate previous findings (Kollat, Engel, and Blackwell, 1970; Pellemans, 1971).

Consumer behavior is still a relatively young discipline, and all the models reviewed here contain considerable scope for revision and development. It is hoped that this development will come as much from market researchers as from researchers in the academic field.

APPENDIX

This appendix contains three flow charts representing the theories of Nicosia, Engel et al., and Howard and Sheth. There is no space here for a definition of the various concepts and interrelationships. Aspects of these theories are outlined in the main text and full descriptions can be found in the references given below. For Figure 3.1 (a flow chart of the Nicosia model), see Nicosia (1966); for Figure 3.2 (a flow chart of the Engel model), see Engel et al. (1968); for Figure 3.3 (a flow chart of the Howard-Sheth model), see Howard and Sheth (1969).

Where applicable, solid lines on the charts indicate flow of information; dashed lines indicate feedback effects.

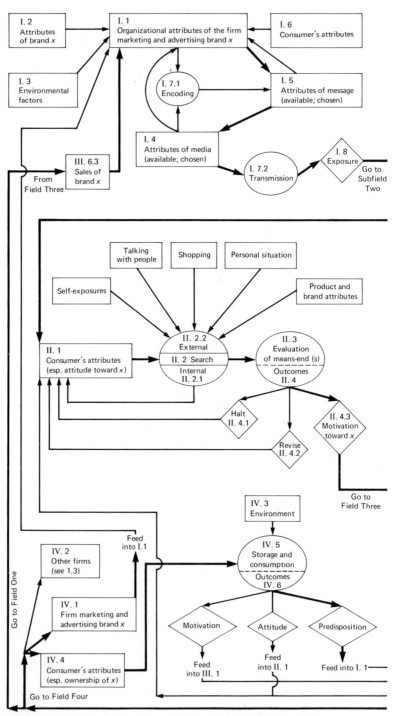

Figure 3.1 Comprehensive Scheme of the Nicosia Model

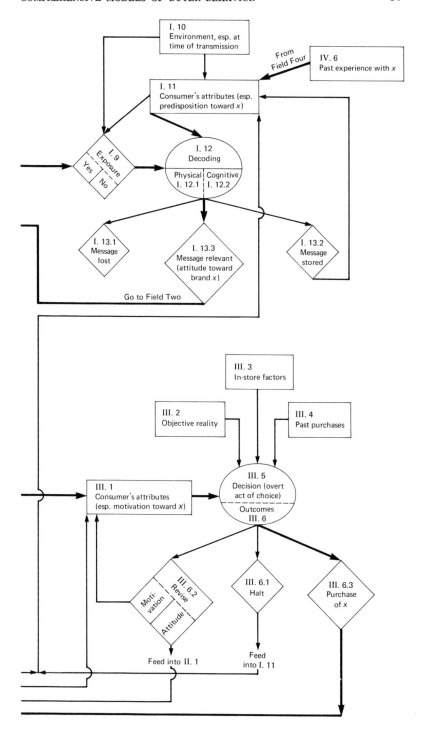

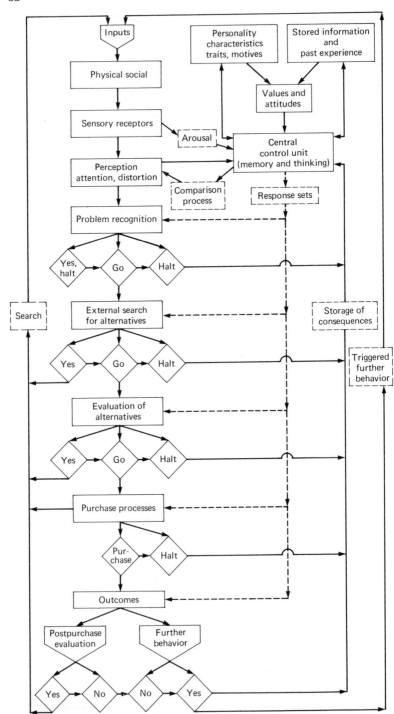

Figure 3.2 Complete Representation of the Engel Model

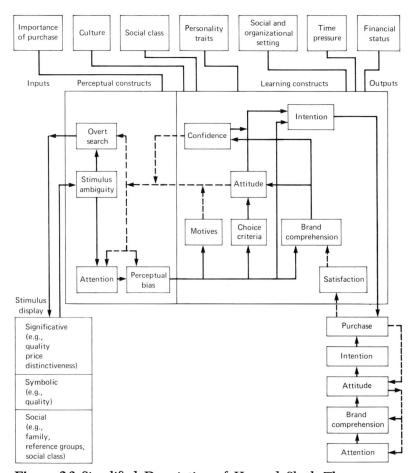

Figure 3.3 Simplified Description of Howard–Sheth Theory

4

SOME GENERALIZATIONS AND PROBLEMS REGARDING CONSUMER PROBLEM SOLVING IN GROCERY STORE CHANNELS

JAMES M. CARMAN

Professor of Business Administration
University of California at Berkeley

Let me begin by stating what I am not going to discuss. The chief constraint placed on this paper limits it to generalizations for products sold in grocery store channels. These generalizations are not inapplicable to other products. However, there are some limits on the range of product attributes under consideration, the most important being the following:

Price. Very expensive products or those frequently purchased on credit are not considered.

Durability. Products used over extended periods of time or requiring service are excluded.

Social significance. Although some grocery store products do have social significance to the buyer, this significance is probably not as great as for, say, apparel.

Frequency of purchase. On the average, the products considered are more frequently purchased than most. However, new or infrequently purchased products can be found on grocery lists, and these do enter into the discussion.

COMPETITIVE RIVALRY
AND RETAIL STRUCTURE

The next limit placed on our general model involves some areas of theoretical development in consumer behavior that are not discussed here in any detail, for to have done so would have taken the paper beyond the topic of consumer problem solving. These areas are learning theory, social class theory, cognitive dissonance, and diffusion of innovation. Learning theory is reflected in the model in the same way as in Howard's (1963) model (i.e., by developing different models at different discrete stages of the learning process).

Social class theory is neglected because we have found it to be of minor importance in the purchase of grocery store products. We do believe that consumer behavior and problem solving may be uniquely influenced by culture (i.e., values and life styles) at the far extremes of the class distributors or in small extreme racial and ethnic subcultures.

Generalization. Our research has elicited no differences in techniques of consumer problem solving for grocery store products attributable to cultural differences among the approximately 90 percent of families in the mainstream of American life. Similarly, we can find no evidence that race has an independent influence on consumer problem solving.

The model we discuss relies on some ideas of cognitive theory. In this spirit, the notion of cognitive dissonance is accepted as correct and operating but is not developed in detail.

This paper is concerned with the acquisition and processing of information. It is not concerned with information transmission. Thus the diffusion of innovation is not covered.

So much for what is not included. What is to be discussed? The challenge of constructing a comprehensive theoretical model led me to review the existing comprehensive models, which fortunately contained more similarities than I had remembered. Where would we be in this field if every comprehensive model had little or nothing in common with others? In short, all the points that I want to discuss in depth could be easily organized into the Howard and Sheth (1969) model, Howard's (1963) model, or that of Engel, Kollat, and Blackwell (1968). I see no reason to begin anew if the work cited provides a conceptual framework on which to hang what I hope will be some useful insights. Therefore, the discussion follows the organization of the Howard model.

This paper approaches a comprehensive model from the direction of empirical work to theoretical work; that is, constructs are suggested that stem from measurable variables rather than from theory. Nonetheless, the constructs are designed to be consistent with theory and to reduce the total number of variables included in such a model. The questions are, What variables one should consider? and What are the effects of each on each element of the decision process? An answer to the first requires that one build and measure constructs from the individual's environment that are logical, theoretically consistent, and efficient predictors of differences in the decision process. Thus, although the questions are independent it is difficult in research to separate them. Similarly, in the organization of this paper, it is difficult to suggest important constructs without stating why they are important. Here are some generalizations we can make.

EXOGENOUS VARIABLES

The exogenous variables in Howard's model are discussed first because most of the generalizations that are offered concern the effects of the consumer's environment on her choice process. This statement takes some liberties with the original model; however, Howard said that the exogenous variables have significant influence on the process of search for information, on the amount and type of perceptual bias, on the state of goals, and on the choice process itself.

Our work certainly agrees with this. Environmental and situational variables play a more important role in determining approaches to problem solving than do generalized typologies of cognitive styles.

Generalization. Observed associations found between demographic characteristics of consumers and their behavior are slight or nonexistent, not because environmental factors are not important determinants of consumer behavior but because these variables have not been organized into constructs that meaningfully reflect the influence of environment on behavior.

The classic example of this is life cycle—a construct of age and family composition that has given more insights into behavior than the sum of its parts. Family composition can also help in understanding other features of behavior. For example, an understanding of brand choice and brand loyalty for a personal product usually requires rather detailed knowledge about the characteristics of all family members. A construct combining usage rate and family structure is one that is seldom tested, but it too may be a powerful predictor of behavior. Usage rate alone has been an important predictor of shopping behavior, but these studies have seldom studied usage in combination with other related demographic variables (Bass, Tigert, and Lansdale, 1969; Carman, 1970).

One family structure construct that has received some attention is the role structure of the family, that is, the functional organization for purchase decision making that the family has developed. In studying grocery shopping, we have found it useful to consider only the role played by the wife versus the role she would like to play.

Generalization. The current and recent employment status of the homemaker is an important determinant of her shopping behavior. Working wives and those who have behavior patterns conditioned by recent work experience demonstrate differences in search patterns, perceptions, and the choice process not found in most full-time housewives (Carman, 1970). This group of women is unique, and careful study by an interested scholar is justified.

Generalization. A woman's perceptions of the roles in life that are important also have a definite impact on her methods of choosing brands and searching for information (Bucklin and Carman, 1967, p. 42).

In studies of brand loyalty, wives who rated the maternal role lower in importance than average were found to be more brand loyal, and those who rated community involvement higher in importance than average were found to be less brand loyal than average. Other more tentative evidence suggests that this construct is a powerful predictor of the internal choice process as well as of external search behavior.

Before leaving the exogenous variables, let us briefly discuss the income variable. Much is said today about the ghetto consumer. "The ghetto consumer" is itself a construct composed of place of residence, race, income, education, work status, and probably many other factors. Because of the activist orientation of the programs that have motivated interest in the subject, this may be a useful construct. In some situations, however, and for the scholar attempting to understand the ghetto consumer's problem-solving process, this construct is too complex to be useful. For example, all the evidence I have found suggests that other things being equal, the more severe the income constraint, the more extensive the problem-solving process.

This finding has not been raised to the level of a generalization because in the research on consumer problem solving it has never been possible to hold "other things equal." Moreover, it is probably not desirable to do so. Low income seldom appears without some interaction effect with other variables. For example, although my attempts to find associations between mobility and the consumer shopping processes have largely been unsuccessful, we have discovered that at low income levels, upward mobiles are more careful shoppers than nonmobiles. But what are the environmental factors that have caused the mobiles to be mobile?

In looking for predictors of shopping behavior, these environmental factors may be more useful from both explanatory and predictive standpoints. In sum, to treat demographic variables in their raw, cold state or to treat them only as constraints will underutilize their value in understanding consumer behavior.

A similar statement can be made about general personality scales. I am willing to agree that self-esteem, role perception, need for cognitive clarity, and a few other reasonably general scales may have a role in understanding consumer problem solving. However, the more specific to the shopping and homemaking tasks these constructs can be made, and the more they can be made to be proxies of surrogates for environment, the more useful they will become for consumer behavior.

Unfortunately, scales of these types do not appear on any of the standard personality batteries. Existing tests are simply not specific enough to the tasks of homemaker, wife, and purchasing agent to be useful predictors of behavior. It is time that consumer behaviorists began to construct personality scales.

The Engel, Kollat, and Blackwell (EKB) model comes closer than the Howard model to showing the way personality influences consumer problem solving. However, even the former model falls somewhat short for my taste. To speak in terms of EKB, general personality—which is, of course, environmentally conditioned—influences values and attitudes but also influences perception and the search for alternatives.

Now Howard and many others tell us that perception influences our evaluation of search information, our interpretation of the state of alternatives, and our stored information of past experience. Thus if general personality influences perception and style of search, and perceptual bias influences every other stage of the internal choice process, personality does play an important role. The interactions are so great and the specifics of the situation so important that given our present state of knowledge, other variables are more efficient than general personality scales in understanding behavior.

Some examples may help to make my position clear on this

point. Donald Cox (1967) has employed some general personality constructs to help predict difference in the choice process. Three that may be useful are the need for cognitive clarity, cognitive style, and the level of self-esteem. Subjects with high need for clarity will try to simplify the problem more rapidly and less objectively than will those with a low need for clarity. Yet if subjects were faced first with a choice between 20 brands and next with a choice between three, we postulate that the differences in the choice process would be greater between the two problems than between individuals on the same problem. Cox's work suggests a second example. He found that subjects who were low in self-esteem were low in socialization and were generally "information avoiders."

Problem. In our own work it has not been clear that personal sources of information can be any more than an indicator of the extent of socialization; that is, they identify people who socialize more, have more conversations with other people, and have a greater opportunity to receive information on purchasing. This suggests that closing the link between socialization and the use of personal sources should precede closing the link between self-esteem and socialization. In particular, it should be very useful now to extend the work of Arndt (1967).

A third example is motivated by the demand theory of Kelvin Lancaster (1968) coupled with the work on multidimensional nonmetric scaling. For the moment, extensive problem solving is assumed to render conceptualization more complete. The more usual case of limited problem solving is considered subsequently.

The model can be described in terms of a simple indifference curve. This discussion is limited to two-space geometry, but the theory is easily extended to n-space. Let us begin by thinking of the classic indifference curve analysis, where the quantities of two goods are plotted on the axes, a budget line is constructed by knowing the price of each good, and the classic solution involves determining the quantities of each good demanded by finding the point of tangency of the budget line with the consumer's indifference curve. (Figure 4.1) Note that in the Lancaster analysis (1968) the indifference curve does not belong on this graph because consumers don't demand goods, they demand characteristics.

Before we make the transformation, however, we have one small complexity to unravel. Are there more goods than characteristics? The same number? Or more characteristics than goods? When the number is the same, the first-stage solutions (not the answers) look very much like the conventional solutions. This case

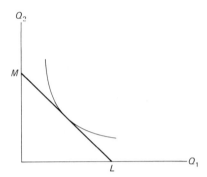

Figure 4.1 G Space

is too unusual to spend time on. However, it is straightforward, and it is also the proper approach when the number of characteristics is greater than the number of goods (e.g., in underdeveloped societies). Perhaps this explains why it is more like the classical case, in which there are no assumptions of affluence.

In the more interesting case, there are more goods than characteristics. This is the situation surrounding most goods in a developed economy like ours (i.e., where there are a number of nonidentical products that provide alternative ways of obtaining similar quantities of similar sets of characteristics).

For this case, it is most interesting to study the characteristics space. In Figure 4.2 we assume two characteristics and four goods. In this figure, the rays represent increasing quantities of characteristics with increasing quantities of the good. The addition of the budget line in C space is easily added, given: (1) the prices of goods and (2) the quantity of each characteristic per unit. Connecting *all* budget points, one will arrive at the quantity of characteristics that can be achieved by buying combinations of goods. This analysis will yield an efficient frontier with combinations that will yield more for the money than other combinations. The exact combination chosen will depend on the point on the efficient frontier that is tangent to the consumer's private indifference curve, Q on the graph. Thus the rays represent product design and promotional strategy decisions of sellers, the budget points represent pricing decisions of sellers, and the indifference curve the private preference decisions of buyers.

It may be well to point out quickly how a price reduction by 1 or the addition of more *a* by 1 could place the frontier at some combination of 1 and 3 and exclude 2 entirely. A bad design or price could place some good completely off the frontier. However,

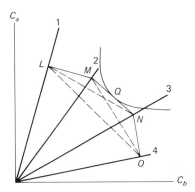

Figure 4.2 *C* Space

even being on the frontier, the seller could appeal to more consumers by price and design changes—or perhaps by trying to shift
the indifference curve. One interesting behavioral fact flows from
the mathematics: the optimum bundle of goods for one individual
will never have any more different goods in it than there are characteristics.

Many more substitutions are possible in this model than in
the classic model of homogeneous goods and price competition
only, simply because of the availability of many different product
alternatives. On the other hand, there are other price changes, say
in 4, that will have no effect on the relevant frontier, hence none
on purchases. This is not true in the classical model.

The problem of defining a product group, which is a major
difficulty in empirical demand studies, is aided only slightly by this
approach. Two goods would clearly be in different product groups
if they had no characteristics in common. Substitutions would then
have to come through income reallocations or private indifference
map changes. It may be, however, that automobiles, home furnishings, and vacations have characteristics in common (e.g., a pleasant
environment for relaxation). If they do, the definition of product
groups is still a problem.

If one can get an operational handle on the product class
problem, the use of the Lancaster approach in planning marketing
strategy has real potential: One locates the indifference curve of a
significant market segment and offers a product with characteristics
and price that dominate the frontier at that point. This fits fairly
well with the way we observe marketing decisions being made.

Perhaps a tougher problem is involved in operationally determining the relevant set of characteristics and ascertaining their

quantities in each good. Refer to *Consumers Reports*, where "best buys" are recommended. You will find that the highest ratings go to products with relatively few characteristics. You will also find fewer "best buys" recommendations of goods whose characteristics are more subjective and hard to measure.

A fair amount of progress has been made on this problem through the use of multidimensional scaling. Measurement and analytical problems remain, but some claims to identification of characteristics, hence product-class definitions, have been put forth.

This long digression but brief summary of Lancaster's theory brings us finally to the third example indicating why personality measures must be made specific to the task being studied. It has been claimed that people are quite homogeneous attributing characteristics to a particular brand. This homogeneity in perceptions, if it exists, is probably a tribute to the communications industry. If it did not exist, a basic assumption of this approach would not be met. Lancaster's model assumes that the quantity of each characteristic of a brand is ordinally measurable and that consumers perceive these quantities in the same way. Notice the complex way in which perception enters at two points: (1) in the quantity, if any, of each characteristic the consumer attributes to each brand, and (2) in the personal importance or utility that the consumer attaches to large and small quantities of each characteristic.

Problem. Does information affect the characteristics attributed to a brand, the consumer's desire to own a particular bundle of characteristics, or both?

In extensive problem solving, this problem looks very much like the hierarchy of effects debate (Palda, 1966). Does information alter the consumer's *knowledge* of what the product has to offer, her *preference* for a particular bundle of characteristics, or both? Is the answer a function of the content of the information? Even if one thinks he knows the answer for extensive problem solving, what happens in limited problem solving?

Generalization. From the evidence we have been able to find, it is suggested that consumers engaging in limited problem solving collapse many dimensions into one and rank the stable brand characteristics on this aggregated dimension. Then brand choices are made, on the basis of the state of a reduced set of usually no more than four dimensions. These are the characteristics that are the most subject to change. The lowest ranked brands on the aggregated dimension are excluded from consideration. The choice criteria then becomes the aggregate dimension, availability, and one or two quality dimensions. In the Lancaster model, price enters strongly into the decision but not as a characteristic.

The use of this reduced-form dimension of the stable dimensions of a brand differs somewhat from the models suggested by others. Howard (1963), Cox (1969), and Hughes and Naert (1970) all suggest models of roughly the following form:

$$P = \sum_{i=1}^{K} b_i A_i C_i$$

where $P =$ predisposition toward a particular brand,

$b_i =$ salience or importance attached to the ith of K product characteristic i

$A_i =$ perceived level of characteristic i contained in the brand

$C_i =$ measure of the confidence attached to one's ability to measure the attitude: the inverse of uncertainty.

These writers postulate (or have found empirically) that on all or most product characteristics, subjects are unable to sort out the independent effects of each b_i, A_i, and C_i. Cox and Wilding seem to believe that b_i will be positively correlated with C_i in the respondent's mind. Other research suggests that A_i will be correlated with the level of the characteristic on many other dimensions. Hughes explains that these intercorrelations and interaction effects occur because all $3K$ terms of the equation are the product of the same cognitive process. Sheth and Hughes, working independently, found that models with equal weighting and no confidence term

(i.e., $P = \sum_{i=1}^{K} A_i$) are superior to the form suggested above.

Problem. Is the saliency unimportant because we lack statistical and methodological technique to identify its independent effects, or has internal simplification gone so far that consumers do not perceive the brand as a set of independent characteristics?

Howard has spoken of a distinction between "choice criteria" and the sum of the subdimension attitudes. This comes closer to the model postulated here and is not much different from the concept of "brand attitude" that is used by most of us.

The key features of the model suggested here are (1) an in-

ternal cognitive problem simplification step that yields some aggregate predisposition toward each brand; (2) the formation of an
evoked set of alternative brands created by dropping brands with
low predisposition on the aggregate dimension; (3) the conscious
separation of availability, variable quality features if any, and
price from the aggregate dimension; and (4) a greater impact of
environmental and situational factors than generalized personality
factors on the results of each of the first three steps.

SEARCH FOR
CLARIFICATION OF ALTERNATIVES

If these features leave the problem-solving process somewhat vague,
it is because so much grocery store shopping is based on limited
problem solving; that is, the learning is so complete that it is difficult
to picture the process clearly. However, when we turn to situations
involving formal search, a more complete problem-solving process
can be observed. In grocery shopping, this complete problem-
solving process is seldom observable. We start by stating some generalizations about formal search and then attempt to put the pieces
together into a summary model.

Generalization. Store loyalty is one of the most important techniques for problem simplification and is thus a key determinant of
brand choice. When the shopper makes her choice in a single store,
she restricts the number of brand alternatives available to her.
However, store loyalty indicates more than a simple decrease in
brand alternatives. It is an indicator of cognitive style. The combined behavioral construct can be called "shopping proneness."

Generalization. Consumers who are not shopping prone will shop
in a small number of stores, and within those stores they will remain
loyal to a small number of brands rather than making careful choices
between the values offered in the customary stores.

I have not yet had an opportunity to develop measures of
shopping proneness. However, a construct that may be the same as
shopping proneness is widely used in commercial research work;
the construct involves a typology of shopper types, and the descriptive names most commonly used are price shoppers, quality
shoppers, methodical shoppers, and experimental (or value)
shoppers.

Demographic and socioeconomic variables, as well as personality measures of consumers, will help to explain differences in
shopping proneness. Even with grocery store products, differences

in problem-solving styles will vary nearly as much between products for the same individual as between different individuals for the same product. "Involvement" with the product or the shopping task may be considered to be synonymous with shopping proneness, but the concept as used here differs from perceived risk. Perceived risk is merely one determinant of shopping proneness.

As a product class, the perceived risk for grocery products is not high, but it is an important cause of the variation in problem-solving styles between products. Risk is perceived as high most often for the following:

(a) Products with status significance (e.g., coffee, meat for company meals)
(b) Products that are not consumed in a single using
(c) Relatively expensive products
(d) Products that have been the subject of well-publicized quality, health, or safety problems.

Information search can also be influenced by differences on the supply side of the market.

Generalization. A good strategy for shopping for one product may not be a good strategy for shopping for another sold through the same channels of distributors and having the same general characteristics.

Differences in the extent of learning, the usage rate, the competition, and the perceived risk all contribute to the differences in problem-solving style that can be observed in the marketplace. These constructs are not just different ways of describing the same phenomenon, and it is important to see that each one has an independent effect. For example, results of Bauer (1967) and Cunningham (1967), as well as our own research, have indicated that perceived risk does not necessarily decrease with learning. Some uncertainty may be reduced with use, but not all. Some products with the characteristics listed above are perceived as inherently risky. Thus problem-solving styles by the same person may differ between products, even though the state of learning is the same for each product. In particular, the evoked set of alternative brands will be *smaller* for high-risk products than for low-risk products.

It is interesting to compare the last statement with the findings of Professor Robertson and others working in the field of diffusion of innovation. Here it is usually assumed that the higher the risk, the more formal the search that takes place. Our findings are not contradictory but reflect only the difference between extensive and limited problem solving. A problem-solving pattern for high-risk products, once established, is more rigid than the pattern that exists for lower-risk products.

Compared with product classes having very different characteristics, on the other hand, the low level of perceived risk, the high level of general performance by the industry, and the high degree of learning displayed in the marketplace for packaged goods, mean that consumers rarely exert any real effort to obtain information; instead, they tend to use what is naturally and easily available. These three characteristics create frustrations for the student of consumer behavior who is attempting to empirically validate sound hypotheses using a grocery store product. The reasons for their frequent use—large number of users, frequency of purchase, availability of commercial panel data—are certainly valid. However, if we are to achieve increased understanding of the consumer problem-solving process, more attention must be given to products with less frequent purchase and a higher unit price. In the following two examples, food products have fallen short in my own research.

First, the generally low level of risk makes grocery store products poor choices for studying the choice between personal and commercial sources of information. Friends and neighbors are used as information sources for these products. Because risk is low, however, the extent of use is related more to the extent of general socialization than to consumer problem solving. Yet socialization is correlated with shopping proneness, working status, and role, which are all constructs that influence the problem-solving process through other avenues. I know of no work that has adequately sorted out these effects.

The second example recognizes that with grocery products the "innovator" of diffusion of innovation fame is much harder to find and identify than is the case with other products. Here the shopping proneness constructs may be the chief predictor of the innovator. Sellers resort to sampling and buyers respond to sampling because delivering of a product into the house at no cost may be the only successful technique for obtaining a significant number of new product triers.

Generalization. Two dominant issues govern behavior related to the use of various sources of information on grocery store products—source credibility and convenience.

Thus some highly credible sources of information for consumers (e.g., consumer group publications, feature articles in shelter magazines, and government pamphlets) are not of great overall importance to the consumer. Experiments in information value that do not involve realistic control over the cost (i.e., the convenience) of the information are doomed to failure. Consequently, symbolic information on purchased goods is very important because of its convenience. However, the frequency with which specific types of symbolic information are used may also be a function of the quantity of information it contains.

The single most important source of information for grocery store products is product trial. It is the most credible and is also convenient and inexpensive. If the product is one with low risk, consumers seem to be more willing to increase risk and try a new product with a coupon. I feel confident that a study of sampling in new product introduction will show that sellers have felt sampling necessary far more frequently with high-risk than with low-risk products.

The importance of advertising as a source of information is also more easily understood if one considers its convenience and credibility. Since advertising is convenient, it would be important if it were credible. However, direct questioning will reveal a high level of skepticism regarding advertising content. But advertising is important. What is the source of its credibility? The answer is the sheer size of the advertising budget. The large sums a manufacturer spends on advertising attests to his reputability. Thus for most consumers the mere presence of national advertising is an indicator of credibility. Repeated reinforcement no doubt helps to increase the importance of advertising as a source of information; but (to tie this point into one made previously in discussing the Lancaster model) our reading of the literature suggests that in many instances advertising can alter attitudes toward a brand and also the importance consumers place on certain features of the brand.

It is no accident if these remarks on convenient information sources are reminiscent of the earlier discussion on the cognitive device of an aggregate brand attitude dimension.

Generalization. Regardless of individual differences in cognitive style, the problem-solving process places strong reliance on problem reduction (i.e., not making all possible comparisons); this simplification process occurs both in internal problem-solving processes and in external search behavior.

SUMMARY

In this long discourse we have attempted to relate a number of constructs that appear to be useful in analyzing the consumer prob-

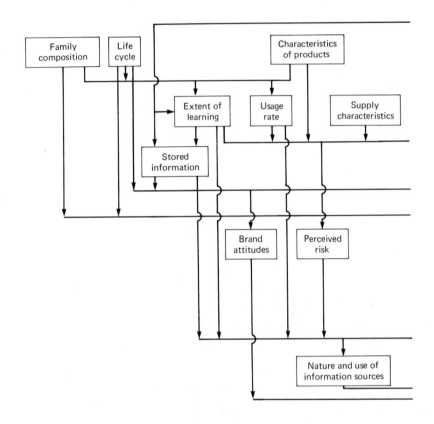

Figure 4.3 Partial Diagram of Consumer Problem–Solving Process

lem-solving process. Believing that a schematic summary of these generalizations will help to sharpen one's understanding of these relationships, we present Figure 4.3. To increase the usefulness of the figure, a brief summary follows. Note that an attempt has been made to keep the model similar to Howard's model. Exogenous variables appear at the top, search and the choice processes in the middle, and the state of alternatives at the bottom. On the other hand, the model is not complete. Some steps, such as triggering, are omitted. Also, to avoid showing schematically concepts that were not dealt with in the paper, only the exogenous variables discussed are represented. There is certainly an implication of cause and effect, but I do not intend that the diagram adequately describe the steps in a time-ordered process. The figure depicts constructs that in-

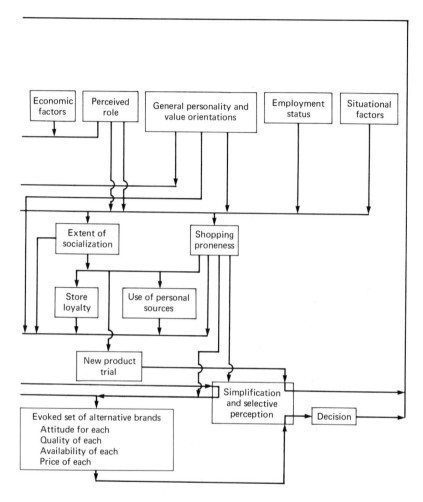

fluence the problem-solving process; it does not describe the steps in this process.

Beginning at the top, the extent of learning and usage rate appear as functions of family composition, life cycle, and the characteristics of the product. Of course the extent of learning also influences the amount of stored information. Brand attitudes are shown to be a function of life cycle, stored information, perceived role, and general personality variables and value orientations.

Perceived risk, showing explicitly in only one box, does not reflect accurately the number of places in which risk or confidence terms have been included in the model. This model involves three individual plus one summary confidence measure. First, the "perceived risk" box refers to *product-specific risk*, the risk stemming from usage rate, product characteristics, supply characteristics, household economic factors, and housewife's perceived role. Second, as discussed earlier, a "brand's attitude" may have associated with it a risk factor reflecting primarily the confidence one has in his stored knowledge about a brand but also reflecting more general personality and environmental influences. Third, the "simplification and selective perception" one employs in internalizing the information obtained from search is strongly conditioned by the credibility or *confidence attributed to each source of information.*

Finally, the evaluation of an "evoked set of alternative brands" is also conditioned by a confidence factor in the final "simplification and selective perception" process. This final confidence consideration is the one I believe Howard and Sheth must be suggesting in their "Confidence" box between "Brand Comprehension" and "Intention to Buy."

Continuing with our summary of the schematic diagram, the extent of socialization and shopping proneness are expressed as a function of family composition, life cycle, perceived role, general personality, employment status, and situational factors. Building on these, store loyalty, use of personal sources of information, and new product trial appear as functions of the extent of socialization and shopping proneness.

The nature and use of information sources in the search for clarification of alternatives are shown to be functions of stored information, the extent of learning, usage rate, perceived risk, values, general personality, the extent of socialization, shopping proneness, store loyalty, and the extent of use of personal sources of information. The information from search is then processed through the internal mechanism of selective perception and data reduction.

For an evoked set of brands, the resulting information, coupled with existing attitudes toward various brands, yields a ranking on general attitude, variable quality features, availability, and price. These ranked data are again distilled through the internal perception and simplification mechanism to produce a decision.

Probably the most striking aspect of this representation is the multiple effects of the first layer of constructs that cycle and recycle through other constructs at lower levels. It might not be possible to make sense out of this diagram without using such summary constructs as brand attitude, perceived risk, extent of socialization, and shopping proneness. The writer might even be accused of suggesting artificial constructs merely to simplify the scheme.

That does not happen to be the case. On the other hand, operational measures of all constructs in the diagram are not readily available from the writer. But this is not the case with some of the first-level constructs and with the four summary constructs just mentioned. In fact, one important objective of this paper has been to suggest that these four summary constructs—brand attitude and preference as developed from multidimensional scaling, product-specific perceived risk as used in a portion of the work of Donald Cox and his students, the extent of socialization as developed through the work on the diffusion of innovation, and shopping proneness as developed in our own work—have not only been employed in empirical work but offer promise of being powerful predictors of choice behavior.

B
QUANTITATIVE MODELS

MICROSIMULATING CONSUMER BEHAVIOR

DONALD E. SEXTON, JR.
Associate Professor of Business
Graduate School of Business
Columbia University

This paper uses an example of a stochastic consumer microsimulation to show the type of structure that may be imposed on the modeling of consumer behavior by digital simulation.[1]

SIMULATION IN MARKETING

Kotler has characterized the processes of the market as "non-linear, dynamic, interactive, lagged, and downright difficult." Any observer of the relative success of management science in production versus marketing must agree that market processes have been difficult to analyze quantitatively.

Perhaps the most flexible but difficult to apply of quantitative methods is simulation. Typically, in the production area it is a last resort in the solution of complex queueing, inventory, or traffic problems. After people in marketing become disillusioned with analytical techniques such as linear programming (often misused as a publicity vehicle for ad agencies), several retreated from quantitative models entirely, others moved to more basic tools (e.g., subjective probability), and some considered simulation.

Reported commercial successes in market simulation are still

---

[1] Originally this model was designed to answer "What if . . ." questions about advertising policy, but it can be used to answer broader questions concerning marketing strategy. In many ways it is similar to the model of Amstutz (1967).

rare (Amstutz, 1967; Beale, 1966; Gersch, 1969; and Sexton, 1968), but interest in them is currently high. A few years ago we visited 20 of the leading consumer products firms and advertising agencies. Most were involved in simulation—at the least as an opinion organization device, at the most (hopefully) as a predictor device.

Simulation has been a more consistent aid to marketing theory than to practice. The expectations of marketing theorists for simulation were well summarized a few years ago by Glock and Nicosia (1963, p. 26):

> While we now have neither the theory nor the body of empirical evidence necessary to construct a fully developed [consumer decision] process model in mathematical terms, attempts toward approximating such a model could add precision to theory construction in the field and provide for testing both the adequacy of existing theoretical statements and for specifying the properties of such statements.

As our reference frame for evaluating the attainment of these objectives by consumer microsimulation, we are examining a simulation that we have formulated and worked with.

THE SIMULATED ENVIRONMENT

The simulated market consists of representative potential consumers and retailers. Only one product or product class is dealt with, although there may be several brands of that product. The product is viewed as a multidimensional object. Each consumer forms his overall attitude toward a brand partly by evaluating it on each dimension.

All the simulated manufacturers sell through retailers. Manufacturers also advertise to consumers and supply promotional material to the retailers. The retailers exhibit these materials and may engage in personal selling for any brand. Consumers are exposed to information; they shop, purchase, and alter their attitudes toward brands. They also spread word-of-mouth messages about the various brands.

DATA INPUT

An initial perspective of the model can be obtained from an inspection of its data requirements. There are three basic sources of data: (1) the manufacturer of the product, (2) his advertising agency, and (3) a sample of potential consumers of the product.

Exhibited in the Appendixes A to C are three rather rough questionnaire drafts—one for the firm, one for the ad agency, and

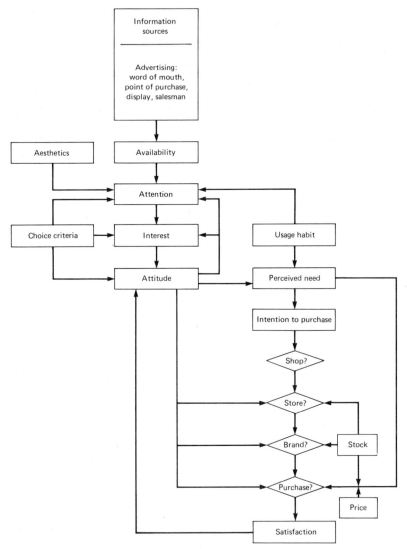

Figure 5.1 Underlying Behavior Model

one for the consumers. Briefly, the firm supplies information about market structure and the possible appeals (dimensions) of the product; the advertising agency describes the theme, intensity, and media schedule of the planned advertising campaign and estimates these variables for the campaigns of competitors; the consumer sample provides data concerning the demographic makeup of the market, the audiences of various vehicles, product usage rates

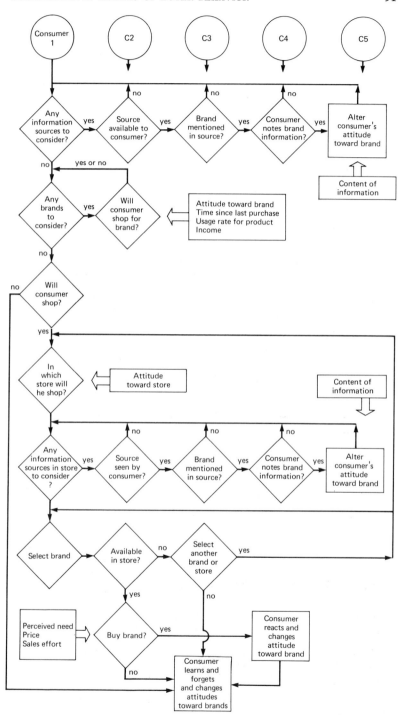

Figure 5.2 Consumer Product Microsimulation

for each consumer, and consumer evaluations of the brands of the product.

SEQUENCE OF
EVENTS IN THE SIMULATION

For each simulated consumer, the pattern of events in the model is based on the chronology of a hypothetical purchasing cycle. This cycle includes the assimilation of information, the shopping decision, the purchase decision, the postpurchase reaction, and learning and forgetting. Figures 5.1 and 5.2 show the pattern of events in the simulation and the underlying behavior model, respectively.

To see more concretely the workings of the model, consider the market for beer. Assumed as given at the start of the periods to be simulated are the data just mentioned on product appeals, advertising campaigns, consumer evaluations, and so on. We shall trace a Mr. Green through a simulated purchase cycle. Following, on the left is a description of what happens to Mr. Green; on the right is a description of the corresponding events in the model. Examples of all functions cited appear in Appendix D.

Events in Mr. Green's Consumer Life

Mr. Green subscribes to *Time* and *Sports Illustrated*, buys *Reader's Digest* occasionally at a newsstand near where he works, listens to WMAQ on his way to work, and watches a wide spectrum of TV shows, but particularly sports events.

He notes an ad on the inside back cover of *Sports Illustrated*. The ad, for Gusto beer, stresses the beer's strong, manly taste and shows it in a chilled glass. Green, who thinks of himself as an ale man who prefers beer, has a liking for a strong taste in beer; since he recently arrived from England, however, he does not care much for coldness in beer. He had previously evaluated Gusto beer as a light beer sold

Corresponding Events in Model

At the beginning of each simulated period, the effects on each customer of information sources such as advertisements and word-of-mouth messages are considered. First, it is determined whether a particular medium (e.g., a magazine or a person) is available to the person.

If it is available to him, then there is a probability that the customer notes the information source (function 2). If he notes the source, his memory must be modified according to the contents of the source and its emphases (function 3).

mainly in cheap bars. After seeing this ad, Green considers Gusto to be a much stronger beer, and slightly colder than he had thought previously, but a beer in the same social class as he had previously judged.

During this period, Green attends a party at the home of a business superior where Gusto beer is served. This event causes him to further alter his opinion of Gusto, particularly his evaluation of its social appeal.

In Green's present opinion, Gusto is a strong, cold, beer that is socially acceptable (although he still has some doubts about the latter). He is a heavy drinker of beer and has not bought any six-packs for more than two weeks. During this period he decides to shop for beer.

Green considers the various stores to which he can go. The ABC Supermarket is usually inexpensive, but shopping there is

After the consumer has been exposed to all these information sources, the model attempts to answer the question, Will he go shopping for beer this period?

The perceived need, an operationally defined variable, of a customer for a given brand is a function of his attitude toward that brand, time since last purchase of the product, and his product usage rate (function 4). The probability that he will shop for the brand is a function of his perceived need for it and of his income level (function 5). The probability that he will shop for at least one brand (i.e., shop for the product at all) is derived from the probabilities of shopping for the various brands (function 6). These values are all calculated, and it is then determined whether the customer will shop for the product.

If he does go shopping, he selects the retailer toward whom he has the highest attitude and goes there.

Events in Mr. Green's
Consumer Life

time-consuming; Joe's Corner
Grocery Store is friendly but gen-
erally expensive; Frank's Corner
Grocery Store is convenient, but
Frank is unfriendly, and so forth.
Green decides to go to Joe's.

In Joe's store there is a Schiller's beer display that emphasizes
the product's "civilized" taste.
Green notes this display and now
feels that Schiller's beer has a
somewhat weak taste—reinforcing what he had thought before.

At this time, Green prefers
Gusto to any brand of beer and
decides to buy two six-packs of
Gusto.

But does Joe have Gusto in
stock? If the merchant does not
now carry Gusto, Green must
make a decision: Will he go to
the next most favorable retailer,
Frank's, and again think of purchasing Gusto, or will he stay at
Joe's and think of purchasing the
next most favorable brand?

Joe does have Gusto in stock
and Green makes his purchase.

Corresponding Events in Model

When he arrives at the retailer, he may be exposed to promotion material for various
brands. There are probabilities
that he will note these materials
(function 2). If he notes any of
them, his memory is altered by
the contents and emphases of this
material (function 3).

At this point there is some
brand toward which he has the
highest attitude.

If the retailer does not carry
this brand, the potential customer compares his attitude toward the brand with his attitude
toward the retailer. If the brand
attitude is higher, he selects and
goes to the retailer toward which
he has the next highest attitude.
If the retailer attitude is higher,
he considers the next most favorable brand and determines if the
retailer carries that brand.

When he finally finds a brand
that the retailer carries, the probability that the potential customer will purchase this brand is
a function of attitude toward the
brand, retail sales effort, and
price (function 7). If he does
not purchase the brand, he considers the next most favorable
appearing brand.

Contrary to the advertising, Gusto Beer has a weak taste, and after drinking one can Green alters drastically his evaluation of that particular appeal of Gusto; that is, he now believes Gusto to be a weak-tasting beer. On the positive side, Gusto has an easy-to-open can, and Green now rates it higher in terms of convenience. However, because he's very disappointed about the taste of Gusto beer, he proceeds to tell his friends about it.

We leave Mr. Green forgetting a little about Schiller's beer as he watches a ballgame on TV, drinking, and learning about Gusto beer.

If he purchases the brand, he compares his previous evaluations of the appeal strengths of the brand with the now firsthand evaluations of the brand's appeal strengths (i.e., the actual values of these appeal strengths.) If there is a large positive or negative discrepancy between the two on any appeal, he may alter his evaluation of that appeal strength (function 8) and/or tell other people about it; that is, a word-of-mouth message whose contents, emphasis, and probability of being noted by others depend on the size of the discrepancy, is generated for succeeding periods. If the potential customer has overestimated the appeal strengths for many of the appeals, he may throw out the brand and shop again the next period.

After this part of the cycle and before the next period begins, learning and forgetting take place. The consumer learns about the brand he has bought; that is, his evaluations of the appeal strengths of that brand become more like the actual values of the appeal strengths (function 9). The consumer also forgets about the brands he does not have; that is, his evaluations of the appeal strengths of those brands decline, but the more information sources there were for a brand in the period, the more slowly his evaluations for that brand decline (function 9).

The simulation next moves to Mr. Blue and the entire cycle is repeated. It proceeds similarly for each consumer in the simulated market.

COSTS AND BENEFITS OF SIMULATION

Although the monetary costs and benefits of simulations may be great, the conceptual costs and benefits of simulations are potentially of more serious concern to marketing theorists. Conceptual costs are incurred when models of consumer behavior are distorted to fit the framework of a simulation. Such unrealistic model constructs can be perpetuated because of the attraction of simulation as a technique. Some of these impositions on the model builder can be easily removed; some cannot.

In the model described as an example, these impositions include the treatment of behavior as an ordered sequence of discrete events, the definition and selection of representative consumers and retailers, the stability and simplicity of the response functions, the use of interval measures of attitudes, and the unambiguous ordering of consumer preferences. Some of these simulation-encouraged distortions occur for reasons that are more pragmatic than theoretical.

The sequencing of events in the purchase cycle is governed mainly by the pragmatic consideration of availability of computer time. For example, in the simulation the consumer is exposed to advertising and word-of-mouth messages and *then* makes the decision to shop or not to shop. The model may be more realistic if these two types of events happen continuously and simultaneously. Any arbitrary level of continuity and simultaneity can be achieved by reducing the unit time period for the purchase cycle from, say, one week to one day, one hour, or one minute. Unfortunately, this increased realism is accompanied by increased demands on computer time.

The need to define and select representative consumers and retailers, as opposed to including all real consumers and retailers in the model, stems from the limited size of a computer's memory. Recent increases in computer size lessen but do not remove the importance of this definition and selection procedure to a simulation.

Although the microsimulation discussed is a stochastic model, its own structure remains rigid throughout the simulated time periods. This may be an important restriction on its ability to mirror the real world, where response functions themselves may vary over time or over situations (e.g., planned vs. impulse buying).

Simulations can be used to examine the logical consistency of various sets of hypothetical behavioral relations. The functions initially placed in the simulation for such purposes are often naïve (see Appendix D), since it is easier to move through analyses dealing first with simpler functions and then with more complex ones than vice versa. However, there is a practical limit to the level of complexity of the relations developed through such a procedure. As new variables are added to a function, the time required for a complete investigation of the effects of these variables mushrooms. Rapidly the model builder may lose contact with the logical consistency of his system. This situation argues for exogenous estimation of as many response functions as possible.

Related to the nature of the response functions are the methods used to measure attitudes and order preferences. The described simulation assumed the availability of interval measures of attitudes and the ability of the consumer to choose quickly and unambiguously between brands, retailers, and even brand-retailer pairs. These assumptions made the model builder's task comparatively easy—the response functions were set up to operate on the evaluations of brands and retailers and to produce new preference orderings. To the model builder, however, this type of attack may be self-deceiving—convenience usurping realism. We would be interested in learning about comprehensive consumer behavior simulations that do not assume interval measures.

Other departures from reality typically found in consumer simulations pertain to uniformity assumptions concerning consumers (e.g., assuming for each consumer the same function for the probability of noting an ad). Although important, these types of unrealities are usually apparent and can be corrected by segmenting the simulated consumer group into subgroups as small as necessary.

Many of the benefits of consumer microsimulations derive from the discipline such models enforce on the marketing theorist. The limits of computer time and space emphasize the need for clearly stating the traits that most fully characterize consumers and retailers, the crucial events in the purchase cycle, the types of response functions that are not only realistic but logically consistent at both the micro and macro levels, the significant variables in the response functions, and the interaction among the various model elements.

Once a marketing simulation is formulated and validated (Naylor and Finger, 1967), a marketing theorist can learn by playing with the model. More formally, he can learn by performing sensitivity analyses; that is, he can vary parameter values and functions within the model and observe changes in the simulation output (e.g., purchases or advertising exposures). With the simulation framework, he can make static and dynamic evaluations of the various pieces of a consumer behavior theory, both separately and in conjunction.

Typically, laymen view sensitivity analyses as the prime benefit of simulations. In marketing, however, we usually feel that the formulation stage provides the chief benefit. This belief is based on observations of several market simulations. Because of the lack of hard information for estimation, the central functions in these models are assumed to be of some particular form (e.g., linear, negative exponential, or Cobb-Douglas). Given the dominance of these functions in the models, modifying parameter values and less central functions will not be likely to lead to incisive revelations into consumer behavior. There is no reason why this must be the case—the central functions can also be varied; but it seems to us, on an empirical basis, that sensitivity analyses with marketing simulations tend to result in findings more reassuring than provocative.

One additional and not inconsequential benefit of simulation is its value as a pedagogical device. In introductory marketing management, we have found that the early presentation of such a model furnishes the student with an initial wide perspective of consumer behavior—a selection that can be fleshed out during the course.

CONCLUSION

Simulation has had some success, and it has great potential for more success for marketers, particularly those concerned with consumer behavior. But before working on a simulation, everyone enamored of the technique should remark a brief interchange between Sherlock Holmes and Dr. Watson. Holmes had been trying unsuccessfully to explain a rather abstruse theory to Watson. Finally, a bit dejected, Holmes said, "Perhaps when a man has knowledge and special powers like my own, it rather encourages him to seek a complex explanation when a simpler one is at hand."

APPENDIX A

DATA NEEDED FROM FIRMS

1. a) Product type _____ b) Brand name _____

2. a) Unit time period (e.g. hour, day, week, month) _____

   b) Number of periods to be simulated _____
3. What was the approximate total unit sales of this product last period? _____

4. a) What are the names of the competing brands? _____

   b) What were their respective market shares last period? _____

Brand	Market share
.	.
.	.
.	.

5. What are the characteristics of the product that could possibly be important to a customer?

Description of characteristics

.

.

.

.

6. a) Roughly how many retailers carry this product? _____

   b) i. What types of retailers carry this product? _____
      (e.g. large food stores, large drug stores, small drug stores, where "large" and "small" are defined perhaps by total sales of *all* products they sell)
      ii. Approximately what percentage of the total number of retailers (5a) are of each type? _____

      iii. About what percentage of the total sales of the product does each type currently account for?

Type	Percentage of Number of Retailers	Percentage of Product Sales
.	.	.
.	.	.
.	.	.

   c) For each type of retailer, what percentage carry Brand A, Brand B, ... ?

Retailer	Percentage Carrying Brand
Type 1	Brand A _____
	Brand B _____
	.
	.
Type 2	.
	.
	.

   d) i. Do any brands have exclusive relationships (no other brand sold) with retailers? yes _____ no _____
      ii. If so, which are they?

Brand	Type and Percentage of Retailer Type Exclusively Carrying Brand
.	.
.	.
.	.

APPENDIX B

AD AGENCY FOR MEDIA RESEARCH

For *each brand* and for *each kind* of ad (e.g. magazine ads, TV ads, point-of-sale displays), please estimate the following information.

1. During the time period to be simulated, how many advertisements with different copy will be used? _____

   .

   .

   .

   .

2. In each of these ads, to what extent are the following product characteristics and the brand name stressed? (0 = not at all, 1 = slightly, 2 = moderately, 3 = heavily)

Advertisement 1	Product Characteristic (as described by firm)	Stress
	.	.
	.	.
	Brand Name	Stress
Advertisement 2		.
.	.	.
.	.	.
.	.	.

3. In what vehicles will these advertisements appear? _____
    _____

    .

    .

    .

4. For each time period, please answer the following:
    a) In which vehicles will each ad appear? (0 = will not appear,
       1 = will appear)

    b) What is the probability that each ad will be "noted" by a
       customer to whom the ad-carrying vehicle is available?

    Time period 1

Advertisement 1	Vehicle 1	Vehicle 2
a)	_____	_____
b)	_____	_____

    Advertisement 2

.	_____	_____
.	_____	_____
.		

    Time Period 2

.	_____	_____
.	_____	_____
.		

APPENDIX C

CONSUMER
QUESTIONNAIRE REGARDING PRODUCT

1. a) Name _____ b) Address _____

2. a) Sex: M _____ F _____ b) Age: Under 20 _____ 21–25 _____
   . . . .

   c) Income: less than $5000 _____ ... d) Occupation: _____
   . . . .

   e) Education: _____ ... f) Family size _____
   . . . .

   g) Etc. _____

3. a) Do you buy this product? yes _____ no _____

   b) If not, might you buy this product? yes _____ no _____
   (If both no, thanks for cooperation, etc.)

4. a) Do you recall the last time you purchased this product and,
   if so, when was it?

   don't recall _____
   last purchase: last week _____ last month _____
   . . . .

b) When might you be likely to purchase the product again?

don't know _____

next purchase: next week _____ next month _____

. . . .

5. When you purchase the product, how much do you usually buy?

size of can: 10 oz. _____ 20 oz. _____ . . . .

number of cans: 1 _____ 2 _____ 3 _____ . . . .

6. Roughly what percentage of your total purchases are

Brand A _____ Brand B _____ . . . .

7. On an overall basis, please rate the following brands with which you are familiar.

(0 = poor, 1 = fair, 2 = good, 3 = excellent.)

	Rating
Brand A	_____
Brand B	_____
.	.
.	.
.	.

8. Following are a number of characteristics of this product. When you are shopping, what is the relative importance of these to you? Allocate 100 points between these characteristics depending on how important each is to you.

[List characteristics as described by firm]	Points
Characteristic 1	_____
Characteristic 2	_____
.	.
.	.
.	.

9. Please rate the characteristics of the following brands with which you are familiar. (0 = poor, 1 = fair, 2 = good, 3 = excellent.)

	Rating
Brand A Characteristic 1	.
Characteristic 2	.
.	
.	
.	

Brand B

.   .

.   .

.   .

10. Following are a number of types of retailers. Please rate them according to how often you shop at a store of each type. [0 = never or rarely (0 to 20% of time), 1 = occasionally (20 to 50% of time), 2 = fairly often (50 to 80% of time), 3 = almost always or always (80 to 100% of time)]

Type	Rating
Type 1	.
Type 2	.
.	.
.	.
.	.

11. Do you subscribe to any of the following magazines?

Magazine A _____ Magazine B _____

. . . .

12. Do you often watch any of the following television shows?

Show A _____ Show B _____

. . . .

Thank you.

APPENDIX D

SAMPLE FUNCTIONS

1. $AB_b = c \sum\limits_{n} (AI_a)(AE_{ab})$

   where AB_b = attitude toward brand b
   AI_a = importance of product appeal to the consumer
   AE_{ab} = consumer's evaluation of appeal a of brand b
   n = number of appeals of product
   c = constant

2. P note information sources = P [exposed to source s (EF_s)]
   where EF = effectiveness of source s (e.g., of ad or person)

3. $AE_{ab} = AE_{ab} + c\,(EA_{as})(AEI_a)e^{EB_s}$
   where EA_{as} = emphasis placed on appeal a in information source s
   ^{EB}s = emphasis placed on brand name in source s
   c = constant

4. $PN_b = ce^{AB_b}(ELS)(US)$

   where PN_b = perceived need for brand b
   ELS = effect on perceived need due to time elapsed since last shopped for product
   = ke^{T-PT}

US = $u$sage rate for product
T = time period
PT = time period when last purchased product
c = constant
k = constant

5. P shop for brand $b = c(PN_b)e^{INC/k}$

where INC = consumer's income
c = constant
k = constant

6. P shop for product $= 1 - \prod_n (1 - P$ shop for brand $b)$

where n = number of brands of product

7. P purchase brand $b = c(EP_b)(ES_b)(EAT)$

where EP_b = effect of brand b price on probability of purchase of brand b
ES_b = effect of retailer's sales effort on probability of purchase of brand b
EAT = effect of attitude toward brand b on probability of purchase of brand b
$= k + AB_b/j$
c = constant
k = constant
j = constant

8. $AE_{ab} = .1\, AR_{ab} + .9\, AE_{ab}$
where AR_{ab} = actual rating of appeal a of brand b

9. For brands not owned,
$AE_{ab} = AE_{ab}(1 - e^{-n})$
where n = number of information sources for brand in period

For the brand owned,
$AE_{ab} = (CL)(AR_{ab}) + (1 - CL)AE_{ab}$

where CL = learning coefficient
$= 1 - e^{T-PT}$

6

INFORMATION AND CONSUMER BEHAVIOR

GEORGE H. HAINES, JR.
Professor of Marketing
School of Business
University of Toronto

This discussion attempts to answer two questions: What is information, and how does information affect consumer behavior? It can be simply demonstrated that the questions are important ones.

During the average business day, the average chain and supermarket warehouse carries 35,000 active grocery items. The average $35,000-per-week store will handle 5800 of these items (Graf, 1967).[1] Almost all consumers will shop at two grocery stores each week (Alexis and Simon, 1967), which means that they must choose a basket of purchased items from more than 5800 available items, on average. (The second store, typically a smaller one, carries fewer items than average.) The statistic relating to items available contains an interesting implication. It is known that people make such decisions in a manner that can be described by a decision tree. In simple problems, simple procedures can be worked out to ensure best answers, for example, search out all

The research reported here was supported by a grant from the Consumer Research Institute, Inc. However, the conclusions, opinions, and other statements in this paper are those of the author and not necessarily those of the Consumer Research Institute, Inc. The author is indebted to Marcus Alexis, James Ferguson, and Leonard Simon for critical comments.

[1] This figure is the total count of separately coded sizes, brands, flavors, and types of items, including private label items.

continuations (extensions of the tree), minimax back, and pick the best one. Let's test the efficiency of this rule in the context of the supermarket basket problem. Let

C = cost per position
B = branch points
D = depth

Time, in terms of the number of elementary processes, is a measure of cost. Now, from algebra it is known that

$$1 + B + B^2 + B^3 + \cdots + B^D = \frac{B^{DH} - 1}{B - 1} \tag{1}$$

and that

$$\frac{B^{D+1}}{B - 1} = B^D \frac{B - B^{-D}}{(B - 1)} \cong B^D \frac{B}{(B - 1)} \tag{2}$$

Therefore, as long as B is large, $T \cong CB^D$, since $B^D[B/(B - 1)]$ measures the number of positions that must be evaluated to reach an optimal decision. If it is assumed that there are about 30 items to be bought, and in each case it is necessary to look forward about 40 steps, then $D = (40)(2) = 80$, since to ensure the best choice, search is "forward" and "evaluation" backward.[2] It follows that $T = C(30)^{80} \cong C(10)^{120}$. The 10^{120} is an immense number—so large that it is impossible to compute (Newell, Shaw, and Simon, 1958). The point is a simple one, and quite obvious: consumers cannot deal with the supermarket basket problem in its entirety on each shopping trip.

Models of consumer behavior that presume rational consumer behavior generally appear to be useful in understanding (and predicting) consumer behavior, yet it is clear that the problem of making the best choices, even for the limited set of consumption items available in the average supermarket, is immense. The puzzle is: How can both circumstances exist?

Previous work has shown that if consumers are assumed to be (1) capable of learning and (2) capable of deciding for them-

[2] This implies an incomplete search of the environment, because (30) (40) = 1200 and the question of store choice is not being considered. The depth would be even greater if it was assumed that all items were "looked at"; this is not necessary, because the answer is unchanged.

selves whether they find use of any particular product rewarding, the resulting general model can be used to explain much of the observed dynamics of consumer behavior. Moreover, it also explains why the traditional economic theory of consumer behavior (or, in other words, the zero-order probability model of consumer behavior) is a sensible model that should have useful explanatory power in certain situations (Haines, 1969).

These arguments rest on the notion that the environment is separable in certain ways, which can be more formally expressed in terms of the concept of a utility tree (Strotz, 1957). Such separability will clearly greatly reduce the problem size but it does not provide the complete answer to the puzzle. Another step can be taken toward solving the puzzle if the two questions asked at the beginning of the paper can be answered; that is our intent here.

AN INFORMATION
PROCESSING VIEWPOINT[3]

The foundation for any analysis of consumer information processing must be empirical knowledge about how consumers process information and data. This implies a theory of choice behavior that deals with individual information processing and choice behavior as a process. One such theory is that proposed by Newell, Shaw, and Simon; an alternative is the Argus paradigm proposed by Reitman (both these theories are discussed in Reitman, 1965). Leaving for future research the question of which alternative is better, we adopt as a means of structuring observed consumer behavior the General Problem Solving model of Newell, Shaw, and Simon.

It is postulated that there exists (1) a memory, (2) search and selection procedures, and (3) a set of rules or criteria that guide the decision-making process. The search and selection procedures fall into one of four basic categories. These categories correspond to four alternate methods (processes) for achieving a given goal: (1) transform process, (2) reduce difference process, (3) apply operator process, (4) apply planning procedures (Alexis, Haines, and Simon, 1968).

The first operation is to establish a list of goals. In some problems, the goals are lexicographically ordered. This implies the

[3] The empirical research reported in this section was performed jointly with my colleagues Marcus Alexis and Leonard S. Simon; data collected was supported by a grant from the Chemstrand Foundation. Thanks are owed to Barbara Reid and Zeena Zidberg for their help in data collection and analysis.

following procedure: once an alternative has been evaluated in terms of its goal-achieving ability, the value of the first goal is compared with the desired goal value. If the value of the alternative is preferable to the goal value in terms of the first goal, the alternative is chosen. If the two are equal, their values in terms of the second goal are examined. If these are unequal in value, the preference for the alternative is determined; otherwise the values relative to the next goal are examined, and so on.

A few further comments on the theoretical structure just outlined are worth stating. First, the creation of a lexicographically ordered list of goals is itself a problem-solving process governed by the theory outlined. Thus the theory is recursive, and it is possible that different goals will be most important at different times and in different situations. (This is an important possibility; however, discussion of the point is deferred until later.) Furthermore, the theory allows for the modification of goal values based on experience. Finally, it is entirely possible that no acceptable alternative will be found. In that case, one of two things happens, depending on whether "no choice" is a feasible alternative. If it is, no choice is made; but if a decision must be made, the most nearly satisfactory alternative is chosen.

Application of this theory to a particular situation requires specification of the general concepts. This is often accomplished in positive studies by the collection of data on how decisions are made in a given case. Such data are gathered by collecting protocols of subjects making decisions.

Figures 6.1 and 6.2 report results of such data collection for two women purchasing raincoats.[4] The following questions and answers are used in the decision trees:

1. Reject item.
2. Is it desired brand?
    a. London Fog.
    b. Misty Harbor.
3. Is it lined?
4. Is my size available?
5. Is it within the desired price range?
6. Style
    a. Does it not have "football" shoulders?
    b. Is it A-line or straight?

---

[4] Details on the data collection methodology are presented in Alexis et al. (1968), where results for women's dresses are presented.

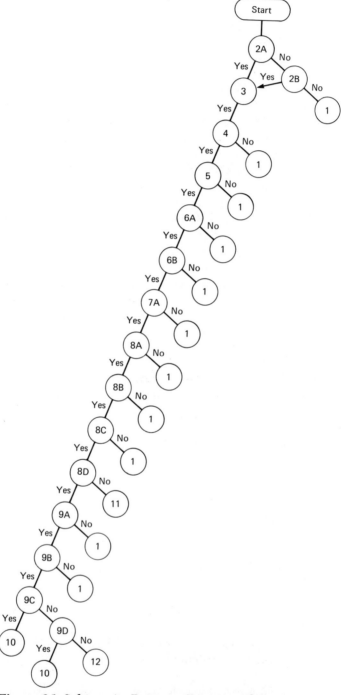

Figure 6.1 Subject A: Raincoat Decision Flow

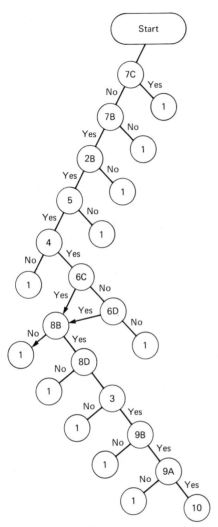

Figure 6.2 Subject C: Raincoat Decision Flow

      c. Turndown collar?
      d. Mandarin collar?
   7. Color
      a. Is it dark blue, black, or beige?
      b. Is it blue or peacock (blue with some green in it)?
      c. Is it orange?
   8. Fit
      a. Is it not tight underarms and without pull across back?

   b. Are sleeves right length?
   c. Does it fit correctly without the lining?
   d. Is the length correct?
9. Practicality
   a. Is it easy to care for?
   b. Can it be worn with most of my clothes?
   c. Is a less expensive lining unavailable?
   d. Is the more expensive lining worth the difference?
10. Purchase coat.
11. Store fact; if coat is otherwise purchasable, purchase if coat can be shortened.
12. Purchase coat with less expensive lining.

This decision process is used recursively. Each time a reject decision is made, the process starts over on a new raincoat. The first satisfactory raincoat is bought, although this does not imply that subject shops in only one store. The question of store choice is deliberately neglected here.

Discussion of Results

There are substantial similarities in the decision processes of the two subjects, although there are some differences in the order in which questions are asked. If the decision structures are essentially correct, however, the subjects exhibit purposeful problem-solving behavior.

Structures such as those in Figures 6.1 and 6.2 clearly rest on a substantial data base in the shoppers' memory, thus representing only the "verbalizable" part of a more complicated underlying process. Some other problems in the analysis of the decision process presented above should be noted. First, choice of color is not a clear-cut matter but tends to be a choice of a shade and tone that is very difficult to express in words. Style and fit are also somewhat intangible. The decision tree considers these major points, but the actual acceptance or rejection at each stage is a much more complex process than these simple diagrams indicate. The mood of the shopper, the responses of salesladies and their availability, and the size of the crowd of shoppers also influence the decision process.

Interestingly such decision processes can be described by the term "attitude structures." As Schroder, Driver, and Streufert (1967) point out, "An attitude structure refers to the conceptual processes utilized in processing information about a particular range of stimuli. . . ." Put another way, an attitude structure is a structure of attitudes ordered to process data and make decisions given relevant stimuli. "An attitude is defined in terms of content properties (magnitude and direction; for example, x degree of conservatism) *and* structural properties (the complexity of conceptual rules invoked in processing information about stimuli relevant to the attitude area)" (Schroder et al., 1967).

Figures 6.1 and 6.2 are attitude structures, and as such they represent a detailed specification of the attitudes of two women toward women's raincoats. This implies that the attitude structure determines what item, if any, is purchased in a purchasing situation. Such a viewpoint replaces motivation as an internal variable with external variables such as noxity (noxious stimuli or unpleasant consequences), reward, interest, and complexity of the environment. Although these variables may have some effect on determining whether an attitude structure is to be invoked, it is known that they affect the structure of the attitude structure. Indeed, one problem with field-study protocols is the difficulty of measuring the influence of such external variables on the observed attitude structure. Field work to date suggests that the influence of motivation centers on determining the ordering of the attitudes in the attitude structure and the number of questions asked. Differences in motivation, it is hypothesized, cause differences in the order in which data from the environment are processed, and the amount of data acquired and processed.

Some theories of consumer behavior claim to view both motivation and attitude as internal variables. Nicosia (1966, p. 197), reviewing this literature, defines attitude as "a driving force that is weaker than M [motivation] and not uniquely crystallized on brand X," whereas motivation is "a strong driving force resulting from some underlying process of interaction that specifically leads a consumer toward brand X more than toward any other brand." The question of whether motivation refers to internal or external variables does not seem to differ in substance in the end, for Nicosia postulates that motivation is uniquely determined by attitude. Nonetheless, the difference is not simply a semantic one when we begin to construct and test positive theories of consumer behavior. If motivation is accepted as an external variable, we must admit that the characteristics of the environment (i.e., task situation) affect consumer behavior. If motivation is taken to be an internal variable, such an admission is not necessary, and although environmental effects may be considered, the theoretical structure focuses attention on the internal states of the consumer. It is not necessary or appropriate that the attitude expressed pre-

viously on attitudes and motivation be accepted as correct, because
(1) empirical evidence on the point is not clear, and (2) the question of what is internal depends at least in part on how the
boundaries of the system being studied are defined. Nonetheless,
this paper adopts as a basis for argument the view that attitude
is an internal variable and motivation an external variable.

Figures 6.1 and 6.2 show that a change in an attitude, or in
an attitude structure, will have abrupt effects because of the discrete, yes–no nature of the attitude structure. This implies that
efforts to measure attitude as a continuous variate will contain a
certain amount of error. However, such a measurement problem
is not nearly as important as the question of what changes attitudes.
Nicosia (1966), for example, has postulated that attitude change
is related to the act of buying, the attitude held when buying, and
communications sent by business firms. But what is meant by the
phrase "a change in attitude"? In terms of the preceding discussion, an attitude change would be called learning, for learning is
"the process by which an activity originates or is changed through
responding to a situation" (Hilgard, 1957), and an attitude structure has been presented as a decision process (i.e., activity). Indeed, it has been argued that attitude structures are merely another
way of representing the long-run behavior of a consumer, sometimes modeled with subject-controlled linear learning models
Haines (1969). If this is true, the difference between theories of
consumer behavior using words such as attitude and motivation
and those using words such as stimulus and response is more one
of language and approach than one of substance. This is an important conclusion, for much of the literature on consumer behavior
is written to delude an unwary reader into thinking that there are
substantial differences between such approaches. Looking at consumer behavior from an information-processing viewpoint gives
concrete evidence to support an argument that the difference between such approaches is not in fact one of substance.

If the study of consumer behavior is approached with a *set*
that consumers seek to maximize their satisfaction subject to certain constraints and achieve this goal by engaging in learning
behavior, the crucial question implied in the foregoing discussion
is: What induces attitude change—in other words, learning? Suppose the argument is that it is information. If this is so, then information affects consumer behavior by inducing learning. Thus one
of the questions posed at the beginning has been answered, although
perhaps not in appropriate detail.

A THEORY OF ATTITUDE CHANGE

If the effect of information is to induce learning, it follows that some consumers will be engaging in learning about at least one product or product class all the time. This raises the question of whether few or many consumers are learning about a given product at any given time. Once the earlier question has been posed, it follows that the argument about whether learning models fit market data has not been very enlightening. This is because it has typically been argued that consumers in the aggregate either are engaged in learning or are not. The viewpoint here is that an accurate response is really a matter of degree. Nevertheless, the particular degree has important practical implications. An example can illustrate this contention.

It is known that under certain conditions the process of consumer response to a new product may be approximated, in the aggregate, by a logistic equation:

$$Y_n = \frac{\lambda}{1 - e^{-a_1 - (1-a_1)\lambda n}} \tag{3}$$

where Y_n = probability of purchasing the new product on the nth/trial (shopping trip)

λ = "long-run" probability of purchasing the new product

a_1 = measure of rate at which the asymptote is approached

a_1 = parameter determined by the initial probability of purchasing the new product (Y_0)

If all consumers are engaged in learning, λ estimates the family share that the new product will achieve at or near the end of the period during which consumers treat it as something new. But if only a fraction f of consumers are engaging in learning behavior, with all other consumers retaining their previous probability of purchasing Y_0, the observed value of λ equals $f\lambda^* + (1 - f)Y_0$, where λ^* is the long-run probability of purchasing that would obtain if all consumers engaged in learning behavior.[5] An observed

---

[5] This analysis presumes that all consumers have the same parameters if they learn, an assumption which is maintained throughout this exposition, despite some evidence that it may not be entirely correct. See Carman (1966).

value of λ of .05 has quite different implications if f is .9 and if f is .1! Most consumers in the first case have learned that the product is unsatisfactory, given the relevant product category for decision purposes; in the latter case most consumers have not considered the new product.

Thus f, the fraction of people engaging in learning, is an important dependent variable. What determines it? Perhaps it can be built up or derived by aggregating knowledge about the probability of individual consumers engaging in learning behavior. Very well, but what determines whether an individual consumer will choose to engage in learning behavior? This more limited question is the one that the last section of the paper attempts to answer. It is useful to reiterate that learning is interpreted here as a process that results in permanent changes in the consumers' attitude structure.

As a start to answering this question, let us list the information sources that people report as influencing their decision to try a new product:

1. Advertising
2. Sampling or other free trial use
3. Personal contacts
4. Availability in store, or salespersons' suggestions[6]

This list can be set as a base list of phenomena to be explained. Each of the information sources represents a process that will affect the probability of a consumer deciding to engage in learning behavior. The effect of each process will be to generate information for the consumer about the product; this information will be imbedded in the relevant attitude structure. Thus the consumer's attitude structure represents a summary of the past information the consumer has obtained. This may be contrasted to data in the immediate task environment about the product: such data are processed by the consumer in making a decision on what to purchase or whether to purchase.

Of course such data also can be summarized and processed into information, and at this point change in the attitude structure of the consumer would be observed. This event will take place only when the consumer is engaging in learning behavior.

---

[6] E. Katz and Lazarsfeld (1955); Haines (1966). This list also seems to be consistent with the general theory of consumer behavior developed by Howard and Sheth (1969), and tested by Farley and Ring in Chapter 8 of this volume.

But what is the nature of this information? Put another way, what problem is the consumer attempting to solve when change in an attitude structure occurs? Possibly consumers engaged in such behavior are assessing the properties of the consumption alternative previously not used, attempting to find relationships common to a class of objects (or ideas, in the case of certain services). That is, the consumer is seeking to discover (1) what attitude structure must be altered if the product is to be considered in the market (product choice) situation, or (2) whether an entirely new attitude structure must be created. If this is so, each of the four influence sources listed previously must represent a different kind of concept learning, for a concept is simply "the properties or relationships common to a class of objects or ideas" (Hilgard, 1957).

Thus, for example, it is postulated that advertising operates to create a preliminary concept of the advertised product in a consumer's mind.[7] These notions can be more formally expressed. When a consumer is exposed to advertising, he is in one of two states:

S: a preliminary concept of the product has been formed
$\bar{S}$: a preliminary concept of the product has not been formed

Of course the consumer begins in state $\bar{S}$ on the first "trial" (i.e., first exposure to the advertising). If this is not true, our initial assumptions about the process being studied are not met. After each exposure, there are two choices: the consumer has formed a preliminary concept or he has not. Let it be assumed further that once a consumer has formed a preliminary concept, it is maintained.[8] Let the probability of not forming a preliminary concept be q (the subject must be in state $\bar{S}$ for this to occur), and let c be the probability that the relevant data in the advertisement are processed after the initial event of not forming a preliminary concept. The qc is the probability that on any given exposure to advertising the consumer, who started the exposure in

<hr>

[7] Advertising may accomplish other tasks, and what follows is not intended to be a general theory of how advertising works. It deals only with advertising as a source of information when information is given the (perhaps limited) definition presented above as something causing an observed alteration in the consumer's attitude structure.

[8] This may not always be true, particularly if the consumer tries the product. But response to trial is a separate question beyond the scope of this paper. The model presented here is an application of a concept learning model in R. C. Atkinson, Bower, Crothers (1965, chap. 2).

state $\overline{S}$, begins the next exposure in state S. The chances that the transition from $\overline{S}$ to S fails to occur is simply $1 - qc$. This can be formally represented as a first-order Markov chain transition matrix:

$$
\begin{array}{c}
S_n \\
\overline{S}_n
\end{array}
\begin{array}{cc}
S_{n+1} & \overline{S}_{n+1} \\
\left[\begin{array}{cc}
1 & 0 \\
qc & 1 - qc
\end{array}\right]
\end{array}
\tag{4}
$$

Let the random variable Y represent the number of exposures necessary before the consumer forms a preliminary concept. Then

$$
\Pr(Y = n) = (1 - qc)^{n-1}qc \tag{5}
$$

where $\Pr(Y = n)$ is the probability that the consumer will have formed a preliminary concept after exposure n.
Furthermore,

$$
\begin{aligned}
\Pr(\overline{S}_{n+1}) &= \Pr(\overline{S}_n)(1 - qc) \\
&= (1 - qc)^{n-1}(1 - qc) \\
&= (1 - qc)^n
\end{aligned}
\tag{6}
$$

where $\Pr(\overline{S}_{n+1})$ is the probability the consumer will be in state $\overline{S}$ after exposure $n + 1$. The probability of not forming a preliminary concept after the $n + 1$ trial is therefore $q\,(1 - qc)^n$. As n becomes very large, this probability becomes very small, and, as $n \to \infty$ the asymptotic probability of not forming a preliminary concept is zero.

Finally, denoting by Z_n the probability of a consumer being exposed to n advertisements, the probability that the consumer will have acquired information from advertising is

$$
(Z_n)\,[1 - q(1 - qc)^n] \tag{7}
$$

This result has some specific implications for measuring advertising results. First, it points up the importance of the number of exposures of consumers to a given ad. Second, as has been noted, a consumer may have acquired information about a product in several other ways. If advertising expresses a concept that is congruent with the concept these other ways would form, or simply with the way the product performs if bought and used, consumers could be aware of the product advertising without ever having seen any advertising at all (Stewart, 1964). In fact, the theory presented predicts that only when advertising leads to a preliminary concept quite different from the preliminary concept formed by other information sources will advertising measure advertising awareness. Nor does anything in the theory suggest that the concept the consumer learns bears any relation to the concept the advertiser thinks the consumer will learn. It follows that a consumer may not be counted as aware of the advertisement and may yet acquire information from it.[9]

Two other issues may be briefly noted. First, the general form of the equation is unchanged if aggregation is performed over sequences of exposures (i.e., if the index n "counts," e.g., in terms of blocks of k exposures). Second, in some circumstances the general form of the equation may be the same in the aggregate as it is for the individual. Although there is limited evidence that this can occur, the issue of deriving aggregate relationships is beyond the scope of the present paper and is not discussed (Twedt, 1965b).

The second item on the list of phenomena to be explained is sampling. Sampling is designed to produce a preliminary concept by delivering a free sample of the product to the consumer. Given the free sample, the consumer may or may not try it; but if the product is tried, the trial use will with probability x_1 generate information. Thus the probability that an individual will have acquired information through sampling can be written as abx_1, where a is the probability of getting a free sample and b is the probability of using it.

The above information highlights the complexity of the process of acquiring information through free use. The model proposes that the process is not very complex. Much more complex process models, such as subject-controlled linear learning models, could be hypothesized and built. But there is no evidence that the simple paradigm presented here is incorrect; and until such evidence appears, there can be no reason for proposing additional complexity.

Evidence for complexity does exist in relation to the third item, personal contacts. Indeed, it might be argued that personal contacts are derivative from other information sources. This is, often

---

[9] The direct-exposure interview technique, in which a consumer is shown an ad and asked to answer questions about it in an effort to learn what information the ad conveys to consumers, does not overcome this problem. The theory developed above clearly implies that more than one exposure is apt to be necessary before a consumer will convert data in an advertisement into information.

true, of course—but not in terms of the receiving consumer (Arndt, 1968d).

At least two possible lines of attack might be followed in trying to construct a formal model of the influence process of personal contacts on attitude change. One approach would be to view personal interactions in terms of a Markov learning model; there is evidence, at least, that such theories are useful in laboratory situations (Suppes and Atkinson, 1960). An alternative would be to base the model on an analogy to an epidemiological model. There is evidence for the usefulness of such an approach when the consumer is an organization or firm (Mansfield, 1968). Certainly there is no evidence to prove that one of these approaches has superior explanatory ability. An approach based on an epidemiology argument is proposed below for the sake of adopting a position and because the theoretical argument has some inherent interest (Bailey, 1957).

Suppose that at some starting time $t = 0$ there are n consumers with no preliminary concept and one opinion leader with a concept of the product. At any time t the probability that n consumers without any preliminary concept remain is $p_n(t)$. Let β be the rate at which information about the product is transmitted. If it is assumed that the entire group of $n + 1$ consumers is homogeneously mixing, as might be nearly the case in small household groups, the chance of one new consumer obtaining a preliminary concept in the time interval dt would be $\beta h(n - h + 1)\, dt$, where h is the number of consumers without a preliminary concept. If the time scale is changed by letting $Y = \beta t$, the resulting equations become dimensionless as far as the rate of information transmission is concerned. The resulting equations, where $P_n(0)$ by assumption are

$$\frac{dP_h(\tau)}{d\tau} = (h+1)(n-h)P_{h+1}(\tau) - h(n-h+1)P_h^{1\tau}; \quad (8)$$

$$0, 1, \ldots, n - 1$$

$$\frac{dP_n(\tau)}{d\tau} = nP_n(\tau) \qquad (9)$$

The explicit solution of such equations leads to a fairly complex result, but it is interesting to note that the shape of the curve plotting the rate at which preliminary concepts are transmitted against βt is unimodal and would be difficult to tell from a normal or a logistic distribution if standard tests of frequency distributions were applied.[10]

These equations express the simple notion that the probability of a consumer receiving information that will result in attitude change is a function of the number of consumers in the reference group, the number who already have received the information, and the rate at which information is transmitted.

The final item on the list is availability in a store. It is hypothesized that the process by which this factor influences attitude change differs sharply in one way from the processes involved in the other three items on the list. The first three items represent efforts by others to induce attitude change; the last one represents the results of the efforts by consumers, without outside prodding, to better their lot as consumers. It might be postulated that on every shopping trip, or at least every few shopping trips, the consumer examines the existing attitude structures or decision processes for structures that have remained unchanged for a long time. Creating a list of such attitude structures, the consumer then

[10] Bailey (1957) shows that the explicit solution where n is an even number has the following form:

$$P_h(\tau) = \sum_{k=1}^{n-h-1} C_{hk} \exp \left[-k(n-k+1)\tau \ h > (1/2)^n \right] \tag{a}$$

$$C_{hk} = \frac{(-1)^{k-1}(n-2k+1)n!\,(n-h)!\,(h-k-1)!}{h!\,(k-1)!\,(n-k)!\,(n-h-k+1)!} \tag{b}$$

$$P_h(\tau) = \sum_{b=1}^{1/2n} C_{hk}\, e^{-k(n-k+1)\tau} + \sum_{k=h}^{1/2n} d_{hk}\tau\, e^{-k(n-k+1)\tau}; \qquad 0 < h \le 1/2n \tag{c}$$

$$P_0(\tau) = 1 + \sum_{k=1}^{1/2n} C_{0K}\, e^{-k(n-k+1)\tau} + \sum d_{0K}\tau\, e^{-k(n-k+1)\tau} \tag{d}$$

where, if $k < h$, C_{hk} is determined by (b), but if $K \ge h$,

$$C_{hk} = \left\{ \frac{(-1)^k(n-2k+1)n!(n-h)!}{h!(k-1)!(n-k)!(n-h-k+1)!(k-h)!} \right\} \tag{e}$$

$$X \left\{ \sum_{u=k}^{n-k} u^{-1} + \sum_{u=k-h+1}^{n-k-h+1} u^{-1} - \frac{2}{n-2k+1} \right\}$$

(When $h = 1$, the first summation in (e) does not arise, and the second is absent when $h = 1/2n$.)

$$d_{hk} = \frac{(-1)^{h+1}(n-2k+1)^2 n!(n-h)!}{h!(k-1)!(n-k)!(n-h+1)!(k-h)!} \tag{f}$$

searches the task environment for potential new information. If he finds such new data (and if the item is in the store) the consumer will try out the product, or perhaps examine it and decide whether to proceed. A probability g of deciding to search the task environment for information about a specific product and finding such search feasible can be postulated, and it expresses the above notions in a form compatible with the previous discussion.

To summarize, the probability of a consumer acquiring information about any particular product over a given, small time interval, denoted f_i^1 (i for the ith consumer), can be approximated as follows:

$$f_i^1 = qc + abx_1 + \beta h(n - h + 1) + g \qquad (10)$$

where dt is 1. If the product or product category were one that consumers did not talk about (perhaps, e.g., toothpicks), then β would be zero and f_i^1 would be a constant. It is an interesting and perhaps not intuitively obvious finding that the only factor that appears to cause a change in the value of a consumer's probability of acquiring information about a product over a short time interval is interpersonal interaction (specifically, the number of people in the consumer's interaction group who are aware of the product). Moreover, this result gives a simple cue on the design of an experiment to test whether the proposed theory has any validity at all. Of course, this result is inherent in the subparts of the theory; if the subparts were designed differently, the result could be altered. Given the present state of knowledge, however, this result seems to be entirely defensible.

Two basic problems remain. First, the theory presented concerns the causes for change in attitude structures, not the final form of the attitude structure after the effects of a change that has occurred have produced an altered, relatively fixed, attitude structure once again. Most existing methods of studying change rely on empirically determining if change has occurred by before-and-after comparisons. Such measurement techniques, telling only if a change has occurred, not when it began, may not be ideally suited to measure f or f_i as defined in the theory presented here.[11]

Second, the aggregation problem has not been attacked, yet

---

[11] I am indebted to John Howard for the observation that changes in product recall can serve as an aggregate measure of f, and that it follows that the rate of change in product recall changes can measure f^1.

use of aggregate data may be necessary to attempt to test the theory.

RECAPITULATION

The two questions initially asked were: What is information? and How does information affect consumer behavior? It was proposed that information is a preliminary concept of a product that induces a consumer to decide to (1) alter his or her decision process for the relevant product category, or (2) if the product category is one the consumer had not previously bought, construct a decision process. In arriving at this proposed answer, a theory was developed for predicting the probability that a consumer will receive information. It was argued that such a theory is not only interesting in its own right but of possible potential practical value, at least in the case of a firm facing the decision of whether a new product should remain on the market.

7

PATTERN RECOGNITION IN STOCHASTIC SERIES

JEROME B. KERNAN
Professor of Behavioral Analysis
School of Business
University of Cincinnati

This paper is concerned with the "make-sense" processes people use to understand the environment within which they make choices. As such, it is relevant to both consumer and industrial or institutional buying, as well as to political behavior, mating, and so on. In short, it is relevant to decision making.

Even the most naïve student soon comes to recognize that decision making is exceedingly complex. In many ways it seems to epitomize the "black-box model" popularized by Buzzell (1964). Since for the most part our present capacities preclude a frontal approach to the problem, investigators typically use inferential tacks. These what-must-be-taking-place approaches are admittedly deficient—all inferential analysis is to some extent—but they represent our only hope of explicating and rendering tractable the terribly complex phenomenon that is displayed when someone makes a choice.

THE FORMALIZED DECISION PROBLEM

One of the inferential games we play in our quest for tractability might be called the formalizing syndrome. We impose an a priori structure on the decision-making phenomenon and model it in terms of this structure. Despite methodological dangers indigenous to it (cogently argued by Halbert, 1968), this has become a popular syndrome, and its archetype is reflected in the now-classic work of Luce and Raiffa (1957).

The Decision Problem
Under Conditions of Uncertainty

The decision problem that appears to be most pregnant for analysis is the so-called game against nature. Formally stated, the problem is this: A choice A_i must be made from among a set of alternatives $A_1, A_2, \ldots, A_m$, but the relative desirability of each depends on which state of nature (SON) prevails, either $N_1, N_2, \ldots, N_n$. The decision maker knows that one of the states prevails, but he does not know which one or even the relative probabilities of the various states occurring. For each pair A_i, N_j consisting of an alternative and a state of nature, there is a consequence, or payoff P_{ij}. The problem, typically displayed in a payoff matrix, reduces to: Given an $m \times n$ array of numbers P_{ij}, choose a row (alternative) that is optimal in some sense—or, more generally, rank the rows according to an optimality criterion.

The problem can be partitioned to some extent. Although the choice maker's problem is clearly bivariate, it proceeds from two issues that can be separated with relative ease. On the one hand, there is the "row problem," which consists of the difficulties accompanying the specification of all the alternatives (elements of the set) available for choosing. "Know thy alternatives," or another such business dictum would characterize the row problem. Otherwise, there is what might be called the "column problem." This comprises the tasks of specifying the various states of nature and predicting their occurrence. Since the decision problem is characterized as "uncertain," the parameters of the column problem are quite sparse. The decision maker knows only that a state N_j, from a set $N_1, N_2, \ldots, N_n$, will occur with some probability p_j, where p_j is an element of the set $p_1, p_2, \ldots, p_n$ and $\Sigma_n \, p_j = 1$ and $p_j \geqq 0$.

Of course simply attending to the row and column problems does *not* resolve the decision. Optimizing the payoff (objective) function P_{ij}, where $P_{ij} = f(A_i, N_j)$, $i = 1, \ldots, m$, and $j = 1, \ldots, n$, requires a *simultaneous* consideration of both issues. Furthermore, experimentation shows that awareness of both issues still occasions variable behavior among decision makers (Kernan, 1968). Humans invoke personal utility (or disutility) functions as they process row and column information to arrive at a choice.

Environmental Entropy

Knowledge of how choosers deal with the column problem (i.e., how they decide which of the environmental states will occur) is interesting in its own right, though it does not itself resolve the decision problem. In large measure it is the key to understanding how people deal with the uncertain world around them, whether the focus of that world is diplomatic negotiation, nuclear retaliation, labor-management bargaining, student demands, competitive reaction, or expected satisfaction with a new instant coffee.

The column problem is basically one of *pattern recognition*. As implied in the Howard-Sheth model (1969), for example, choosing a particular brand includes recalling how that (or a similar) brand sufficed on past occasions that are nearly equivalent to the present occasion. An "occasion" here may be considered in the Bauer-Cox sense of an event involving a combination of performance and psychosocial risk for the chooser (Cox, 1967). Occasions are not altogether deterministic; one rarely knows exactly the environmental state that will prevail when a product is used. Occasions (states of nature) therefore must be predicted and, depending on how disordered the environment seems to be, differing prediction strategies are appropriate.

The thermodynamic concept of *entropy* affords a useful analogy for consideration of the relative disorder in the decision-making environment. In statistical mechanics, entropy refers (roughly) to the amount of available energy in a substance. This is analogous to the amount of available information in a series of events or states of nature. Where entropy is high, disorder is high and the amount of available information is high. Where entropy is low, disorder is low and the amount of available information is low.

A simple illustration clarifies these notions. If in a game against nature there are four possible environmental states, N_1, N_2, N_3, N_4, and these states occur with equal frequency—$p(N_j) = .25$—a condition of maximum entropy exists; there is the greatest possible amount of disorder (unpredictability) in the series of states. The amount of information available in such a case is great because to know which state will occur adds materially to one's stock of information. At the other extreme, if one of the states is known to occur with probability 1.0, a condition of zero entropy exists; there is complete order or predictability in the series. And one's stock of information remains the same each time that state occurs, since the occurrence tells nothing that was not already known.

Entropy H is measured in information bits. Maximum entropy is given by

$$H_{max} = -\log_2 1/N \tag{1}$$

where N is the number of equally likely events (SONs).

The logarithmic measure is used because it has the property of additivity when dealing with the joint occurrence of independent events. The base 2 reflects the number of binary choices that must be made to specify one state from a number of equally likely states. The resulting measure of information is reckoned in "bits" (*binary digits*). Such bits emerge positively, despite the negative sign; recall that logarithms of decimals (in this case, $1/N$) are themselves negative.

D. W. Miller and Starr (1960) suggest a partitioning of the decision environment according to its entropy. They invoke the notion of redundancy R, which refers to the relative degree of *order* in a series of environmental states.

$$R = 1 - \frac{H}{H_{max}}; \qquad 0 \leq R \leq 1 \tag{2}$$

When $H = 0$, $R = 1$, and perfect order exists in the series, a condition of "certainty" exists in the Luce-Raiffa sense. When $R = 0$, however, $H = H_{max}$, and a condition of "uncertainty" exists. Finally, when $0 < R < 1$, the decision environment is described as one of "risk."

This partitioning is convenient but perplexing. It suggests that many of the series we commonly designate as "uncertain"—specifically, nonrectangularly distributed ones—are not uncertain but merely "risky."

In any event, it seems reasonable to consider the column problem of the decision maker in terms of the amount of entropy (or redundancy) present. When the environment is completely ordered (only one SON), effectively there is no column problem. When the environment is completely disordered (H_{max})—and the chooser knows this—the principle of insufficient reason seems to be optimal. Finally, when there is some disorder ($0 < H < H_{max}$), the problem ought to be optimally handled by ascertaining the SON distribution and applying an expected value strategy—unless, of course, the chooser opts for a mixed strategy in which he attempts to "outguess" the series.

PREDICTION IN AN
INFORMATION-THEORETIC CONTEXT

The preceding section implies a relationship between decision making and information theory, or the mathematical theory of communication, as it is sometimes called. This section seeks to explicate that relationship.

The literature of information theory is vast and diverse. In a gross way, however, it falls into two categories. By far the most research has been done on *physical* systems, as reflected in the works of Wiener (1948) and Shannon and Weaver (1949). This work has since been applied to *human* systems, as reflected in Garner and Hake (1951), G. A. Miller (1953), Cherry (1957), Garner (1962), Lanzetta and Kanareff (1962), and Green (1964). Cherry's book is largely expository; however, Green treats a specific decision problem in a marketing context, and the other authors deal specifically with human choice problems.

It is not feasible to "treat" information theory within the confines of this paper—only to draw from it. Accordingly, reference is made only to aspects of the theory that seem to be germane to the environmental state problem.

Nature as a Communicator

Figure 7.1 depicts an information-theoretic model of communication. The model pertains to the transmission of information about the state of the decision environment "from nature" (the source) to a decision maker (the receiver). Two basic entities comprise the model. First, there is the *actual* environmental condition, the average amount of information available, which is given by $H(N)$. Second, there is the decision maker's *inference* of $H(N)$, the average amount of information available, which is given by $H(M)$. To accommodate the unequal frequency of occurrence of the states comprising the environment (actually or inferentially), a generalized computational form for $H(N)$ and $H(M)$ is given in the legend to Figure 7.1. If either set should form a rectangular distribution, the formula previously given for $H_{\max}$ would suffice. Also, the sets are assumed to represent discrete probabilities. For example, if $H(N)$ reflects a continuous distribution, its entropy would be given by

$$H(N) = \int_{-\infty}^{\infty} p(N) \log_2 p(N) \, d(N) \qquad (3)$$

Our interest, of course, lies in the extent to which correct inferences of the empirical world are made by the decision maker —that is, in the correspondence of $H(N)$ and $H(M)$. Morphologically, four boundary cases seem to be obvious. These are dis-

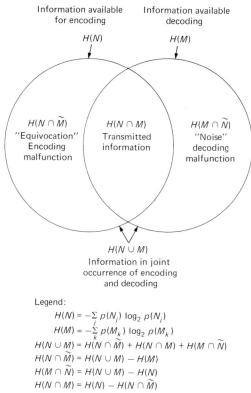

Figure 7.1 Theoretical Model of Information Communication

played in Table 7.1, which should be read with benefit of the Boolean algebras listed in the legend of Figure 7.1. If decision maker draws perfect inferences about the environment, $H(N)$ will be the same as $H(M)$ and their intersection will be complete. Under such conditions (case I in Table 7.1), all the information in the system is contained in the intersection $H(N \cap M)$. Transmission from nature to decision maker has been perfect; nature has revealed all and no more, and the chooser has deciphered all and no more. There have been no malfunctions in the nature–man communication interface, no information loss, and no noise.

At the other extreme (case IV), we conceive of a (completely) "lossy" and noisy case, where, all nature's information is lost. All the information in the chooser's inference is noise. The intersection of $H(N)$ and $H(M)$ is empty; $H(N)$ and $H(M)$ are disjoint. This occurs because nature "fails" to encode the state of

TABLE 7.1

LOGICAL CASES OF INFORMATION TRANSMISSION

	CASES			
VALUE OF PROPERTY	I LOSSFREE, NOISEFREE	II LOSSFREE, NOISY	III LOSSY BUT NOISEFREE	IV LOSSY AND NOISY
$H(N)$	$H(M)$	0	$H(N \cap \widetilde{M})$	$H(N \cap \widetilde{M})$
$H(M)$	$H(N)$	$H(M \cap \widetilde{N})$	0	$H(M \cap \widetilde{N})$
$H(N \cup M)$	$H(N)$	$H(M)$	$H(N)$	$H(N) + H(M)$
$H(N \cap \widetilde{M})$	0	0	$H(N)$	$H(N)$
$H(M \cap \widetilde{N})$	0	$H(M)$	0	$H(M)$
$H(N \cap M)$	$H(N)$	0	0	0
Interpretation	No malfunctions	Decoding malfunction	Encoding malfunction	Encoding and decoding malfunctions

the environment in a language understandable to the decision maker, who simultaneously misinterprets what is transmitted. Thus all $H(N)$ is lost in transmission and all $H(M)$ is added in transmission with the result that $H(N \cap M)$ remains empty because of encoding and decoding errors.

Case II reflects a lossfree but (completely) noisy situation. There is no loss of information in transmission; there is no equivocation in the sense of uncertainty regarding the environmental state. The *amount* of information in $H(N)$, nevertheless, is zero precisely because we *do* know the environmental state. Somehow, in this case, the chooser completely misinterprets the state of the environment, with the result that although there is no encoding malfunction, the chooser's abortive decoding yields all noise. All the information in the system, then, resides in $H(M \cap \widetilde{N})$, and $H(N)$ and $H(M)$ remain disjoint. No information is transmitted.

Finally, case III depicts a (completely) "lossy" but noise-free situation. All the information available in $H(N)$ is lost in transmission because of encoding malfunction—that is, $H(N) = H(N) \cap \widetilde{M})$. In effect, nature has no adequate language for "telling" man about his environment. In this case, nevertheless, the chooser is not at all ambiguous about his inferences (although they are wrong). There is no noise in $H(\widetilde{M})$, therefore, but neither

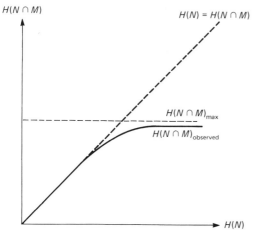

Figure 7.2 Transmitted Information as a Function of Information Available for Encoding

is there any information in the sense of reduction of uncertainty. Thus all information in the system resides in $H(N \cap \widetilde{M})$, and $H(N)$ and $H(M)$ remain disjoint. No information is transmitted.

The Decision Maker's Capacity

The boundary cases described are simply that: They are unlikely to be observed in an empirical situation. Rather than all loss and/or all noise or all transmission, then, what can be expected?

George A. Miller (1953, 1956) has suggested that when humans are considered as "channels," they have information capacities just like physical channels (e.g., coaxial cables). Although information can be encoded in differential ways to "compress" it, there remains a limit to how much information an individual can "receive."

Figure 7.2 depicts a model of information transmission as a function of the amount available for transmission. It simply says that as the average amount of information $H(N)$ available for transmission (encoding) increases, the amount $H(N \cap M)$ actually transmitted will increase proportionately (45°), but only to a point. At that point, transmitted information will begin to converge on an asymptote—$H(N \cap M)_{\max}$ or the decision maker's capacity—and will remain asymptotic to that capacity no matter how large $H(N)$ becomes.

This phenomenon holds interesting consequences. It suggests, for example, that there is a definite limit to the amount of uncertainty with which a decision maker can cope. Since $H(N)$ depends on both the number of environmental states and their respective probabilities of occurrence, the chooser's information capacity is likely to compel him to apply rather gross taxonomic heuristics to render the bewildering array of states even tractable. Perhaps this is an important antecedent of the "evoked set" component of the Howard-Sheth model. Brian M. Campbell (1968), for example, found that laundry detergent and toothpaste buyers rarely had evoked sets larger than seven brands—out of awareness sets at least twice as large. In any event, it would seem useful to have more empirical validation of the notion of a decision maker's information capacity.

TOWARD RELEVANCE: TWO HYPOTHESES

We have suggested that games against nature might usefully be cast into an information-theoretic perspective. The advantage to such an approach would seem to be that its logarithmic measure of information affords a useful metric for analysis. Such quantification comes as a mixed blessing, of course. It must be recalled that we are dealing only with the *amount* of information and not its *meaning*. We are at the level of syntactics, not semantics.

Introducing a subjective note, one might question the validity of the popular proposition that the amount of information is independent of its value. In the general case, of course, this is logically irrefutable. In the case in point, however, it seems tenuous. To know an SON distribution (which can be measured by the amount of information contained in it) is valuable to a decision maker if the consequence of his decision is a function of both the alternative chosen and the state prevalent when the alternative is implemented.

Insofar as an information-theoretic approach to games against nature is relevant, more empirical work is necessary to establish its contribution. To this end, two hypotheses for testing might be considered. These are in the form of hypothesized decision rules that choosers would be expected to use in an experimental game against nature.

Hypothesis I: On Information Capacity

Our first concern is with the decision maker's capacity to receive information. We wish to validate empirically the model depicted in Figure 7.1. An appropriate hypothesis might be

$$H(N \cap M) < H(N) \qquad \text{for some } H(N) \qquad (4)$$

This hypothesis, of course, is largely a ruse of classical statistics. Our concern is not merely with testing it but with determining the chooser's capacity.

This is a decision rule implicit in this hypothesis. As the entropy $H(N)$ of the environmental series increases, the chooser becomes increasingly aware of his inability to absorb all its available information. Accordingly, as a one-to-one discrimination of states becomes increasingly impractical, *homogenizing* strategies become necessary. Thus purple "becomes" increasingly red or blue. Practically speaking, we wish to know not only the individual's capacity for discrimination but also his methods. In the terms of Schroder, Driver, and Streufert (1967), we are concerned with both the *content* variables and the *structural* variables that comprise an individual's information-handling heuristic.

Hypothesis II: On Event Dependence

Our second concern—not unrelated to our first—is with the individual's search behavior as he seeks to decipher the SON environment. In a stochastic series of states, the question is how to reckon entropy. It is one thing if states are inferred to be independent events and another if they are dependent. In other words, the disorder perceived in a series depends on how the series is perceived. An hypothesis to test would be

$$0 < p \left(N_{jt} \mid N_{jt-1}, \ldots \right) \leqq 1 \qquad (5)$$

This hypothesis contends merely that individuals perceive SON series as compromised of dependent events—specifically, as at least first-order Markov processes. As with the first hypothesis, accepting it is virtually certain. The real interest lies in ascertaining what search heuristics individuals use to "figure out" a series, to explicate its order, and to reduce its entropy.

The decision rules implicit in hypothesis II are of the form: "N_j always occurs in clusters of three; therefore, after it has occurred once, assume it will occur twice more," and so on.

Both hypotheses assume that when confronted with stochastic series of SON outcomes (i.e., when the environment is not deterministic), decision makers seek to cope with the entropy of the environment by searching for patterns, regularities, or orderliness in it. They do this because, as humans, they have information-processing limitations and an innate desire to know—whether as subjects in the experimental laboratory or as *Homo sapiens* struggling with the human condition.

AN APPROACH TO
ENVIRONMENTAL SEARCH

An extension of the foregoing notions likely resides in the search behavior of human organisms, whether this search involves the perception of advertising, choice among brands, or whatever.[1]

If search is construed in the form of a maze, consisting of k steps and m_k choices at each step, the information-theoretic model is useful in describing the search behavior of the organism through the maze.

A random search of such a maze requires that the organism process $\Sigma_k \, m_k$ bits of information (assuming each "choice" is a binary one between equally likely alternatives)—a most formidable task given any appreciable size m or k. Of course search rarely occurs randomly; people engage heuristics to reduce the amount of information (m or k) they must process.

In an information-theoretic context, search heuristics represent intentional equivocation—$H(N \cap \widetilde{M})$—introduced by the organism (decision maker) in an effort to reduce the environmental entropy—$H(N)$. As such, they have a "power" P, which is given by the ratio $H(N \cap M)/H(N)$. Thus P reflects the amount of entropy—information—*left* in the environment after the organism has *purposely* reduced $H(N)$ by applying search heuristics.

The reader will recognize that the concerns of hypotheses I and II for information capacity and event dependence, respectively, prompt the decision maker to engage the search heuristics noted in this final section. Therefore, P is perhaps a summary measure of the individual's behavior as he scans the uncertain decision environment.

---

[1] I am indebted to Professor George H. Haines, Jr., of the University of Toronto, for the substance of this section.

C
EMPIRICAL TESTING

8

DERIVING AN EMPIRICALLY TESTABLE VERSION OF THE HOWARD-SHETH MODEL OF BUYER BEHAVIOR

JOHN U. FARLEY
Professor of Business
Columbia University
L. WINSTON RING
Associate Professor of Business
University of Wisconsin
Milwaukee

Marketing research is slowly developing some theoretical underpinnings that promise to bring the field a giant step closer to maturity. The Howard-Sheth theory of buyer behavior is an example of these developments. Such a general theory can handle many different classes of behavior, but it is not so general that it becomes either tautological or definitionally void. It helps discipline the work of the empirical researcher, and it also helps avoid the aimless data massages of which we are all occasionally guilty. On the other hand, as any empiricist can testify, casting such a theory into a form that can handle data on a given problem is often a substantial task in its own right. This paper makes an initial attempt to adapt the full Howard-Sheth model of buyer behavior for a specific empirical test.

SOME DIFFICULTIES IN ADAPTING
A THEORY FOR EMPIRICAL TESTING

There are a variety of difficulties encountered in deriving empirically manageable formulations of general theories. These can be conveniently brought into focus by examining problems facing empirical work in the context of the neoclassical theory of demand, a much older general theory that has been undergoing rigorous refinement for almost a century. The theory states, quite innocently, that the quantity demanded of a product depends on its price, the prices of goods that are its substitutes or complements, incomes, and tastes. A variety of thorny problems arise in empirical applications of this elegant and useful aggregate theory of buyer behavior:

1. The dependent variable is clearly specified as the price of the good in question, the independent variables being other prices, income, and tastes. Suppose, though, that we wish to analyze the demand for one of the complements; the price of the first good is then an independent variable and the price of the complement is dependent. Joint causation, of course, raises empirical as well as theoretical problems. In theoretical work, joint causation can be handled by extending the partial theory involving only one good to a more general equilibrium theory involving a number of goods. Unfortunately, the general theory quickly becomes cumbersome and difficult to manage, even in principle. Furthermore, the ambiguity about whether a variable is dependent or independent in this more general framework means that quite advanced types of multivariate statistical techniques are needed (at least in principle) for the testing, and simpler correlational techniques can be hopelessly ambiguous. Early contributors to the theory probably never dreamed that such advanced techniques of analysis would be needed.

2. The benign-looking phrase "depends on" turns out to be a source of even greater problems. It is easy to write "demand = f (price, etc.)"; but what is the functional relationship—linear, multiplicative, sinusoidal? Unfortunately, the theory itself gives little help in solving this problem, and there is an endless choice of relationships. Work based on utility theory and various maxims of choice has identified certain functional relationships that are admissible (Russell, 1966)—consistent in principle with the general theory of demand—and some that are not. Fortunately, all the relationships that are commonly used in empirical testing of demand functions are admissible. Even so, the theory offers little assistance in choosing among elements in the set of admissible functions. This is one reason why so many analysts have decided

to retreat to the simplest and most manageable, acceptable specification—the linear one. Of course previous empirical work may
provide solid evidence about the form of the relationship, but this
really involves adapting empirical results to the theory and not
the reverse.

3. Once the hurdles of identifying and specifying the functional relationships are cleared, we still face a morass of variable
definition problems. The theory itself almost never helps in solving
these problems. Are market prices adequate definitions of price
under the theory? Or should we, as Stigler (1961) and Mincer
(1964) have suggested, try to evaluate the subjective value of the
time of the buyer and add it to the market price to get a true
value of foregone resources involved in the transaction? How big
is the array of relevant substitutes and complements, and how
should their prices be specified? Is current monetary income an
adequate definition of the income variable, or do we have to perform the arduous task of evaluating the total wealth of the buyer
and estimating a probable total income stream from it? Do buyers
respond to current income and price levels, or are there significant
lags and delays? Or perhaps we have to worry about whether the
consumer preceives current income as the relevant definition for
planning expenditures, or whether there is some other income
measure, free of temporary windfall gains or momentary setbacks
(Friedman, 1957), which the consumer perceives as his income for
planning purposes. Furthermore, the theory deals with movement
of goods within a market; thus the arena of activity must also be
circumscribed—a major definitional problem in itself.

4. Finally, enormous problems associated with the collection
of relevant data. Some of the variables are abstract concepts (e.g.,
utility measures); these may be virtually impossible to measure
empirically and must often be subsumed into the analysis in other
ways. Other data (prices, incomes, etc.) are subject to significant
measurement errors. Of course, the theory is not (and probably
should not be) concerned with worldly data inaccuracies of various
types, but in testing the theory we are often preoccupied with
measurement error management at every stage in the analysis. A
useful theory, however, will not present the empiricist with a long
string of unmeasurable theoretical concepts.

A FIRST PASS AT
EMPIRICIZING THE HOWARD-SHETH THEORY

These four matters (joint causal interdependencies among the variables, uncertainty about the forms of the functional relationships,

definition of variables, and data collection and error management) form the nucleus of problems involved in casting a general theory like the Howard-Sheth theory of consumer behavior into a form amenable to empirical investigation. On the one hand, the situation presents some advantages. The theory evolved from painstaking examination of empirical and theoretical evidence concerning what the patterns of individual interrelationships ought to be and how many of the variables might be defined. This means that model building can concentrate on specifying the form of relationships and estimating parameters. In addition, variety of research projects have dealt in detail with some of the individual relationships (e.g., Lampert, 1969). This particular application, moreover, involves developing a testable version of the model that is useful for a specific purpose—to test the theory on data collected in a four-month, intensive research project dealing with a grocery product in Portland, Oregon. This narrow definition of product class and geographic market simplifies the task of testing the theory. The data collection procedures are described in Appendix B.

A General Specification of
the Structure of the Model

The now-familiar chart of influence flows (Figure 8.1), which is the basis of the theory, provides an extremely convenient starting point for empirical work on the theory. The chart is a preliminary version of the theory, which has been modified partly on the basis of this test. For our purposes, the theory is taken as given and self-contained, although the results of the empirical research suggest modifications in the theory. It is striking how much the explicit statement of what depends on what helps resolve the fuzziness and uncertainty that pervades many marketing discussions about the dependence of purchasing on past history, attitudes, intentions, and various socioeconomic and psychological characteristics of the buyer. Simply by specifying interrelationships among variables, and the order in which the variables affect the causal chain, we can divide the set of variables into working categories for further analysis. Since the data inputs involve behavior of individual families, there are no serious data aggregation problems at this point.

It is convenient to start by dividing the variables into two sets—those whose values are determined by interactions within the system (i.e., the endogenous variables), and those that are viewed as fixed data, read in from the outside environment, on which interactions within the model have little effect, (i.e., the

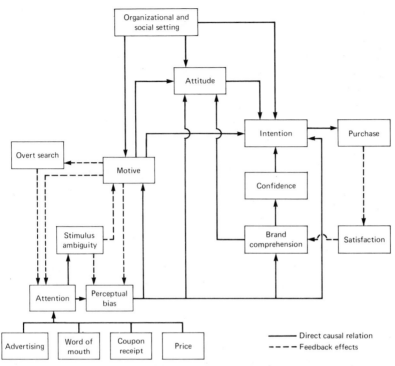

Figure 8.1 Conceptual Model of Buyer Behavior

exogenous variables). This initial step is important for several reasons. First, it helps circumscribe the order of magnitude of the empirical model itself; second, it suggests the measurements that are needed to deal with various aspects of the model; and third, it suggests the schedule for collecting various data. For working purposes, all the variables within the rectangle are endogenous, as all are determined or affected by various feedback relationships. The "output" variables—purchase and satisfaction—feed back into the system and are, of course, also endogenous. The exogenous variables are the components of the marketing program and sociopsychological characteristics of the buyers. Although buyers' decisions in the aggregate ultimately feed back to the firm, causing it to modify its marketing program, the data collection period in this case is so short that price, receipt of samples, advertising, and display can be viewed as being determined outside the system. It is eminently reasonable to assume that no changes occur in the sociopsychological variables as a result of a consumer's being aware of or purchasing a product of the type under study.

The variables include 11 endogenous measures and a set of exogenous variables; the size of this set is discussed later. The lists are:

Endogenous	Exogenous
Y_1 Attention level	X_1 Advertising exposure
Y_2 Perceptual bias	X_2 Level of word-of-mouth activity
Y_3 Stimulus ambiguity	X_3 Receipt of coupon
Y_4 Motive	X_4 Price
Y_5 Overt search activity	X_5 Various characteristics of the social and organizational setting
	.
Y_6 Attitude	.
Y_7 Intention	.
Y_8 Brand comprehension	X_K
Y_9 Confidence	
Y_{10} Purchase	
Y_{11} Satisfaction	

A quick perusal of the list of variables indicates that there are probably some substantial definitional and measurement problems, particularly involving some of the endogenous variables; these are discussed later. The set of organizational and social variables need not be fully defined for the moment, as long as they are all assumed to affect only the three variables into which they flow—motive, attitude and intention. This point is also discussed later.

Configuring the Model for Tests

The distinction in Figure 8.1 between endogenous and exogenous variables is critical in empirical analysis, but in the present analysis the distinction between direct and causal relationships and feedback effects is not important. The latter are simply relationships among endogenous variables. It is clear, for example, that although all the endogenous variables are interrelated, many of the relationships are fed through intervening variables. To configure the entire model in a manageable form, we consider values of each of the endogenous variables in boxes as dependent or explained variables in a set of equations, and we consider the immediate origin of flows of influences into these boxes as explanatory variables. (The flows are indicated by the arrows with the heads indicating the direction of flows.) The strength of these influence flows are the effects of these explanatory variables on the variables designated in the boxes; the goal of the empirical analysis is to evaluate the strength of these influences. Suppose we label each of the connecting links in Figure 8.1 using the following labeling conventions:

    1. If the link connects two endogenous variables, it is labeled β, and if it connects an exogenous variable with an endogenous variable, it is labeled γ.

    2. Each of the labels bears a two-element subscript. The first element is the variable that is being influenced and the second the variable that is doing the influencing. Thus, we are using the label $\beta_{i,j}$ to represent an influence link, and the magnitude of $\beta_{i,j}$ represents the net influence on variable i per unit magnitude of variable j. The entire set of labels, with explicit subscripts denoting the paths linking the variables, appears in Figure 8.2. For example, the endogenous variable motive (Y_4) is influenced by perceptual bias (Y_2) to the extent of $\beta_{4,2}$, by stimulus ambiguity (Y_3) to the extent of $\beta_{4,3}$, and by all the exogenous organizational and social variables to the extent indicated by $\gamma_{4,5}, \ldots, \gamma_{4,k}$. Motive, in turn, influences attention (Y_1) as measured by $\beta_{1,4}$, overt search (Y_5) as measured by $\beta_{5,4}$, intention (Y_7) as measured by $\beta_{7,4}$, attitude (Y_6) to the extent of $\beta_{6,4}$, and perceptual bias (Y_2) to the extent of $\beta_{2,4}$. These coefficients, called the structural parameters of the system, are to be estimated.

    We now face a major decision about the functional form to be adopted for the model, since the flow chart implies only general "depends on" relationships. Econometric techniques provide an appropriate avenue for the empirical attack, and the relationships are configured as a multiple equation econometric model. Assuming linear relationships among the variables (nonlinearities are better handled by transformations on the variables than by developing a nonlinear multivariate model), we cast the model in the following form:

$$Y(i) = \sum_{j \neq 1}^{11} \beta_{i,j} Y(j) + \sum_{k=1}^{K} \gamma_{i,j} X(k) + \gamma_{i,0} + \mu(i); \qquad i = 1, \ldots, 11 \quad (1)$$

where each $Y(j)$ and $X(k)$ is a single-valued observation on endogenous variable k, $\gamma_{i,0}$ is the additive constant in the ith equation,

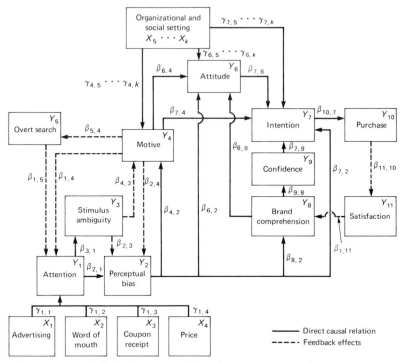

Figure 8.2 Labeled Conceptual Model of Buyer Behavior

and $\mu(i)$ is an error term related to the model's ability to predict values of the endogenous variables.

The linear system (1) clearly has as many equations as there are endogenous variables. These 11 equations are written compactly using matrix notation as

$$\mathbf{B}Y + \tau X + \mu = 0 \qquad\qquad (2)$$

where $\mathbf{B}$ is an 11×11 matrix of coefficients of the endogenous variables, Y is an 11-component column vector of observations of the endogenous variables for one sample point, τ is an $11 \times (K + 1)$ matrix of coefficients of the exogenous variables, X is a $(K + 1)$-element column vector of values of the exogenous variables for the same sample point (including $X(0) = 1$), and μ is an 11×1 column vector with elements $\mu_{(i)}$. The relevant elements of $\mathbf{B}$ and τ in (2) can be read directly from Figure 8.2 using the standard convention that $\beta_{i,j}$ is the entry in the ith row and jth column of

$$B = \begin{bmatrix}
-1 & & & \beta_{1,4} & \beta_{1,5} & & & & & & \\
\beta_{2,1} & -1 & \beta_{2,3} & \beta_{2,4} & & & & & & & \\
\beta_{3,1} & & -1 & & & & & & & & \\
& \beta_{4,2} & \beta_{4,3} & -1 & & & & & & & \\
& & & \beta_{5,4} & -1 & & & & & & \\
& \beta_{6,2} & & \beta_{6,4} & & -1 & & \beta_{6,8} & & & \\
& \beta_{7,2} & & \beta_{7,4} & & \beta_{7,6} & -1 & & \beta_{7,9} & & \\
& \beta_{8,2} & & & & & & -1 & & & \beta_{8,11} \\
& & & & & & & \beta_{9,8} & -1 & & \\
& & & & & & \beta_{10,7} & & & -1 & \\
& & & & & & & & & \beta_{11,10} & -1
\end{bmatrix}$$

$$\Gamma = \begin{bmatrix}
\gamma_{1,1} & \gamma_{1,2} & \gamma_{1,3} & & & & & \gamma_{1,0} \\
& & & & & & & \gamma_{2,0} \\
& & & & & & & \gamma_{3,0} \\
& & & \gamma_{4,5} & \cdots & \gamma_{4,K} & & \gamma_{4,0} \\
& & & & & & & \gamma_{5,0} \\
& & & \gamma_{6,5} & \cdots & \gamma_{6,K} & & \gamma_{6,0} \\
& & & \gamma_{7,5} & \cdots & \gamma_{7,K} & & \gamma_{7,0} \\
& & & & & & & \gamma_{8,0} \\
& & & & & & & \gamma_{9,0} \\
& & & \gamma_{10,4} & & & & \gamma_{10,0} \\
& & & & & & & \gamma_{11,0}
\end{bmatrix}$$

Figure 8.3 Configuration of Parameters for Endogenous and Exogenous Variables

B, and similarly for $\gamma_{i,j}$ in τ. These two matrices appear in Figure 8.3. All blank entries in the matrices are identically zero.

First we must examine the characteristics of B and τ to determine whether empirical work is feasible on the model in its original form. Several things are clear from the entries in the B and τ matrices. Many elements in both matrices are identically equal to zero, meaning that the two variables in such row and column pairs are not functionally related to one another except through intervening variables. These zero entries in the matrices are very important for other purposes, as we shall see. Each row in B and τ represents the coefficients of one of the 11 individual equations, each of which looks like an ordinary regression equation. For instance, the first equation is

$$Y_1 = \gamma_{1,0} + \beta_{1,4}Y_4 + \beta_{1,5}Y_5 + \gamma_{1,1}X_1 + \gamma_{1,2}X_2 + \gamma_{1,3}X_3 + \gamma_{1,4}X_4 + \mu_1 \tag{3}$$

[The convention of placing -1 for the diagonal elements $B_{i,i}$ of the B matrix in effect moves the explained variable to the left side of (2), with a positive sign.] Here $\gamma_{1,0}$ plays the role of an additive constant term. Note also that there are no exogenous variables in some of the equations like the second; this causes no trouble. Of course, (3) is not an ordinary regression equation; it is one of 11 interdependent regression equations in (1) or (2), and the explanatory variables are a mixture of endogenous and exogenous variables. Before empirical analysis can begin, though, the configuration of parameters in the set of equations must be examined to see if parameter estimation is possible even in principle. In econometric jargon, this is called examining the system for "identifiability"—a set of conditions that must be met before estimation of the individual structural parameters (the β's and γ's) can proceed.

It is important to remember that identification is a precondition to estimation and not a part of any particular statistical apparatus. For estimation to be feasible, a variety of restrictions must be imposed on elements of the B and τ matrices; in fact, if every variable affects every other in the sense that every variable occurs in every equation with a nonzero coefficient, parameter estimation is impossible. The required restrictions generally involve some of the coefficients being identically equal to zero. Several rather complex matrix conditions constitute necessary and sufficient conditions for identification, but a simple counting rule is usually the starting point for examining whether a set of equations are identified (Johnston, 1963). The counting rule is: the number of exogenous variables *excluded* from each structural equation must be as great as the number of endogenous variables *included* in the equation, less one. This counting rule is a necessary condition; but in this application, as in many others, it is also sufficient. For the set of equations in Figure 8.3, the counting conditions are presented in Table 8.1.

The number of social and organizational variables is not a problem, as long as there are four or more variables in this set (i.e., $K - 4 \geq 2$, remembering that there are four exogenous marketing variables). An increase in the number of exogenous marketing variables will have no influence on identification, but a reduction will cause immediate problems in the seventh equation. Since the social and organizational variables include all demographic variables, prior preferences, and so on, there are undoubtedly three variables in the set. It appears, then, that all equations in the system are identified and that parameter estimation can proceed.

TABLE 8.1
ENDOGENOUS AND EXCLUDED EXOGENOUS VARIABLES
IN THE STRUCTURAL SYSTEM

EXPLAINED	NUMBER OF ENDOGENOUS VARIABLES LESS 1 INCLUDED IN EQUATION	NUMBER OF EXOGENOUS VARIABLES EXCLUDED FROM EQUATION	MINIMUM VALUE OF K
Y_1	2	$(K-3)$	5
Y_2	3	K	3
Y_3	1	K	1
Y_4	2	4	2
Y_5	1	K	1
Y_6	3	4	3
Y_7	4	4	4
Y_8	2	K	2
Y_9	1	K	1
Y_{10}	1	$K-1$	2
Y_{11}	1	K	1

FITTING THE MODEL

As was mentioned earlier, parameter estimation for this type of model poses some difficult statistical problems. Consider, for example, the fourth equation:

$$Y_4 = \gamma_{4,0} + \beta_{4,2}Y_2 + \beta_{4,3}Y_3 + \sum_{i=5}^{K}\gamma_{4,i}X(i) + \mu_4 \tag{4}$$

and the second equation:

$$Y_2 = \gamma_{2,0} + \beta_{2,1}Y_1 + \beta_{2,3}Y_3 + \beta_{2,4}Y_4 + \mu_2 \tag{5}$$

The standard linear regression model is in some ways inadequate because it is built on the assumption that the explanatory variables in the equation are independent of the error term in the same equation. But substitution of (4) into (5) for Y_4 shows that Y_2 is a function of μ_4, and Y_2 is an explanatory variable in (4) containing μ_4. As a result of this problem, there is no way to make unbiased estimates of the structural parameters of the system.

There are, however, several statistical approaches that eliminate this bias asymptotically—that is, for endlessly large samples. The techniques, variants on regression analysis, provide estimated values of the parameters that are consistent. Examples of such techniques are two-stage least-squares and limited or full-information maximum likelihood techniques.

However, it is often useful to make an initial pass at estimating ·the parameters of a model such as (2) with ordinary regression —that is, with ordinary least squares (OLS). Besides its computational simplicity, OLS has a number of virtues relative to alternative procedures like two-stage least squares (TSLS), especially for exploratory analysis on large systems such as this. For example, OLS stands up well to both multicollinearity and specification problems (Friedman, 1957; Lampert, 1969)—two difficulties that nearly always arise in initial work with a large system of equations. It is important to remember that all statistical methods produce estimates that are biased for small samples; the more sophisticated estimation techniques produce only consistent and asymptotically unbiased estimators. Further, OLS and TSLS estimates are often quite similar.

TESTING THE MODEL

The most convenient attack on a large model is through an examination of joint hypotheses involving sets of coefficients. In this case, these hypotheses are nicely divisible into four categories: (1) those concerning coefficients of the endogenous variables; (2) those concerning coefficients of the exogenous marketing variables, some controllable and some uncontrollable by the firm; (3) those dealing with the exogenous social and demographic variables; and (4) those related to the magnitude of the goodness of fit measures. These tests are extremely harsh, as they are applied to data on the behavior of individual households rather than to aggregates of consumers, which tend to produce more stable estimates (Farley, 1964).

Coefficients of the Endogenous Variables

The 11 endogenous variables are defined so that positive relationships are implied theoretically between each pair of partial relationships. By implication, then, all 21 coefficients in the first 11 columns of Table 8.2 should be positive and significant. Furthermore, each coefficient provides a statistical test of an individual hypothesis within the model. In both senses, the results are satisfactory. Of the 21 coefficients, 20 are positive as expected, and 14 of these are significant at $a = .05$ or better. The negative coefficient $\beta_{8,2}$, not significantly different from zero, is in the relationship determining "brand comprehension," which is the least satisfactory in terms of variable definition. Each of the endogenous variables,

TABLE 8.2

ORDINARY-LEAST-SQUARES ESTIMATES OF STRUCTURAL
PARAMETERS IN LINEAR FORMULATION OF
HOWARD-SHETH BUYER BEHAVIOR MODEL

	EXOGENOUS VARIABLES										
EQUA-TION	Y_1	Y_2	Y_3	Y_4	Y_5	Y_6	Y_7	Y_8	Y_9	Y_{10}	Y_{11}
1	−1			.028	.384[a]						
2	.040	−1	.061	.100[a]							
3	.380[a]		−1								
4		.167[a]	.132[a]	−1							
5				.047	−1						
6		.224[a]		.312[a]		−1		.251[c]			
7		.141[a]		.142[a]	.292[a]		−1		.253[a]		
8		−.014		.142[a]				−1			.043[c]
9								.212[b]	−1		
10							0.91[a]			−1	
11										.436[a]	−1

[a] Significant at $\alpha = .01$.
[b] Significant at $\alpha = .05$.
[c] Significant at $\alpha = .10$.
Endogenous Variables: Y_1 Attention, Y_2 Perceptual bias, Y_3 Stimulus am-

moreover, enters at least one of the relationships as a statistically
significant predictor variable.

Coefficients of the Exogenous Market Variables

The four exogenous market variables include two related to the
tendency of the subject to be exposed to information (from media
and from verbal communication with other people). The other two
variables measure controllable elements of the marketing program
—receipt of samples and average prices paid. The results in this
section of the test are disappointing because there is only one
statistically significant relationship among the four variables involved.

Two factors are probably at work here. First, the effects of
these variables have historically been extremely difficult to estimate
on a disaggregated level. Second, the variables occur only in the
first equation (attention) and the tenth (purchase). The definition
of attention as recalling advertising is not particularly satisfactory.
The significance of the coefficient for X_4 is somewhat surprising,
since there is very little variability in the price series—in fact, just
barely enough to permit its inclusion in the analysis.

TABLE 8.2 (*Continued*)

EXOGENOUS VARIABLES

MARKET				SOCIAL, PERSONAL, DEMOGRAPHIC			
X_1	X_2	X_3	X_4	X_5	X_6	X_7	X_8
.018	−.006	.016					
				−.120	.023	$.176^b$	$.125^a$
				$−.237^c$	$.111^c$	.093	.017
				−.084	.028	.056	$.062^b$
			$.122^a$				

biguity, Y_4 Motive, Y_5 Overt search, Y_6 Attitude, Y_7 Intention, Y_8 Comprehension, Y_9 Confidence, Y_{10} Purchase, Y_{11} Satisfaction.
Exogenous Variables, Market: X_1 Advertising, X_2 Word of mouth, X_3 Receipt of sample, X_4 Price paid; Social, Personal, and Demographic: X_5 Breakfast

Coefficients of the Exogenous
Social and Demographic Variables

The exogenous social-demographic variables occur as a set in the fourth (motive), sixth (attitude), and seventh (intention) equations. Each of the 10 variables enters at least one of these three equations significantly in two-tailed tests; 14 of the 30 coefficients are statistically significant. There are few surprises in the signs of the significant coefficients. Consumption of the product (a convenience food) tends to occur when a small number of people eat the meal in question at home. Strong motive is positively related to household size and leadership, and negatively related to education and to size of the city in which the family lives. Favorable attitudes are also related to small meal groups, homemaking skill (a little surprising), urbanism, and the age of the housewife. Intention is related positively to household size, housewife's working hours, housewife's age, and family income. Intention is related negatively to housewife's education.

As a set, the variables are useful in the analysis and cover both the socioeconomic characteristics of the households and some of the product-specific variables.

| | | | | EXOGENOUS VARIABLES | | | | |
| | | | | SOCIAL, PERSONAL, DEMOGRAPHIC | | | | |
X_9	X_{10}	X_{11}	X_{12}	X_{13}	X_{14}	CONSTANT $\gamma_{i,0}$	R^2
							$.05^a$
							$.03^a$
							$.03^a$
$-.253^b$	$-.320^b$	$-.013$	$-.081^a$	$-.017$	$-.029$		$.10^a$
							$.02^a$
$.243$	$.341^c$	$.218^a$	$-.039$	$-.012$	$.016$		$.13^a$
$.159$	$.168$	$.069^b$	$-.053^a$	$.051^b$	$.081^a$		$.43^a$
							$.01$
							$.01^b$
							$.12^a$
							$.05^a$

consumption, X_6 Homemaking skill, X_7 Leadership, X_8 Household size, X_9 City, 10,000 to 100,000, X_{10} City, over 100,000, X_{11} Wife's age, X_{12} Wife's education, X_{13} Wife's employment (hr/wk), X_{14} Household income.

Goodness of Fit

Ten of the 11 coefficients of determination of goodness of fit are significantly different from zero, but most are extremely small. (With almost 700 observations, it is hardly surprising that the R^2's are significant.) Very little can be done about this situation, but some observations may be useful in the design of future studies. First, the fits are particularly poor for the dependent variables that are difficult to measure or for which the measures available for this study are not particularly good (e.g., attention and brand comprehension). The fits are relatively good when the definitions are better or the measures are more closely related to the phenomenon—attitude, intention, and purchase, for example. The noise is much worse for variables early in the theoretical sequence, where interpersonal variability is especially large. Second, relatively poor fits characterize large cross-sectional studies such as the present, in which variability across subjects is to be expected and the consumption phenomenon in question is subtle. Third, we are assuming, in this first approximation, that there are no significant segments in the market. That is, we are assuming that the same set of regression coefficients is appropriate for all members of the sample. Convenient statistical procedures for handling this problem are only now under development, but any significant segmentation will markedly affect the goodness of fit.

Finally, there is the matter of the sharpness of the data instruments themselves. Even if the variables have been defined correctly, the measurement techniques are quite blunt in several cases. Some measures are simply two-value dummy variables. Others are four- to seven-point category scales. These have reasonable ordinal interpretations, but they add levels of noise to the system that are statistically almost impossible to reduce. As an aside, the noise level in pairwise relationships made it impossible to use scatter diagrams reasonably to look for nonlinear relationships.

SOME IMPLICATIONS

The results of this first try at testing the Howard-Sheth theory of buyer behavior are generally very encouraging. The empirical values of the coefficients are generally consistent with the theory, and the theory has been extremely useful in developing the empirical procedures. As might be expected from exploratory empirical work, however, a major outcome of this set of tests implies more by way of advice for sharpening the theory and for developing future field studies than it does in suggestions for this product and market. The following particular advice should be kept in mind:

1. Data collection in any future research project should concentrate on explicitly measuring each of the endogenous variables and the exogenous market variables. Even a careful survey asking all sorts of conventional market research questions fails to provide good measures for some of the variables that are key elements of the Howard-Sheth model. This results in some of the deficiencies now apparent in both the definitions and the empirical results.

2. Particular attention should be paid to precise definition and measurement of the exogenous marketing variables. A complex structure like that implied by the theory should give a good opportunity to assess the influence of advertising, sampling, and so on. In the present case, however, these were the least satisfactory measurement aspects of the field study that produced the data. These very important variables are required for statistical system identification, and they also include the key control variables for the firm's marketing activities. When more precise estimates of the system parameters are available, the same control variables will be paramount in evaluating a firm's marketing activities.

3. A great deal of attention should be devoted to developing

sensitive data collection techniques. Once noisy data are collected, it is virtually impossible to clean them up. Furthermore, careful design of data collection procedures will probably allow a study to collect a smaller amount of data than is usually involved in omnibus market research projects.

4. Distribution plays a very important role, not only in determining the aggregate rate of purchasing but in obtaining good estimates of the parameters of the model. When distribution is significantly less than 100 percent, it is difficult to determine *ex post* whether an individual's rate of purchase was low because of lack of availability, failure to act on intentions, or other reasons. The distribution level of approximately 50 percent for two of the three major brands in the present product class clearly explains some of the noise in the present analysis.

5. Data should be coded simply and configured in a straightforward way in conventional data files. It is always tempting to pack data and code esoterically to save time and data storage space; this temptation should be resisted. Unpacking and decoding costs far outweigh any minor savings in cards, tape, or disc space achieved at earlier stages of the study.

6. Some particular points on this version of the theory and the collection of relevant data should receive attention. (It is worthwhile to note that considerable modification of any relationship—with the possible exception of the intention equation—is possible without raising any serious identification problems.) First, the "attention" variable confounds passive receiving of various messages and active attention to the product; these aspects of attention should probably be divided explicitly. Similarly, arousal motive and directive motive should probably be measured separately, as an argument can be made that they are affected by different outside forces. The confidence variable might also be divided; perhaps generalized self-confidence is exogenous and product-specific confidence is endogenous. The confidence variable might also receive some further attention with regard to the other endogenous variables that it affects.

SUMMARY

The Howard-Sheth model of buyer behavior proved amenable to formulation as a system of simultaneous equations. Ordinary-least-squares estimates of the system's parameters for the endogenous and social-organizational variables were reasonable, but those of a set of market-oriented exogenous variables were unsatisfactory.

Goodness of fit measures were generally very low, indicating very high levels of noise in the system. For future work in the context of this type of model, the first order of business is to improve vastly the data collection technology to be used in field work.

APPENDIX A

DEFINITION OF VARIABLES

This section describes how the variables are defined and presents the variables and the stage of the data collection process at which this information was gathered. A number of subsidiary details about variable definition, various adjustment procedures, and the like are included.

Endogenous Variables

Attention (Y_1). Recollection of seeing ads for instant breakfast. Data collected on second telephone interview.

Perceptual bias (Y_2). A filter variable, related to a tendency to use new products and to rate them well. Data collected in the mail questionnaire.

Stimulus ambiguity (Y_3). The ability to describe the product accurately. Results from the first telephone interview. The characteristics chosen were "powdered," "in a box," "many flavors," "drunk," and "individual portions." The variable is the total number of correct identifications among the five categories.

Motive (Y_4). A scale variable collected in the first mail questionnaire on interest in differences among brands of milk additives.

Overt search (Y_5). Endogenous, experience-induced search for information by talking to someone else. Data collected on the first telephone interview.

Attitude toward product (Y_6). Scaled overall evaluation of the product. Collected in the mail questionnaire.

Intention to purchase (Y_7). Answer on the mail questionnaire about likelihood of buying instant breakfast in the next month.

Brand comprehension (Y_8). Ability to recall at least one brand of the product. Collected on the first telephone interview.

Confidence (Y_9). General confidence in ability to make judgments about products such as these. Scaled from "extremely confident" to "not confident at all"; data collected on the first telephone interview.

Purchase (Y_{10}). Number of units purchased, as reported in purchase diaries.

Satisfaction (Y_{11}). Postpurchase scaled satisfaction with the product, measured in the second telephone interview.

Exogenous Variables

Exposure to advertising media (X_1). Recall measure in the mail questionnaires of tendency to be exposed to advertising media.

Word-of-mouth conversation activity (X_2). General index based on subject's tendency to socialize and communicate on matters concerning the home. Data collected in the mail questionnaire.

Brand stimulus (X_3). Receipt of sample or coupon, reported in the first telephone interview.

Prices paid (X_4). Average of prices reported paid for product in the raw purchase data reported in the purchase diaries.

Mealtime group (X_5). Index constructed from data in the mail questionnaire, involving tendencies to eat a relevant meal alone versus with others.

Homemaking skill (X_6). Self-evaluative scale in the first mail questionnaire rating interviewee's homemaking skills.

Leadership (X_7). Index constructed from self-evaluation of leadership roles described in the mail questionnaire.

Household size (X_8). Number of people reported in household on the screening questionnaire.

Size of city lived in (X_9, X_{10}). Also from the screening questionnaire. Two dummy variables, the first for cities greater than 100,000 and the second for cities less than 10,000.

Age of housewife (X_{11}). From the screening questionnaire.

Education of housewife (X_{12}). Number of years of formal education of the housewife, from the screening questionnaire.

Housewife's employment (X_{13}). Number of hours per week that the housewife works, reported in the screening questionnaire.

APPENDIX B

DATA COLLECTION PROCEDURE

The data used in this analysis were gathered as a part of the comprehensive Buyer Behavior Project directed by Professor John Howard, Columbia Graduate School of Business.

In the summer of 1966, two consumer panels were established in a test market to monitor the introduction of a new branded product sold in supermarkets and grocery stores. This product class had only one brand at the time of formulation of the consumer panels, and it was available in almost every retail grocery store in the test market. The new brand was similar to the old brand in packaging, price, and product attributes. During the test period, another new brand was also introduced into this test market; this brand was likewise very similar to the old brand.

One result of this dual introduction was that each new brand obtained only about 50 percent distribution in the test market. From an analysis of distribution, it appears that stores decided to stock one of the new brands but seldom stocked both.

The test market selected for this Buyer Behavior Project contained approximately 300,000 households and 1 million persons. A sample of 70,000 persons was selected in a systematic manner from the telephone directories in the test market. A recruitment letter and screening questionnaire were sent to each of these persons. Respondents were offered a choice of a set of cutlery or kitchen tools if they were selected for participation in the panel.

The individual pieces of the set were to be sent to panel members as their completed purchase diaries were received. About 8300 persons responded to the invitation, and from these respondents, 2200 were selected for panel membership. Prior users of the old brand were twice as likely to be selected as nonusers. The 2200 persons were allocated evenly to a control panel and an experimental panel. The two panels were matched so that the number of members in different Nielson areas who were prior users of the old brand were closely comparable between panels.

After the screening questionnaire, members in the control panel and the experimental panel made reports every two weeks on their purchases of five food product classes. The members in the control were not contacted in any other way during the 20-week period during which both panels were in existence. As shown in Figure 8.4, the members in the experimental panel were interviewed extensively; however, they were never told in advance that they would be interviewed.

One week before the purchase reporting periods began, the members of the experimental panel were mailed an 18-page questionnaire. This instrument was used to obtain measures of breakfast eating habits and predispositions such as involvement in homemaking, impulsiveness, gregariousness, perceived time pressures, and concern with nutrition. Respondents were also asked whether they had ever heard of the old brand and two other brands in the related product class. For each brand they had heard of, respondents were asked who in their house used it, their attitudes concerning 14 attributes of each brand, the importance of these attributes in their purchase decisions, how likely 13 specified categories of persons were to use the brand, and the likelihood that they would purchase the brand in the next month.

The response rate of 86 percent for the mail questionnaire, which seems very high, was primarily due to two factors. First, the panel members were more willing to respond than the average consumer, since they had already agreed to participate in a panel. Second, a cover letter sent with the mail questionnaire informed the panel members that a three-piece Party Knife Set had already been mailed as a gift in appreciation of their cooperation.

At the beginning of the fifth week of purchase reporting, the members of the experimental panel were interviewed by telephone. Respondents were asked to name as many brands as they could in the product class. After the spontaneous response, each brand that had not been mentioned was named and the respondents were asked if they had heard of it. If they had heard of it, either un-

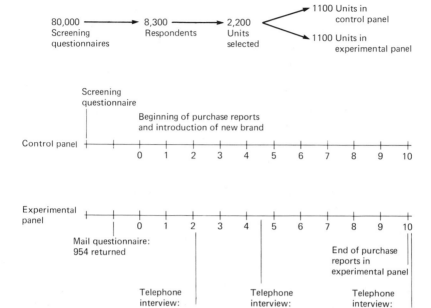

Figure 8.4 Panel Schedules: Time—2–Week Intervals Correspond to Ends of Purchase Report Periods

aided or aided, the respondents were asked if they had discussed the brand with anyone. Next they were requested to rate their attitudes on eight attributes, to rate their confidence in evaluating each brand, and to state how likely they were to purchase each brand next month. The new brand was used by the interviewer in explaining how to answer the questions.

A second telephone interview was conducted five weeks later and a third 11 weeks later, immediately after the tenth diary report. These interviews were similar to the first telephone interview described above.

9

CONFIDENCE AS A VALIDATED CONSTRUCT

JOHN A. HOWARD
Professor of Business
Graduate School of Business
Columbia University

Confidence in making a brand choice, we postulate, is a central construct in explaining buying behavior. In this role it explains both the buyer's *search effort*—the amount, source, and timing—and his probability of overt action of *purchasing* the brand. It regulates his information input, and it influences his purchase act (Howard and Sheth, 1969).

Our purpose here is to assess the extent to which confidence can be viewed as a validated construct. Although it is perhaps belaboring the obvious, we ask, Why is the validation problem important to those of us researching the buyer? The answer, of course, is that the things we work with are so often not observable. For example, who ever observed—touched, tasted, smelled, heard, or saw—an attitude? Confidence has the same characteristic of unobservability. To create substantial knowledge with such idealistic constructs—concepts representing things whose existence in some physiological sense we are not necessarily willing to accept—does indeed complicate the task of research. However, unless we are willing to pay attention to validating these constructs, research on buyer behavior is a hopeless task, and we should transfer our energies to more productive pursuits.

On the other hand, if we do recognize the validation problem and attempt to deal with it, we should not be unduly discouraged with our difficult task of creating knowledge about unobservables. The great developments in atomic energy, for example, have been based on a construct postulated more than two thousand years ago by Democritus, and not until recently could physicists have any real hope of observing—seeing, smelling, feeling, tasting, or hearing—an atom.

As an aid to the reader, the first letters of the labels of all postulated constructs are capitalized. The operationally defined counterpart of this construct—sometimes termed "an intervening variable"—is identified by the same term but followed by a prime.

DEFINITION OF CONFIDENCE

At the grossest level, Confidence is the buyer's subjective certainty—his state of feeling sure—in making his judgment of the quality of a particular brand.

One of the central complications in defining the term is time. Because we wish to predict the purchase act some time before it occurs, we are interested in knowing the buyer's Confidence prior to the purchase act. The longer this period, the greater the number of decision aspects involved in his Confidence in contemplating the future act. To add concreteness to the discussion, it is helpful to distinguish between his buying a brand in a product class of short purchase cycle, such as a food item in which the purchase cycle may be as short as a week, versus his buying a large consumer durable in which the purchase cycle may be longer than five years.

With a short purchase cycle, logically, the buyer can be uncertain about (1) his ability to judge the *current* value of the brand (the current dimensions of the evaluative beliefs that constitute his Attitude), and (2) his ability to judge the current value of the elements that constitute the inhibitors underlying his Intention (to buy). By inhibitors we mean the factors in his purchase situation that constrain him from following the direction of behavior implied in his Attitude for each of the brands in the product class.

When we turn to the more complicated durables case, the buyer could in addition be uncertain about (1) the future values of his inhibitors, and (2) the future values of the dimensions that enter into his Attitude.

Given these complications, the question is: What is the best way to simplify and thus conceptualize Confidence to make it a useful construct? I suggest that we use three dimensions of certainty with respect to (1) evaluation of the brand (current Attitude), (2) judgment of the current values of inhibitors, and (3) estimates of future values of inhibitors (future Intention), and that we omit the buyer's estimates of the future values of the dimensions of Attitude.

CONSTRUCT VALIDATION

Having postulated Confidence, we must ask: Is it a valid construct? Or is it an ad hoc, isolated, and even a meaningless concept?

One might attempt to answer this question in terms of whether the thing represented by the construct exists; for example, is there some physiological counterpart that we have not yet measured? I would not care to take this realistic position, however. I prefer to attempt only to answer it at a more idealistic level—namely, whether it is a useful construct here and now in guiding our research and interpreting our data for policy purposes, both public and private. Even if a person is more realistic, however, and says he is interested in it only in some physiological but currently unobservable sense, construct validation is still a problem because he still must be satisfied only with indirect measures.

How does one evaluate a concept? How does he say that it is good or bad, useful or not useful, satisfactory or unsatisfactory? To answer these questions is to make use of the process of construct validation.

Construct validation is important because if the construct has been validated, the researcher can predict performance for a measure that has not yet been employed in empirical studies. The lack of construct validations is the enormous weakness of current market research. In market research, we discover a measure and use it repeatedly in a habitual, mechanical way. We do not attempt to validate the construct that lies behind it; thus we are incapable of predicting what values we will obtain on new measures of it. In market research, for example, we take an "attitude" measure that is in fact merely the buyer's verbal response to a question over the telephone. The probe is often "Tell me how well you like this brand: very much, some, not at all." Then we take the consumer's responses and begin to theorize from them—conjecturing about what causes attitude to have the value it has or about the extent to which attitude influences purchase—but the theorizing is almost always implicit, seldom explicit.

An illustrative consequence of lack of validation is the practice sometimes observed among market researchers of using "attitude" to refer both to a measure of the buyer's *evaluation* of a brand and to his *intention* to buy that brand in the future.

There are certain rules according to which we can say that we have or have not validated a construct (Cronbach and Meehl, 1955).

1. We need to make it clear what the construct is. To "make clear what something *is*" is to describe the laws by which it occurs. These laws are contained in an interlocking system or set of relations that make up a theory and are called a nomological network, where "nomological" deals with laws of the mind.

2. We must describe these laws for our construct; they relate (a) observable attributes to each other, (b) hypothetical constructs to each other, or (c) hypothetical constructs to observable attributes.

3. At least some of the laws must pertain to observable attributes.

4. In the process of validating a construct, we learn more about our construct. "Learning more about" a hypothetical construct involves either (a) elaborating the nomological network or (b) increasing the definiteness of the components by providing more empirical evidence on the existing links.

5. Validation can be furthered by elaborating the nomological network. The network can be elaborated, for example, by adding a construct or a relation (a) if it generates nomologicals that are confirmed by observation or (b) if it reduces the number of nomologicals required to predict the same observations.

6. We must be able to identify the case of quantitatively different measurement operations that are measuring the same construct. Measurement operations that appear quite different "measure the same thing" if their positions in the nomological network tie them in to the same construct. Our confidence in making this identification is determined by the amount of empirical support for that particular region of the overall network that contains this construct.

Thus necessary conditions for a construct to be validated are that in the network containing the construct, the links make contact with observable reality and that these links exhibit explicit, public steps of inference. The construct must, in other words, be *behavior relevant*.

With these essential conditions in mind, let us describe the nomological network surrounding Confidence, then proceeding to examine some of the empirical evidence on the links in the network.

NOMOLOGICAL NETWORK OF CONFIDENCE

In discussing the links that constitute the networks surrounding Confidence, let us distinguish them according to the direction of causality.

We first examine the outbound links—the consequences of Confidence. Confidence is positively linked to Intention and through Intention exerts an effect on overt action, purchase of the brand. Confidence is also linked as a feedback inversely to the arousal aspect of the buyer's Motives, which in turn regulates search effort. When the Motives satisfied by this product class are operative, the value of Confidence will be one of the influences on the intensity of the Motives. By "search" we mean the activities of the buyer that affect the amount of information that he takes into his nervous system. Search activities extend all the way from merely opening and closing his sensory receptors in response to certain stimuli to talking with other people and such acts as obtaining *Consumer Reports* from the public library.

The inbound links—the constructs influencing the level of Confidence—are, first, the buyer's comprehension of the denotative or descriptive aspects of the brand concept (Brand Comprehension). Second, there is a feedback from Satisfaction to Confidence—the degree of Satisfaction resulting from the purchasing act and the consumption of that brand. These two links are positive.

Although it is often more important to say what a construct is not than what it is, this delimiting role of theory is sometimes neglected. Confidence is not postulated to be Attitude or any component of it. Some scientists view confidence as merely another way of describing the intensity of Attitude. We believe it will be more fruitful to treat it as being separate from Attitude.

Confidence illustrates the benefit of juxtaposing cognitive theory and behavior theory from psychology. Cognitive theory, by leaning heavily on attitude, has developed a comprehensive system that is manipulable but difficult to make operational because so many of the variables cannot be observed. Behavior theory has been highly operational, but at the price of being an exceedingly complex system—one that is so much more implicit than explicit that for our kinds of complex problems the system becomes impossible to manipulate. Thus I believe we must break apart some of the cognitive concepts to achieve greater operationality. We are here separating the usual concept of attitude into its evaluative (Attitude) and Confidence components. Not only will this separation yield greater operationality, it will give us the opportunity to sort out the differential effects of the great variety of stimuli impinging on the buyer. As we know, the marketer is far more interested in some of these stimuli—advertising, for example—than others.

EMPIRICAL EVIDENCE FOR NETWORK

We now move to the observable counterparts of the hypothetical constructs, the variables that link the nomological network with reality. We postulate that an intervening variable and its hypothetical counterpart are at least monotonically related. The reader should bear in mind the problem of surplus meaning: a hypothetical construct contains meaning that is never fully captured by its intervening counterpart.

To validate Confidence, we must determine whether relations among observables (intervening variables) conform to the postulated relations among the hypothetical construct. As we noted in discussing the nomological network, Confidence has certain causes and certain consequences. Let us first examine the consequences and then the causes.

Consequences of Confidence'

Confidence' is hypothesized to influence both overt purchase behavior and behavior directed to obtaining information about the brands in the buyer's evoked set of the relevant product class.

Effect on Overt Behavior. Our evidence from buying behavior is limited, but research is under way. Johnson (1968) found confirming evidence in a purchase panel established in the test market for a new food product. Consumers with a given level of Intention' (intention to buy within a given time period) were more likely to execute that Intention' if their Confidence was high.

In an 11-equation model of the system, Farley and Ring (Chapter 8 of this volume) found a clear relation between Confidence' and Intention', and the proportion of variance explained in this equation was better than any of the other 10 equations.

That confidence in Intention as contrasted with the more general confidence in judging a brand also makes a difference in behavior is shown by Juster (1964) in evaluating consumer plans to buy groups of consumer durables, such as houses, automobiles, refrigerators, television sets, and radios. The usual intentions question is:

Do you expect or plan to buy a car in the next 6 to 12 months?

DW _____ (Definitely will)
PW _____ (Probably will)

DK _____ (Don't know)

No _____

Juster argues that the replies are estimates of the probability that the item will be purchased within the specified time. He believes a more direct approach should be used and he asks:

Taking everything into account, what are the prospects that some member of your family will buy a _____ sometime during the next _____ months, between now and next _____ ?

Certain, practically certain	(99 in 100)	10
Almost sure	(9 in 10)	9
Very probable	(8 in 10)	8
Probable	(7 in 10)	7
Good possibility	(6 in 10)	6
Fairly good possibility	(5 in 10)	5
Fair possibility	(4 in 10)	4
Some possibility	(3 in 10)	3
Slight possibility	(2 in 10)	2
Very slight possibility	(1 in 10)	1
No chance, almost no chance	(1 in 10)	0

In the case of automobiles, the probability scale predicts purchase considerably better than does the intention measure. For household durables, it improves the predictions but not by nearly so much.

Search Effort. Turning now to the evidence on the effects of Confidence on search behavior, we postulate an inverse relation between the level of Confidence and the tendency to look for information. Actually the relationship is more complicated than this, but except for the extremes, an inverse relation is satisfactory.

In a related way and in the buyer behavior area, Bauer and his group have presented extensive ideas and findings under the rubric of perceived risk (Cox, 1967). The results, however, do not bear closely on the issue here because the measures were conceived in terms of the product class, not brand choice. In terms of more general human behavior, Berlyne (1963) has assembled a great amount of evidence in simple laboratory experiments. Lanzetta (1967), following Berlyne, has done some of the most extensive laboratory work.

To validate his measure of subjective uncertainty, Lanzetta uses the information theoretic concept of uncertainty:

$$H = -P_i \log_2 P_i$$

where H is the amount of uncertainty and P_i is the probability of occurrence of the ith response. This equation provides an objective estimate of the amount of uncertainty in the stimulus (response uncertainty), since P_i is obtained by computing the relative frequencies of response from a sample of people who are asked to interpret each stimulus in the set of stimuli of varying complexities. Lanzetta finds that subjective uncertainty measured by the subject's magnitude estimation of "felt degree of uncertainty about the choice" varies directly with this objective measure of uncertainty. Then having validated his measure of subjective uncertainty, he goes another step and finds that subjective uncertainty (the inverse of Confidence) varies directly with the person's preference for additional information. Later work has carried this analysis further.

On the other hand, in data from a food product in test market, O'Brien (1969) found that level of word-of-mouth discussion and level of Confidence' vary directly instead of inversely. O'Brien's analysis was especially relevant because by his methodology he was able to trace causality from Confidence' to word of mouth. How can these contradictory findings be reconciled? It can be hypothesized, first, that in a naturalistic setting a certain level of Confidence must be attained before the person feels he knows enough about a product to discuss it. This conclusion is prompted in part by Arndt's (1966) finding that there is a bit of game playing in word-of-mouth discussion, where the receiver tries to minimize revealing his ignorance. Second, and also in a naturalistic setting, even after the person has acquired adequate information, he continues to talk about the new product because he is now telling others about it: he is an "opinion *leader*" and he thus enhances his status. His motives for talking have changed.

Causes of Confidence

Finally, it is equally important to examine the empirical evidence on the postulated causes of the level of Confidence in order to assess the validity of the construct. Recall that we postulated in the nomological network two causes of confidence: Brand Comprehension and Satisfaction. Farley and Ring found a positive relation between Brand Comprehension' and Confidence'.

We should ask about the effects of informational input, since it is a central issue. O'Brien (1969) found a clear relation between word of mouth and Confidence'. Word of mouth affected unaided brand awareness, which in turn affected level of knowledge about the brand, and I would accept these two measures as the equivalent of Brand Comprehension. This finding suggests that information can affect Confidence without first changing Attitude or Intention.

The finding that Attitude seemed to be bypassed by information in changing Confidence is important because of the common belief that Confidence is a dimension of attitude as usually defined. Clearly Confidence and Attitude as defined here are correlated, perhaps with $r = 0.4$. If the line of argument being pursued here (i.e., that they are separate entities) is correct, we conclude that the same things are not causing both.

CONCLUSIONS

We have formulated a nomological network that contains Confidence as one of its elements (Howard and Sheth, 1969). The relations among the constructs that make up the network have been specified regarding the direction of causation. Some empirical evidence on these relations among observables has been assembled. In this way we have cònformed to the rules of construct validation. Perhaps the most accurate statement to be made is that Confidence as a hypothetical construct appears to be partly validated.

If Confidence can be fully validated, significant progress will have been made because Confidence appears to occupy an equilibrating role in buyer behavior. Assuming the buyer is experiencing a need for the new product in the market—he is experiencing motivational *dis*equilibrium with respect to this product class—his Confidence is less when he is first confronted by the new product. This low Confidence motivates search effort, but as he receives information, his Confidence rises and his motivation to collect information recedes; and particularly as he buys the product and consumes it, his Confidence rises. Thus he attains an informational equilibrium at which he no longer needs information. This equilibrium will most likely occur if the item is a frequently purchased one and he buys additional units of it. He will develop brand loyalty, which we can think of as a state of purchase equilibrium. Hence we can say that he has achieved information-purchase equilibrium that presumably will continue through repetitive cycles of motivational disequilibrium-equilibrium, until some external event (e.g., as another new product, or possibly his internally generated need for variety) pushes him off dead center.

10

THE INFLUENCE OF PERSONAL COMMUNICATION ON A BUYER'S CHOICE CRITERIA IN THE SALESMAN/BUYER DYAD

JOHN O'SHAUGHNESSY
Associate Professor of Business
Graduate School of Business
Columbia University

A decision to buy stems from a perceived need, and the intended result of the decision is the satisfaction of the perceived need. The nature of the need guides the overt search for product information and determines the appropriateness of suggested products and the choice criteria used in their evaluation.

CONCEPT OF CHOICE CRITERIA

Choice criteria are the factors used by the buyer in evaluating competitive makes within an evoked set. Thus the factors in column 1 of Table 10.1 might be the product attributes considered by a prospective office equipment buyer. For the factors to be operational as criteria, they must be weighted (either explicitly or implicitly) according to their relative importance. Such a weighting is shown in column 2. The weighting of product attributes cannot be an objective process, since establishing the relative importance of a particular attribute to the satisfaction of needs requires weighing different kinds of evidence, and this inevitably involves a large element of judgment. After weighting the various factors, the buyer rates each product in his evoked set for its likely performance on each of the factors. Such a rating (see column 3) would be subject

TABLE 10.1
OFFICE EQUIPMENT EVALUATION

PRODUCT ATTRIBUTES	WEIGHT	POINTS AWARDED PRODUCTS			WEIGHTED RATING PRODUCTS		
		A	B	C	A	B	C
(1)	(2)		(3)			(4)	
Quality							
Quality of output	2	2	2	3	4	4	6
Durability of equipment	3	−1	1	2	−3	3	6
Reliability of equipment	3	3	−1	2	9	−3	6
Distinctiveness							
Ease of operation	3	2	2	2	6	6	6
Machine speed	1	3	2	1	3	2	1
Space used	1	2	1	1	2	1	1
Preference of clerical operators	2	−2	1	3	−4	2	6
Appearance	1	−2	1	3	−2	1	3
Flexibility	1	2	2	2	2	2	2
Ease of maintenance	−						
Service							
Reputation of supplier in servicing	3	1	2	3	3	6	9
Availability							
Delivery	1	−1	2	2	−1	2	2
Price							
Original cost	1	−1	2	3	−1	2	3
Maintenance cost	2	2	2	2	4	4	4
Running cost	3	2	2	2	6	6	6
Payoff					30	38	61

to perceptual bias resulting from previous experience and motives and also influenced by the extent to which the prospective buyer has (or believes he has) adequately comprehended the various product features. There is even likely to be a halo effect, whereby a single factor on which a product excels or is inferior may, in Thorndike's words, cast a halo over the other factors, thus raising or lowering ratings. (The halo effect may be related to feature substitution, which occurs when a customer evaluates one product feature in depth and ignores those remaining.) Finally, the points awarded in the rating would be multiplied by the weights to produce a weighted rating on each factor (column 4). The overall sum of the weighted factor ratings constitutes the overall weighted product assessment, and the ranked assessments constitute the relative evaluation of the products. They could be taken as a reflection of likely attitudes toward the products in question. In outlining this systematic, though crude, approach to product evaluation, we do not suggest that it is descriptive of buying behavior. The outline is meant to be a guide to likely deficiencies in the actual decision process used by a buyer to evaluate products. It is argued that knowledge of such deficiencies can help the salesman in his task of persuasion.

We can distinguish the following choice criteria situations:

1. **Choice criteria are absent or inactive.** The choice criteria in terms of product attributes are inactive or nonexistent; thus the buyer may even reach the stage of purchasing a product without reference to any implicit or explicit list of product attributes such as shown in column 1. The basis for the belief in the efficacy of the product is past experience of its performance, faith, intuition, or authority.
2. **Choice criteria are inadequate or vague.** Although the buyer does possess some criteria in terms of product attributes, they are inadequate and imprecise. In other words the buyer is vaguely aware of some product attributes that he believes the products he buys should possess.
3. **Choice criteria are in conflict.** The buyer is aware of the product attributes he desires, but these attributes are in conflict. As in item 2, criteria may be inadequate and vague.
4. **Choice criteria are explicit.** Choice criteria in terms of product attributes are known; they do not conflict, and they are regarded by buyer and seller as comprehensive and explicit.

Choice Criteria Absent or Inactive

We infer that choice criteria exist as a hypothetical construct because we can articulate our reasons for buying one product rather than another. Is this sufficient evidence, however, for asserting that choice criteria always play a part in the purchase decision process? Can a distinction be drawn between "mere choice" and "decision"? I may choose this cigarette rather than that simply because "I like it better"; but I decide to buy this car rather than another because, on the basis of my criteria in terms of product attributes, it is more likely to satisfy my perceived need. Could the first case be labeled "mere choice" because that selection appears to be based on tastes and values not open to inspection? Should only the second situation be called "decision," since the process involved evaluation or selection that stemmed from deliberation on criteria that are potentially open to inspection?

The distinction is less contrasting than it appears to be. Some purchases stem from the process of habit formation; thus there is a one-to-one correspondence between perceived need and product choice. This is not to suggest that such behavior is nonrational, unless we adopt Weber's definition of rational behavior as "the deliberate and logical choice of means to attain explicit goals, in the light of existing factual knowledge." Watkins (1953, p. 741) regards this definition as unsatisfactory for two reasons:

> (a) Whitehead said somewhere that "civilisation advances by extending the number of important operations we can perform without thinking about them." This morning's tooth-brushing was not irrational because done from habit and not from deliberations on dental hygiene. Our pursuit of goals need not be conscious in order to be rational. (b) Behaviour often does not conform to the end-means pattern. I may tell the truth, or go fishing, simply from a desire to do so, with no further end in mind.

Buying habits serve to economize on search effort and mental deliberation. There are, however, choice criteria. There is first the criterion "to economize on effort by buying the product that satisfied the need previously," or the buyer might be using a standard evaluation strategy. Probing might even reveal choice criteria in terms of product attributes that led initially to the selection of the product. However, choice criteria in terms of product attributes are not necessarily deliberated on or even consciously present as the buyer makes his purchase decision.

How does such a situation arise? We have already suggested that buying through habit might replace buying through deliberation. When buying is based on habit rather than deliberation on product attributes, satisfaction with the product currently being bought is implied. Or, at least, it appears that the extent of the dissatisfaction is not sufficient to induce the buyer to take the trouble in seeking and the risk in sampling competitive makes. However, the absence of choice criteria in terms of product attributes can lead to random purchase behavior and may stem from a failure to diagnose precisely the buyer's need.

If there are no choice criteria based on product attributes, how can the salesman steer a prospect to his product? As a hypothesis, it is suggested that the salesman's best strategy is to *educate* the prospect on the effects generated by a satisfactory product or the relationship between increases in quality and the effects of such increases on product performance. Only then should the salesman discuss with the prospect the signs that indicate the product's potential to produce certain effects. Then the salesman may claim that a particular attribute is:

1. A sign of a superior product or even essential for the product to produce the effects described.
2. More important (or less important) than appears, since it could produce undesirable side effects later if ignored (or will produce no side effects if ignored). In the first case the emphasis lies in implanting attributes to enter into the buyer's choice criteria. The second case suggests how the buyer should weight the attributes.

Choice Criteria Inadequate and Vague

When the buyer's choice criteria are inadequate and vague, the potential range of products falling within the buyer's evoked set will be correspondingly wide, and two strategies will be open to the salesman. On the one hand, he may find it easy to show that his product meets the buyer's choice criteria because these are very broad, thus are satisfied by any product that is not specifically excluded. There is little selling here but merely *recommending*, and the buyer, perhaps aware of the vagueness of his needs, may prefer to shop around before making a final choice. The hypothesis put forward is that the salesman's best strategy is to *solve* the customer's problem by helping him diagnose and define it—assuming the salesman has a range of products to offer and is interested in repeat business and customer goodwill. The emphasis lies not in discussing the characteristic effects of a "good" product but in discovering the effects that the prospect himself desires. Only after this process of mutual problem solving has been completed will the salesman put forward a product from his range. He then discusses its attributes in a way that allows the customer to perceive the instrumentality of the product to meet his redefined need. Unfortunately, the strategies of education and their solution are too difficult to distinguish at the verbal level; thus they form a combined strategy below.

Choice Criteria in Conflict

The conflict situation is dealt with in psychological choice theory. The psychologist distinguishes three situations in which two or more motives block one another.

1. The "approach-approach" conflict, where the choice lies between two or more mutually exclusive but positive goals, is regarded as unstable because indecision is momentary.

2. The avoidance-avoidance conflict, where choice lies between two negative goals, is recognized as stable because the subject seeks to avoid both alternatives.

3. The "approach-avoidance" situation, where goals possess both negative and positive features, introduces the strengths of an individual's tendencies to approach a positive goal and also to avoid a negative goal. Both tendencies are decreasing functions of the subject's distance from the goal. The tendency to approach predominates at a distance, whereas near the goal, the tendency to avoid predominates. The situation is regarded as stable, since there is a strong tendency for the subject to remain at the point where the two tendencies cross. This point of intersection can be moved toward the goal, either by increasing the value of the positive features of the goal or by reducing the perceived negative features of the goal. Psychologists argue that inducing a movement toward the goal by enhancing the goal's more positive features is at the expense of increasing fear and anxiety, whereas reducing the perceived negative features is more effective because it results in a movement toward the goal with a lesser increment of fear.

Only conflict situations 1 and 3 are of interest in this paper. Situation 1 corresponds to the buyer choosing between two or more mutually exclusive attributes. Unless the attributes are only mutually exclusive in the salesman's product (which means that the problem falls into category 3), the buyer decides quickly which attribute he prefers. The salesman helps in this process by depreciating one of the alternatives.

Situation 3 represents the purchase situation in which a product or attribute is accompanied by negative features. At its simplest, this represents the traditional price-versus-desire conflict: approaches are made toward buying, but guilt at spending increases near the point of buying intention and purchase. (Subsumed perhaps in this heading of approach-avoidance is the problem of closing the sale; fear of failure to make a sale increases as the interview nears its end, and the salesman is apt to "drag out" the interview.)

Situation 3 opens two strategies to the salesman: He can

enhance the positive features, or he can depreciate the consequences of having the undesirable features in terms of the buyer's perceived need. For the reasons given in discussing the approach-avoidance situation, the depreciation strategy is the one most likely to be effective.

Choice Criteria Explicit

When a buyer's criteria are explicit and well formulated, it is hypothesized that the salesman's best strategy is to *match* each attribute of his product to each item of the buyer's specifications. The salesman guides the prospect into agreeing that each attribute of his product matches the attributes of the buyer's choice criteria. If the prospect does not agree to the salesman's proposition at the end of the sales talk, he appears to be denying what he had previously admitted. This approach should be distinguished from "barrier selling," which is common in door-to-door sales. In barrier selling, the salesman also guides the prospect into approving statements made by him. These statements, however, do not confirm a match between the prospect specification (choice criteria) and product attributes but between some generally accepted principle and the suggestion that application of the principle implies buying the salesman's product.

Table 10.2 summarizes the four choice criteria situations and the corresponding persuasive strategy, attitude theory emphasis, and likely product characteristics. Table 10.3 shows the aim of each strategy with respect to changing preferences on objectives (effects), attributes, or attribute weighting.

These tables constitute merely a set of hypotheses that have been deduced from an analysis of buyer decision making, assuming that the concept of choice criteria plays a role in that process. They have a certain face validity in being consistent with the various theories of attitude change. This is usually important, since the probability of a hypothesis being true is enhanced if it coheres with existing knowledge. Propositions that are related to a wider theory receive support not only from the corroborating evidence for the proposition but also from the evidence supporting the other propositions in the theory. However, the theories themselves are not so well supported by evidence that they can be accepted as dogma; such overarching theories seldom are. They do not really arise from attempts to synthesize and systematize existing corroborated hypotheses; rather, they are developed to suggest hypotheses that can lead later to a modified and truer theory. In any case, the theories only lend support to the approaches in general; they do not help

TABLE 10.2
FOUR CHOICE CRITERIA AND STRATEGIES

	CHOICE CRITERIA INACTIVE OR NON-EXISTENT	CHOICE CRITERIA VAGUE AND INADE-QUATE	CHOICE CRITERIA IN CONFLICT	CHOICE CRITERIA EXPLICIT
Strategy	Educate	Solve (Recommend[a])	Depreciate (Enhance gain[a])	Match
Attitude Theory Emphasis	Learning	Perceptual and functional		Consistency
Product Purchasing Characteristics	Low-price convenience product	Technical product and infrequent purchase		Important purchase with specific application

[a] Less effective strategy.

in the selection of actual strategy. There is thus a strong need to collect empirical data to corroborate the hypotheses regarding the most effective persuasive strategy given the choice criteria situation.

**MODEL OF
INTERPERSONAL INFLUENCE PROCESS**

The difficulty in testing the set of hypotheses in Tables 10.2 and 10.3 stems from the recognition that persuasive strategy is only one of the factors contributing to making a sale.

TABLE 10.3
STRATEGIES AND CHANGING PREFERENCES

	PREFERENCES[a]			
STRATEGY	OBJECTIVES (EFFECTS)	ATTRIBUTES	WEIGHTING OF ATTRIBUTES	RATING OF PRODUCT BY PROSPECT
Educate	C	C	C	C
Solve	U	C	C	C
Depreciate	U	U	C	C
Match	U	U	U	C

[a] C = potentially changed; U = unaffected.

Appendix A includes a model of the interpersonal influence process. It is mainly derived from Kelman's (1961) model on the process of opinion change and Etzioni's (1961) model of power and its correlative compliance. Merely adding together these two models would yield nothing new; they have been fused so that their hypotheses are mutually self-supporting to provide a synthesis that it is hoped will be fruitful for further hypotheses.

Kelman distinguishes three processes of social influence:

Compliance. Subject accepts an opinion to avoid punishment or achieve reward. In such circumstances, there may be public acquiescence without private commitment.

Identification. Subject accepts influence in order to be identified with the source of the influence. The subject believes in the opinions he adopts but the maintenance of the belief depends on the source's continued advocacy of it.

Internalization. Subject accepts the opinion because it is congruent with his existing values. Here the subject's belief is independent of the change agent, and the subject may maintain the belief even if it is abandoned by the influencing party.

Kelman argues that the perceived characteristics of the change agent corresponding to compliance, identification, and internalization are:

1. Means control (compliance)
2. Attractiveness (identification)
3. Credibility (internalization)

Kelman (1961, pp. 67–68) further argues that:

(a) To the extent that the individual is concerned—for whatever reason—with the *social effect* of his behavior, influence will tend to take the form of compliance. (b) To the extent that he is concerned with the *social anchorage* of his behavior, influence will tend to take the form of identification. (c) To the extent that he is concerned with the *value congruence* of his behavior (rational or otherwise), influence will tend to take the form of internalization.

This part of Kelman's model has been incorporated with modifications into the model in Appendix A. The first change was made

because Kelman's basic classification (into compliance, identification, and internalization) is defective in that compliance emphasizes
behavior, while identification and internalization suggest mental
constructs. Identification and internalization could in fact be simply
two of the possible consequences out of a set of consequences aris-
ing from compliance.

In Appendix A, under the heading of "anchorage of opinion,"
the terms "intimidation" and "expectations" are substituted for
compliance. In Kelman's model, the perceived characteristics of the
influence source that corresponds to compliance is "means control."
Substituted for this term are "force" and "strategy," including use
of patronage, to correspond to intimidation and expectations. The
relationship between force and the mental state of intimidation is
clear, but that between strategy (including use of patronage) and
expectations requires defining. Where the influence source is perceived as able to supply material rewards, it has influence based on
its ability to conjure up such perceptions, and a person becomes influenced by such a source because he expects to receive a material'
benefit. Finally, concern with social effects, social anchorage, and
value congruence are regarded in Appendix A as goals sought by the
subject, though once again with modifications.

1. In the context of compliance being the anchorage of opinion
(or, as in the model, intimidation and expectations being the basis),
concern with social effects must surely be concern to avoid punishment and reap reward. Hence social effects, in the model, are split
into "security" (avoiding punishment) and "gain" (seeking reward).

2. Social acceptance has been substituted for social anchorage
to emphasize the incentive aspect that makes people seek social
anchorage. This assumes that we anchor our behavior to that of
some reference group in order to be accepted by that group.

Etzioni (1961) argues that power differs according to the
means used to achieve compliance. These means could be physical,
material, or symbolic, or a mixture of the three. Corresponding to
these means are coercive power, remunerative power, and normative
power. Where coercive power is used, the involvement of the subject to the change agent tends to be alienative. When remunerative
power is used, the involvement tends to be calculative, and corresponding to symbolic power, the involvement tends to be moral.

In Appendix A, the classification of means is retained, but
symbolic means are subclassified into those stemming from the characteristics of the communication source and those stemming from
the subject's own set of values. Etzioni's corresponding classification
of involvement is used, but it is felt that in substituting the term

"orientation" for "involvement," the right emphasis is given and it becomes possible to split moral involvement into "responsive orientation" and "respectful orientation" to correspond to the suggested split of symbolic means. Thus it is legitimate to assume that a person who seeks to win social acceptance will be responsive to those in a position to give it.

We can now interpret Appendix A in terms of the salesman/buyer dyad. There are four suggested distinct flows of influence; in practice, however, there are likely to be combinations of flows. The first flow is irrelevant and is merely mentioned for completeness.

MATERIAL MEANS APPROACH

The second flow suggests that a salesman using purely material means to influence a buyer is given a potential source of influence if he adopts the appropriate persuasive strategy and/or is allowed some discretion over what the buyer receives for his dollar or possesses information (e.g., on availability of product or performance details) required by the buyer for his evaluation of the product. We have given the two labels "strategy" and "patronage" to this source of influence. Patronage can be used to reinforce the persuasive strategy adopted by the salesman. Tables 10.2 and 10.3 can be regarded as a classification of persuasive strategies according to the extent of the buyer's awareness of the tangible product characteristics he seeks.

Patronage, for example, is possessed by the salesman who can exert discretionary authority over trade-in price. On the other hand, a shop assistant acting merely like a vending machine, offering a standard product for a fixed price, has no delegated influence; actual influence (if any) must stem from his sales strategy and personal qualities of attractiveness and credibility. Patronage must be used with subtlety, embodying as it does uncertainty for the buyer. There is always the possibility that a prospect will agree with the salesman in the hope of getting favorable terms, but he may also be less likely to deal with the salesman again. Thus, much depends on how patronage is exercised and perceived.

It is argued that a buyer, if questioned after being influenced merely by appeal to his self-interest, will tend to *justify* his acceptance of the salesman's opinions. (Outside the salesman/buyer dyad, e.g., in cases of bribery, the subject may tend merely to acquiesce to the change agent's opinions.) The anchorage of the buyer's opinion change is likely to be based on his expectations of what the product will do. In other words, if these expectations are not fulfilled, the opinion ceases to have an anchor. The incentive thus to maintain the opinion is the expectation of personal gain. The prospect's orientation to the salesman is calculative—What's in it for me?

The model forms an interacting system rather than one of simple cause and effect. A salesman may want to use symbolic means to influence the prospect, but if the prospect has a predisposition to be purely calculative, either the prospect must change his orientation or the salesman must change his appeal.

SYMBOLIC MEANS

A salesman may use symbolic means, in which case his attractiveness and/or credibility to the buyer are his sources of influence. The appeal is to the buyer's self-concept and/or his values and frame of reference. The self-concept (self-image or ego-identity) refers to a person's perceptions of himself. One reason for social interaction is to develop a distinct, consistent, and satisfactory self-concept. In social interaction, when a person perceives that his audience does not accept and support the self-image he wishes to present, he is likely to feel embarrassment and a loss of face. Of course the self-image presented may not be the real self-image but nearer to the person's ego-ideal (i.e., the kind of person he would like to be). The model assumes that the main factor making for a salesman's "attractiveness" lies in his being perceived by the buyer as helping him to develop a distinct, consistent, and satisfactory self-concept. In general this would involve two requirements.

1. *That the salesman enhance the buyer's self-esteem by indicating his approval of the buyer.* There is evidence that the greater the need for approval, the more the conformity (Crowne and Marlowe, 1965); hence the more likely it is that such people will be influenced by appeals to reference groups. R. W. Brown (1965) has argued that the authoritarian personality is distinguished less by the content of his beliefs than by his susceptibility to influence from authority figures. This is in contrast to Adorno (1950) and others who argue that the content of belief characterizes the authoritarian personality. Thus according to Brown the authoritarian personality's anchorage of opinion is identification with those individuals or groups who form positive reference groups for him. Liam Hudson (1966, 1968) quotes evidence to support his claim that the scientific converger is more likely to adopt attitudes that are authoritarian than the artistic imaginative diverger. Accepting these assumptions, the scientific converger—contrary perhaps to intuitive belief—is more likely to be influenced by an attractive source and reference group appeals.

2. *That the salesman possess characteristics that allow the buyer to identify with him.* Thus Evans (1963) found that the more alike the salesman and buyer are, the more likely it is that a sale will occur.

A value judgment is a conclusion that expresses approval or disapproval or the assessment of the worth of some event or idea in terms of its contribution to human needs. All moral, ethical, and esthetic judgments are value judgments. Behind a value judgment lies the personal system of values that act as premises from which value judgments stem. Attitudes can be regarded as reflecting values held.

A person's value system owes much to his current frame of reference, which is the sum total of his experience and knowledge on which he bases his interpretations of new experience. A person's frame of reference limits his perception and the ability to acquire new knowledge. As defined here, appeals to values should be distinguished from appeals to self-interest. An appeal to a person's values and current frame of reference is an appeal to his current beliefs, attitudes, and prejudices. The perceived credibility of an argument will depend on whether it coheres with the values and frame of reference of the buyer; a logical argument that runs contrary to the buyer's value system, or is couched in terms outside the buyer's frame of reference, is not likely to make much impact. (This might explain the conflicting evidence on the relationship between intelligence and persuadability.)

Appeals to self-interest are specific and not generalized appeals. They relate to observable product attributes, features, effects, and functions. They attempt to demonstrate material benefits and have premises that are grounded in statements about the performance of the various product attributes. It would seem that value appeals are more likely to come unstuck because the salesman may be obliged to "guess" the prospect's values, whereas appeals to self-interest, grounded as they are in demonstrating specific material benefits, are less likely to backfire. The main reason for distinguishing the two, however, is to isolate material appeals on choice criteria to test the set of hypotheses in Tables 10.2 and 10.3.

Whether appeals to self-concept and appeals to values are distinguishable is a matter of empirical investigation. Certainly the two are interrelated, for value systems help to shape a person's self-concept. For example, a person who values truth is likely to visualize himself as a seeker of truth. The distinction, though, between appeals to self-concept and appeals to values is in line with

Riesman's (1961) distinction between other-directed people, who look to others and depend on others for guidance and leadership, and inner-directed people, whose behavior is guided by internalized values. Other-directed people should be more susceptible to social influence and more responsive to an "attractive" change agent.

The buyer's overt expressive behavior after buying will tend to indicate loyalty to the source with which the buyer wishes to be identified (a positive reference group, to which the salesman may or may not belong) or fidelity to the opinions expressed by the salesman. The salesman's attractiveness, based on liking or ideological similarity between himself and the salesman, can help the buyer identify with the source of the message. On the other hand, the salesman's credibility leads to an internalization of the opinions of the salesman.

When identification occurs, the buyer seeks social acceptance of the salesman or the anticipatory approval of the reference groups quoted by the salesman. The incentive behind internalizing the opinion is the buyer's desire to incorporate into his set of values the opinions that are *congruent* with those already there. The orientation toward the salesman is *responsive* under conditions of identification, since the buyer is predisposed to comply with the salesman's opinions. When opinions are internalized, the orientation toward the salesman is *respectful* of the salesman's competence or veracity. Again, a buyer may seek a salesman who uses symbolic means and may remain unmoved by one who relies on purely material means.

Although a sharp distinction has been drawn between strategy (including use of patronage), attractiveness, and credibility, these qualities are likely to reinforce one another. Perhaps in most cases some attractiveness is a necessary condition. Thus we might refer to Kurt Lewin's (1952) three-step model for implementing attitudinal change:

1. Unfreezing the system
2. Moving to a new pattern
3. Refreezing into this new pattern

Without some attractiveness, the salesman would have difficulty with the first stage of "unfreezing the system" when he attempts to establish rapport. However, the strategy, attractiveness, and credibility of the salesman have their greatest impact at stage two, and successful consumer experience is the main aid in establishing the third stage.

OTHER FACTORS IN THE
INTERPERSONAL INFLUENCE PROCESS

A number of other factors might determine the degree of influence attained by the salesman over the buyer. These factors are briefly stated below:

1. The salesman's speed of delivery and, within limits, the percentage of the interview time that he is talking. Thus Carment, Miles, and Cervin (1965) hypothesize that one person will dominate another if he speaks first and talks more. Chapple and Donald (1947) found that the most successful salesmen simply spoke a great deal in the standard interview. It may be true then that within limits a salesman should talk more, faster, and with shorter pauses before replying than the buyer.

2. If a buyer has done business with the salesman on previous occasions, the salesman is likely to have more influence on the buyer. There is evidence that frequent interaction is likely to increase interpersonal sentiment in the direction of increased liking (Homans, 1950; Warr, 1965).

3. When relevant (i.e., when issues are complex), the clarity of the salesman's message makes for easier comprehension, and this can add to the salesman's influence. Making conclusions explicit and repeating an argument where necessary can also aid comprehension.

4. When a prospect brings up a competitor's arguments, the salesman is likely to achieve more influence if he combats such arguments. However, in so doing he follows a "depreciate" strategy.

5. The salesman will be more influential if he gets the prospective buyer involved, but the buyer should not dominate the discussion.

PROPOSED FIELD STUDY
IN PREPARATION FOR FIELD EXPERIMENT

A field study is initially proposed to establish the relationships suggested by the hypotheses and to explore the possibilities of making the various concepts operational. Later it is hoped to carry out a field experiment in which conditions are manipulated to determine the contribution made by the various factors to the influence of the salesman on the buyer.

The field study will involve recording sales interviews (pref-

erably on videotape). This initial study will be concerned with car
salesmen and prospective buyers of cars. The recording sheets for
buyer and salesman appear in Appendix B. On these sheets will be
recorded the kind of verbal communication that occurs between
the buyer and the seller. Recording in the form of a time ladder
will allow the sequence of interaction to be recorded, as well as
the percentage of the sales interview devoted to the different types
of communication and to the different participants. The definitions
of the communication categories (given in Appendix C) are discussed below. The classification of categories has been refined
through preliminary testing by Morris Holbrook and other students.
However, the categories will no doubt require further refinement.

So far we have simply discussed the factors that appear, on
theoretical grounds, to be relevant to selling effectiveness; namely
selling effectiveness depends on:

1. Use of appropriate strategy by salesman.
2. Patronage of salesman as perceived by buyer.
3. Extent to which salesman is attractive to the prospective
   buyer and uses appeals that bolster the prospect's
   self-concept and self-esteem.
4. Extent to which the buyer perceives the salesman as
   having credibility, and the extent to which the salesman
   appeals to the buyer's values and frame of reference.
5. Extent to which the salesman contributes to discussion
   ($>$ 50 percent, and $<$ 75 percent) and speaks faster
   than the buyer.
6. Extent to which the buyer is involved in discussion ($>$
   20 percent, $<$ 40 percent).
7. Clarity of salesman.

If we are to assess the validity of the factors, we need to reduce
to a minimum the amount of inference required of observers by
stating operational definitions both of the factors themselves and of
selling effectiveness.

MEASURES OF SELLING EFFECTIVENESS

A. Commitment to buy plus rating on each of the dimensions
listed in question 4 of the buyer questionnaire (Appendix D). It
will be assumed that the higher the rating, the higher the influence.

B. No commitment to buy, but the prospect indicates (question 5 of buyer questionnaire) influence of salesman, the degree of
influence being indicated on a serial five-category scale.

C. Other evidence of salesman's effectiveness (e.g., selling record or rating by superiors).

MEASURES OF INFLUENCING FACTORS

A. Use of Appropriate Strategy

SALESMAN STRATEGY	CHOICE CRITERIA SITUATION	RECORD OF EVIDENCE OR JUDGMENT
1. Educate and diagnose	1. Choice criteria absent or vague	1.
Educate—salesman discusses characteristic effects of products and/or attributes *Diagnose*—salesman seeks effects sought by prospect (problem-solving approach).	Prospect unable to offer, without salesman's help, information on product attributes sought. Alternatively, those mentioned are too few or too vague to form an adequate basis for defining buyer's exact requirements.	Communication time ladder, categories SIB SIIB (1) } See BIB } Appendix C BIIB (1) } dix C Buyer questionnaire question 7, answers 1 and 2.
2. Depreciate	2. Choice criteria in conflict	2.
On discovering that the buyer seeks attributes that are in conflict, the salesman depreciates the attribute he can less conveniently provide.	Buyer states his requirements, and these encompass attributes that are in conflict.	Communication time ladder categories SIB SIIB (2) } See BIB } Appendix C BIIB (2) } dix C Buyer questionnaire question 7, answer 3.
3. Match	3. Choice criteria explicit	3.
Salesman matches each of his product attributes to each item in the prospect's specification, persuading the buyer to agree with each match.	Prospect provides clear specification of attributes sought. There is no conflict (as far as salesman concerned) between these attributes.	Communication time ladder categories SIB SIIB (3) } See BIB } Appendix C BIIB (3) } dix C Buyer questionnaire question 7, answer 4.

B. Patronage of salesman as perceived by buyer. See communication time ladder categories SIIA and BIA in Appendix C.

C. Extent to which salesman is attractive to the prospective buyer and uses appeals that bolster the prospect's self-concept and self-esteem.

DESCRIPTION	RECORD OF EVIDENCE OR JUDGMENT
1. Extent of similarity in socioeconomic status.	1. Buyer questionnaire question 8.

2. Extent of liking as indicated by:
   a. Sentiments expressed, specifically the ratio of time spent in SIIB, SIIC, SIID, and also in BIIB, BIIC, and BIID. (Note: SIIC includes persuasive device of praise, e.g., "I hadn't thought of that."
   b. Length of acquaintance between buyer and seller.
	2. In communication ladder ratio of time or occasion spent between SIIB, SIIC, and SIID and also between BIIB, BIIC, and BIID. Buyer questionnaire question 2.

3. Salesman or buyer seeks or appeals to preferences of likely reference groups.	3. In communication time ladder, categories SIC(1), SIIC(1), BIC(1), and BIIC(1).
4. Establishes rapport (using warm friendly manner) by seeking common ground and/or discussing interests of a social anchorage nature.	4. Communication time ladder categories SIC(2), SIIC(2), BIC(2), and BIIC(2).

D. Perceived credibility of salesman and extent to which salesman appeals to buyer's values and frame of reference.

DESCRIPTION	RECORD OF EVIDENCE OR JUDGMENT
1. Perceived degree of competence (technical expertise) of salesman.	1. Buyer questionnaire question 4.
2. Perceived trustworthiness of salesman.	2. Buyer questionnaire question 4.
3. Salesman or buyer seeks or appeals to values and attitudes.	3. Communication time ladder categories SID(1), SIID(1), BID(1), and BIID(1).
4. Establishes rapport by discussing interests related to values.	4. Communication time ladder categories SID(2), SIID(2), BID(2), and BIID(2).

E. Extent to which salesman contributes to the discussion ($>$ 50 percent and $<$ 75 percent) and speaks faster than the buyer. Calculations made from analysis of recordings to discover percentage of time salesman communicating.

F. Extent to which the buyer is involved in discussion ($>$ 20 percent, $<$ 40 percent). Calculations made from analysis of tape recordings.

G. Clarity of salesman as measured by Flesch test and according to whether conclusions made clear as noted by observer. The study will also test the interrelationships between parts of the model, specifically the suspected high correlations between the main appeals used and the corresponding orientations toward the salesman.

MAIN APPEAL	ORIENTATION TO SALESMAN
1. Appeal to self-interest Indicated by percentage of sales interview devoted to persuasive strategies under various choice criteria situations. Communication time ladder categories SIB, SIIB, SIA, SIIA, and SIIIA.	1. Calculative Prospect negotiates and bargains during sales interview. Communication time ladder categories BIA, BIIA, and BIIIA. Buyer questionnaire question 3, answers 4 and 5.
2. Self-concept and self-esteem Salesman scores high in attractiveness and social anchorage appeals (see factor C above).	2. Responsive Prospect constantly voices agreement with salesman, offers opinions and information on self. Ratio of BIIIC to BIIIB in communication time ladder. Buyer questionnaire question 3, answer 3.
3. Salesman high in credibility and appeals to values (see factor D above).	3. Prospect voices agreement. No disagreement or disapproval. Seeks opinions and information. Buyer questionnaire question 3, answers 1 and 2.

APPENDIX A

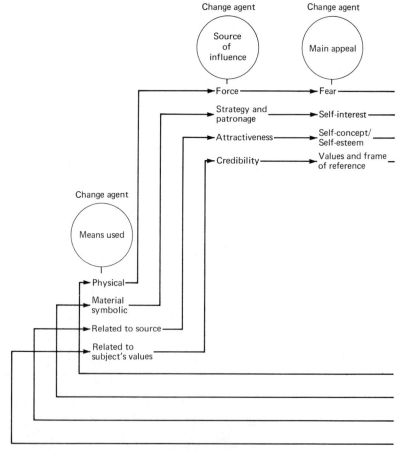

Change agent

Source
of
influence

Change agent

Main appeal

→ Force ——————————— ► Fear ——————

→ Strategy and ——————— ► Self-interest ——————
   patronage

→ Attractiveness ——————— Self-concept/ ——————
                          Self-esteem

► Credibility ——————— Values and frame —
                       of reference

Change agent

Means used

► Physical

Material
symbolic

► Related to source —

Related to
subject's values

Appendix A Model of the Interpersonal Influence Process

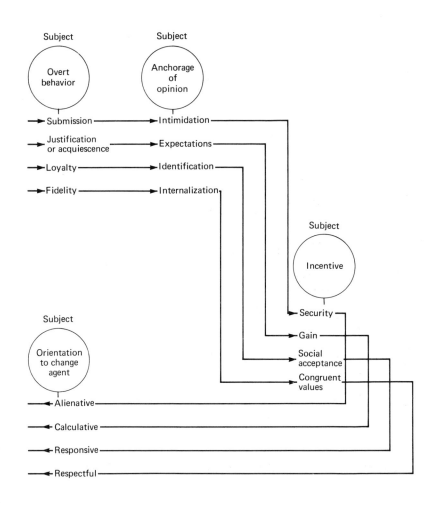

APPENDIX B

NOTE: Mark in different colors for each participant if more than one buyer involved.

No. _____

Communication Time Ladder
Buyer Analysis Sheet

Salesman _____ Distributor _____ Town _____

Start _____ Finish _____ Total _____ Buyer _____

TIME	BUYER PROSPECT COMMUNICATION					
	BO	BI	BII	BIII	BIV	BUC
1						
2						
3						
4						
5						
6						
7						
8						
9						
10						
11						
12						
13						
14						
15						
16						
17						
18						
19						
20						
21						
22						
23						
24						
25						

APPENDIX B (*Continued*)

NOTE: Mark in different colors for each participant if more than one
buyer participates.

No. _____

Communication Time Ladder
Salesman Analysis Sheet

Salesman _____ Distributor _____ Town _____

Start _____ Finish _____ Total _____ Buyer _____

TIME	SALESMAN COMMUNICATION					
	SO	SI	SII	SIII	SIV	SUC
1						
2						
3						
4						
5						
6						
7						
8						
9						
10						
11						
12						
13						
14						
15						
16						
17						
18						
19						
20						
21						
22						
23						
24						
25						

1. Comprehension level

———————

2. Patronage
   Yes ☐   No ☐

CONCLUSIONS
1. Always explicit
2. Mostly explicit
3. Seldom explicit

RESULTS
1. Product bought
2. Product not bought

APPENDIX C

COMMUNICATION TIME LADDER
Salesman Analysis Sheet

(SO) *Introductory greeting:* a comment—most often made on meeting or parting—that conveys no information or affect classifiable under I, II, III, IV (which take precedence), but that serves the function of creating or maintaining interaction. *Examples:* Hello; May I help you?; My name is . . . ; Welcome to Jones Olds; Call again soon; Here's my card; I'll call you in the morning.

(SI) *Seeks information:* a comment—most often a question or a probe—intended to prompt an answer of type II from the other dyad member. *Examples:* What model are you driving now? How much horsepower does it have? Where do you work? Did you watch the moon landing last night?.

    (SIA) Buyer's bargaining limits.

    (SIB) Buyer's choice criteria.

    (SIC) (1) Buyer's social anchorage, (2) Establishes rapport, seeking common social anchorage.

    (SID) (1) Buyer's values, (2) Establishes rapport, seeking common values.

(SII) *Offers information via persuasive strategy or device:* a comment that informs the other dyad member about A, B, C, D; this category includes comments conveying sentiment as long as those comments carry some new information or confirm previously unconfirmed facts or values. *Examples:* I can't spend more than $2000; I like that shade of blue; I'm a doctor; I voted for Nixon; I want an economical car; Yes, or I agree (in response to a question of fact or value *other* than a response to a question intended merely to elicit agreement or commitment).

(SIIA) Own bargaining limits or patronage.

(SIIB) Choice criteria: (1) Educate or diagnose, (2) Depreciate, (3) Match.

(SIIC) (1) Social anchorage, (2) Social anchorage not related to purchase.

(SIID) (1) Values, (2) Values related to purchase.

Bargaining limits, patronage, threat: a comment related to *any aspect* of some reward (negative or positive) that the speaker can presumably influence, such as *any* reference to trade-in (the car itself, its value, etc.), price, delivery date, special features. *Examples:* I could give you $350 for your old model; What car are you driving now? That lists for $3500; I think we could get it by Christmas; Our mechanic, Jim, will take it around the block and see what he thinks it's worth.

Choice criterion: a comment referring to some tangible product attribute—that is, any aspect of the car that is not subject to patronage and that can be *measured* and *quantified* by a mechanical device, although not necessarily by the buyer himself. *Examples:* color, miles per gallon.

(1) *Social anchorage:* a comment related to role or role performance—that is, to expectations of behavior based on position or status; the reference could be to a dyad member's role and associated expectations (e.g., occupation, education, income) or to some members of a role set who have reciprocal role expectations such as a positive or negative reference group (e.g., family, friends, club, prestigious figures). *Examples:* I'm a lawyer; Are you married? Your kids would love this; Rockefeller drives one of these; (2) *Social anchorage not related to purchase:* a comment regarding subject that (by assumption or revelation) interests the other dyad member but has no established relevance to the purchase. *Examples:* Wow, they had a great football team last year; Did you see Bernstein's farewell concert?

(1) *Values related to intangible product attributes:* a comment referring to some intangible product attribute—that is, any aspect of the car that *cannot* be measured or quantified by

a mechanical device but may still be a purchasing goal. *Examples:* economy, practicality, patriotism, prestige, sportiness, masculinity; I need an economical car; I think 4-doors are very practical; See the U.S.A. in your Chevrolet. (2) *Values related to the purchase:* a comment similar to C2 *except* that a connection is established between the interest and the purchase situation. *Examples:* My boss has a kid who played the flute in Bernstein's farewell concert; Our agency sponsors the Little League; You'll need a good rugged car like this for those trips to Shea Stadium.

(SIII) *Offers expression of sentiment, commitment, or decision:*
   (SIIIA) Rejects bargaining limits or offer; threatens.
   (SIIIB) (1) Disapproval, (2) Disagreement, (3) Negative decision.
   (SIIIC) (1) Approval, (2) Agreement, (3) Positive decision.
   (SIIID) (1) Mixed approval, (2) Equivocation, (3) Postponement of decision.

   (A) *Rejects bargaining limits or offer; threatens:* any bargaining maneuver of a negative variety—that is, one that rejects an offer of type IIA without stating any new information. By convention, we include threats (negative offers) in this category. *Examples:* That's the lowest trade-in I've ever heard of; If you don't give us a better offer than that, I'll take my business down the road; OK, but this car will be gone by tomorrow. (B,C,D) (1) *Disapproval, Approval, Mixed approval:* initiations that are purely affective—such as spontaneous praise—which carry no new information but are intended as expressions of sentiment. *Examples:* Why did you show me this red convertible when I said I wanted a blue sedan? Thank you so much for being so kind; you seem like a nice man, but. . . . (2) *Disagreement, agreement, equivocation:* a response to IV; most often these will be made by B. *Examples:* Yes, it is nice; Well, it seems very desirable, but. . . ; (silence); Yes. (3) *Negative decision, positive decision, postponement of decision:* a statement of intention to purchase, not to purchase, or to postpone such a statement; this category does not apply to bargaining (see A), but to whether a buyer (seller) wants to buy (sell) a particular car, independent of terms. *Examples:* I'm afraid that car just doesn't suit me; I think I'd like to take the one you showed me first; I'll have to think about it.

(SIV) *Seeks expression of sentiment, commitment, or decision:* a comment—most often made by salesman as a persuasive device—intended merely to elicit agreement or commitment.

Examples: Isn't that a dandy? Isn't that a beautiful shade of green? Wouldn't you like to drive right out of here today in that one?

(SUV) *Unclassifiable comments:* this is a residual category. By convention it includes any verbal interaction referring to physical movements, such as the logistics problems involved in showing a buyer a car. *Examples:* Come right this way; If you'll just come into my office.

Buyer Analysis Sheet

Same categories as above, but initial coding letter B instead of S.

APPENDIX D

Classification of Choice Criteria Situation
Absent or Vague .... ☐
Choice Criteria in Conflict .... ☐
Choice Criteria Explicit .... ☐
(FILLED IN AFTER SALES INTERVIEW)

We are engaged in research on car buying on behalf of a research unit at Columbia University. One aim of this work is to help the buyer feel satisfied that he has been given every assistance in making a wise purchase. We hope you will assist us in this research by answering a few questions. Naturally your replies will be treated in the strictest confidence. We are only interested in the broad picture that emerges.

1. Do you already own a car?   ☐ Yes   ☐ No
   If Yes,
   A. How long have you had it? ....
   B. Did you purchase it from this dealer?   ☐ Yes   ☐ No
2. Had you previously known the salesman who just dealt with you?   ☐ Yes.   ☐ No
   If Yes, in what capacity?
   ☐ Bought from him previously
   ☐ Met socially
   ☐ Other
3. Buying a car represents a major purchase to most people.

In seeking out a dealer who sells a car in which you are interested, in which order would you arrange this list? (Hand card to respondent)

4. (Hand the second card to respondent). Could you rate the salesman who has just dealt with you anywhere along these scales on each of the characteristics of technical expertise, trustworthiness and understanding of my needs, and likeability?

5. After talking to the salesman, do you consider yourself more likely or less likely to purchase this car? Could you please indicate on this card? (Hand card to respondent).

6. Do you believe the salesman has any influence over the terms of the sale? For example, over the trade-in price of a car or the price of the car itself?   ☐ Yes   ☐ No

7. (This question to be asked only if a commitment to buy has been made) Can you tell me in what way the salesman most helped you to reach a decision to buy? Could you check the most appropriate box on this card? (Hand third card to respondent).

Card attached to Question 3

Arrange the following in order of importance to you.

1. ☐ Whether I thought salesmen could be trusted
2. ☐ Whether salesman seemed to me to be technically competent
3. ☐ Whether salesman seemed to understand my needs and was easy to talk to and helpful
4. ☐ Trade-in price for my current car
5. ☐ Location of dealer to ensure convenient aftersales service

Card attached to Question 4

Please record your rating of the salesman who just dealt with you anywhere along the three following scales.

Technical expertise

High ⌐─────────────────────────────────┐ Low
   100% 90% 80% 70% 60% 50% 40% 30% 20% 10% 0

Trustworthiness

High ⌐─────────────────────────────────┐ Low
   100% 90% 80% 70% 60% 50% 40% 30% 20% 10% 0

Understanding of my needs, and likeability

High ⌐─────────────────────────────────┐ Low
   100% 90% 80% 70% 60% 50% 40% 30% 20% 10% 0

Card attached to Question 5

1. ☐ Much more likely than before
2. ☐ Somewhat more likely than before
3. ☐ About as likely as before

4. ☐ Somewhat less likely than before
5. ☐ Much less likely than before

Card attached to Question 7

1. ☐ Salesman helped most in pointing out the features that are important if a car is to be satisfactory and/or relative importance of various features.

2. ☐ Salesman helped most in clarifying my own thoughts about what I wanted from a car.

3. ☐ Salesman helped most in showing that on the whole this car was the best I could get for the money—what I have lost in the way of additional features or lower price I have gained overall.

4. ☐ Salesman simply demonstrated that this car met the specification I had laid down for the car I wanted.

11

ATTITUDE CHANGE AND THE RELATIVE INFLUENCE OF MEDIA AND WORD-OF-MOUTH SOURCES .

GEORGE S. DAY
Associate Professor of Marketing
Stanford University

Empirical evidence and common sense generally support the conclusion that media communications are most effective in creating awareness and providing information about a candidate, product, or issue, whereas word-of-mouth communications are more influential in forming or reinforcing attitudes once they reach a person [The relevant studies are summarized in Engel, Kollat, and Blackwell (1968, table 19.3)]. This is particularly true with media advertising of products, which is designed to reach a large number of people who will frequently ignore or misperceive the specific appeal but will at least have achieved brand awareness as a result of their exposure. By contrast, fewer people are likely to be exposed to word of mouth. Typical is the finding by Haines (1966) that 58 percent of the buyers of new supermarket items reported a recent exposure to television advertising, 26 percent mentioned sampling, and only 18 percent reported word-of-mouth exposure. This represents a change in relative emphasis from the pretelevision-era study by E. Katz and Lazarsfeld (1955), which found 38 percent of a sample

Comments and suggestions by Russell Haley of D'Arcy Advertising are gratefully acknowledged.

who bought a new or different product were exposed to word of mouth, whereas approximately 60 percent[1] were exposed to radio, newspaper, or magazine advertising. More important than the relative reach, however, is the much greater impact on those who are exposed of word of mouth over media communications, because (1) there is an opportunity for feedback and clarification; (2) word of mouth is regarded as providing more reliable, trustworthy advice; and (3) personal contacts are generally able to offer social support and encouragement (Arndt, 1967c).

This body of research poses several challenges to those interested in evaluating the effect of advertising. For a start, word of mouth is seldom taken into account in evaluation schemes based on the hierarchy-of-effects notion (even though the stimulation of information seeking is sometimes an explicit advertising goal). The consequence of not isolating the role of word of mouth is that the observed changes in awareness and attitude are likely to be attributed to advertising or promotion by default. However, the extent to which the importance of these marketer-controlled variables is inflated is uncertain, since the applicable research is usually based on high-priced, high-risk durable goods. In fact, it is most often found in the diffusion of innovation tradition (Rogers and Beal, 1958). But what about the minor product improvements or well-established products in frequently purchased food and drug categories? It could be argued that the minimal risks associated with this type of product do not justify the high acquisition costs of word-of-mouth information. On these grounds, word of mouth should have little aggregate influence on low-risk purchases because very little is generated. This would seem to justify the lack of explicit consideration of this form of communication by advertising decision makers. However, there are competing hypotheses that should not be dismissed. For example, how do buyers who are not exposed to media advertising, or pay no attention to it because they don't believe it, learn about the brand and form attitudes toward it? One possibility—scanning the store shelf and display area (Fisk, 1959)—may provide sufficient information about products that are reasonably familiar from past experience; but apparently it is not adequate for justification of a trial purchase of an unfamiliar product (Haines, 1966). This does not necessarily mean that the need for

---

[1] This figure is arrived at by assuming that half the people who reported being exposed to newspaper and magazine advertising were also exposed to radio advertising.

information, or the perceived risk of trial, is great enough to trigger further search from personal sources. The most likely event, according to the much debated "two-step flow" of communications is that someone occupying the role of opinion leader may offer unsolicited information (E. Katz and Lazarsfeld, 1955; see also Cerha, 1967, for criticisms of the two-step flow). A supported argument is that friends and relatives may be even more willing to offer unsolicited advice on low-risk products than on high-risk products, because any adverse consequences would not be likely to jeopardize the personal relationship (Sheth, 1969c).

Thus products perceived as low in risk may generate word-of-mouth advertising. It is more likely that there will be significant individual differences in the perception of risk, hence in consumer needs for information. For example, Cunningham (1966) separated risk into two components: (1) the *uncertainty* that an unfamiliar brand would work as well as the present brand, and (2) the seriousness of the *consequences* in the event of unsatisfactory performance. On these grounds, he found that as much as 24 percent of a sample rated products such as analgesics as high in risk, but there was strong consensus that quasi-commodities such as dried spaghetti were low in risk. He also discovered that up to 60 percent of those who perceived a regularly purchased product as high in risk had also discussed the product category within the past six months. However, his study emphasized word-of-mouth activity in the overall product category. Thus our first objective is to move from the usual focus on the product alone and examine the extent of word-of-mouth versus media exposure to specific new and established brands (of a regularly purchased convenience food product). The relative influence of these two sources is then evaluated by measuring differences in rates of attitude change and formation (obtained from a three-wave reinterview panel) between exposure conditions.

DESCRIPTION OF THE DATA

The research design[2] was based on two matched mail diary panels that were used to monitor the introduction of a new branded convenience food product into a statewide test market area. Both panels started with 1,100 households. One panel was used as a control, and members of the second panel were sent a mail questionnaire at the

[2] The data were collected as part of the Columbia University Research Project on Buyer Behavior.

beginning of the study and were interviewed three times by telephone. The mail questionnaire was completed by 955 households,
and telephone reinterviews were limited to this group. The three
interviews were spaced 5, 10, and 21 weeks from the date of introduction. In each interview, the same data on awareness, preference,
intentions and usage, recall of advertising and word-of-mouth exposure, and sample receipt were asked for all brands that the respondent could *recall*, in three related product classes. Despite the
heavier work load imposed on the analysis panel, the attrition rate
was the same for both panels.

Choice of Variables to Monitor

Two different brand-attitude measures were used during each of
the three interviews. One was a seven-point semantic differential
evaluative scale with opposite poles reading "In general I like it . . .
In general I don't like it." The other was a five-point intentions
scale. Both these scales were collapsed somewhat into the categories
shown in Table 11.1. To compare their sensitivity, both scales were
used for all the analyses reported here. In almost every instance, the
conclusions were not influenced by the scale that was used. This is
to be expected, given the strong pressure for congruency of brand
evaluation and intentions measures within well-defined product
classes (Day, 1970a). Overall, the evaluative measure was more
meaningful for evaluating the effectiveness of marketing communications, and it is used here. The first advantage of the evaluative
measure can be seen in Table 11.1.

The evaluative measure includes the distinct and important
"aware only" category. These are respondents whose information
about the brand is limited to the name. In the interview situation, the
"aware only" respondents refuse to state a degree of preference but
are willing to say that they don't intend to buy the brand. The
result is that the intention-*not*-to-buy response category includes
respondents with very little information, along with others who have
strongly held reasons for not wanting to buy the brand. Of course
there is also some heterogeneity in the amount of information held
by respondents within each category of evaluation. But this heterogeneity is reduced by separating out the "aware only" respondents,
and the key advertising objective of forming favorable attitudes can
be more realistically evaluated. A further advantage of the general
evaluative scale is that it can be correlated directly with scales that
are used to evaluate specific attributes, if it is desired to look further
into the performance of the brand.

TABLE 11.1
DISTRIBUTION OF ATTITUDE RESPONSES TOWARD A NEW
AND AN ESTABLISHED BRAND OVER FIVE MONTHS
(PERCENTAGE OF TOTAL SAMPLE)

RESPONSE CATEGORY	NEW BRAND (A)			ESTABLISHED BRAND (B)		
	t_1 ($n =$ 695)	t_2 ($n =$ 695)	t_3 ($n =$ 640)	t_1 ($n =$ 695)	t_2 ($n =$ 695)	t_3 ($n =$ 640)
Favorable	12%	27%	30%	46%	49%	49%
Neutral and unfavorable	17	26	36	34	33	38
Aware (no attitude expressed)	13	23	17	17	17	12
Unaware	58	24	17	3	1	1
	100	100	100	100	100	100

Measures of Attitude Change

The data in Table 11.1 yield some interesting patterns of change in the aggregate distributions. However, many possible patterns of individual change could produce similar distributions. The obvious next step is to form a turnover table for cross-tabulating individual responses at two points in time (e.g., see Table 11.2A). Much more information about the process of change is obtained, but not all questions can be readily answered. The most immediate problem is that cells are hard to compare within and between turnover tables. One solution is to normalize the rows by computing the probabilities of changing or remaining in a response category between time periods (see Table 11.2B). We are dealing now with the familiar first-order, discrete-time Markov model, which assumes that no respondent can make more than one jump (or change between response categories) in the period between interviews. Yet if the hierarchy of effects has anything to say about attitude change, it is that the progression from the unaware state to a positive attitude may take place in several jumps. If the period between interviews is long enough, all these jumps may occur in that time interval. If we ignore this possibility, the measure of rate of change may be substantially understated. To overcome this problem, we have used a continuous-time Markov model (Coleman, 1964), which assumes that the process of change operates continuously through time rather than at discrete intervals. The transition rate parameter that describes this continuous process is the limiting form of the transition probability when the time interval approaches zero. See Table 11.2C for a matrix of transition rates.

Each transition rate q_{ij} is an estimate of the proportion of all respondents, starting in some attitude response category i, who moved to another category j at any time between interviews. The estimation procedure considers all those who moved from i to j regardless of whether they remained in j, returned to i, or made a further jump in the same time period. Thus the size of the q_{ij}'s is dependent on the number of jumps that are possible in a given time period. If there is a great deal of change in a particular category, the row sum of the transition rates will be considerably greater than 1.0. A good illustration is the "aware only" category (see Table 11.2C), which is very unstable. Since these rates are also time dependent, the longer the period between interviews, the larger the q_{ij}. By dividing each q_{ij} by the number of months between interviews, the rate of change per month can be obtained. This is an important advantage of the model, for it permits direct comparisons of data collected over time from interview periods of varying duration. Here as in the case of the discrete-time Markov model, we assume that the q_{ij}'s are constant during the period between interviews and that they apply to all respondents (homogeneity condition).

A METHOD FOR EVALUATING
THE RELATIVE INFLUENCE OF EXPOSURE
TO COMMUNICATION SOURCES

Our method provides the opportunity to consider simultaneously a number of kinds of attitude change and multiple, overlapping sources of information. We start by characterizing the change activity in a matrix of transition rates as either building awareness (q_{43}), attitude formation (q_{41} and q_{31}, where 1 is the favorable category), attitude change (q_{21} and q_{12}), or forgetting (q_{13} or q_{14}). This classification is illustrated in Table 11.2C.

The next step is to isolate the effect of exposure to various marketing stimuli. This requires partitioning the total sample on the basis of the type of exposure, then estimating all transition rates for each of the resulting subsamples. The relative influence of a marketing stimulus on each type of attitude change can be evaluated from the ratio of the various transition rates for the exposed and not-exposed conditions. The "not-exposed" group is useful as a base-line because it accounts for the impact of other opportunities for attitude change (1) through other forms of communication, such as store displays or shelf facings, (2) through delayed response to earlier communications, or (3) forgetting an exposure situation that did trigger attitude change. Thus the incremental effect of media advertising on the rate of formation of favorable attitudes among previously unaware buyers (q_{41} in Table 11.2C) would be evaluated from the size of the ratio

TABLE 11.2
ILLUSTRATION OF TECHNIQUES FOR ANALYZING ATTITUDE PANELS: SHOWING CHANGES IN AWARENESS AND ATTITUDES TOWARD BRAND A BETWEEN T_1 AND T_2

(A) Turnover Table

		ATTITUDE T_2				
		FAVOR-ABLE (1)	NEUTRAL OR UNFA-VORABLE (2)	AWARE ONLY (3)	NOT AWARE (4)	COL-UMN Σ
ATTI-TUDE T_1	Favorable (1)	46	15	14	12	87
	Neutral or unfavor-able (2)	25	53	29	14	121
	Aware only (3)	27	27	21	14	89
	Not aware (4)	79	99	93	127	398
	Row Σ	177	194	157	167	695

(B) Matrix of Transition Probabilities

		(1)	(2)	(3)	(4)	Σ
ATTI-TUDE T_1	Favorable (1)	.53	.17	.16	.14	1.00
	Neutral or unfavor-able (2)	.20	.44	.24	.12	1.00
	Aware only (3)	.30	.30	.24	.16	1.00
	Not aware (4)	.20	.25	.23	.32	1.00

TABLE 11.2 (*Continued*)

(C) Matrix of Transition Rates

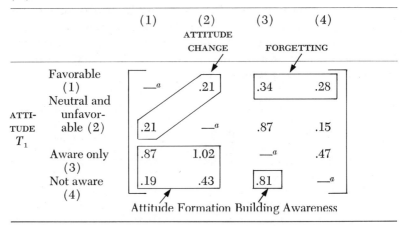

		(1)	(2)	(3)	(4)
			ATTITUDE CHANGE	FORGETTING	
ATTITUDE T_1	Favorable (1)	$—^a$	.21	.34	.28
	Neutral and unfavorable (2)	.21	$—^a$	.87	.15
	Aware only (3)	.87	1.02	$—^a$	.47
	Not aware (4)	.19	.43	.81	$—^a$

Attitude Formation Building Awareness

$^a q_{ii}$ is arbitrarily set as $— \sum\limits_{j=1}^{k} q_{ij}$, for $j = 1, 2, \ldots, k$.

$$\frac{q_{41} \text{ (saw advertisement)}}{q_{41} \text{ (not exposed)}}$$

Each of the following categories was investigated *separately* for both time periods:

Type of Exposure	*Partitioning Categories*
1. Communications exposure	A. Saw media advertisement
	B. Talked about brand
	C. Saw ad and talked about brand
	D. Not exposed
2. Sample receipt	A. Received sample
	B. Not sampled

Unfortunately, because of sample-size constraints, it was not possible to make further partitions. For example, partitioning on the basis of communications exposure and sample receipt together would give eight subgroups. Most of these groups would have fewer than the 75 to 100 respondents necessary to obtain stable estimates of transition rates.

The Validity of Recall Measures of Exposure

The basic question is whether observed differences in rates of attitude change between exposure groups are due to the effects of marketing stimuli or to other, possibly irrelevant, differences between the groups. D. T. Campbell and Stanley (1966) argue for the latter explanation on the grounds that a report of exposure is likely to be correlated with the response on both the before (pretest) and after (posttest) reinterviews. But are these two invalidating correlations large enough to warrant concern?

Correlation of Report of Exposure with the Pretest Attitude Response. First, we should note that such a correlation is not wholly invalid because of the operation of selective exposure, perception, and retention. Respondents who are favorable toward a brand are more likely to become buyers, to initiate conversations, to notice advertisements, and to recall this activity. A problem arises only when favorable respondents report nonexistent exposures and unfavorable or unaware respondents fail to recall or mention actual exposures. As a result, physical exposure and recalled exposure are not likely to be the same. Our investigation of this problem was limited to bivariate cross-tabulations of the exposure categories against a large number of descriptive variables (ranging from standard demographics to measures of product interest and buying style). Out of 46 variables, only three demonstrated a significant relationship. These were interest in differences between brands in the product class, prior usage of the product class, and initial attitude response. By far the strongest relationship was between the initial attitude response and the subsequent report of exposure. The results for brand A (Table 11.3.) are generally encouraging, since the groups who recalled exposure to television advertising or receiving a sample were not significantly different from the not-exposed group in the proportion with favorable attitudes at the beginning of the period. The worst that can be said about the word-of-mouth exposure groups is that the evidence of bias is ambiguous. That is, the significantly larger proportion having initially favorable attitudes may reflect only the greater tendencies of satisfied users and others with very favorable attitudes to initiate word of mouth.

Correlation of Report of Exposure with the Posttest Attitude Response. The problem here is that "any two items in the same questionnaire tend strongly to correlate more highly than do the same two if in separate questionnaires" (D. T. Campbell and Stanley, 1966). In an effort to reduce this problem, the exposure and attitude-

TABLE 11.3
EXPOSURE TO BRAND A AND FAVORABLE ATTITUDES

EXPOSURE GROUP DURING PERIOD	PROPORTION OF EXPOSURE GROUP WITH FAVORABLE ATTITUDES AT BEGINNING OF PERIOD	
	T_1 TO T_2	T_2 TO T_3
No exposure	.10	.24
Saw advertisement	.13	.31
Talked about brand	.21	.53
Saw advertisement and talked about brand	.22	.40
Received sample	.11	No sampling during this period

response questions were separated by several minutes in the telephone interview and were asked of five or six brands at a time. The extent to which these tactics reduced the memory biases could not be determined. There seems to be no completely satisfactory alternative that will overcome this problem. A true experimental design that varied advertising plans (Haskins, 1968) would be much more complex and still would not provide information on word-of-mouth exposure. Another possibility is to infer advertising exposure from media habits, which means disregarding selective perception and retention tendencies.

On balance, recall measures appear to be acceptable because they provide the only standardized approach to identifying both word-of-mouth and media exposure. This is an important advantage in our study because of the need to compare directly the consequences of different kinds of exposure. Of course, there are many opportunities to go beyond the crude dichotomies of exposed/not exposed that are used in this study. This is most evident with the word-of-mouth exposure variable, which presently ignores the direction of initiation and influence, the motives of the communicators, and the content of the message.

RESULTS AND INTERPRETATION
Exposure to Media
and Word-of-Mouth Sources

The most striking feature of Table 11.4A is the large proportion of panelists who reported being exposed to some kind of communication about both the new and the established brand within the two weeks of the beginning of the interview. No doubt some of these exposures

TABLE 11.4
RECALL OF EXPOSURE TO MEDIA AND WORD-OF-MOUTH
INFORMATION ABOUT NEW AND ESTABLISHED BRANDS

(A) Proportion of Sample Reporting Exposure[a] (*During Two Weeks Prior to Interview*)

TYPE OF EXPOSURE	T_2		T_3	
	NEW BRAND (A)	ESTAB-LISHED BRAND (B)	NEW BRAND (A)	ESTAB-LISHED BRAND (B)
	$(n = 695)$	$(n = 695)$	$(n = 640)$	$(n = 640)$
1. Saw media advertisement	.25	.31	.25	.34
2. Word of mouth	.05	.12	.03	.10
3. Both media and word of mouth	.08	.16	.04	.11
4. No exposure to communication	.62	.41	.68	.45
	1.00	1.00	1.00	1.00

(B) Proportion Reporting Exposure to Word of Mouth

ADVERTISING EXPOSURE GROUPS	NEW BRAND (A)	ESTAB-LISHED BRAND (B)	NEW BRAND (A)	ESTAB-LISHED BRAND (B)
1. Not exposed to advertising[a]	.08 $(n = 469)$	.24 $(n = 368)$	.04 $(n = 457)$	.19 $(n = 353)$
2. Exposed to advertising	.25 $(n = 226)$	.34 $(n = 327)$	.14 $(n = 183)$	.25 $(n = 287)$
Ratio of rows 2 and 1 (2/1)	3.1	1.4	3.5	1.3

[a] *Note* that 24 percent of the sample was unaware of the new brand between T_1 and T_2; 17 percent were unaware between T_2 and T_3. (See Table 11.1.)

are attributable to the reactive nature of the reinterview design. But if the bias was severe, in which case most of the exposures would be due to yea-saying tendencies or unusual sensitivity to the product class, we would expect that proportion reporting *no exposure* to communication to have increased more than the average of 10 percent observed between T_2 and T_3. This is because any unusual interest in the product class attributable to panel membership would probably have dissipated after five months. Specific precautions were taken to reduce biasing sensitivity to a single product class by asking similar questions about brands in other product classes.

In interpreting the exposure results, it should be noted that they apply to a market that was in an unusual state of flux. This is generally true when new brands are striving to gain a niche and was particularly so of this market when a second new brand (C) entered the market shortly after the introduction of the new brand under study. These introductions apparently provoked the dominant brand to defend its franchise by increasing advertising. Thus, in the two weeks prior to T_2, 48 percent of the sample was exposed to a media advertisement for the established brand (B), compared with 33 percent for the new brand (A).[3] During the same period, however, 20 percent of the sample received a sample of brand A, and half those who received the sample were not exposed to any other communication.

Table 11.4B was designed to focus on the interaction between word of mouth and media advertising. One of the desirable by-products of a successful advertising campaign is the generation of word of mouth. This is most apparent for the new brand (A), where the probability of exposure to word of mouth is an average of 2.4 times as great as in the group exposed to advertising.[4] This effect is much less pronounced for the established brand (B), which is very familiar and so strongly identified with the product class that all discussions would be likely to mention it.

Some tentative insights into why advertising triggers word of mouth can be seen in Table 11.5 from a question aimed at determining with whom the brand was discussed (without regard to who initiated the conversation). Discussions with family members are more likely to result from joint viewing of advertising and are probably not as influential as discussions with friends or relatives, which are more likely to be motivated by a desire for more information. According to this criterion, there were no significant differences between brands A and B in the impact of word-of-mouth messages because nonfamily sources occurred with roughly equal frequency for all brands. This conclusion is further supported by a question that asked whether the word of mouth was favorable,

---

[3] These recalled-exposure proportions were divided about equally between print media and TV for both brands.

[4] Causality cannot be inferred here, since the order of advertising and word of mouth is not known, and exposure to both communication sources is somewhat dependent on the initial attitude.

TABLE 11.5

COMPARISON OF DISCUSSIONS ON BRANDS A AND B

PERCENT OF TOTAL MENTIONS PER BRAND

BRAND DISCUSSED WITH	NEW BRAND (A) (T_2)	NEW BRAND (A) (T_3)	ESTAB-LISHED BRAND (B) (T_2)	ESTAB-LISHED BRAND (B) (T_3)	AVERAGE OF BRANDS IN TWO OTHER PRODUCT CATEGORIES $(T_2 + T_3)$
	$(n = 92)$	$(n = 45)$	$(n = 194)$	$(n = 134)$	$(n = 352)$
Husband	.23	.15	.18	.18	.19
Child	.31	.28	.33	.28	.32
Friend or friends	.28	.37	.35	.37	.35
Other (including relative)	.18	.20	.14	.17	.14
	1.00	1.00	1.00	1.00	1.00

unfavorable, or mixed in content. Again, no significant differences were found between brands.

Attitude Change During a New Product Introduction

The results in Table 11.6 summarize the attitude change experience of a new brand during the period between two and seven weeks from the date of introduction. This was a crucial period for the brand, for it began with 71 percent of the sample without an attitude (see Table 11.1). The problem for the advertiser was to build awareness from a low base and to create sufficient favorable attitudes to ensure an adequate trial rate. The question is, which communication source (or combination of sources) was most effective in achieving these dual objectives, given that 33 percent of the sample was exposed to media advertising and only 13 percent to word of mouth. In this situation, the contribution of product sampling to the objective must also be taken into account. All conclusions about the relative influence of information sources are based on a comparison with the rates of attitude change in the absence of exposure to communications about the brand.

According to Table 11.6, media advertising performed as ex-

TABLE 11.6
INFLUENCE OF COMMUNICATIONS EXPOSURE ON ATTITUDE CHANGE DURING INTRODUCTION OF NEW BRAND (T_1 TO T_2)

(Ratio of Transition Rates of Exposed to Not Exposed Subgroups)

	TRANSITION RATES
GOAL IS TO MAXIMIZE THESE RATIOS	Building awareness q_{43} Forming favorable attitude q_{41} q_{31} Attitude change (unfavorable to favorable) q_{21}
GOAL IS TO MINIMIZE THESE RATIOS	Attitude change (favorable to unfavorable) q_{12} Forming unfavorable attitudes[a] q_{32} Forgetting[b] q_{13}

[a] In the not-exposed subgroup q_{12} was very small, while q_{13} and q_{14} were relatively large. An examination of the turnover table showed that of those leaving the favorable category, 83% went to categories 3 and 4. Apparently the favorable attitudes formed prior to T_1 were based on very little information, hence were very unstable.

pected, its primary contribution being to build awareness (q_{43}). More important, however, is the finding that advertising alone was relatively ineffective in moving people the rest of the way into the favorable category (q_{41} and q_{31}). This analysis is somewhat unfair to advertising, for it neglects the beneficial effects of the word-of-mouth communications that were apparently triggered by exposure to advertising. If the definition of advertising exposure is broadened to include those who may also have been exposed to word of mouth, advertising appears slightly better. The improvement

EXPOSURE SUBGROUPS			
EXPOSED ONLY TO MEDIA ADVERTISEMENT $(n = 171)$	EXPOSED TO MEDIA ADVERTISEMENT $(n = 226,$ INCLUDES 55 ALSO EXPOSED TO WORD OF MOUTH)	EXPOSED TO WORD OF MOUTH $(n = 92,$ INCLUDES 55 ALSO EXPOSED TO TV ADVERTISING)	RECEIVED SAMPLE $(n = 146)$
2.5	2.7	4.0	0.7
1.5	1.6	2.5	2.3
1.0	1.0	2.0	1.4
1.1	3.5	9.6	5.9
8.0	10.0	1.8	4.0
0.5	0.4	0.4	0.9
0.4	0.4	0.5	0.0

[b] By definition, q_{14} is zero; that is, if a person forgot the brand name he or she was asked about exposure to advertising or word-of-mouth communication.

from the redefinition comes largely from facilitating favorable attitude changes (q_{21}). The reason becomes clear if we isolate the effect of word-of-mouth exposure on attitude change. According to Table 11.6 word of mouth is nine times as effective as media advertising in changing unfavorable or neutral attitudes to favorable attitudes. However, most people who made this shift (from category 1) had very little information about brand A on which to base an attitude, thus were very prone to shift when exposed to credible information. Since 66 percent of those in response category 2 at T_1

TABLE 11.7
PROPORTION OF SUBSAMPLE REPORTING EXPOSURE
TO WORD OF MOUTH (T_1 TO T_2)

SUBGROUP	PROPORTION
Received product sample $(n = 79)$	.24
Exposed to advertisement $(n = 162)$	.22
Saw advertisement and received sample $(n = 64)$	.30
No exposure to advertisement or sample $(n = 390)$	.05

had low confidence in their judgments of brand A (compared with 29 percent with low confidence in category 1), it appears that advertising alone is unable to establish firm attitudes toward a brand, or even to improve neutral and unfavorable attitudes when they are in a highly malleable state. For these tasks, both word of mouth and sampling are much more effective.

The importance of sampling as part of the introductory campaign is persuasively documented in Table 11.6. Since a sample provides a direct usage experience, it comes close to maximizing the rate of change from the unaware to the favorable response state (q_{41}). Of course this will only occur when the product provides a satisfactory usage experience, as appeared to be the case with brand A. We were surprised to learn that sampling was no more effective in generating word of mouth than was media advertising Table 11.7. This conclusion assumes that the subsamples do not differ significantly in the direction of initiation and influence, which is debatable.

Changes in Attitudes
Toward an Established Brand

Once a brand has found a niche in the market, the advertising objectives become more defensive. While creating brand preference remains important, more attention must be directed toward ensuring that the brand continues to be considered acceptable by past and present buyers,[5] or, at least is not forgotten. The need to avoid erosion of the presently established position becomes doubly pressing in this situation, where almost 50 percent of the sample has a favorable attitude toward the brand and two new entrants appeared

[5] Sometimes this goal also includes reinforcing presently favorable attitudes among present and prospective users. This goal can be evaluated with the procedure outlined here, but it requires supplementing the attitude measure with data on attitude stability.

on the market. As Table 11.1 showed, the established brand suc-
ceeded in maintaining, and to some extent reinforcing, its initial
position. What role did advertising and word of mouth play in this
achievement?

Again, we can use as a baseline the group that did not discuss
the brand or see an advertisement. Fortunately, this group was a
minority (41 percent), for within this group there was a definite
erosion in the size of the favorable category. In particular, the ratio
of q_{21}/q_{12} was only .70, and this is of concern because the favorable
category was initially larger than the unfavorable category. In both
the information exposure groups, this ratio shifted in favor of the
growth and maintenance of the favorable category (q_{21}/q_{12} was 1.2
for advertising and 3.4 for word-of-mouth communications). These
results parallel the pattern observed earlier with the newly established brand, in which word-of-mouth communications are much
more effective than advertising in inducing positive attitude change.
It is equally important in this context that word of mouth reduced
the rate of unfavorable attitude change (q_{12}) well below the rate
for the not-exposed subgroup, counteracting the partially negative impact of the advertising. This can be seen in column 1 of Table
11.8 where q_{12} in the advertising subgroup is well above the rate
for the not-exposed group. Fortunately, the undesirable consequences of the advertising alone are considerably lessened when
we take into account the effects of word of mouth that are either
associated with the advertising exposure or generated by the advertising (see columns 2 and 3 of Table 11.8). In terms of the advertising goals, however, there is certainly a problem when the
advertising is apparently unable to effectively change attitudes unless it is accompanied by word of mouth.

In the aware-only group (3), the critical variable is the ratio of
the formation of favorable versus unfavorable attitudes (q_{31}/q_{32}).
Anything greater than 1.0 is acceptable. On this basis, the results
shown in Table 11.9 for the established brand are disquieting.

Not only is the overall attitude formation performance poor,
but it is accentuated by word-of-mouth and media exposure. This
contrary situation is not really a serious problem, for it largely
reflects the lack of involvement of the aware-only group in the
product or brand. A large proportion of this group is nonusers and
consequently lacks confidence in their judgments about the brand.
The proportions of response categories at T_2 with *low* confidence
ranged from 12 percent in the favorable group to 43 percent in the
neutral/unfavorable group to 48 percent in the aware-only group.

TABLE 11.8
INFLUENCE OF COMMUNICATIONS EXPOSURE ON
CHANGES IN ATTITUDE TOWARD AN
ESTABLISHED BRAND (T_1 TO T_2)

(*Ratio of Transition Rates of Exposed to Not Exposed Subgroups*)

	Forming favorable attitudes
GOAL IS TO MAXIMIZE	q_{31}
THESE RATIOS	Attitude change (unfavorable to favorable)
	q_{21}
	Attitude change (favorable to unfavorable)
	q_{12}
GOAL IS TO MINIMIZE	Forming unfavorable attitudes
THESE RATIOS	q_{32}
	Forgetting
	q_{13}

It is not clear why exposure to media or word-of-mouth sources increases the likelihood that the aware-only group will express neutral or unfavorable opinions. Fortunately for the established brand, this group is not likely to be part of the market for the product (Day, 1970a).

CONCLUSIONS

Advertising was found to play an essential role in the acceptance of a new brand and an established brand of a convenience food product. Very simply, the role of advertising was to provide the *preconditions for success*; for the new brand this meant primarily building awareness, and for the established brand it involved main-

---

TABLE 11.9
ADVERTISING VERSUS WORD-OF-MOUTH EFFECTS

EXPOSURE GROUP (T_1 TO T_2)	q_{31}/q_{32} (T_1 TO T_2)
Total sample	.65
Talked about brand	.48
Saw advertisement	.30

EXPOSURE SUBGROUPS		
EXPOSED ONLY TO MEDIA ADVERTISEMENT ($n = 207$)	EXPOSED TO MEDIA ADVERTISEMENT (INCLUDES 112 ALSO EXPOSED TO WORD OF MOUTH) ($n = 327$)	EXPOSED TO WORD OF MOUTH (INCLUDES 112 ALSO EXPOSED TO TV) ($n = 198$)
0.8	0.7	1.2
1.5	1.7	2.7
1.6	1.0	0.6
2.5	3.6	3.6
2.5	1.1	0.1

taining existing favorable attitudes. In both cases, ultimate success, in terms of creating and reinforcing favorable attitudes, largely rested with the ability of the brand to generate favorable word-of-mouth communications and to provide a satisfactory usage experience.

These general conclusions are not at all surprising, having been articulated in various forms for years. What is significant is that these results furnish a quantitative estimate of the relative impact of various kinds of communications and usage experiences. And since the results have considerable face validity, they provide grounds for greater confidence in the basic procedure of partitioning attitude change groups to evaluate advertising campaigns.

12

FOOD SHOPPING BEHAVIOR OF LOW-INCOME HOUSEHOLDS

MARCUS ALEXIS
Professor of Business Administration
University of Rochester

How low-income consumers engage in shopping (search) behavior, the quantities they purchase, their consumption expenditures, and the variables influencing these behavioral acts are of increasing concern to economists, behavioral scientists, and makers of public policy. The literature on the subject is extremely limited, but enough is known to be of value to serious students.

This paper is divided into two parts: (1) a study of food shopping behavior and (2) a study of prices paid. In both parts the socioeconomic status of the household is an explanatory variable. The reported results are from the published research of myself and my colleagues at the University of Rochester (Alexis, 1959a, 1959b, 1960, 1962; Alexis and Simon, 1967; Alexis and Smith, 1969). There are some suggested directions and areas for additional research that represent research in progress by members of the marketing faculty and graduate students at the University of Rochester.

I am indebted to George H. Haines, Jr., and Leonard S. Simon for their continued stimulation and advice. Much of what appears in this paper is the product of our joint efforts. It is only because of their insistence that this paper not bear their names as joint authors. Responsibility for any defects is solely mine.

FOOD SHOPPING, FOOD
PURCHASES, AND PRICES PAID

The results in this section are taken from work by the author and colleagues (Alexis, 1962; Alexis and Simon, 1967). The studies seek answers to the questions about the effect of income (and socio-economic status in general) on types of stores shopped, distances traveled to make food purchases, dollar level of food expenditures, and the variables affecting these factors.

Two areas of particular interest are expressed in the following hypotheses:

Hypothesis 1. Consumers in the lower-income classes ($5000 or less) are more likely to patronize small neighborhood stores than consumers in the middle- and upper-income groups.

Hypothesis 2. There is a negative correlation between the physical mobility of the consumer and the number of services offered by the retail units at which he shops, irrespective of the economic class.

Sample Selection

Respondents were selected from the Rochester (New York) metropolitan area. The 130 census tracts comprising this area were classified into high-, middle-, and low-income groups based on median income. Low tracts were defined as those with median family incomes of $4999 or less, middle as $5000 to $9499, and high as $9500 and over. This categorization resulted in 18 low-income tracts, all contained within the City of Rochester; 102 middle-income tracts; and 10 high-income tracts, all located in the suburban areas.

The low-income group represented 7.3 percent of the population, the middle group represented 83.3 percent, and the high group 9.3 percent. Since the principal objective of the study was to compare groups, the census tracts were stratified to obtain a random sample of 10 tracts from each stratum. Ten interviews were taken in each tract, two from each of the 150 predesignated locations.

In the course of the questioning, respondents were asked to state their family income. Table 12.1 compares published 1960 census tract median income data with the income reported on the questionnaires for those tracts. Census tract designations as high, middle, or low income were based on the median income in the tract, and all tracts contained some high-, low-, and middle-income

TABLE 12.1
1960 CENSUS TRACT INCOME DATA VERSUS
REPORTED INCOME DATA

	QUESTIONNAIRE INCOME			
CENSUS TRACT INCOME (MEDIANS)	LOW ($0– $4999)	MIDDLE ($5000– $9999)	HIGH ($10,000 AND OVER)	TOTALS
Low ($0–$4999)	74	21	5	100
Middle ($5000–$9499)	21	71	8	100
High ($9500 and over)	1	40	59	100
	96	132	72	300

families. Therefore, it was not expected that low-income tracts, for example, would yield only low-income families. One test of the sampling procedure was how consistently a tract designated as low, middle, or high produced respondents with the corresponding incomes. An inspection of Table 12.1 reveals that 204 of the 300 respondents, or better than 2 out of 3, had incomes corresponding to the designation of their tract. Of the remaining respondents, 90, or exactly 30 percent, were one income group higher or lower, and only 6, or 3 percent, were two income designations away from their tract designation. Considering that the census data were four years old and that the tracts were quite hetergeneous, the sampling results seem to be quite reasonable.

Relationships Among Variables

Analysis of the relationships between income, occupation, age, and education for the respondents showed that the sample group conformed to known interrelations among the variables. As income increased, for example, both the level of occupational skill and the level of education increased. Similarly, the low-income groups contained proportionately more older people than either the middle or high groups. An interesting but not unexpected observation was that more than 50 percent of the low-income group were unemployed, on relief, retired, or widowed.

Families with annual incomes of $3000 or less were separated out and scrutinized to determine what, if any, differences exist between this "poverty group" and the other low-income groups as defined herein. Significant differences are reported as each subject area is discussed rather than devoting a whole section to the $3000-and-below group.

STORES SHOPPED
Major Stores

Respondents reported the name and location of the store used most often in major shopping for food and groceries. Table 12.2 breaks these replies down by income. Analysis of the replies showed that about 70 percent of all families made the bulk of their purchases at the outlets of one of four food chains located in Rochester. Another 6 percent bought from large food discount centers, and the remaining 24 percent from one type of independent grocer or another. The χ^2 of this distribution is significant at the .01 level, clearly indicating a difference in store patronage by income group.

There are no major differences in the shopping patterns of high- and middle-income groups. However, a substantially different pattern exists for the low-income group, where 35 percent of the shopping is not done in chain or discount stores, compared with about 14 percent for the middle- and high-income groups.

Lack of physical mobility may be a major reason for the lower frequency of food chain patronage by low-income families. Car ownership is presented in Table 12.3. The middle- and high-income car ownership rates are about 94 and 99 percent, respectively. On the other hand, only 43 percent of the low-income families owned cars. An examination of families in the $3000-or-less income group and those in the $3001–$5000 income group reveals that auto ownership in the latter is more than three times the rate of the former, but shopping patterns are nearly identical.[1] This suggests that factors other than mobility are also operating.[2]

When distances to major stores are considered (by income level), further support is given to the mobility hypothesis. A breakdown of distances traveled is contained in Table 12.4. The low-income family median distance traveled is less than the other income groups. The medians are, respectively, 0.5 to 0.75 mile for

[1] The rates are, respectively, 72.5 percent in the $3001–$5000 income group and 22 percent in the $3000 or less income group.

[2] Unfortunately, we did not uncover these other factors although a method to detect them was built into the research design. The income elasticity of services (as defined on p. 228) was not significantly different from zero. To what extent this is due to the configuration of food stores in Rochester is unknown.

TABLE 12.2
MAJOR STORE SHOPPING PATTERNS BY INCOME LEVEL

INCOME LEVEL	INDE-PENDENTS (%)	DISCOUNT STORES (%)	CHAINS (%)	NO MAJOR STORES (%)
Low ($0–$4,999)	33 (34.4)	2 (2.1)	57 (59.3)	3 (4.2)
Middle ($5,000–$10,000)	18 (13.6)	9 (6.8)	102 (77.3)	3 (2.3)
High ($10,000 and over)	10 (13.9)	6 (8.4)	56 (77.7)	0
Totals	61 (20.3)	17 (5.7)	215 (71.7)	7 (2.3)

$$x^2 = 23.2$$
$$x^2_{.01} = 16.8$$

the low-income group, 0.75 to 1 mile for the middle-income families, and more than 1 mile for the highest income group. For the $3000-or-less income class, the median distance to major stores is 3 to 5 blocks—this is also the model class.

Correlation analysis indicated that the greater the distance to the major store shopped, the greater also the distance to the fill-in store. The total pattern reveals that wealthier people are less constrained by distance and may be able to select from a wider array of major stores.

Additional findings relating to mobility and major store shopped were the following: the more school years completed, the greater the likelihood of car ownership; the higher the income, the greater the likelihood of car ownership; and the lower the level of occupational skill, the less the likelihood of car ownership. Combining these factors with those just given, it becomes apparent that many poor persons are quite immobile and, therefore, must choose

TABLE 12.3
CAR OWNERSHIP BY INCOME LEVELS

	LOW INCOME ($0–$4999)	MIDDLE INCOME ($5000–$9999)	HIGH INCOME ($10,000 AND OVER)	TOTAL
Owner	46	124	71	241
Nonowner	50	8	1	59

TABLE 12.4
DISTANCES TRAVELED TO MAJOR STORES BY INCOME LEVELS

DISTANCE	LOW INCOME ($0–$4999)	MIDDLE INCOME ($5000–$9999)	HIGH INCOME ($10,000 AND OVER)	TOTALS
1 block or less	13	6	1	20
1–2 blocks	11	9	1	21
3–5 blocks	21	22	7	50
0.5 to 0.75 mile	22	15	9	46
0.75 to 1 mile	3	16	14	33
More than 1 mile	24	64	39	127
Totals	94	132	71	297

stores in an area within walking distance or possibly within a short bus ride.

The next categorization considered was the number of major stores shopped by the respondents. Of the shoppers interviewed, 98 percent reported making the major amount of their food purchases at only one store. The results of this investigation clearly indicate that most shoppers have a major store they consider to be "their major store," indicating an extremely high level of store loyalty for the purchase of foodstuffs.

Only 9 percent of the respondents shopped at *two major stores*, but some of the findings for this group were quite interesting: the greater the distance to the major stores, the greater the likelihood that the shopper is white; the higher the level of occupational skill, the less the likelihood of the spouse accompanying the shopper; a larger number of adult equivalents[3] are associated more with black than with white shoppers; the greater the age, the more likely the shopper is to be white—that is, blacks shopping in two major stores tend to be younger. The two-major-store shopper is the principal case in which consumption differences between blacks and whites appeared so decisively, with black consumers reporting a much higher proportion of multistore usage. But the size of the black cell is quite small, and the results are not statistically significant, but potentially important.

In no more than 10 percent of the cases did major stores offer

---

[3] A standardization of family size based on caloric intake of children and adults to permit comparison of families of different sizes and age structures. For a more detailed explanation, see p. 228.

services other than check cashing and the giving of trading stamps (other possibilities were payment of utility bills, delivery, credit and telephone ordering) as reported by the respondents.[4] The importance of trading stamps and check-cashing services is revealed by the fact that 66 percent of the respondents shopped at stores offering trading stamps and 78 percent at stores providing check cashing. Check-cashing service in major stores was much more common as income increased; this seemed to be the only income-sensitive service. Finally, more than 50 percent of those who shopped major stores with delivery service or telephone ordering also used fill-in stores providing the same services.

A weak verification of the hypothesis that low-income families have higher credit use is contained in the observation that for major stores, low-income families reported the greatest number of stores offering credit. Also, these families were heavier users of stores providing telephone and delivery service than either middle- or high-income families. These observation, taken together, tend to indicate that low-income families are more likely to patronize service-oriented stores. However, high-income families do not exhibit this tendency to any greater extent than middle-income families. Thus we have only partial confirmation of the high/low-income service store orientation thesis, which argues that high-income families, because of their financial ability, are willing and able to pay for such services. The argument further states that low-income families will be inclined toward service-oriented stores because of their need for credit and, in the case of the aged poor, toward telephone and delivery as well.

Fill-in Stores

Almost 80 percent of the respondents indicated that they used a "fill-in store." "Fill-in" shopping was defined as shopping for items one either forgot to buy at the regular store or that he unexpectedly needed more of. The percentage of "fill-in" store users is given by income level in Table 12.5. Surprisingly, the differences among the groups are not significant at the .05 level when subjected to a χ^2 test.

A significantly lower figure was expected for the low-income group, since slightly more low-income families shop in neighborhood independent grocers for *all* their purchases (if a store was mentioned by a respondent as his major store, the same response

---

[4] It is recognized that trading stamps are not a service, but the goal of this section was to establish "extras" that stores utilized to attract patrons.

TABLE 12.5
FILL-IN STORE USERS BY INCOME LEVEL

PERCENTAGES

	LOW INCOME ($0–$4999)	MIDDLE INCOME ($5000–$9999)	HIGH INCOME ($10,000 AND OVER)
User	72	80	81
Nonuser	28	20	19

was not permitted for his fill-in store). In addition, the $3000-or-less income class does not have a significantly greater percentage of non-fill-in store users than the $3000–$5000 income class. Table 12.6 shows the distances traveled to fill-in stores by those indicating such use. As in the case of distances to major stores, the medians progress upward one distance category at a time as income increases; but all income levels use fill-in stores substantially nearer to their home than the major stores patronized.

As with the major store, the majority of respondents (76 percent) had only one fill-in store; thus it would seem that people are store loyal for both major and fill-in stores, and clearly the bulk of the respondents shop one major and one fill-in store. Two findings concerning fill-in store users not covered by the correlation analysis were: (1) as income increased, the distance traveled to the fill-in store became greater, and (2) whites tended to travel further to fill-in stores than blacks. It appears that poorer people, especially blacks, patronize fill-in stores nearer their homes. Since

TABLE 12.6
DISTANCE TRAVELED TO FILL-IN STORE BY INCOME LEVELS

DISTANCE	LOW INCOME ($0–$4999)	MIDDLE INCOME ($5000–$9999)	HIGH INCOME ($10,000 AND OVER)	TOTALS
1 block or less	30	21	5	56
1–2 blocks	17	20	4	41
3–5 blocks	16	23	7	46
0.5 to 0.75 mile	3	13	17	33
0.75 to 1 mile	2	14	10	26
More than 1 mile	3	15	15	33
Totals	69	106	58	233

a similar finding was uncovered for major stores, it would be reasonable to believe that the low-income family's shopping pattern is decidedly more constrained by the distance of stores from the home.

A sizable group of the respondents (about 22 percent), however, have no fill-in store. Some interesting findings were uncovered specifically within this group: shoppers who own automobiles are more likely to have freezers at home; the higher the level of occupational skill and the greater the distance to the major store, the higher the likelihood of auto ownership and the greater the number of adult equivalents; also, the higher the level of occupational skill, the larger the (unadjusted) family size and the higher the amount spent weekly on food; and as the number of children under 14 years of age increases, weekly food expenditures also increase.

In contrast to the major stores, the distribution of services (sale of stamps, station for payment of utility bills, etc.) reported for fill-in stores was much more evenly spread among the potential services, including the offering of no services, with the following exceptions: check cashing was reported for 48 percent of the cases (and was approximately three times more frequently used than any other service), and utility payments were not reported at all. Although a wider variety of services were available at the fill-in stores, a large number of the stores were reported not to offer these services; and for both the major and fill-in stores, the highest incidence of services being offered occurred in the middle-income groups. Cell frequencies in the fill-in store data are so small that they preclude drawing inferences.

INCOME
Income—All Cases

The only two remaining correlational findings for the sample as a whole that centered on reported family income were as follows: as the level of occupational skill increased and a greater number of years of schooling was completed, the family income was greater.[5] The percentage of families in which both spouses did the shopping had an inverted, U-shaped distribution when plotted against family income. Joint shopping occurred most frequently (about 55 percent of the cases) in families with incomes between $3,000 and $10,000; that is, in both the very-low-income groups and the high-income groups, spouse-accompanied shopping occurs in only 25 percent of the cases. The total sample was divided into three

[5] Other correlational relationships including income are reported under the major and fill-in store analysis.

subsets by low, middle, and high income, and correlation analysis was conducted within each subset.[6] The results are reported below.

Low Income

There was a stronger relationship in the low-income class than in the all-cases classification, showing that as age increased, the level of occupational skill decreased—this relationship was even more marked for those with incomes of $3000 or less. This is to be expected because unskilled older persons are very likely to be poor. A finding, which did not exist in the all-groups class, was that as age increased, weekly food expenditures decreased. Other results that did not appear in the all-cases category were the following: as age increased, the race of the respondent tended to be white; as total family size and the number of adult equivalents increased, the likelihood of shopping accompanied by one's spouse decreased; and as total family size or the number of children under 14 years of age increased, color tended to be black. The low-income families might then be characterized as older whites with lesser occupational skills and young blacks with large families. Most of the black families in the sample fell in the latter class, but there were not significantly more of them in the $3000-and-less income group as compared with the $3000–$5000 group.

Among the very-low-income families ($3000-and-less annual income), a rather interesting result was obtained: the more years of schooling completed, the greater the distance to the major store. Perhaps in low-income families additional years of schooling lend a type of sophistication to purchasing habits that causes the purchaser to search further from his home to maximize his shopping objectives or utility.

Middle Income and High Income

There were no significantly new or different findings in the middle- and high-income categories. A hypothesis to explain this lack of particular results, at least for the middle-income group, might be that the middle-income group exhibits the normative behavior toward which the higher- and lower-income respondents tend.

FAMILY SIZE

Table 12.7 presents the mean family size and the mean number of children 14 years old or younger, according to reported income.

---

[6] Findings in subsets are reported only if they differ significantly from the all cases group.

TABLE 12.7
MEAN FAMILY SIZE ACCORDING TO INCOME GROUP

INCOMES	MEAN FAMILY SIZE	MEAN NUMBER OF CHILDREN 14 YEARS OR LESS
Low		
Up to $2,000	1.92	0.52
$2,001 to $3,000	3.10	1.07
$3,001 to $5,000	4.07	1.29
Middle		
$5,001 to $7,000	4.83	2.15
$7,001 to $10,000	4.91	2.03
High		
$10,001 to $15,000	4.21	1.00
$15,001 and over	4.48	1.48

The largest families are in the two middle-income groups, which are homogeneous. The two high-income groups also show considerable homogeneity. These four groups might all be approximately equal in family size if their age composition were the same. The high-income shopper was, on the average, 10 years older than the middle-income shopper, which might account for the smaller number of children under 14. In the low-income classifications, family size and small children increase with increasing income level. This is explained by observing that the oldest members of the low-income group are the poorest and that the sizes of younger families in the low-income group increase as incomes rise. The highest income category within the low-income classification exhibits characteristics more closely associated with the middle- and upper-income levels.

COMMODITIES PURCHASED—
ANALYSIS BY INCOME LEVELS

This set of findings primarily deals with family purchases of food commodities, by income levels. Since varying sizes of families can influence the results, a means was developed for standardizing family size. Children under 14 years of age were defined as members of the household. This basis was selected for two reasons: first, the daily food intake of a child older than 14 years is probably roughly equal to that of an adult; second, someone older than 14 may be capable of contributing to household income, and this income might be used for food expenditures. A conversion factor relating the food consumption of children under 14 to that of an adult was developed. Through use of this factor, the number of adult equivalents in each family was determined. All the analysis for specific commodities is based on mean consumption per family in each income class, where family size was defined in terms of adult equivalents. Two findings from the correlation analysis should be reported here: As total family size increased, the number of children under 14 increased; and as either total family size or the number of adult equivalents increased, the amount spent weekly for food increased.

This study is only concerned with actual food purchases from grocery stores and not with other food purchases made by consumers, such as meals purchased away from home. The figures reported here, therefore, are an understatement of the total food bill. This difference between grocery purchases and total food purchases increases as income rises.

There is an important limitation in the analysis of commodities purchased. It is extremely difficult to take into account differences in the quality of similar items purchased at various income levels; for example, the mean amount of ground beef purchased is about the same in the high- and low-income classes, but it is readily conceivable that the quality may vary considerably. We recognize that this drawback clouds the results, but we have been unable to devise an economic, easily administered means of accounting for quality differences.[7]

If it is true that quality improves with income, although the mean amounts purchased remain constant, the effect would be to magnify any differences found in this study. Higher-income families not only buy more of goods with positive income elasticities, but frequently they also buy better quality in that good. This is almost certainly the case with the fruit and vegetables in column 1 of Table 12.8.

The sensitivity of various commodities to income effects is given in Table 12.8. This information is based solely on the quantities purchased, standardized for variations in the size of the unit of purchase; it does not reflect differences in quality. In addition to the items already mentioned, information was collected on three

[7] The Consumer Price Indexes of the U.S. Bureau of Labor Statistics do not take account of quality differences adequately, probably because of the not insignificant difficulties involved. See Kruskal and Telser (1960).

TABLE 12.8

EFFECT OF INCOME ON FAMILY PURCHASES OF FOODSTUFFS

As Income Rises, the Mean Amount Purchased Per Family[a] of These Commodities

INCREASES	REMAINS THE SAME	DECREASES
Frozen orange juice	Onions	Bread
Frozen vegetables	Fresh milk	Pork chops
Fresh tomatoes	Margarine	Pork and beans
Fresh fruit	Ketchup	Canned soup
Cartoned orange juice	Peanut butter	Canned orange juice
Regular coffee	Laundry soap	Canned milk
Butter		Spam
		Chicken
		Canned vegetables
		Potatoes
		Instant coffee
		Tea
		Powdered milk
		Jelly
		Rice
		Sugar

---

[a] Standardized, as explained in text, in terms of adult equivalents.

---

other commodities, but these exhibited quite different patterns: Ground beef and canned fruit exhibited a U-shaped pattern, being purchased in about equal amounts by the high- and low-income groups and in substantially smaller amounts by the middle-income group; chili had an inverted U shape, being purchased mostly by the middle-income group.

It would be appropriate to view Table 12.8 in terms of the shifts in behavior patterns that occur as income for the family unit changes. This table also has important implications for the product assortment a grocery store should offer, dependent on the types of clientele it serves. Only three items that fall into classifications seem surprising on an a priori basis. These are regular coffee, instant coffee, and tea. It was thought these results might be due to the correlation of age and income, and it was suggested that convenience was a factor in the consumption of both instant coffee and tea. Older people were hypothesized to be more convenience conscious, and poor. Regression analysis of sales of regular and instant coffee and of tea, with age and income as independent variables, failed to uncover any such effect. Whether the results in Table 12.8 are general can only be determined by observing a sample from a wider geographical area.[8]

Family Food Expenditures

One of the objectives of our study was to determine total family expenditures for food and to relate those expenditures to a set of economic and demographic variables. The expenditures were treated as the dependent variable in a regression analysis in which the independent variables were as follows:

1. Freezing capacity
2. Distance to major store
3. Distance to fill-in store
4. Spouse accompanied on shopping trips
5. Car ownership
6. Total family size
7. Number of children under 14
8. Number of adult equivalents
9. School years completed
10. Age
11. Income
12. Race
13. Sex
14. Occupation

Variables 1, 4, 5, 12, and 13 are "dummy variables" in that they are discrete and can have only one of two states. In the case of 1, 4, and 5, it is "yes" or "no." Variable 12 is either "white" or "nonwhite," and 13 is "male" or "female."

Four of the variables—car ownership, number of adult equivalents, income, and race—explained almost one-third of the total variance. Equation (1) is the final regression with b weights. The second equation contains the same four variables and gives their β weights,

where E_F = total food expenditures

X_1 = car ownership $\qquad \left. \begin{array}{l} 0 \\ 1 \end{array} \right\} \begin{array}{l} \text{car} \\ \text{no car} \end{array}$

X_2 = number of adult equivalents

---

[8] At a prepublication reading of this paper, a member of the audience pointed out that instant coffee is less expensive than regular coffee on a per-cup basis. Given that understanding, the coffee results make sense.

$X_3 =$ family income

$X_4 =$ race of respondent $\left.\begin{matrix}0 \\ 1\end{matrix}\right\}$ $\begin{matrix}\text{white} \\ \text{nonwhite}\end{matrix}$

$$E_F = -4.5956X_1 + 3.1169X_2 + 0.0311X_3 - 5.0871X_4 \qquad (1)$$
$$(1.8619) \qquad (0.3947) \qquad (0.0132) \qquad (1.8704)$$

$R^2 = .3169,$ multiple $R = 0.5630$

$$E_F = -0.1418X_1 + 0.4201X_2 + 0.1295X_3 - 0.1472X_4 \qquad (2)$$
$$(0.0575) \qquad (0.0532) \qquad (0.0548) \qquad (0.0541)$$

where the quantities in parentheses are the standard errors of estimate.

Considering the inherent variability in consumer behavior, the results reported in this section indicate that the four predictor variables in (1) and (2) do a good job of accounting for total family food expenditures. Of particular interest is the significance —both statistical and practical—of car ownership and race.[9]

RECAPITULATION

Many of the findings in the preceding section reinforced already existing knowledge; for instance, it was known that low-income families in the $5000-and-under class are made up mainly of retired white persons or young black families. Nor are the foodstuff profiles and their implications for grocery store product assortment based on type of clientele a marked departure from what would have been expected. There are, however, several findings that are new in that they offer some quite unexpected results, as well as evidence of ideas that have previously been discussed primarily on a theoretical basis.

Consumers in the lowest economic group are more likely to patronize independent neighborhood stores than consumers in the middle- and upper-income groups. This tendency is primarily a function of the lack of mobility due to a lower level of automobile ownership; but a lesser amount of schooling may also be an important influence in reducing purchasing sophistication and causing consumers in the $3000-and-less income group to remain closer to home. Generally, wealthier people are less constrained by geographical considerations in their choice of stores. Also, low-income

---

[9] The negative effect of the dummy variable $\left.\begin{matrix}0 \text{ white} \\ 1 \text{ nonwhite}\end{matrix}\right\}$ is consistent with this author's earlier findings relating race and food expenditures.

families have a higher relative frequency of patronizing service-oriented major stores—those offering delivery, credit, and telephone service. Delivery and telephone are mobility-related services; credit reflects the financial constraints. If the same phenomena were observed in the high-income class, the explanations would be a positive income elasticity for these services, since neither poor mobility nor stringent financial limitations would be operative.

Store loyalty is extremely strong. Most families use only one store each for their major and fill-in shopping. In addition, with the exception of check cashing and the offering of trading stamps, the array of services offered as patronage inducements to either low- or high-income shoppers is quite limited at both major and fill-in stores, but less so for middle-income shoppers.

An unexpected finding was that the shopping patterns of families with incomes of $3000 and less do not differ significantly from those of families earning $3001 to $5000 annually. The significance of this is that the families with incomes of $3000 or less are frequently considered part of a "poverty class." This paper suggests that their shopping behavior is very much like those in the $3001–$5000 income class; thus their situation is not relatively worsened by the way in which they purchase their foodstuffs. This statement does not apply to particular commodities purchased, inasmuch as the $3000-and-less groups purchase either greater or lesser amounts per family of certain foods depending on whether the commodity has a positive or negative income elasticity. One explanation for the observed similarity in shopping patterns may be that it results from the transition of families who retain their prior shopping patterns as they move out of the $3000-and-less class into the next higher class. Implicit in this statement are two additional hypotheses: (1) the $3001–$5000 income class is a "trapping state" (in an ergodic process) for certain family types (with given education, skills, etc.); (2) a behavioral change takes place as families move from the $3001–$5000 income level to higher plateaus. In essence, very poor people exhibit shopping behavior that is consistent with the hypothesis that their objectives are to emulate upper-lower- or lower-middle-class standards.

LIMITATIONS

The findings of this study are limited by several considerations. First, the sample is comprised entirely of families living in the Rochester, New York, metropolitan area. On the average, Rochester is a well-to-do area, having, for example, the third highest county income level in New York state and one of the lowest unemployment rates in the nation. On the other hand, it can be argued that this prosperity should only serve to heighten the differences between the low-income group and the other groups.

Second, some of the methodology employed, although statistically significant, has practical limitations in terms of application—for example, the use of $r = .4$ or greater as a basis for determining whether to report correlation analysis results. Third, the inability to account for quality variations in the commodities purchased may cloud the results, although as explained earlier, we would expect determination of quality differences to reinforce the present findings. Despite the preceding reservations, we believe that many of the behavior patterns uncovered here are probably appropriate descriptions of many of America's urbanized areas.

FOOD PRICES

Using the consumer survey information as a base, we set out to determine the shelf price in chain and independents given by respondents. This approach differs from that used by the National Commission on Food Marketing and others who have simply collected prices available in different socioeconomic neighborhoods. Many respondents shopped in neighborhoods they did not live in. This was especially true of mobile low-income consumers. Thus the weight to be given to food prices in neighborhoods is the proportion of food sales they account for and the proportion of people who reside in the neighborhood(s).

Selection of Stores for the Sample

In the family interviews, we obtained the names of the major and fill-in stores where food purchases were made by each family. The characterization of a store as low, middle, or high income was dependent solely on the socioeconomic grouping of the customers reporting shopping in that store, not on the surrounding neighborhood. A random sample of these stores, with slightly more stores taken from the group shopped by low- and middle-income families, was then selected. In all, 31 stores, including both chains and independents, were included in the sample (see Table 12.9). This procedure produced a sample in which the proportion of independent stores shopped by low-income consumers was somewhat greater than in the actual population.

On the basis of the food items for which information was collected in the original family interviews, a market basket of items to be studied in the stores was constructed. To be included in the

TABLE 12.9
CHARACTERISTICS OF STORES IN SAMPLE

INCOME LEVEL OF SHOPPERS	MAJOR STORE		FILL-IN STORE		TOTAL
	CHAIN	INDE-PENDENT[a]	CHAIN	INDE-PENDENT[a]	
Low	2	4	1	4	11
Middle	5	1	1	4	11
High	5	0	2	2	9
Total[b]	12	5	4	10	31

[a] Stores that belong to a buying cooperative such as I.G.A. are classified as independents.

[b] Lower frequency of patronage of independents for major shopping by middle- and upper-income families is shown in Alexis et al. (1969). The low-income selection of majors is weighted more heavily in favor of independents than the relative use of independents as major food sources in our 1965 study (Alexis and Simon, 1967). The fill-in store selection is proportional to use in the designated categories.

store market basket, an item only had to show noticeable use across all income classes.

Design

Some of the problems in making shelf-price comparisons were as follows: the quality comparability of food items because of branding effects, width and depth of product lines as they affect alternative choices, and special deals (e.g., loss leaders) in some of the sample stores during the weeks in which data was collected.[10]

The problems were resolved in the following manner. Specific sizes of canned merchandise, for example, were selected for inclusion in the market basket, and information was collected on the prices for such size cans in all stores on all brands offered in the stores, with one exception—the second- and third-quality lines of private-label merchandise of large chain stores were excluded. Second, stores were checked during subsequent periods to determine whether certain prices being used during the period of the study were lead prices. In such cases, the normal or usual price was substituted for the lead price. One important observation at

[10] One of the interesting by-products of this research is that the notion of product width and depth as now used is not satisfactorily defined. Graduate students at the University of Rochester are working on this problem and have made progress in making these terms operational.

this point was that the occurrence of lead prices was generally greater in chain stores than in independents. With the exception of the check-backs in the cases of special merchandise offers, information was collected only once from each store.

To analyze the data, two price estimates were prepared: a high market basket and a low market basket. The low market basket was calculated by taking the lowest price quotation in the appropriate size for each item and summing over all items. The high market basket was calculated similarly, but the highest price in the store was used in the summation. Such a procedure makes for the strongest possible comparison of price-level ranges in different stores. For example, if the low-income people buy the least expensive items available to them at the stores of their choice, one obtains the minimum price they would have to pay for the market basket. Similarly, if a person bought the lowest-priced item at other stores, the procedure described also gives the minimum total price at which the basket could be obtained in those stores. If an individual follows the policy of always buying the lowest-priced items, regardless of the store in which he is shopping, there is a standard basis on which to compare the stores. Some of the problems that arise in comparing brands are avoided through this procedure if quality levels are equal, or nearly so, for the different brands compared. If this assumption is incorrect and, say, private-label merchandise is inferior, real prices would be higher for items in stores where such merchandise is sold.

The information collected was divided into five separate indexes (a descriptive term to indicate the summed prices of the relevant items for each store). The five indexes were as follows: meat, dairy, coffee, laundry, and miscellaneous. The five were also summed to form a grand index for each of the stores. The general goods index consists of canned fruits and vegetables, canned soups, baby food, frozen food, bread, rice, and sugar.

Low Prices

Table 12.10 shows the mean of the low-price market baskets by chains and independents for each of the above indexes and a cross classification by income level and major or fill-in store. The grand index shows that the total market basket cost in either major or fill-in stores is significantly less for low-income families who shop in chain stores. Interestingly, the only category in which chain stores shopped by low-income families do not have a significant advantage is meat. It is also surprising that there is no significant difference for low-income major stores by type on the dairy index.

Middle-income shoppers could pay less for their fill-in shopping (i.e., depending on whether they bought low-priced goods) at chain stores as shown in the grand index, particularly on items in the laundry soap and meat categories. Upper-income families who do their major shopping at chains also pay less.

High Prices

Table 12.10 also gives the high prices of the market basket items. Here, chains shopped by low-income families for fill-in purposes are less expensive, as evidenced in the grand index; this may be largely due to the lower prices in the coffee and dairy categories. In contrast, the coffee index shows chains shopped by lower-income families for major shopping to have significantly higher prices than independents. The grand index also shows, for the upper-income group, higher prices for chains used as the major source of shopping than for independents; this effect is partly due to the relatively high prices for meat products. Furthermore, since the independent category in our study includes contract chains that sell over a narrower price range, this effect may be the result of definition of store types. Also, independents in high-income areas are likely to be outlets with larger sales volume and price appeal.

Other Evidence

In a study in Los Angeles, Harry Fendrick (1965) used as his basic hypothesis Holdren's (1960) comment that "there is no discernible relationship between location and price levels." He intentionally selected a sample stratified by the income areas that the store served and compared prices for the standard list of items given by Holdren. Although the sample was small, the evidence obtained further reinforced the findings reported in this paper. To quote Fendrick, "The results of the price comparison show that the location variable should not be dismissed as a factor in store price structure."

Limitations

The ability to generalize from this section of the study is limited because the work was done entirely within the confines of Monroe County, New York. For this reason, certain ethnic influences exist in the merchandise offered in sample stores. For example, the predominance of southern blacks in certain areas in the central core of Rochester influences the selection of goods available. The comparability of items, a second kind of problem discussed earlier, posed particular difficulties in developing the meat index.

TABLE 12.10
LOW AND HIGH PRICES OF MARKET BASKET ITEMS[a]

	LOW PRICES			
	MAJOR STORES		FILL-IN STORES	
	CHAINS	INDE-PENDENTS	CHAINS	INDE-PENDENTS
Income	GRAND INDEX			
Low	1298.3^a	1412.1^a	1292.1^b	1474.9^b
Middle	1299.2^b	1319.9^b	1298.1^a	1386.6^a
High	1301.5	—	1295.1	1545.7
	GENERAL GOODS INDEX			
Low	364.5^a	404.8^a	363.3^a	417.5^a
Middle	365.2	362.6	368.9	387.3
High	364.9	—	366.1	447.3
	LAUNDRY SOAP INDEX			
Low	213.0^b	236.0^b	202.0^b	243.3^b
Middle	219.5^b	232.0^b	219.0^a	234.3^a
High	224.0	—	210.5	246.5
	COFFEE INDEX			
Low	267.0^a	314.5^a	275.0^b	351.5^b
Middle	279.7	285.0	261.0	303.0
High	285.5	—	268.0^a	336.0^a
	DAIRY INDEX			
Low	213.8	217.2	209.8^a	225.5^a
Middle	210.6	214.3	213.2	214.3
High	210.2	—	211.5	228.9
	MEAT INDEX			
Low	240.0	239.7	242.0	237.2
Middle	224.3	226.0	236.0^a	247.8^a
High	217.0	—	239.0	287.0

[a] Significant at the 5-percent level.
[b] Significant at the 1-percent level. Student's t was used to test differences of means or, when a cell contained only one store, the likelihood of the store's

MAJOR STORES		FILL-IN STORES	
CHAINS	INDE-PENDENTS	CHAINS	INDE-PENDENTS

HIGH PRICES

GRAND INDEX

CHAINS	INDE-PENDENTS	CHAINS	INDE-PENDENTS
1484.7	1445.1	1427.7[a]	1523.3[a]
1460.7[b]	1413.1[b]	1438.6	1443.2
1474.4	—	1433.2	1568.9

GENERAL GOODS INDEX

434.0	425.0	409.0	426.9
426.4[a]	364.9[a]	416.8	412.8
433.2	—	412.9	458.5

LAUNDRY SOAP INDEX

247.0	243.6	239.0	263.0
243.3	245.0	240.0	242.9
245.3	—	239.5	253.0

COFFEE INDEX

345.0[a]	317.0[a]	313.0[a]	358.8[a]
326.3	319.0	321.0	322.8
331.0	—	317.0	338.0

DAIRY INDEX

218.7	220.3	210.7[a]	225.8[a]
216.5	214.7	214.8	217.0
218.5	—	212.8[a]	232.1[a]

MEAT INDEX

240.0	239.7	256.0	237.2
248.0[b]	226.0[b]	246.0	247.8
246.5	—	251.0	287.0

having come from the same population as stores in the other half of each pair.

[a] Taken from Alexis and Simon (1967). Errors in the original table are corrected here.

A third possible source of error is the ability of the individual store to respond to fluctuations in price levels; certain commodities, such as potatoes, experienced wide fluctuations during the time in which the survey was made. Because of inventory positions, such prices may have been more stable in the small independents. There may also be the problem of "traditional" prices which independents may feel more reluctant to violate. Still another drawback is the scheme used for classifying stores as low-, middle-, or high-income units. This kind of error is probably not too great, since the shopping at many independents by low-income people was confirmed in the earlier study.

Conclusions

The 30 to 40 percent of low-income families who do their shopping in independent stores (whether because of actual preference or constraints such as lack of mobility) and who shop the bottom end of the price range, pay higher prices than they would pay if they shopped in chain stores. In actual dollar terms, this premium appears to be of the order of 10 percent. Chains seem to sell over a much wider price range than do independents; the grand index for chain stores used for major shopping by low-income families shows almost a $2.00 spread from the low to the high prices of the market baskets. Similar effects hold for the relative spread between high and low in other income groups too, but the magnitudes are smaller. Generally speaking, it may be argued that chains present a greater opportunity for price savings on an item because of the greater width and depth of their product line.

The market basket may cost low-income families more in independent stores at the low end of the price range and the chains may offer a broader selection of opportunities. Both conditions are due to the same cause—the inability of the small independent to develop privately branded merchandise.

An investigation of the structure of the high-price market baskets shows that differences between independents and chains and between fill-ins and majors are smaller than for the low-price market baskets because in almost all cases the items included are national brands; furthermore, the dispersion of prices for similar items of the national brand, say, one-pound cans of Del Monte peaches, is much smaller than for the generic food item as a whole (i.e., peaches). The work of Boyd and Frank (1966) supports this finding.

Another effect that has been noticed is a U-shaped distribution of prices for independent fill-in stores (see Table 12.10). It was originally speculated that prices might be higher in both lower- and upper-income fill-in stores than in middle-income stores, but obviously for very different reasons. Our data seem to lend some support to this speculation.

In general, the weight of the accumulated evidence suggests that families of lower income pay higher prices for the food commodities they purchase. Additional data collected from the diaries of consumer panel members would be useful in finally establishing the point. Also, none of the studies to date have examined the operating costs and risks for grocery stores serving lower-income families or the rationales of the consumers who shop in these stores. That is, it may now be possible to state that higher prices exist, but their cause is still largely uninvestigated.

13

A FIELD STUDY OF ATTITUDE STRUCTURE AND THE ATTITUDE-BEHAVIOR RELATIONSHIP

JAGDISH N. SHETH

Professor of Business
Department of Business Administration
University of Illinois at Urbana-Champaign

Several researchers in social psychology have suggested a close relationship between *affect* (the individual's like or dislike of an object, concept, or act), *beliefs* (the cognitive structure representing bits of information related to that object, concept, or act), and *behavioral intention* (the tendency to respond to the object, concept, or act by approaching or avoiding it). Rosenberg (1956, 1960), for example, hypothesized that affect is a function of beliefs related to the perceived instrumentality of an object or concept in attaining or blocking a set of relevant valued states, weighted by the relative importances of those valued states. Fishbein (1967), based on Dulany's (1968) theory of propositional control, considers behavioral intention to be a function of two factors: (1) attitude toward a specific act defined in terms of beliefs about the consequences of performing that act, weighted by the evaluation of those beliefs, and (2) social and personal normative beliefs, weighted by motivation to comply. Fishbein (1966), McGuire (1969b), and Scheibe (1970) furnish reviews of different viewpoints.

The underlying objective of all these theories and propositions is to search for an invariant linkage among the three broad areas of psychology that deal with cognitions, affect, and conations (Krech, Crutchfield, and Ballachey, 1962). Unfortunately, this quest for an invariant relationship is still unattained because of a number of factors:

1. Although extensive theoretical thinking is available, there are relatively few studies.

2. Whatever studies have been carried out have suffered from a number of methodological and analytical limitations.

3. Most studies have been conducted in the controlled environment of the laboratory, which makes substantive inferences to the naturalistic environment difficult.

4. Finally, and probably most important, the linkage between attitude or behavioral intention and actual behavior has been elusive even in laboratory settings. This has generated a great deal of pessimism about attitude's power to predict subsequent behavior (Insko, 1967). Worse yet, others have proposed that the causality may be in the opposite direction: attitudes may indeed be determined by the behavior that precedes the formation and, more important, the change in attitude structure (Cohen, 1964; Festinger, 1964). It seems that we need more realistic theories of attitudes as predictors of behavior in which situational factors are consciously taken into account as mediators between attitude and behavior. Rokeach (1968), for example, has emphasized the situational aspects in his distinction between attitude-toward-the-object and attitude-toward-the-situation.

There are two major objectives of this paper:

1. To present a conceptual framework that links cognitive, conative, and affective aspects in a more realistic and comprehensive manner. In particular, it attempts to isolate situational factors that systematically intervene between attitude and behavior.

2. To report a large-scale field study that (a) investigates the structure of attitude components, (b) causally relates attitude with behavior, and (c) provides some operational measures of situational factors.

A THEORY OF ATTITUDE STRUCTURE
AND THE ATTITUDE-BEHAVIOR RELATIONSHIP

Based on the thinking of several researchers, notably Rosenberg (1956, 1960), D. Katz (1960), Dulany (1968), and Fishbein (1967), I have attempted in Figure 13.1 to develop a conceptual framework of the structure of attitudes and the attitude-behavior relationship. This section describes the conceptual framework.

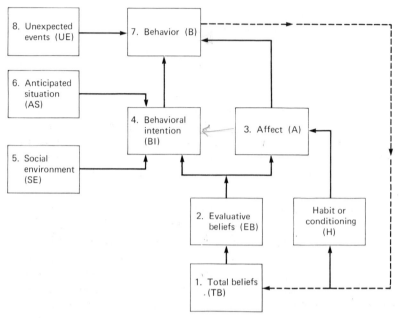

Figure 13.1 Conceptual Theory of Attitude Structure and Attitude–
Behavior Relationship

Total Beliefs

At a point in time, it is hypothesized that an individual has a set
of beliefs about an object or concept. These are his Total Beliefs
(TB). They constitute both the denotative and connotative meanings of the object or concept, regarded from the psycholinguistic
viewpoint (Carroll, 1964; Osgood, 1962). Thus Total Beliefs consist of the descriptive, evaluative, and normative knowledge that
the individual possesses about the concept or object. The Total
Beliefs can be classified into the following six types based on Fishbein's thinking (1967, p. 259):

A. Descriptive Beliefs
    1. Beliefs about the component parts of the object.
    2. Beliefs about the object's relation with other objects.
    3. Beliefs about the characteristics, qualities, or
       attributes of the object.
B. Evaluative Beliefs
    4. Beliefs about whether the object will lead to or block
       the attainment of various goals or valued states.

C. Normative Beliefs
  5. Beliefs about what should be done with respect to the object.
  6. Beliefs about what the object should or should not be allowed to do.

Alternatively, we can think of Total Beliefs as a belief system serving all the four functions suggested by D. Katz (1960). The descriptive beliefs serve the knowledge function; the evaluative beliefs serve the instrumental, utilitarian function; and the normative beliefs serve the ego-defensive function as well as the value-expression function.

Total Beliefs are learned by the individual from both informational sources and personal experiences. The former has been the major study area among the mass communications researchers such as the Yale group of experimental psychologists (e.g., Hovland, Janis, and Kelley, 1953) and the Columbia group of survey sociologists (e.g., E. Katz and Lazarsfeld, 1955). The latter, consisting of cognitive restructuring that arises from behavioral consequences, has been the major thrust of the dissonance theory (Festinger, 1957; Brehm and Cohen, 1962), as well as among the cognitive psychologists who have relied on the learning theory (Doob, 1947; Fishbein, 1967; Osgood, 1957; Osgood, Suci, and Tannenbaum, 1957; Rhine, 1958; Staats, 1967). In Figure 13.1, the dynamics of the interdependent relationship between behavior and the cognitive world is incorporated in the feedback loop.

Evaluative Beliefs

Evaluative Beliefs (EB), by definition, are an element of Total Beliefs. They refer to the cognitions about an object that portray the connotative meaning and knowledge about the object as the goal-object. In other words, Evaluative Beliefs represent the potential of the object to satisfy a set of relevant motives. Therefore, Evaluative Beliefs as defined here are equivalent to the perceived instrumentality component of Rosenberg's (1960) theory of attitude structure. Similarly, the belief structure underlying N. E. Miller's (1959) approach-avoidance gradients would constitute Evaluative Beliefs. Finally, Howard and Sheth (1969) consider Evaluative Beliefs to be the profile of assessment of an object relative to competing objects on a set of choice criteria.

Evaluative Beliefs are the primary determinants of the individual's affective reactions toward an object or concept. In other words, a person has a favorable-unfavorable, like-dislike, love-hate, or good-bad reaction toward an object or concept because of the connotative meaning of that object as a relevant or salient instrument of satisfying some motive. We are here ignoring the development of affective tendencies that are due solely to habit or conditioning as suggested by, for example, D. Katz and Stotland (1959). Later we shall incorporate affective tendencies both with and without a cognitive structure.

Evaluative Beliefs are likely to vary from object to object in complexity and intensity. Furthermore, it is presumed that in repetitive goal-directed behaviors, the structure of Evaluative Beliefs becomes more streamlined and stable as learning of the behavior becomes greater. Evaluative Beliefs, however, are at least multivariate (several distinct although interrelated cognitions) with some fundamental underlying multidimensional structure.

Affect

Affect (A) represents the positive or negative predisposition toward the object as a goal-object. To that extent, affective tendencies not anchored to the goal-attaining or goal-blocking properties of the object are ignored here. Therefore, affect here is close to the classic definition of attitude as "a disposition to evaluate certain objects, actions, and situations in certain ways" (Chein, 1948).

As stated earlier, Affect is a function of Evaluative Beliefs. However, I also believe that affective tendency exists without a structure of Evaluative Beliefs because it is likely to be determined by the habit or conditioning process (H). Affective tendency is likely to be especially common among infants and young children.

Affect is likely to be determined differentially by each Evaluative Belief. It is, therefore, possible to examine the structure of Evaluative Beliefs in terms of the degree to which each Evaluative Belief, relative to others, governs affective tendency. I presume that only a handful of Evaluative Beliefs typically determine, therefore correlate with, Affect, although theoretically one can find a large number of "salient" Evaluative Beliefs. This phenomenon can be partly explained in terms of George Miller's (1956) theory of "The Magical Number Seven." Another point to keep in mind is the possibility that there may be individual differences in regard to whether Evaluative Beliefs are greater or lesser determinants of affective tendency.

Affect is presumed to be univariate and unidimensional, although we should realize that there is a complex cognitive structure underlying it.

The algebraic function of Affect is stated as

$$A_{ij} = f\ (\mathrm{EB}_{ijk},\ H_{ij}) \tag{1}$$

where $A_{ij} =$ individual i's affect toward object j
  $\mathrm{EB}_{ijk} =$ individual i's kth evaluative belief about the object j
  $H_{ij} =$ habit or conditioning toward object j.

This general equation can be made more explicit in a specific investigation by determining a priori a finite number of criteria that the individual utilizes to evaluate the object or concept as the goal-object. However, we often lack such a priori judgment and are obliged to rely on empirical findings regarding which Evaluative Beliefs correlate with Affect.

It is also possible to think that each Evaluative Belief partially and incrementally contributes toward a fuller determination of Affect. Furthermore, Evaluative Beliefs may be positively or negatively related to Affect because most choice situations tend to be of the approach-avoidance type: the goal-object both attains and blocks a set of motives or goals underlying the choice criteria. To bring these ideas into focus, we can reformulate the first equation in terms of a linear additive model:

$$A_{ij} = b_1[\mathrm{EB}_{1ij}] + b_2[\mathrm{EB}_{2ij}] + \cdots$$
$$+ b_n[\mathrm{EB}_{nij}] + b_{n+1}[H_{ij}] \tag{2}$$

In formulating this linear additive model, I am departing from the standard thinking in social psychology (e.g., Fishbein, 1967; Rosenberg, 1960) of summing the beliefs to produce a univariate attitude score, which is then correlated with Affect. I have found (Sheth, 1973) that prior summing of beliefs consistently lowers the correlation between Evaluative Beliefs and Affect. In addition, we can give at least the following arguments against the summing of beliefs:

1. We have no reason not to expect the individual to retain a *profile* of his beliefs rather than a sum score. Most evidence in the literature on information processing supports the argument that the individual distinctly retains or files his beliefs about the object.

2. Beliefs are typically measured on a bipolar scale; therefore, summing them entails a compromise (average) value that may be nothing more than a statistical artifact.

3. Beliefs can be positive or negative. Summing them pre-

sumes that one cancels out the other. Another major difference is the explicit possibility of Affect being present in some situations without a cognitive structure. Such a possibility was first systematically suggested by D. Katz and Stotland (1959) and amplified by Triandis (1971).

Behavioral Intention

Behavioral Intention (BI) refers to the plan or commitment of the individual expressed at time t about how likely he is to behave in a specific way toward the object or concept at the time $t + 1$. We must remember that the individual can behave toward an object or concept in many different ways; however, we are primarily concerned with his behavior that treats the object or concept as the goal-object. In other words, we want to investigate behavior toward the object or concept that will lead to attaining or blocking a set of motives or goals.

Behavioral Intention is hypothesized to be a function of (1) Evaluative Beliefs about the object and, therefore, also Affect toward the object; (2) the Social Environment (SE) that surrounds the individual and normatively guides his behavior (i.e., what he should and should not do); and (3) the Anticipated Situation (AS), which includes the situational factors related to behavior that he could anticipate, and thus forecast at the time of expressing his plan or commitment.

Implicitly, therefore, Behavioral Intention is a *qualified* expression of behavior: given such-and-such environment and other contingencies to happen at $t + 1$, when behavior is likely to be manifested, the individual estimates at t whether he would or would not behave. This is important to emphasize because we may predict Behavioral Intention very well but not the actual behavior, since (1) anticipated social and situational factors may change and, therefore, behavior may not materialize as planned or forecasted, and (2) other unanticipated factors may impinge on behavior in a manner that deviates considerably from the individual's plan.

Evidently the influence of anticipated and unanticipated social and situational factors can be minimized if the time interval between Behavioral Intention and actual behavior is reduced. Theoretically, we can produce a very high positive correlation between Behavioral Intention and actual behavior if the two are measured contiguously in time and space, because then we allow no freedom for outside factors to intervene and mediate.

Algebraically, we can write the following function of Behavioral Intention:[1]

$$BI_{ij} = f \ (EB_{ijk}, SE_{ij}, AS_{ij}) \tag{3}$$

where BI_{ij} = individual i's plan to behave in a certain way toward object j
$EB_{ijk}{}^1$ = individual i's belief k about object j
SE_{ij} = individual i's Social Environment impinging on his behavior toward j
AS_{ij} = individual i's anticipation of events at the time of his behavior toward j.

It is possible that the three factors (EB, SE, and AS) may act as opposing forces, resulting in conflict. For example, an individual may very much want to buy and use a Rolls Royce but be unable to afford one; or he may like a Cadillac and be able to afford it but be inhibited by his social environment from buying one if Cadillacs are socially unacceptable as goal-objects. Consumer psychologists have learned that it is common among working housewives to encounter such conflicts regarding many convenience (instant) foods. Reciprocally, it is also possible for the three factors additively to contribute or facilitate the qualified expression of behavior. Perhaps it is more common to find this facilitating or supportive role.

We can express the facilitating or inhibiting relationship among the three factors with respect to the determination of Behavioral Intention by writing the general equation as a linear additive model:

$$BI_{ij} = b_1[EB_{ijk}] + b_2[SE_{ij}] + b_3[AS_{ij}] \tag{4}$$

It should be pointed out, however, that this model is simply a hypothesis that should be tested because we do not know how the three factors interact with one another.

Social Environment

Social Environment (SE) includes all the social factors that are likely to impinge on and provide a set of normative beliefs to the

[1] It is possible to use Affect as a surrogate for Evaluative Beliefs, since it is determined by the latter. In fact, when Affect is primarily determined by conditioning, it may be superior to Evaluative Beliefs as a predictor variable.

individual about how he should behave toward the object or concept at time $t + 1$. Most of these social factors are likely to be anchored to the demographic, socioeconomic, and role-oriented images of the object or concept. For example, the individual may have the image of hair spray as a feminine product, used mostly by the lower socioeconomic class and clerical workers. In consumer psychology, we think the following specific factors and their categorizations may be relevant: (1) sex, (2) age, (3) education, (4) occupational styles, (5) wealth, (6) life cycle, (7) family orientation, and (8) life styles. This list is by no means exhaustive, nor is it postulated that all the factors are impinging on a specific behavior. Indeed, it would be suggested that beliefs about the influence of the Social Environment should be empirically determined for each situation under investigation. However, Social Environment clearly includes a brand's stereotype.

Anticipated Situation

The Anticipated Situation (AS) factor includes all the other activities that the individual is likely to engage in at the time of future behavior as he perceives and forecasts them now when expressing his plan or intention to behave. These anticipated events may enhance or inhibit the Behavioral Intention as determined by Affect or Social Environment, or they may do both. For example, because of a planned move to a large metropolitan area, the individual may commit himself to riding on the mass transit system even though he dislikes it and his social environment is neutral to the situation. Similarly, the individual may desire a new personal luxury car and his social environment may also support this desire, but financial constraints as projected to the next one or two years inhibit his intention to buy it.

The Anticipated Situation factor is presumed to be much more situation bound and ad hoc than the Social Environment factor. Accordingly, it is very difficult to develop an invariant list of variables as indicators of the Anticipated Situation factor. Once again, we must empirically determine the presence or absence of this factor in each investigation. However, based on some existing empirical evidence, we can list the following general causes that lead to the presence of Anticipated Situation affecting the neat relationship between Evaluative Beliefs or Affect and Behavioral Intention: (1) cyclical phenomena such as holidays, vacations, birthdays, schooling, and education; (2) anticipated mobility (since mobility is very prevalent and increasing, a number of buying decisions may be strictly due to this factor); and (3) financial status of the decision maker, including anticipated incomes and expenditures.

Behavior

Behavior (B) refers to a specific act under investigation that is manifested at a specific time and under specific conditions. In the buyer behavior area, for example, this may mean the purchase of a brand of television set from a particular store on a particular day. We are not, therefore, interested in predicting generalized behavior that has no situational influences. For example, brand loyalty of the individual in buyer behavior, measured either by actual observations of repeat patterns of purchases or by a verbal self-reporting scale, is likely to be a generalized act in which situational influences at each purchase occasion are ignored or at least deemphasized.

Behavior is hypothesized to be a function of the individual's Affect (with or without cognitive structure), Behavioral Intention, and a set of Unexpected Events (UE) that impinge on Behavior and that the individual could not predict at the time of verbally expressing his Behavioral Intention. By definition, if Affect and Behavioral Intention were expressed just prior to the act of behavior, the Unexpected Events factor would probably be absent. Thus in most laboratory experimental studies both Affect and Behavioral Intention can be treated as equivalent to Behavior because they are expressed contiguously to Behavior both in time and space, which means that very few nonpredictable or unexpected events cause Behavior to deviate from the verbally expressed Behavioral Intention. However, in the naturalistic settings of the real world, we must expect a lack of contiguity between Behavioral Intention and Behavior due to the problems of data collection. This enables the Unexpected Events factor to exert an influence on Behavior. The greater the lack of contiguity in time and space, the greater should be the opportunity for the Behavior to be also influenced by the Unexpected Events factor. In buyer behavior, considerable empirical evidence exists in the area of durable appliances to support this hypothesis.

Mathematically, we can state that

$$B_{ijt} = f(A_{ij,t-n}, BI_{ij,t-n}, UE_{ijt}) \qquad (5)$$

where B_{ijt} = a specific act of behavior manifested by individual i at time t toward object j

$A_{ij,t-n}$ = Affect toward the object (with or without cognitive structure), expressed at time $t - n$

$BI_{ij,t-n}$ = individual i's plan to behave in a certain way toward object j, as expressed at some time interval n, prior to actual behavior

UE_{ijt} = Unexpected Events experienced by individual i at the time of behavior t toward object j.

We also presume that Affect and Behavioral Intention are uncorrelated with Unexpected Events and that Unexpected Events can either enhance or inhibit the conversion of Affect and Behavioral Intention into actual Behavior. Under these assumptions, the following linear additive model can be established:

$$B_{ijt} = b_1[A_{ij,t-n}] + b_2[BI_{ijt,t-n}] + b_3[UE_{ijt}] \tag{6}$$

It is my belief that the failure of attitudes (Affect or Behavioral Intention) to predict subsequent Behavior is primarily due to the presence and influence of the Unexpected Events factor and not, as suggested in social psychology, simply due to the problems of definition and measurement.

The foregoing model also provides an explanation for habitual behavior based on conditioning, reasoning (intentional behavior), and unplanned or random behavior. Therefore, it allows for the possibility of behavior being determined both by a plan and by random events.

Unexpected Events

The Unexpected Events (UE) factor refers to the antecedent and contiguous stimuli that impinge on the individual at the time of the behavior under investigation. In other words, it refers to the situational environment surrounding the specific act of behavior. In buyer behavior, the Unexpected Events factor can be illustrated by the announcement of the supermarket sale of a competing brand, which influences the purchase plan of the housewife. It is my contention that the influence of Unexpected Events is very much underrepresented in studies of buying behavior because of our zeal to give a rational explanation for all behavior. In other words, in buyer behavior we have based our thinking on the assumption that all buying decisions are intentional behavior. We all know very well that this is not the case. It is therefore critical to examine more fully the nature and typology of the Unexpected Events factor. Some research has already begun under the rubric of impulse purchase behavior, novelty seeking, and venturesomeness of the buyer.

CANONICAL CORRELATIONS FORMULATION

In the preceding section I described the conceptual model of the structure of attitudes and the attitude-behavior relationship. We may test each of the linkages in the model by simply obtaining relevant data for each of the equations in the preceding section (see Sheth, 1971). However, it is obvious that the conceptual theory has a set of constructs that are in a sequential form; thus a given construct is determined by other constructs and also determines some other constructs. This enables us to use the method of canonical correlations to test simultaneously all the relationships proposed in the theory. The rationale is developed below.

In Figure 13.1, Behavior (B) is a function of Affect (A), Behavioral Intention (BI), and Unexpected Events (UE). Thus

$$B = f(A, BI, UE) \tag{7}$$

Behavioral Intention (BI) itself is a function of Evaluative Beliefs (EB), Anticipated Situation (AS), and Social Environment (SE). Hence

$$BI = g(EB, AS, SE) \tag{8}$$

Finally, Affect (A) is a function of a set of Evaluative Beliefs (EB). Therefore

$$A = h(EB_k); \quad k = 1, 2, \ldots, n \tag{9}$$

It is obvious that Evaluative Beliefs are central both to the understanding of various dimensions of attitude structure and to the prediction of behavior. If we assume that all the above functions are at least monotonic and probably also linear, we can set up a canonical correlation function in which B, BI, and A are all simultaneously a function of the set of Evaluative Beliefs. Thus we have

$$(B, BI, A) = p(EB_1, EB_2, \ldots, EB_n) \tag{10}$$

Since SE, AS, and UE are also determinants of BI and B but not of A, it is logical to assume that Evaluative Beliefs will predict Affect much better than they will predict Behavioral Intention and that they will predict the latter better than they will predict Behavior. To see the difference in predictive power, we can set up another canonical correlation function that includes these environmental factors. Therefore,

$$(B, BI, A) = f(EB_1\ EB_2, \ldots, EB_n, SE, AS, UE) \qquad (11)$$

This equation represents a full test of the conceptual theory. Now to include the individual differences and lack of contiguity between behavior and attitudes, (11) can be made specific to an individual i behaving toward an object j at time t:

$$(B_{ijt}, BI_{ij,t-n}, A_{ij,t-n}) = f(EB_{1ij,t-n}, EB_{2ij,t-n}, \ldots,$$
$$EB_{nij,t-n}, SE_{ij,t-n}, AS_{ij,t-n}, UE_{ijt}) \qquad (12)$$

The canonical function in (12) represents a full test of the model.

DESCRIPTION OF DATA
AND OPERATIONAL DEFINITIONS

The empirical investigation of the relationships among beliefs, affect, behavioral intention, and behavior is based on data collected in a large-scale study that attempted to test the Howard-Sheth (1969) theory of buyer behavior. The theory of buyer behavior provides a description and explanation of the consumer's brand choice process and the development of brand loyalty over time. At the core of the theory is the concept of expectancy developed primarily by the process of learning from informational and experiential sources.

Based on standard probability sampling procedures, a longitudinal panel of 954 housewives was established. The panel members recorded in diaries their purchases of several convenience food products, including instant breakfast, for a five-month period (May through October 1966). In addition to recording their buying behavior, including the place of purchase, the time, the amount, and the price of the products, the panel members were interviewed four times. The first interview was by way of a mail questionnaire sent out at the time of recruiting, requesting information on the housewife's home involvement, her family's breakfast eating habits, and her attitudes and opinions on several milk additive products, including instant breakfast, and so on. One month later, during a telephone interview, information was obtained on the respondent's awareness, knowledge, preference, and intentions regarding three brands of instant breakfast. Two of these brands were introduced to the market soon after the recruitment and establishment of the panel, whereas the third brand was well known because it had been on the market for at least two years prior to the study. The second and third interviews were also conducted by telephone and essentially obtained the same information as the first telephone interview.

The data relevant to this study pertain to a well-known brand of instant breakfast, which we shall call CIB. The object in question is, therefore, a *brand* of instant breakfast, and this investigation examines the interrelationships among Evaluative Beliefs, Affect, Buying Intention, and buying Behavior toward the CIB brand of instant breakfast. The attitudinal data utilized in this study came from the mail questionnaire and the first two telephone interviews. The behavioral data came from the recorded diaries.

The following are the operational definitions of Affect, Buying Intention, Evaluative Beliefs, buying Behavior, Social Environment, Anticipated Situation, and Unexpected Events:

Affect (A). Overall like or dislike of a brand of instant breakfast at the time of interview. The specific rating scale used was the following:

> In general, I
> like it very   □ □ □ □ □ □ □   In general I
> much   don't like it

Buying Intention (BI). Verbal expression of intent to buy the brand of instant breakfast within some specified time period from the time of interview. The particular scale used was the following:

> How likely are you to buy____in the next month?
> □ Definitely will
> □ Probably will
> □ Not sure one way or the other
> □ Probably will not
> □ Definitely will not

Evaluative Beliefs (EB). Evaluation of a brand of instant breakfast in terms of certain characteristics that are anchored to blocking or attaining a set of valued states or choice criteria. Seven Evaluative Beliefs were obtained from the respondent about each of the three brands of instant breakfast during each of the three telephone interviews. The particular characteristics of the brands and the associated criteria of choice were based on a prior depth-interviewing of 100 housewives on milk additive products including instant breakfast. The seven Evaluative Beliefs about a brand were obtained by the following bipolar rating scales.

.

Delicious tasting ☐☐☐☐☐☐☐ Not delicious tasting
Good substitute for ☐☐☐☐☐☐☐ Poor substitute for a meal
a meal
Very nutritious ☐☐☐☐☐☐☐ Somewhat nutritious
Very good for a ☐☐☐☐☐☐☐ Not good for a snack
snack
Very filling ☐☐☐☐☐☐☐ Not very filling
Good buy for the ☐☐☐☐☐☐☐ Not a good buy for the money
money
Good source of ☐☐☐☐☐☐☐ Poor source of protein
protein

Behavior (B). Purchase of a brand of instant breakfast during the five months of panel operation was the specific act of behavior under investigation. It was operationally measured from the reported purchases of a brand of instant breakfast as recorded in the diary that panel members filled out every two weeks. Two types of measures were used in this study. One was the number of purchases of a brand between two telephone interviews; the other was a classificatory measure of buying at least once or not buying at all. The latter is utilized in the canonical function tested in the next section.

Social Environment (SE). Social normative beliefs about the appropriateness of buying and consuming instant breakfast. These normative beliefs were obtained from a projective-type question in which respondents were asked to agree or disagree with the following characterizations of persons who consume instant breakfast:

A. People who are health conscious
B. People who have a health problem
C. People who want quick energy
D. People who are in a hurry at meals
E. People who like snacks
F. People who are lazy
G. People who don't like breakfast

Anticipated Situation (AS). The anticipated situational factors that are likely to impinge on the purchase of CIB. Howard and Sheth (1969, chap. 4) present a number of "inhibitors" that presumably dampen a buyer's affect in expressing behavioral intention. The following factors were extracted from the mail questionnaire as indicators of AS:

A. Budget determines what we eat
B. Do check prices of food items
C. Differences in price among brands are interesting to compare
D. Go to other stores for sale items

Unexpected Events (UE). The situational factors impinging on the purchase of CIB that could not be anticipated or forecast by the respondent. The factors were obtained by direct questioning of the respondent if she did not buy CIB although she had expressed an intention to buy it. Two such factors were used in this study:

A. Tried to buy, but CIB wasn't available
B. Number of hours per week the housewife works

It must be pointed out that whereas the operational definitions of B, BI, A, EB, and SE seem to be quite satisfactory, those of AS and UE are probably not exhaustive. To that extent, the study suffers from weak data. However, both AS and UE are very much situation bound and mostly empirical. They are, therefore, most difficult to observe and measure.

In using data from this large-scale, naturalistic study, as opposed to several experimental studies found in social psychology, we seem to obtain the following advantages:

1. The study was conducted in naturalistic environment that dealt with a real situation. It was conducted in cooperation with a large grocery company that was test marketing one of the brands of instant breakfast. It thus reduced the burden of substantive and statistical inference from a simulated laboratory-type situation to reality. In short, many of the differences that Hovland (1959) pointed out between experimental and survey findings are absent here.

2. The sample size of this study was large enough to justify statistical faith in the findings. In addition, the sample was based on standard probability sampling procedures.

3. Due to the cooperation of the company, a unique situation was created in which beliefs, affect, and behavioral intention preceded actual behavior, since the product had not been introduced to the market at the time of the first interview and, therefore, no one could buy it.

4. This was a longitudinal study in which we could use time as a factor to build the direction of causation between attitude and behavior. Therefore, it was possible to measure prior attitudes for predicting subsequent behavior and also use prior behavior as a predictor of subsequent attitudes.

FINDINGS AND DISCUSSION

The model presented earlier was tested in two stages. The first stage consisted of the canonical correlation of Affect, Behavioral Intention, and Behavior only on Evaluative Beliefs. This was done primarily to examine the relative predictive power of Evaluative Beliefs across three criterion variables. The model appropriate for this stage of the analysis is given in (10).

Three separate canonical analyses were performed by utilizing measurements of (1) Evaluative Beliefs, Affect, and Behavioral Intention from the mail questionnaire and the first two telephone interviews, and (2) Purchase Behavior from the biweekly diary records between the mail questionnaire and the first telephone interview, between the first and the second telephone interviews, and finally between the second and the last telephone interviews.

If the conceptual theory and the mathematical models are correct, we should expect to predict Affect best, Behavioral Intention less well, and Purchase Behavior even less well from a set of Evaluative Beliefs. This is because Behavioral Intention is also governed by other factors and Behavior is governed by still one more factor, as shown in Figure 13.1.

Results of the canonical analysis are presented in Table 13.1. The first two canonical correlations were significant at least at the 5-percent level, and they are retained for interpretation and discussion. However, the canonical correlation of the second linear compound is only around .200, and it explains only about 5 percent of the additional variance in the criterion set. Therefore, it obtains its significance status primarily from the large number of degrees of freedom that result in the chance expectation of near-zero canonical correlation.

Examination of the variance explained in each of the criterion variables confirms quite well the expectations of the model. The variance in Affect is explained the most (between 53 and 65 percent), in Behavioral Intention the second most (between 32 and 37 percent), and in Purchase Behavior the least (between 8 and 10 percent). The extreme drop in the ability of Evaluative Beliefs to predict Purchase Behavior simply confirms the findings of other studies conducted in naturalistic settings regarding the limited usefulness of attitudes in predicting subsequent behavior. Evidently many Unexpected Events or random factors vitiate the presumed neat attitude-behavior relationship so popular in experimental and social psychology.

Another aspect of interest in the canonical analysis is the structure of the relationship between the predictor and the criterion variables. In other words, which Evaluative Beliefs are more salient as determinants of Affect, Behavioral Intention, and Behavior? Do the same Evaluative Beliefs have equal saliency for the prediction of all the three dependent variables, or is there a classification (typology) of beliefs such that some are determinants of Affect, others of Behavioral Intention, and still others of Purchase Behavior? According to the theory presented in Figure 13.1, we should expect some beliefs to determine Affect and others to determine Behavioral Intention; but both types of beliefs should determine Behavior by being mediated through either Affect or Behavioral Intention.

To examine the typology or structure we need two things. First, the Evaluative Beliefs must be uncorrelated, allowing us to avoid the problem of multicollinearity. Fortunately, this was true for our data, since we had eliminated six other Evaluative Beliefs, such as flavor, reasonable price, and calories, based on the high intercorrelations with the seven beliefs kept in the analysis. Second, the canonical axes solution suffers from the same problem of lack of invariance as does factor analysis or discriminant analysis because all are special cases of one another and utilize the same theory of characteristic equations. The only difference among these three multivariate methods is the manner in which the researcher partitions his data matrix. In factor analysis, the variance-covariance of the total matrix is maximized; in discriminant analysis, the sampling observations are partitioned into mutually exclusive and exhaustive groups based on some theory of group differences; and in canonical correlation analysis, the variables are partitioned into two or more groups based on some theory of the structure of variable relationships. In all these methods, we need to utilize principles of judgment that will enable the researcher to choose the one set of canonical coefficients that is most meaningful from a certain viewpoint. These judgments are Thurstone's principles of simple structure for rotating axes in a way that brings out in bold relief the structure of relationships among variables. Accordingly, a rotation was performed on the canonical analysis results given in Table 13.1 with the use of orthogonal varimax rotation.

The rotated canonical coefficients are presented in Table 13.2.

TABLE 13.1
CANONICAL ANALYSIS OF AFFECT, BEHAVIORAL
INTENTION, AND PURCHASE BEHAVIOR AS A
FUNCTION OF EVALUATIVE BELIEFS

| | MAIL QUESTIONNAIRE | | |
| | CANONICAL AXES | | |
	I	II	R^2
Criterion Set			
Affect	.873	−.983	.528
Behavioral intention	.166	1.239	.322
Purchase behavior	.029	.124	.103
Predictor Set			
Delicious tasting	.617	−.653	
Good buy	.195	.678	
Meal substitute	.176	.695	
Snack	.141	.168	
Protein source	.097	−.501	
Filling	.094	−.101	
Nutritious	.015	.013	
Canonical R	.733[a]	.236[a]	
Canonical R^2	.537	.056	
		$n = 668$	

[a] Significant at .05 level.

An examination of the large coefficients in that table suggests that Affect was primarily determined by "taste" and somewhat by "protein source" and "filling quality of the instant breakfast." On the other hand, Behavioral Intention and to some extent Purchase Behavior were primarily determined by "good buy" and "meal substitute" and somewhat by "nutritious" and "filling quality of the instant breakfast." Finally, Affect lies in one domain of the two-dimensional space and Behavioral Intention and Purchase Behavior lie in some other domain. In other words, if Affect and Behaviorial Intention were used as predictors of Purchase Behavior, Behavioral Intention would prove a better predictor than Affect. This is also expected from the model presented earlier in the paper.

A final point to discuss is the role of feedback from Purchase Behavior in the development of habit or conditioning. As the consumer buys the product, he should develop conditioning effects

FIRST TELEPHONE INTERVIEW (T_1) CANONICAL AXES			SECOND TELEPHONE INTERVIEW (T_2) CANONICAL AXES		
I	II	R^2	I	II	R^2
.806	−.935	.538	.850	−.736	.646
.281	1.010	.345	.237	.716	.367
−.004	.391	.080	−.025	.682	.084
.710	−.670		.701	−.676	
.176	.754		.213	.399	
.121	.518		.118	.617	
.072	.190		.123	.383	
.082	−.271		.010	.453	
.116	.238		.101	−.737	
.020	−.415		−.017	−.008	
.751[a]	.181[a]		.818[a]	.200[a]	
.564	.033		.669	.040	
	$n = 604$			$n = 553$	

that must at least strengthen the relationship of Affect and Behavioral Intention with Evaluative Beliefs. We see this from the slight increase in the explained variance in the second telephone interview as compared with the mail questionnaire.

Having examined the magnitude and structure of the relationship between Evaluative Beliefs and Affect, Behavioral Intention, and Purchase Behavior, let us test the full model presented in Figure 13.1 and in (12). We should expect an increase in the explained variance of the criterion set by including variables related to Social Environment, Anticipated Situation, and Unexpected Events. Furthermore, the increase in the explained variance should come primarily in Behavioral Intention and Purchase Behavior, since these are all directly related to the three added factors. In short, the variance explained in Affect should remain unchanged but the explained variance in Behavioral Intention or Behavior or both should increase depending on the impact of the three factors.

TABLE 13.2

ROTATED CANONICAL AXES OF BELIEF MODEL

| | MAIL QUESTIONNAIRE | | |
| | CANONICAL AXES | | |
	I	II	R^2
Criterion Set			
Affect	1.30	−.20	.528
Behavioral intention	−.66	1.06	.322
Purchase behavior	−.06	.11	.103
Predictor Set			
Delicious tasting	.89	−.11	
Good buy	−.28	.65	
Meal substitute	−.31	.65	
Snack	.00	.22	
Protein source	.39	−.32	
Filling	.14	−.02	
Nutritious	.00	.02	
		$n = 668$	

A second set of canonical analyses was performed on a smaller set of individuals; the criterion set remained the same, but the predictor set now consisted of Evaluative Beliefs, Social Environment, Anticipated Situation, and Unexpected Events. The results are summarized in Table 13.3. All the three canonical axes were significant at least at the 5-percent level, even though the last canonical correlation hovered around .200 and the additional variance explained by the third canonical axis was only around 5 percent. Once again the significance was due to the large number of degrees of freedom in the data.

As the explained variances of each of the criterion variables indicate, the variance explained in Affect remained virtually the same despite the additional predictor variables included in the analysis. This is clearly a very good support for part of the full model specified in Figure 13.1. The amount of variance explained in Behavioral Intention jumped somewhat; thus the additional variables contributed toward an increase of about 10 percent in the explained variance. Behavioral Intention's variance changed from around 35 percent with Evaluative Beliefs alone to around 45 percent with the additional variables.

FIRST TELEPHONE INTERVIEW (T_1) CANONICAL AXES			SECOND TELEPHONE INTERVIEW (T_2) CANONICAL AXES		
I	II	R^2	I	II	R^2
1.19	−.33	.538	1.11	−.18	.646
−.33	1.00	.345	−.17	.73	.376
−.22	.32	.080	−.38	.57	.084
.96	−.16		.95	−.21	
−.27	.72		−.03	.45	
−.19	.50		−.22	.59	
−.05	.20		−.10	.39	
.22	−.18		−.23	.39	
−.04	.26		.47	−.58	
.25	−.33		−.01	−.02	
$n = 604$			$n = 553$		

Finally, the variance explained in Purchase Behavior jumped considerably with the utilization of the full model. From an average of about 9 percent with Evaluative Beliefs alone, the explained variance increased to around 24 percent with the additional variables.

To allow us to examine the source and structure of covariances with the predictor variables, the canonical axes were rotated with the use of orthogonal varimax rotation. The rotated canonical coefficients are given in Table 13.4. Examination of the third canonical axis on which Affect loads heavily shows that none of the additional variables relates significantly to Affect through it. This is what we should expect if the full model is correctly specified.

Examination of the canonical axis on which Behavioral Intention loads heavily reveals that a number of variables from the Social Environment and Anticipated Situation factors are loaded on it. These include "lazy," "have health problem," "like snacks," "want quick energy," and "don't like breakfast" from the Social Environment factor, and "brand price differences interesting" and "check food prices" from the Anticipated Situation factor. Unfortunately,

TABLE 13.3

CANONICAL ANALYSIS OF AFFECT, BEHAVIORAL INTENTION,
AND PURCHASE BEHAVIOR AS A FUNCTION OF EVALUATIVE
BELIEFS AND SOCIAL AND SITUATIONAL FACTORS

MAIL QUESTIONNAIRE

CANONICAL AXES

	I	II	III	R^2
Criterion Set				
Affect	.731	−.990	.440	.555
Behavioral intention	.307	.794	−1.098	.439
Purchase behavior	.094	.605	.960	.242
Predictor Set				
Delicious tasting	.500	−.501	.592	
Good buy	.175	.121	−.449	
Meal substitute	.162	.241	.260	
Snack	.080	−.023	.015	
Protein source	.095	−.254	.317	
Filling	.062	−.263	−.262	
Nutritious	.024	.052	.085	
Lazy	.096	−.074	−.485	
Have health problem	.062	−.027	.113	
Health conscious	.051	.158	−.211	
Like Snacks	.033	−.059	−.211	
Want quick energy	.019	.095	−.190	
Rushed at meals	−.026	.057	.278	
Don't like breakfast	−.113	.006	.432	
Brand price differences interesting	.003	−.075	.006	
Switch stores for sales	−.015	.001	−.252	
Budget determines menu	−.070	.003	.262	
CIB unavailable	.276	.800	.280	
Hr/wk wife works	.044	.065	.057	
Check food prices	.022	−.196	−.171	
Canonical R	.765[a]	.448[a]	.219[a]	
Canonical R^2	.585	.201	.048	

$n = 631$

[a] = Significant at .05 level.

there is no stability among the three separate analyses. This may
be due to the likelihood of multicollinearity among the variables
comprising the two factors.

Finally, most of the increased variance in Purchase Behavior

FIRST TELEPHONE INTERVIEW (T_1) CANONICAL AXES				SECOND TELEPHONE INTERVIEW (T_2) CANONICAL AXES			
I	II	III	R^2	I	II	III	R^2
.715	−.771	−.727	.582	.806	−.676	−.698	.681
.328	.404	1.233	.445	.268	.481	1.191	.459
.111	.865	−.675	.241	.026	.842	−.679	.233
.591	−.551	−.457		.647	−.528	−.440	
.190	.323	.533		.186	.072	.186	
.076	.171	.079		.130	.217	−.100	
.073	−.009	.046		.118	.064	.102	
.020	−.204	.169		.017	.214	.144	
.092	−.090	.290		.055	−.355	−.137	
.013	−.194	−.407		−.016	−.062	.454	
.115	−.359	.499		.059	−.291	.397	
.070	.475	.297		−.010	.234	−.142	
−.023	−.311	−.482		−.074	−.160	−.270	
−.120	−.208	.571		.028	−.291	.929	
.136	.284	.394		.081	.361	.345	
−.001	.522	−.540		.037	.356	−.658	
−.115	−.049	−.276		−.186	.141	−.710	
.002	.258	−.380		.028	.199	.688	
−.049	−.054	.147		−.011	−.302	.035	
.072	.072	−.011		.002	.069	.181	
.301	.747	−.256		.184	.789	−.073	
.071	.001	−.354		−.005	−.042	−.162	
−.015	−.619	−.221		.009	−.294	−.416	
.793	.390	.223		.843	.447	.203	
.629	.152	.050		.711	.200	.041	
	$n = 502$				$n = 454$		

comes from a single situational variable, namely, nonavailability of CIB brand of instant breakfast. This is a dramatic example of the role of the Unexpected Events factor in the prediction of behavior in natural settings. Unfortunately, there are too many situational events that inhibit or precipitate actual behavior that is often contrary to the cognitive structure about the object and the situation.

TABLE 13.4
ROTATED CANONICAL ANALYSIS OF THE MODEL

| | MAIL QUESTIONNAIRE | | | |
| | ROTATED AXES | | | |
	I	II	III	R^2
Criterion Set				
Affect	−.36	−.37	1.20	.555
Behavioral intention	1.31	.19	−.41	.439
Purchase behavior	−.55	.99	.04	.242
Predictor Set				
Delicious tasting	−.43	.04	.82	
Good buy	.49	−.07	−.03	
Meal substitute	−.06	.37	.09	
Snack	.01	.01	.08	
Protein source	−.30	−.02	.28	
Filling	.15	−.32	.10	
Nutritious	−.04	.09	.01	
Lazy	.42	−.27	−.01	
Have health problem	−.07	.05	.09	
Health conscious	.25	.04	−.09	
Like snacks	.17	−.14		
Want quick energy	.20	−.01	−.08	
Rushed at meals	−.22	.18	.03	
Don't like breakfast	−.41	.18	.02	
Brand price differences	−.03	−.05	.04	
Switch stores for sales	.20	−.13	−.08	
Budget determines menu	−.25	.12	.01	
CIB unavailable	.16	.87	−.07	
Hr/wk wife works	−.01	.09	.02	
Check food prices	.09	−.24	.06	
		$n = 631$		

In addition, some of the variables in the Social Environment and Anticipated Situation factors also seem to contribute toward the prediction of Purchase Behavior. These include "rushed at meals," "like snacks," and "brand price differences interesting." Since all these variables seem to be compensatory to Evaluative Beliefs, even a negative evaluation of the brand is not enough to stop Purchase Behavior due to these variables.

Once again we see that the explained variance in Affect and Behavioral Intention improves slightly in the second telephone interview analysis compared with the mail questionnaire analysis. This somewhat supports the feedback aspects of the model.

FIRST TELEPHONE INTERVIEW (T_1) ROTATED AXES				SECOND TELEPHONE INTERVIEW (T_2) ROTATED AXES			
I	II	III	R^2	I	II	III	R^2
−.71	.06	1.05	.582	−.01	−.27	1.23	.684
1.19	−.60	−.07	.445	−.24	1.18	−.50	.459
.16	1.08	−.04	.241	1.06	−.15	−.08	.233
−.44		.82		−.06	−.12	.93	
.63	−.15	−.03		−.01	.27	.04	
.19	.06			.25	.08	.04	
.05	−.03	.06		.01	.16	.02	
−.02	−.26	.05		.09	.19	−.14	
.16	−.26	.06		−.20	−.19	.26	
−.39	.17	.15		−.32	.29	−.17	
.13	−.60	.12		−.45	.21	.01	
.53	.11	−.14		.26	.02	−.05	
−.52	.14	.17		.01	−.29	.13	
.19	−.57	−.16		−.75	.57	−.22	
.50	−.08	−.04		.11	.43	−.24	
	.75	.06		.67	−.31	.13	
−.26	.16	−.03		.50	−.51	.16	
−.08	.45			−.22	.58	−.35	
.04	−.15	−.05		−.26	−.09	.12	
.07	.06	.04		−.04	.15	−.10	
.43	.71	.08		.71	.35	−.18	
−.55	−.26	.23		.06	.13	.31	
−.56	−.26	.23			−.41	.31	
$n = 502$				$n = 454$			

It may appear from the foregoing results that the model is supported and validated by empirical evidence. However, this is not completely true. For the model to be validated, we would have to obtain a much larger percentage in the explained variance for both Behavioral Intention and Purchase Behavior. It should have been at least comparable to that obtained for Affect. Why is this not the case in the study? There are several reasons, but the most obvious and critical explanation lies in the weaknesses of the variables chosen to measure Social Environment, Anticipated Situation, and Unexpected Events. As stated earlier, many of them are at best surrogates for the type of variables that comprise these three factors in the model. A second explanation is related to the low explained variance of Purchase Behavior. The addendum to the diary asked the housewife to record the reasons for the discrepancy between intentions and actual behavior. The listing of these reasons is large and is specific to each customer. The only common variable that could be isolated was the lack of availability of the brand. If we had specified other reasons as binary variables, it is certain that the model could have been considerably improved in its empirical validation.

One last point on the validation of the model. In an attempt to relate cognitive aspects of attitudes and the attitude-behavior relationship, this paper has ignored the role of conditioning or habit in determining Affect and Behavior. We need to examine carefully whether cognitively determined Affect and Behavior or habitually determined Affect and Behavior are more prevalent in consumer behavior. This is critical in building any control models from the point of view of the marketing management. The cognitively determined attitudes and behavior will suggest the usefulness of persuasive communication as the strategy of change, and the behaviorally determined attitudes and behavior will suggest the strategy of some form of behavior modification.

The model of attitude structure and the attitude-behavior relationship presented in this paper do not represent a definite, final viewpoint or theory. It simply marks an advanced stage of evolutionary thinking that began at the time of writing the Howard-Sheth theory of buyer behavior. I hope that it will not be mistaken for a final invariant position on my part.

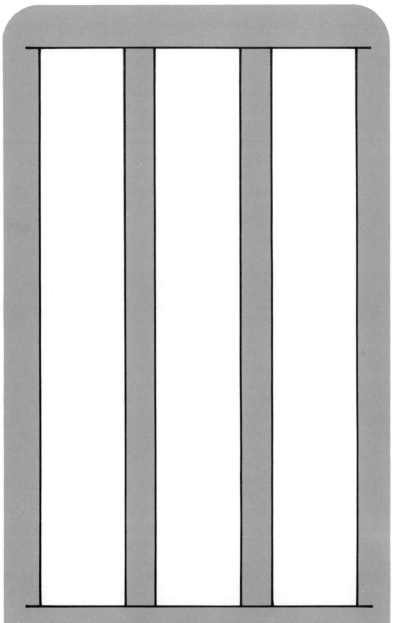

MODELS OF
INNOVATIVE BEHAVIOR AND
PRODUCT ADOPTION

A
CONCEPTUAL MODELS

14

A CRITICAL EXAMINATION OF "ADOPTION PROCESS" MODELS OF CONSUMER BEHAVIOR

THOMAS S. ROBERTSON
Associate Professor of Marketing
Wharton School
University of Pennsylvania

This paper critically examines the concept of an "adoption process" and suggests that there is no specified form, number of stages, or sequence to which the adoption process must conform. As used here, *adoption* refers to the acceptance and continued use of a product or brand. Since adoption is a behavioral output, it has been traditional to specify its antecedents. The *adoption process* is the mental and behavioral sequence through which the consumer progresses and which *may* result in acceptance and continued use of a product or brand.

Several adoption and purchase decision models have been postulated. Although similar in their conceptualization of a flow of events rather than an "instant metamorphosis," they differ considerably in the number of stages proposed and in the identification of these stages. It should be recognized that all such schemes are conceptual frameworks only, therefore, neither true nor false.

A distinction should be made between the adoption process and the purchase decision process. The adoption process refers to the possible acceptance and continued use of an item, while the purchase decision process generally refers to a single buying decision. Furthermore, the adoption process concept is derived from literature dealing with innovations, whereas the purchase decision process has been used in a variety of contexts not necessarily related to new product adoption decisions.

The distinction is not nearly as clear as suggested, however. It is very difficult to specify what constitutes adoption, since this criterion varies with the product category under consideration. For an appliance product, for example, the adoption process and the purchase decision process would be almost synonymous, since the low extent of purchase frequency makes the very concept of "acceptance and continued purchase" questionable. For a product such as detergents, characterized by a high rate of purchase frequency and considerable brand switching, what number of repeat purchases would constitute adoption—three in a row, three out of four, . . . ? What determines adoption also varies for heavy versus light users of a product. Nakanishi (1968) has distinguished between the "regular user" and the "occasional user" modes of adoption. The regular user mode involves purchase of the product at regular intervals, exclusive of available alternatives; the "occasional user" mode entails occasional but consistent purchase of the product and purchase of substitutes at in-between times. Because of such inherent difficulties in distinguishing adoption from purchase, the two concepts are often used interchangeably and that will be the practice here also.

THE "ADOPTION PROCESS" SCHEME

The adoption process, as first defined in the rural sociology literature in the mid-1950s, consists of five sequential stages. These stages and their commonly accepted definitions are as follows:

1. **Awareness.** The individual knows of the new idea but lacks sufficient information about it.
2. **Interest.** The individual becomes interested in the idea and seeks more information about it.
3. **Evaluation.** The individual makes a mental application of the new idea to his present and anticipated future situation and decides either to try it or not to try it.
4. **Trial.** The individual uses the innovation on a small scale to determine its utility for him.
5. **Adoption.** The individual accepts the innovation and commits himself to its use.

This scheme does not allow for the individual "skipping" stages, nor are any feedback loops provided. For example, after trial the individual might return to an interest stage and seek further information, or he might go back to an evaluation stage (which would seem to be implicit in trial) and continue to evaluate the item's utility for him. The model does propose that the innovation may be *rejected* at any stage in the process and that individuals will proceed through these stages at varying rates of speed.

THE "HIERARCHY OF EFFECTS" SCHEME

The "hierarchy of effects" scheme was proposed in the marketing literature by Lavidge and Steiner (1961) and labeled by Palda (1966). This concept consists of six steps to purchase which are related, according to Lavidge and Steiner, to three basic psychological states—*cognitive, affective,* and *conative.* The cognitive dimension is the realm of thoughts, the affective dimension is the realm of emotions, and the conative dimension is the realm of motives. Definitions of stages in the hierarchy of effects model are as follows:

1. **Awareness.** The individual is aware of the product's existence.
2. **Knowledge.** The individual knows "what the product has to offer."
3. **Liking.** The individual has favorable attitudes toward the product.
4. **Preference.** The individual's favorable attitudes have "developed to the point of preference over all other possibilities."
5. **Conviction.** Preference is coupled "with a desire to buy" and confidence "that the purchase would be wise."
6. **Purchase.** "Attitude" is translated into actual buying behavior.

In elaborating on this model, Lavidge and Steiner have noted that the stages are not necessarily equidistant. The difficulty and time involved in moving up each step in this hierarchy will depend on both product and consumer characteristics. Thus they offer the hypothesis that

> The greater the psychological and/or economic commitment involved in the purchase of a particular product, the longer it will take to bring consumers up these steps, and the more important the individual steps will be [p. 60].

They have further pointed out that a buyer may sometimes move up several steps simultaneously (e.g., in an impulse purchase). Thus they are arguing that each stage is necessary and that any apparent skipping of stages reflects a collapse of the hierarchy into a shorter time interval. Again in this model, there are no feedback loops to earlier stages, and a unilateral and continuous process is envisioned.

The hierarchy of effects model is perhaps the first such model to rely explicitly on an information-attitude-behavior theory of communication effect. It has been assumed for some time that communication functions by providing information (awareness and knowledge), forming or changing attitudes (liking and preference), and thus inducing behavior (conviction and purchase). In fact, Lavidge and Steiner specified the hierarchy of effects model as a framework for measuring advertising effectiveness. Their basic thesis was that although the end objective of advertising is to produce sales, immediate sales results do not constitute a valid measure of advertising impact. Yet "if something is to happen in the long run, *something* must be happening in the short run, something that will ultimately lead to eventual sales results" [p. 59]. They contend that short-run effects of advertising can be measured in terms of movement on the purchase decision process.

OTHER PURCHASE DECISION SCHEMES

A variety of other schemes has also appeared in the literature. The most familiar in marketing and advertising texts is the AIDA scheme, which was formulated within the context of personal selling. The salesman was advised to (1) attract attention, (2) maintain interest, (3) achieve desire, and (4) get action (Tosdal, 1925, p. 61). Hovland, Janis, and Kelley (1953) have delineated three stages in achieving audience response—attention, comprehension, and acceptance. The AIDA model is compared with the adoption process and the hierarchy of effects models in Table 14.1.

The adoption process may also be viewed in terms of a basic problem-solving model, as follows:

1. **Perception of the problem.** For adoption to occur, a problem must be felt to exist. (This statement assumes that perception of the problem precedes awareness of the innovation. It could also be argued that awareness of the innovation might induce perception of a problem.)
2. **Setting the stage.** A configuration of information and solution alternatives (including the innovation) is brought together.

TABLE 14.1
ALTERNATE MODELS OF THE ADOPTION DECISION PROCESS

	HIERARCHY OF EFFECTS MODEL	AIDA MODEL	ADOPTION PROCESS MODEL
Behavioral level	Purchase ↑ Conviction ↑	Action ↑ Desire ↑	Adoption ↑ Trial ↑
Attitude level	Preference ↑ Liking ↑		Evaluation ↑
Information level	Knowledge ↑ Awareness	Interest ↑ Attention	Interest ↑ Awareness

3. **The act of insight.** Here the solution is found. The innovation is chosen over the other alternatives. (It could also be rejected.)
4. **The critical revision.** The innovation is analyzed by the consumer to determine how practical it is (cost, availability, etc.).

A major difficulty of the problem-solving model is that adoption need not be based on problem-solving behavior. The consumer could be playing what Bauer (1964) calls the psychosocial game and adopting a product by a process quite different from that outlined above. A further difficulty is that except for important purchases consumers are not likely to engage in much data collection, and the information they use is usually far from complete. Furthermore, the beginning stage of adoption behavior need not be problem perception but a potential solution to a problem not yet specified, unless we consider the problem to be latent.

CRITIQUE OF ADOPTION PROCESS MODELS

The discussion to follow summarizes several critiques directed to either the adoption process model or the hierarchy of effects model. In general, the critiques apply with equal force to either model.

Mason (1963) has argued that five stages leading to adoption are not necessary and that, in fact, only two stages are "necessary and sufficient"—awareness and adoption. Using the Guttman technique of scalogram analysis, Mason found that the sequence of stages proposed by rural sociologists did not occur and that several forms of an adoption process varied "according to practice and the individual farmer." He also found that evaluation apparently occurred before interest and that adoption was not the terminal stage but that interest and information seeking occurred after adoption. Active information seeking after adoption would seem to indicate the existence of cognitive dissonance. There was no single process of adoption for all the items studied, except that awareness preceded adoption (and there was even one exception to this).

It seems unlikely that a consistent adoption process conceptualization would hold across any range of consumer goods. Inexpensive, low-risk products, would not require the same deliberateness in purchase necessary for expensive, high-risk products. Important differences would seem to exist in the adoption processes for continuous versus discontinuous innovations.

Rex Campbell (1966) has presented a paradigm of the adoption process that differs in two important respects from the standard scheme. His first point is that the adoption process may not be as rational as is commonly assumed. There is an inherent rational bias in the model in that it suggests deliberate information seeking and "evaluation" of alternatives and consequences. His second point is that the starting point in the adoption process may not be awareness. This assumes a passive consumer. The beginning of the adoption process may instead be perception of a problem (as in problem-solving models).

Based on these two distinctions, four forms of the adoption decision process can be specified. Campbell calls the first of these *rational/problem solving*. The consumer becomes aware of a problem, looks for a solution, and carefully evaluates any product that potentially solves his problem. The adoption stages are problem (defined by Campbell as synonymous with interest), awareness, evaluation, rejection—or trial followed by adoption or rejection. The second adoption process form is *rational/innovation*, whereby the consumer becomes aware of the innovation before he recognizes the problem. This corresponds to the traditional specification of the adoption process, that is, awareness, interest, evaluation, rejection— or trial and adoption or rejection. The third form is *nonrational/ problem solving*, whereby the problem is perceived in advance of product awareness, but "in seeking a solution, he [the consumer] impulsively accepts the innovation without careful consideration or evaluation." Adoption process stages are problem (interest), awareness, adoption or rejection, and resolution. The resolution stage is to overcome dissonance. It is debatable, however, that a resolution stage would be unique to "nonrational" adoption. The fourth adoption decision process form, *nonrational/innovation*, occurs when the individual "sees something new and impulsively adopts the item without deliberation as to its utility." Adoption process stages are awareness, adoption or rejection, and resolution.

Palda (1966) has been the leading antagonist of the hierarchy of effects model. He finds no evidence for a hierarchy of effects as such and, more basically, he believes that no evidence exists *proving* the relationship between each step on the hierarchy and final purchase of the product. Thus he argues that there is "no logical necessity for awareness of brand to precede the purchase by any significant fraction of time, particularly in self-service stores." He further discounts research evidence that buyers of a product are more exposed to product advertising on the grounds that (1) buyers may be better rememberers, since all product stimuli may then be more salient, and (2) buyers may selectively expose themselves to ads to reduce cognitive dissonance. Palda further argues that there is no documented connection between attitude and behavior. Moreover, research showing buyers to possess more favorable attitudes than nonbuyers is methodologically unsound, since the before-and-after conditions could create the differences in results, rather than buyer-nonbuyer predispositions.

Palda's basic contention, then, is that sales results are the only meaningful measure of advertising effectiveness. The marketer who chooses advertisements to move consumers along the purchase decision process may be using a suboptimal strategy if other criteria would be more relevant to ultimate product purchase. However, Palda does not specify conditions to measure sales effect due to advertising. His thesis represents a valuable point of view, but of course lack of proof for a purchase decision process does not refute the existence of such a process; nor does the difficulty of measuring cognitive and affective changes mean that they do not occur; nor does our inability to document cognitive-affective effect on purchase deny the existence of such effect. Yet Palda does place the proponents of the purchase decision process in a somewhat uncomfortable position.

THE INFORMATION-
ATTITUDE-BEHAVIOR RELATIONSHIP

All the adoption process models assume implicitly or explicitly that information must precede attitude and that favorable attitude toward the product must precede behavior. Little documentary evidence is available to justify these assumptions. A number of researchers have concluded that information can be communicated without consonant attitude change and that attitude change can occur without subsequent behavioral change. This, of course, poses further difficulties for the adoption process models, especially since measures of change in knowledge or change in attitudes then may not be valid criteria for the evaluation of advertising effectiveness.

Perhaps the most completely documented study showing the communication of facts without opinion change is that of Hovland, Lumsdaine, and Sheffield (1953), who exposed groups of American soldiers during World War II to a film entitled *The Battle of Britain*. The film was found to be highly effective in communicating factual information but almost entirely ineffective in eliciting attitude change regarding British or American participation in the war and in changing motivation to serve in the war.

The attitude-change-behavior relationship has been subject to considerable debate. Cohen (1964), in a summary volume on attitude change, pointedly concludes:

> Most of the investigators whose work we have examined make
> the broad psychological assumption that since attitudes are
> evaluative predispositions, they have consequences for the
> way people act toward others, for the programs they actually
> undertake, and for the manner in which they carry them out.
> Thus attitudes are always seen as precursors of behavior, as
> determinants of how a person will actually behave in his daily
> affairs. In spite of the wide acceptance of the assumption,
> however, very little work on attitude change has dealt explicitly with the behavior that may follow a change in attitude
> [pp. 137–138].

Festinger (1964), in an article prompted by Cohen's conclusion, states that he was at first skeptical but that prolonged search brought to light only three relevant studies that focused on the relationship between attitude change and behavior. He points out that it is not the attitude-behavior relationship that is being questioned, only the attitude-change-behavior relationship. Examining these studies, Festinger discovered that the "obvious" relationship between attitude change and behavior did not hold. This led him to suggest that when an attitude change is based on persuasive communication, such a change "is inherently unstable and will disappear or remain isolated unless an environmental or behavioral change can be brought about to support and maintain it" [p. 415]. This almost seems to put us in the awkward position of having to change behavior before we can change behavior. Attitude change will not serve as a sufficient condition for behavioral change if "the same factors that produced the initial opinion and the behavior will continue to operate to nullify the effect of the opinion change" [p. 416].

It has been further suggested that behavioral change can occur without a preceding attitude change. Instead, attitude change can follow behavioral change. Several dissonance experiments suggest this behavior-attitude change possibility. In one such experiment by Brehm (1956), for example, young women were asked to rate the desirability of eight products; they were then offered a choice between two of these products and asked to rate them again. Results indicated that after making the choice, subjects showed a marked increase in preference for the product chosen and a marked decrease in preference for the product not chosen. Commitment to the decision apparently set in motion an attitude change process to result in cognitive consistency. In a later study by LoSciuto and Perloff (1967), involving a similar experimental design, the same order of results was obtained.

An example may illustrate the implications of this behavioral change mode of attitude change. A marketer may be successful in gaining new product trial, perhaps by the distribution of product samples. It can be assumed that some triers of the product will have what amounts to an initially favorable attitude toward it, and others will have an initially unfavorable attitude. Use of the product by those possessing a favorable attitude is cognitively consistent and should reinforce the already favorable attitude (assuming that the product is good). However, use of the product by those possessing an unfavorable attitude suggests a dissonant relationship. The experience of dissonance under these conditions can be reduced by revoking the behavior, by minimizing the importance of the trial behavior, or by changing one's attitude toward the product. If the product were reevaluated positively, this attitude would be consistent with the behavior and consonance would be achieved.

It has been reported in experiments by Festinger and Carlsmith (1959) that the smaller the incentive to produce behavior, the greater the dissonance and the greater the change in attitude. Thus a 10-cents-off deal, if it induces behavior, is more likely to result in attitude change than a 25-cents-off deal or free sampling. Change in attitude under these conditions of low inducement must, of course, be balanced against the extent of behavioral response obtained by these inducements. Large inducements, it is reasoned, may lead to rationalization for engaging in the induced behavior, whereas small inducements force the individual to face his behavioral response without a ready excuse. Therefore dissonance reduction is more likely to occur via attitude change under low-inducement conditions.

There are a number of other ways to encourage attitude change by inducing behavior inconsistent with existing attitudes. Cohen (1964) has provided perhaps the best summary of means and effects of "enforced discrepant behavior." Most such means, though experimentally interesting, cannot be used as part of a marketer's attitude change program; but of course social scientists are not necessarily interested in generating usable research findings.

Attitude change occurring after a behavioral response has also been noted by Krugman (1965). In accounting for the impact of television advertising, he attributes much of such impact to "learning without involvement." Such learning tends to be incidental, resembling the learning of nonsense syllables and other meaningless material. Constant exposure to trivia, coupled perhaps with a lack of perceptual defense due to low involvement, may lead to learning and alteration in cognitive structure regarding a product, but not, according to Krugman, to attitude change. When the individual is faced with the item in a purchase situation, he may see it "in a new, 'somehow different' light although nothing verbalizable may have changed *up to that point*" [p. 354], and purchase may result. Attitude change may then follow product purchase.

In Krugman's thinking, such postpurchase attitude change is not a form of "rationalizing" the purchase. His explanation, therefore, is not in terms of dissonance theory. He argues instead that attitude change is "an emergent response aspect of the previously changed perception" [p. 354]. Attitude change following behavior may give meaning to the behavior. Moscovici (1963), stating a similar position, has noted the dual direction of attitudinal and behavioral change:

> When attitude is changed first, the aim is to cause change
> in behavior. On the other hand, if behavior changes first,
> a change in attitude is involved and serves to give a meaning
> to the already achieved behavior. Attitude may thus be viewed

either as a mechanism directing behavior, or as a modality which confers on behavior its meaning.

Krugman expects the typical attitude change-behavior relationship under high-involvement conditions and the behavior-attitude change relationship under low-involvement conditions. If this is in fact the case, it would suggest different forms of the adoption process.

Bauer (1966) has since contended that behavioral change *cannot* occur without attitude change. An attitude, according to Bauer, is an intervening variable defined as a "disposition to act." It is also a hypothetical construct that must be inferred from samples of individual behavior. Thus two arguments arise. First, any change, even a perceptual change as alluded to by Krugman, is an intervening state—an attitude. Second, lack of measured attitude change may reflect lack of refinement in our instruments, since the change involved is so minor. But does this argument hold for the dissonance experiments?

If we posit that behavioral change cannot occur without attitude change of some sort, we must rely on a distinction made by Rokeach (1966) between attitudes toward objects (products) and attitudes toward situations. If an individual is induced to buy a product because of a 30-cents-off deal, this represents a situational change and a changed attitude toward the situation. Behavior is preceded by attitude change, although not necessarily product attitude change. Based on trying the product, attitude change toward the product may then occur, but only because a preceding situational attitude change had already occurred.

MULTIPLE ADOPTION
DECISION PROCESS MODELS

The adoption process concept in the abstract makes implicit sense. If a behavioral act is to occur, it must have antecedents. As a conceptual framework, the adoption process can be of value in focusing attention on such antecedents. It can also perform a disservice for marketers to the extent that it specifies an order of antecedents that does not universally or even generally hold. While recognizing the limitations of the concept, however, it appears on balance that it can increase our understanding of consumer behavior.

Several refinements of the adoption decision process concept can be made to increase its utility. These refinements should be based on the following three conclusions:

1. There is no single *form* to which the adoption process must

conform. It may be useful to suggest at least three alternate forms—
the "rational/decision-making" form, the "nonrational/impulse" form,
and the "nonrational/psychosocial" form.

2. There is no specified *number* of stages that will always
occur. The minimum number of stages seems to be two, whereas
the maximum number of stages is probably a function of our
ingenuity in drawing distinctions.

3. There is no specified *sequence* of stages that must occur.
Any such model must make allowances for consumers to *skip* stages
and must also provide *feedback* loops, since such a process will not
necessarily be linear and unidimensional.

Alternate Forms

Most adoption process models have a rational, problem-solving
bias. The consumer is seen as securing information, processing it, and
evaluating it. We assume that he makes his decision in the rational
manner of an economic man based on the intrinsic qualities of the
information obtained. This is one form of the adoption process,
and it approximates reality for certain classes of decisions. This
form is closest to the problem-solving models and can be referred to
as the rational/problem-solving form.

However, the consumer may also make decisions in a nonrational manner, that is, *nonrational in the sense of not securing,
processing, and carefully evaluating all available information.* He
may make adoption decisions on impulse, or he may make decisions
to ingratiate himself with other people. Thus two alternate forms
of the adoption process are suggested—the nonrational/impulse
form and the nonrational/psychosocial form. These models do not
follow the same stages or truly resemble the rational/decision-
making form. Both models will be noted for their lack of information
seeking and evaluation.

The form of the adoption process will vary with (1) the importance of the decision, (2) the extent of meaningful product
differentiation, (3) the extent of product conspicuousness, (4) the
extent to which the consumer can afford to take risks, and (5) the
decision-making ability of consumers. There are undoubtedly other
factors to be considered, as well. We would expect that the more
important the decision, the more likely the adoption process would
be to approximate the rational/decision-making form. We would expect that the lower the amount of meaningful product differentiation,
the more likely the consumer would be to decide on impulse or on
the basis of psychosocial influence. Product conspicuousness would
more likely lead to the nonrational/psychosocial adoption process.

We would expect that the more able consumers are to take risks (financially and socially), the more the adoption decision process would depart from a rational/decision-making form to a non-rational/impulse or psychosocial form. Finally, the more capable consumers are to engage in rational decision making (which is a learned problem-solving approach), the more likely is such an adoption form. Thus Fliegel, Kivlin, and Sekhon (1968) found that Pennsylvania farmers were considerably more likely to review factors such as expected payoff and saving of discomfort in arriving at adoption decisions, whereas Punjabi farmers were much more apt to use such factors as social approval and clarity of results.

Number of Stages

Adoption is the outcome of a *flow* of psychological and mental processes. It is convenient and meaningful for the social scientist to divide this flow into stages. Such stages are arbitrary, however, and no specified number of stages can be considered right or wrong, just as no specified number of periods in history can be considered right or wrong.

Mason (1963) has argued that only two stages in the adoption process are necessary—awareness and adoption. This can be accepted as the minimum number of stages, since it hardly seems possible for a person to be able to adopt a product without being aware of its existence. In contrast, it is conceivable that a vast number of stages could actually occur. For example, the following decision sequence might be suggested. The adoption process might begin with *perception of a problem* that caused the individual to engage in *information seeking*, resulting in *awareness* of the new product and subsequently *knowledge* about it. A favorable *attitude* might come about, followed by *legitimation* leading to *trial*. The consumer would then engage in *evaluation*, which could lead to further *information seeking*. *Adoption* (which could lead to *dissonance*) or *rejection* would be the outcome, with *discontinuance* perhaps at some future time.

Sequence of Stages

Whatever the adoption process used, it must make allowances for consumers to skip stages, and it must provide for the occurrence of feedback. In a comprehensive study of the adoption of new grocery products, Nakanishi (1968) has argued that the sequence of stages used by consumers is a function of the product category's attributes. The most significant attributes for new grocery products are (1) low unit prices, (2) divisibility into small sizes allowing trial, and (3)

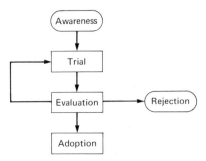

Figure 14.1 Simple Flow Diagram for Adoption of New Grocery Products
Based in Part on Nakanishi (1968)

reversibility of decisions. These attributes, argues Nakanishi, "contribute to a striking characteristic of their acceptance process, namely, the integration of the interest, evaluation, and trial stages" [p. 36]. Because trial for grocery products is inexpensive and easily conducted, consumers tend to skip from awareness to trial thus gaining product knowledge and engaging in product evaluation by this route rather than seeking information in advance of purchase. Figure 14.1 is a flow diagram for the adoption of new grocery products. The arrow from evaluation back to trial takes into account the possibility that one trial purchase will not provide sufficient information for the consumer to make an adoption decision.

Consumer attributes will also govern the adoption sequence. For example, a consumer is more likely to skip from awareness to attitude to adoption or rejection to the extent that he already possesses product category knowledge and holds attitudes about products in that category. To the extent that the consumer is venturesome (a risk taker), he will be more likely to go from awareness to trial without any intervening stages.

RESPECIFICATIONS OF THE
ADOPTION DECISION PROCESS

A number of marketing scholars have recently proposed more comprehensive accounts of the consumer decision-making process. These accounts, particularly the works of Nicosia (1966), Andreasen (1965), and Howard and Sheth (1968), account more fully for the dynamics of consumer decision making and attempt to specify the operating variables and their interrelationships.

In the Nicosia model (Figure 14.2) it is assumed that the firm is introducing a new product or brand and that the consumer has no prior attitudes, either toward the brand or toward its product

Field 1: From source of message to a consumer's attitude

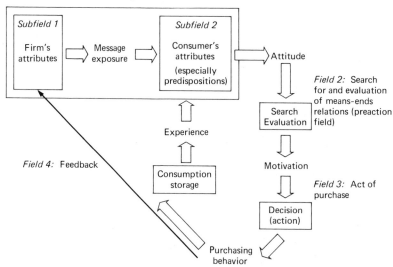

Figure 14.2 The Nicosia Conceptualization of the Purchase Decision Process
Source: Nicosia (1966)

class. The decision flow consists of the following components: the firm's sending out an advertisement, the consumer's possible exposure to it, the interaction of consumer attributes with message content, the resulting possibility of attitude formation, the possibility of this attitude's invoking search/evaluation procedures leading to motivation, the possibility of motivation's converting into purchase behavior, and the feedback of purchase information to the firm and to the consumer that will lead to modification of the consumer's predispositions toward future purchase and perhaps to modification of the firm's future communication strategy. The model as proposed is in the form of a summary flow chart indicating major fields, but Nicosia has also specified the subfields of each major field and the possible outcomes.

Several important differences between this model and the earlier adoption process accounts can be noted. Perhaps the most important difference, according to Nicosia, is that this concept is amenable to simulation techniques, since the process is in the form of a computer flow diagram. Thus, hopes Nicosia, computer simulation can be used to explore and specify the interactions, among the large number of variables, that will result in a model with dynamic properties. This may be possible, since specific variables are defined and their overall interrelationships discussed. Moreover, this model

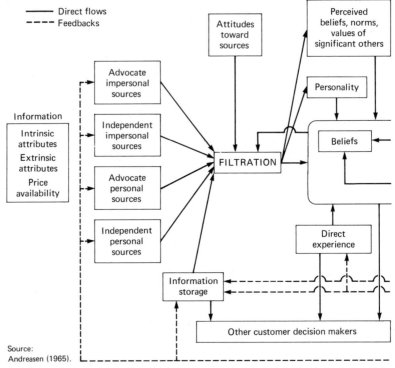

Figure 14.3 The Andreasen Conceptualization of the Purchase Decision Process
Source: Andreasen (1965)

indicates the occurrence of feedback and successfully integrates communication input and response output variables, unlike the original adoption process or hierarchy of effects specifications.

   This model, however, and others like it, including those to be discussed, are not without their faults. Ehrenberg (1968) has criticized the Nicosia model for consisting mainly of "long listings of variables that might possibly enter into such a [consumer behavior] model with little, if any, explicit treatment of how they are interrelated." He also levels the complaint that such models should be derived from empirical knowledge rather than starting with concepts. In defense of Nicosia, it can be argued that little systematic empirical knowledge exists, and more important, that all researchers have concepts in mind when doing research. Both empirical research to test theories and models and theoretical elaborations and systematizing of empirical knowledge are necessary.

   Andreasen (Figure 14.3) has proposed yet another conceptual

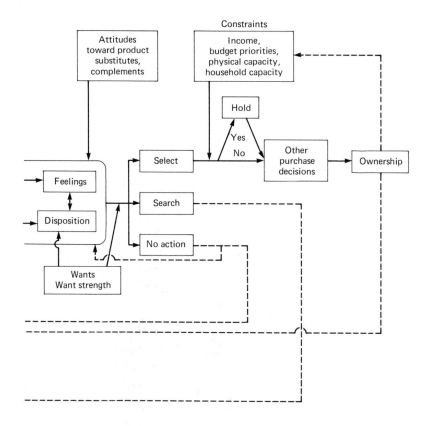

scheme of the adoption process. Again, innovative consumer behavior is assumed, since this will either be a new product or a new
product for the individual consumer.

The process begins, therefore, with a consumer who is unaware of a product or brand and concurrently, therefore, holds no
attitude toward it. *Information* then reaches the consumer, communicated by one of a number of *sources*, and is *filtered* by the
consumer (selective processes). Such information will affect consumer *attitude*, defined in terms of its belief, feeling, and disposition
components. Attitude may result in a decision to *select* the product,
to *search* for more information, or to take *no action*. A select decision
will be mediated by certain *constraints*, and other *purchase decisions* (store selection, quantity, etc.) will have to be made before
ownership is final. Appropriate mediating variables are also indicated, and feedback flows are traced. This model contains almost all
the advantages of the Nicosia model over traditional models, as
well as the faults of even more incomplete specification of variable
interrelationships and lack of firm empirical footing.

Howard and Sheth (1968) have presented a theory of buyer behavior, as summarized in Figure 14.4. Unlike the preceding models, their model focuses on repeat purchase behavior. The theory has four major components: stimulus inputs, hypothetical constructs, exogenous variables, and response outputs. The *inputs* to the buyer's internal state are stimuli from the marketing and social environments, including "significative" stimuli as communicated by the brand itself and "symbolic" stimuli as communicated by information channels. The *hypothetical constructs* appear within the heavy solid line representing the consumer's internal state. These constructs include perceptual constructs (for information processing) and learning constructs (for concept formation). The perceptual constructs include sensitivity to information, perceptual bias, and search for information, whereas the learning constructs include motives, evoked set, decision mediators, predispositions, inhibitors, and satisfaction. The *exogenous variables* (top of diagram) are influences on the hypothetical constructs, which provide for adjustment for interpersonal differences. *Response variables* are in the form of outputs, closely resembling the hierarchy of effects model but taking account of feedback.

It is difficult to do justice to these models in such abstract form. Each of the variables and constructs in the Howard-Sheth model, for example, is defined at length, and interrelationships are approximately specified. However, this discussion may provide a general idea of form. The three models now briefly summarized represent a significant step forward from the original adoption and purchase decision process specifications. Say Howard and Sheth: "We hope that our theory will provide new insights into past empirical data, and guide future research by instilling coherence and unity into current research, which now tends to be atomistic and unrelated" [pp. 486–487].

A SUMMARY MODEL

Figure 14.5 is offered as an outcome of the discussion to this point. No attempt is made to present a "new" or "improved" or "modified" adoption process model, but several features of the model should be emphasized.

1. The information-attitude-behavior conceptualization is kept, since it appears to provide a meaningful format for viewing adoption. It ties directly to common understanding of how advertising functions.

2. It is possible to trace the different *forms* of the adoption process. The rational/decision-making form follows the full sequence

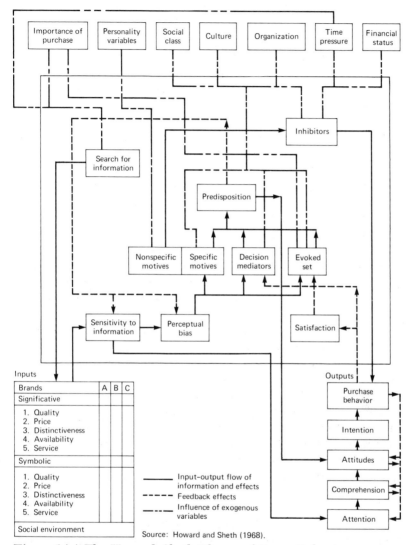

Figure 14.4 The Howard–Sheth Theory of Buyer Behavior
Source: Howard and Sheth (1968)

of stages, whereas the nonrational/impulse form goes from awareness to trial and the nonrational/psychosocial form goes from
awareness to legitimation to trial, or possibly to adoption without
trial.

3. Feedback effects are noted by broken lines. Thus adoption
affects legitimation and attitude (as argued earlier by Palda) and

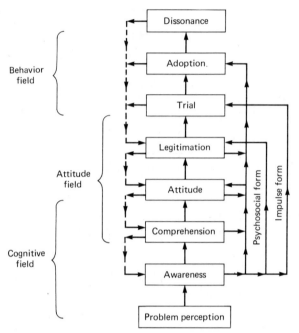

Figure 14.5 Summary Adoption Decision Process Model

adoption also adds to knowledge and heightens product awareness.
Other feedback effects could be similarly detailed.

4. Problem perception (as proposed by Rex Campbell, 1966)
and dissonance are two basically new stages added to the process to
account more fully for the possible *sequences* that may occur.

Explanation

It should be noted initially that *rejection* can occur at any stage as
soon as the individual is aware of the innovation. Many adoption
process models have included an *interest* stage, but I do not feel that
interest is a useful, distinguishable stage. Instead, interest is a prerequisite for the occurrence of every stage of the process. Similarly,
evaluation has been discarded, since this stage, too, does not appear
to be useful and distinguishable. Again, evaluation occurs throughout the process and not at any one time. The consumer evaluates
the item based on initial awareness and knowledge, again as part
of attitude formation, again in legitimizing trial, and, of course,
again in considering the trial experience.

Definition of Stages

Problem Perception. The adoption process will at times begin with the consumer's perception of a problem. The natural result should be a search procedure in which the person evaluates his existing knowledge and set of alternatives and turns to his environment for further information and alternatives. It is during such environmental search that the innovation alternative can become known to him.

Awareness. This is the common start of the adoption process—the product stimulus registers with the consumer, having passed his filtration process. Awareness assumes only that the consumer knows of a product's existence.

Comprehension. Based on knowledge, comprehension represents the consumer's conception of what the product is and what functions it can perform. Differential comprehension among consumers will occur in terms of consumers' abilities to handle and reason with information. Some consumers, for example, may characteristically simplify and assimilate information into a small number of categories, while others may complicate and contrast information into a large number of categories. Thus some consumers can perceive a product as basically the same as all other offerings, but other consumers can note individual differences and perceive the product as "new."

The awareness and comprehension stages are the information-processing stages. Together they comprise the cognitive field of the purchase process. Comprehension, however, overlaps with the attitude stage because knowledge, defined in terms of beliefs, is recognized as an attitude component.

Attitude. Attitude is an interrelated system of beliefs, feelings, and action tendencies toward an object (Krech, Krutchfield, and Ballachey, 1962). It goes beyond comprehension in terms of the feeling and action tendency components. An attitude is most generally thought of as the predisposition of the individual to evaluate an object of his environment in a favorable or unfavorable manner. A favorable evaluation is necessary in almost all cases for the adoption process to continue.

Legitimization. If the individual realizes a favorable attitude toward the product, he will be disposed to purchase it on a trial basis. However, whether trial occurs will depend largely on the result of the legitimization stage. Legitimization means that the individual must become convinced that purchase is the appropriate course of action. He may reach this decision based on the information that he has accumlated to this point, or he may turn to his environment for further information. Relevant here are such questions as, Do my friends buy this product? or Is the cost in line with other such products? The legitimization stage often stands as a barrier between favorable attitude toward the product and actual purchase.

The comprehension, attitude, and legitimation stages may be considered to comprise the attitude field of the adoption process. As noted, comprehension is also part of the cognitive field and legitimization can also be considered part of the behavioral field, since the individual is, in a sense, acting toward goal achievement.

Trial. The consumer uses the product on a limited scale. Trial may represent a commitment to adopt or a means of evaluating the product based on experience.

Adoption. Here the consumer accepts the product and continues to purchase and/or use it.

The legitimation, trial, and adoption stages comprise the behavioral field in the adoption process. The process is now complete, except for a consideration of the occurrence of cognitive dissonance.

Dissonance. Commitment to a decision, as adoption implies, may tend to place the individual in a state of cognitive dissonance, since he has adopted a certain product yet typically believes that other products have desirable features as well. Dissonance is psychologically uncomfortable, and the individual will seek to reduce it and to obtain consonance (e.g., by seeking social support or selectively perceiving advertisements for the product purchased in order to justify behavior). This may mean that the individual in effect repeats the legitimation stage; or, if dissonance is not successfully reduced, he may discontinue use of the product.

USING THE ADOPTION
PROCESS CONCEPT: A CASE EXAMPLE

The new product marketer is often hampered in arriving at meaningful sales predictions because the sales data base is so small and, frequently, unpredictable. Thus early heavy sales rates may indicate a large potential market or a small potential market that is highly interested in the product and highly motivated toward trial. Slow beginning sales rates may be due to the complexity or lack of com-

TABLE 14.2
CLASSIFICATION OF CONSUMERS BY STAGE OF THE
ADOPTION DECISION PROCESS FOR A HYPOTHETICAL INNOVATION

ADOPTION DECISION PROCESS STAGE	CUMULATIVE PERCENTAGE OF CONSUMERS[a]	
	JUNE 1969	DECEMBER 1969
Awareness	55	85
Knowledge	45	70
Favorable attitude	25	30
Legitimation	16	18
Trial	10	14
Adoption	3	10

[a] One hundred percent is assumed to represent the entire market potential for the product.

municability of the product and may not reflect long-run sales potential. In other words, *sales* figures in the short run need not be the best indicator of long-run adoption rates.

The Adoption Progress Concept

A more reliable and potentially more usable form of data may be acquired by measuring *adoption progress*. In this approach, as proposed by Klonglan, Coward, and Beal (1968), the focus is on the classification of consumers in the defined market segment at stages on the *adoption process*, instead of merely classifying consumers as buyers or nonbuyers. Consumers will be distributed along the various stages of the adoption process.

A hypothetical illustration of the utility of the adoption progress approach is given in Table 14.2. Let us assume that a new product is introduced to the market on January 1, 1974. Using adoption rates only, it is evidenced that 3 percent of the potential market has adopted by June and 10 percent has adopted by December. At this point, management may be plotting sales figures and noting what appears to be the take-off point on the traditional S-shaped curve (see Figure 14.6). The product manager may be a strong contender for a bonus. If adoption *progress* rates are used, however, quite a different picture is seen. While awareness and knowledge levels have shown significant gains, the relative percentage increase in number of consumers holding favorable attitudes toward the product is indeed small, and an even smaller relative percentage increase appears in number of consumers advancing as far as legitimation. This is clearly shown in Figure 14.6. According

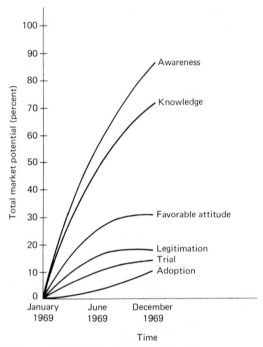

Figure 14.6 Adopted Progress Rates
(Based on Table 14.2)

to the additional data, sales levels will soon stabilize rapidly, since other consumers in the population are not progressing toward adoption.

These data suggest either that the market share for this product is limited but quickly cornered or that promotional efforts are not successfully gaining attitude change—perhaps because they are still focusing on informational messages for the "new" product even though 85 percent of consumers are at or beyond the awareness level. Using the adoption progress index, the marketer would be able to check these hypotheses in December 1974, and not many months later when adoption has stabilized after production has been expanded. It would also be possible to modify the promotional campaign to correct, if possible, the indicated difficulties.

CONCLUSION

This paper has strongly suggested that there is no particular *form* to which the adoption process must conform. As developed within diffusion theory by rural and medical sociologists, the adoption process has stressed communication of knowledge under the assumption that adoption would logically follow. This model is implicitly one of problem solving and rational behavior. Marketing researchers on diffusion, who have focused on this theoretical perspective relatively late compared with researchers in other disciplines, have tended to use whatever literature seemed to be relevant and have included concepts from the attitude change tradition of research to enrich the adoption model. A number of adoption forms are possible, including, for example, Bauer's problem-solving and psychosocial ideal types.

It is further suggested that the adoption process need not contain any specified *number* of stages. Any adoption sequence is essentially arbitrary, based on the observer's theoretical position and his ability to draw fine distinctions among hypothetical constructs.

Finally, it is concluded that there is no specified *sequence* that the adoption process must follow. Instead, the sequence depends on product attributes; thus, for example, more information seeking might be expected for expensive or high-risk products than for inexpensive or low-risk products. The sequence of adoption stages also depends on consumer characteristics; for example, individuals with risk-taking characteristics will tend to seek less information and to engage in less deliberation than risk-minimizing individuals. Using these distinctions should increase our understanding of the process leading to consumer actions, producing more valid marketing strategies to encourage adoption.

B
QUANTITATIVE MODELS

15

NEWS REPORT: A DISCUSSION OF THE THEORY AND APPLICATION OF THE PLANNING PORTION OF DEMON

ABRAHAM CHARNES
Professor of Management Science
University of Texas, Austin
WILLIAM W. COOPER
Professor of Industrial Administration
Carnegie-Mellon University
J. K. DE VOE
Cargill, Wilson & Acreer, Inc.
DAVID B. LEARNER
Applied Devices Corp.
LAWRENCE LIGHT, L. PRINGLE, and E. F. SNOW
Batten, Barton,
Durstine & Osborn, Inc.

The collection of concepts and relations examined in this paper can be grouped together under the single name NEWS. This is an acronym for New-Product Early Warning System and is motivated by the "new-product context" in which NEWS was originally conceived. NEWS was developed as part of the *"planning"* component in a model called DEMON designed for use in new product marketing at Batten, Barton, Durstine & Osborn, Inc. Via this component, DEMON can supply early warning on the parts of a marketing system that merit attention.

It is important to emphasize that DEMON was designed with NEWS as a separable component. Other components may be inserted in place of NEWS as part of the DEMON system. NEWS may also be used in other contexts. For example, NEWS is available as a component of a system for planning media schedules. It will also be useful as a guide in data-collection systems that will be required for extending present media scheduling models to dynamic applications. Advertising expenditures might then be related to actual sales via trier-user relations, advertising awareness, and other such intervening variables and relations.[1]

In subsequent sections of this paper we examine some of the concepts and methods that NEWS brings in new product marketing and advertising. In later sections we shall examine some extensions or modifications of NEWS.

NEWS: BASIC CONCEPTS AND METHODS

NEWS was intended to be separable from other aspects of DEMON. The model was designed to conform as closely as possible to current practice and present data availability—all the variables and relations were selected to permit assignment of operational significance as part of any new product marketing study. This was to be accomplished while synthesizing the NEWS elements and mechanisms that would produce a model capable of guiding subsequent extensions (including data assembly).

Focusing on only the advertising component of new product marketing systems, it is clear that total advertising expenditures (AD $) delineate one instrumental variable.[2] Gross rating points (GRP), reach, frequency, advertising awareness (AW), and triers and users of the product or brand are also variables that are usually considered in the planning of the advertising component of a new product marketing strategy.[3]

These variables are related in ways that violate the assumptions underlying any use of a single least-squares regression equation.[4] In particular, the usual assumption of independence does not hold; in fact, some of the variables are actually *defined* in terms of the others.[5]

---

[1] See Charnes, Cooper, De Voe, and Learner (1968) for further discussion of the "planning" and other components of DEMON. See also Kempthorne (1952) and De Voe (1965).

[2] GRP is the term used by J. Tinbergen (1952). (But see also the citation to a memo by R. Frisch in Tinbergen, 1952, p. 9.)

[3] See Batten, Barton, Durstine & Osborn (1966) for definitions of these and other terms.

[4] That is the so-called Gauss-Laplace-Markov assumptions (as discussed in, e.g., Kempthorne, 1952).

[5] See the discussion of the relations between awareness, triers, and users in the next section.

This kind of difficulty can be overcome in a variety of ways, including the utilization of constrained regressions under known specified relations and the replacement of each such set of inter-dependent variables with a new one, to eliminate the collinearities that cause the trouble. The latter approach is not satisfactory because it eliminates some decision and diagnostic possibilities. The former (i.e., constrained regression) possibility is also unsatisfactory because (1) it does not appear to correspond to the situation that is observed or (2) it does not provide relations that are readily usable in the usual new product marketing context.

Figure 15.1 depicts the causal relations that appear to hold. This suggests the use of a "recursive regression system."[6] The parts of the NEWS model examined here exclude the promotion, distribution, usage rate, price, and dollar demand components. Therefore, these components are aggregated in the representation of Figure 15.1 and only the remaining parts of the diagram correspond to the causal assumptions we are making for the recursive relations between the indicated variables:[7]

$$GRP = f_1 \ (AD \ \$)$$
$$AW = f_2 \ (GRP)$$
$$Triers = f_3 \ (AW)$$
$$Users = f_4 \ (Triers)$$

The variables are defined and these relations are discussed in detail in the immediately following sections. For the present we simply observe that they conform to the ways in which data are usually obtained for insight and decisions in new product marketing management.

NEWS: BASIC RELATIONS AND PARAMETERS

The considerations leading to such a recursive system of relations supply general guidance and useful insight. The relations that are utilized still need to be considered, as do the methods of estimation and the parameter values. We should emphasize that the latter are regarded as unique to each application. The form of the relations, however, should cover many situations. It would be premature to claim that the relations used in this paper will cover all situations,

---

[6] See, for example, Wold (1964) and Wold and Jureen (1953). A discussion of approaches to measuring *econometric* relations involving *simultaneous* estimation may be found in Bass (1967). See also Farley (1968).

[7] Note that some additional relations and artifactual variables are utilized. These are described in the next section.

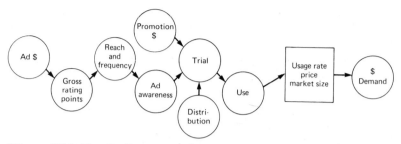

Figure 15.1 Simple Diagram of "News" System

but several years of application preceded by an extended period of testing seem to indicate that these relations hold surprisingly well for new consumer packaged goods products.

Let us now develop these relations. The first one is:

$$GRP = b_1 \times AD\ \$ \tag{1}$$

where b_1 is an empirically determined constant and AD $ is measured cumulatively (in millions of dollars) from time $t = 0$ to the present. For each media vehicle, GRP is the initial rating (in percent) of each specific media vehicle multiplied by the number of insertions in the vehicle.[8] The GRPs for each vehicle in a product's media schedule are summed to yield total GRP for the schedule. This gives a total in which GRPs are conveniently expressed in thousands when total AD $ are expressed in millions.

By means of the next expression we introduce a variable called "virtual reach," which serves as an artifact for reach-frequency considerations. It is defined with the following expression:

$$VR = 0.451\ (\log_{10} GRP) - 0.418 \tag{2}$$

where VR means virtual reach and $\log_{10}$ GRP refers to the logarithm of GRP taken to the base 10.

The next expression for use in the indicated recursive system is

$$AW = \frac{b_3}{\exp\ VR^{-a_3}} \tag{3}$$

where AW is "advertising awareness," measured as the proportion of a target audience who claim to recall having seen or heard an

---

[8] "Rating" refers to the percentage of a target audience reached on a single insertion in a particular media vehicle.

advertising message for the brand during some specified time period.[9] Constants b_3 and a_3 are determined empirically, exp is the base of the natural logarithms, and VR is "virtual reach."

The parameters in (3) reflect the relative impact of an advertising budget, and other such factors. Specifically, b_3 is the maximum level of AW that is approached asymptotically with increasing values of VR. The other parameter, a_3, reflects the *rate* at which advertising awareness accumulates (see Figure 15.2 for an illustration). When b_3 remains fixed, as in Figure 15.2, AW increases with increasing values of a_3 to the right of VR $= 1$. Thus higher values of a_3 produce greater AW in this region. Of course, this purely hypothetical situation is displayed only for purposes of illustration, since as a rule the values of b_3 and a_3 are not independently determined.

The form of the awareness to trial (TR) relation is

$$TR = a_4 + b_4(AW) \qquad (4)$$

The relation of trial to use is formulated as

$$Use = b_5(TR) \qquad (5)$$

"Trial" is the proportion of a target population who remember having purchased or otherwise tried the brand within a specified time period. "Use" represents the proportion of a target population who purchased the brand as the most recent purchase made in this product category.[10] Note that, by definition, $0 \leq b_5 \leq 1$, since b_5 is an estimate of the *ratio* of triers to users.

Of course some allowance must be made for transient behavior during the time that is needed for consumers to familiarize themselves with a product. A "shakedown period" should be incorporated in the experimental design (i.e., before the data-collection surveys are initiated) or else the foregoing model will have to be extended to allow for dynamic transient terms.[11]

The parameters in (4) provide measures of the selling power of the advertising (along with promotion and distribution) in obtaining triers for the brand (see Figure 15.1). Unlike expression (5), the graph of (4) does not necessarily go through the origin since

---

[9] Usually unaided recall is understood.

[10] These definitions differ in some respects from those employed in Learner (1968).

[11] This course should be taken when it is believed that these dynamic transient terms could cause different decisions or action recommendations.

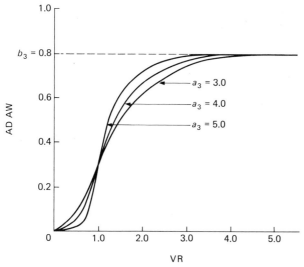

Figure 15.2 Relation of Virtual Reach to Advertising Awareness

allowance must be made for the effects of promotion and distribution in producing triers of the brand.[12]

We can collect these last interpretations and summarize them by saying that a_4 and b_4 represent the quality of the advertising, promotion, and so on, in producing "triers", while b_5 represents the quality of the product as perceived by the target population relative to their expectations and perceived alternatives.

PARAMETER ESTIMATES:
AN ILLUSTRATIVE EXAMPLE

As already noted, the parameter values for NEWS usually must be determined for each application. Data availability and decision possibilities need to be considered in each different application, along with the kind of estimating and testing procedures that are available in the statistics and economics literature. Pursuit of the latter topics is best reserved for a subsequent paper where they may be dealt with in adequate technical detail. Then we can utilize the present paper to describe a recent application of the NEWS model in evaluating a new product marketing strategy. We will also be able to examine the possible extensions to other uses that were noted in the opening sections of this paper.

---

[12] Negative values of a_4 are sometimes obtained, suggesting a subsequent extension via constrained regressions or related techniques. See, for example, Charnes and Cooper (1961, chap. X).

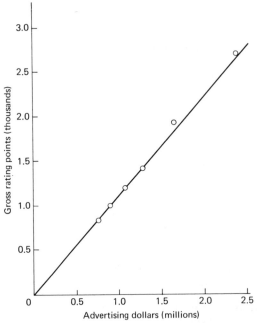

Figure 15.3 Relation of Advertising Dollars to Gross Rating Points
(GRP)

APPLICATION OF NEWS

The NEWS model has been used in a variety of applications in the
United States and elsewhere. Rather than simply repeating these
results, it might be of interest to report on an in-process application
in which NEWS is being used in analyzing test market data for
a new consumer packaged goods product. The following analysis is
based on these data.

Figure 15.3 indicates the relationship between AD $ and the
obtained GRP as estimated from the empirical data for this case.
Note that the relationship conforms to the linear model assumed in
NEWS; see (1). The corresponding regression equation shows that
the media schedule will deliver about 10^3 GRP/10^6AD $. This is
quite efficient, considering the type of media that were acceptable
to the brand management.

Figure 15.4 depicts the relationship between GRPs and AW.
In this case, "total" brand awareness (unaided plus aided) was the
criterion. The two parameter values, $b_3 = 99$ percent and $a_3 = 3.0$,
suggest that the advertising is performing quite well in generating
brand awareness; see (3) and (2). Projecting this function, a 60-

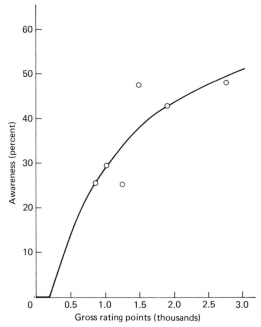

Figure 15.4 Relation of Gross Rating Points to Awareness

percent level of awareness is predicted for the end of year 1 (5000 GRPs; see Figure 15.5).

The next phase of NEWS involves analyzing the power of the marketing plan, particularly the advertising and promotion, in motivating people to try the brand. Figure 15.6 shows the Awareness-to-Trial relationship along with the observations used for (4) in this case. The coefficient $b_4 = .24$ indicates that as awareness increases, about one-fourth of those aware of the brand tried it. It should be noted that the confidence level associated with this regression coefficient is only 75 percent. The Awareness-to-Trial conversion appears to be quite low, but additional data might be collected here if the level of confidence is considered inadequate.

The next step in NEWS is an examination of the Trial-to-Use conversion rate. The relationship (5) between trial and use for this brand appears in Figure 15.7 along with a plot of the pertinent observations. The conversion rate for this brand was .45. (The confidence level is .90.) This is a reasonable conversion rate, the average in this class being about .50.

Table 15.1 summarizes the observed NEWS relations for the brand under investigation. Using these relations, we can now com-

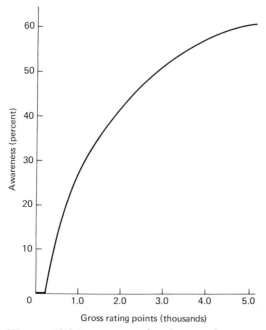

Figure 15.5 Projection of Relation of Gross Rating Points to Awareness

pare the forecast of the advertising and marketing effort with goals initially specified by management. Table 15.2 compares first-year goals with the NEWS forecast. Instead of the desired 19-percent share at the end of year 1, NEWS forecasts that an 8-percent share will be obtained. Examination of the parameter values suggested that the advertising was generating a satisfactory level of awareness, but the goal of 75 percent will be difficult to achieve. In any case, al-

TABLE 15.1
OBSERVED NEWS RELATIONS

ITEM	RELATION
AD $ GRP	GRP = 1.015 (AD $/1000)
GRP to AW	AW = 99/(exp x^{-3})
	where $x = 0.451$ (log$_{10}$ GRP) − .418[a]
AW to TR	TR = 3.2 + .24 (AW)
TR to Use	Use = .45 (TR)

[a] x is the virtual reach described in the next section; see expression (2).

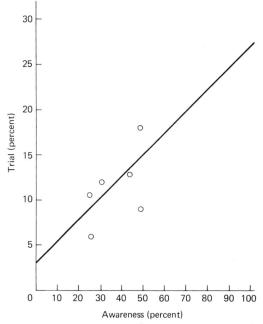

Figure 15.6 Relation of Awareness to Trial

ternative advertising might be considered and the possibility of getting more GRPs per dollar should also be investigated.

The major problem appears to lie in obtaining triers. Again, changes in copy approach should be tested. Additional promotions might be implemented. Finally, certain product characteristics might be changed to increase the Trial-to-Use conversion rate. These involve the brand's price, its quality, the package size, and so on.

After consideration of several alternative strategies, the following modifications of the marketing plan were recommended:

TABLE 15.2
COMPARISON OF YEAR 1 GOALS WITH NEWS FORECAST

PERCENTAGES		
YEAR 1 GOALS		NEWS FORECAST
Awareness	75	60
Triers	38	18
Users	19	8

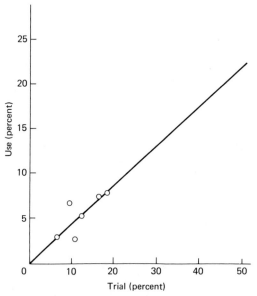

Figure 15.7 Relation of Trial to Use

1. Consider alternative media strategies that provide more GRPs per dollar.
2. Develop new copy strategies to generate a higher level of awareness and more triers.
3. Introduce an additional promotional event to get more triers.
4. Introduce a new package size to be more competitive with other major brands.
5. Conduct research to suggest improvements in product performance.

These recommendations involve only minimal additional marketing expenditures. They have all been adopted and are reported here for purposes of the record in evaluating NEWS, even though the activities needed to validate the recommendations have not been undertaken. Presumably they will begin in the near future, however, whereupon results will be available and can be reported as part of the evaluation of NEWS in a subsequent report. For the present, we can observe that NEWS was designed for use as a *continuing forecasting and evaluative* system; hence it can at least serve as an effective approach for "tracking" new product introductions.

SUMMARY AND CONCLUSIONS

1. We have now covered NEWS both by general discussion and by an illustrative application. The latter was selected to show how the NEWS system could be employed, on an in-process basis, apart from the DEMON context for which it was originally developed. In this case, as in others, we can see how the specific aspects of data assembly are related to the customary decision variables in a chain that admits of intervention and alteration on strategic dimensions available in the product. The advertising programs being employed or available for consideration can also be placed in relation to data assembly.

2. We now turn to some of the ways in which NEWS might be modified and used as an aid (and a guide) in other areas of potential application. For example, we might focus on the potential value of NEWS as a way of extending present models and methods for developing media schedules, to reflect the dynamic considerations that are evidently present when effecting such schedules over a sequence of periods.

An extension that deals with all aspects of media scheduling must ultimately be reflected in a stochastic conditional (decision-rule) approach because the schedules utilized in any period will alter the kinds of phenomena that are encountered in succeeding periods. Procedures for assembling data that will help to determine these effects, along with rules for determining whether and when such additional studies are to be executed, must be incorporated in the model along lines similar to those now used in other parts of the DEMON system. See Charnes, Cooper, De Voe, and Learner (1968) and other references in the bibliography.

3. A great deal can (and should) be accomplished, however, before such conditional stochastic extensions are attempted. Here too, NEWS can furnish considerable help. As observed earlier, it already provides insight and aids for an advertising program at a comprehensive aggregate level. Additional features would include a detailed treatment of the media vehicles. Specific quantitative constraints might be imposed on the media selection possibilities—at least in goal-programming fashion—to achieve suitable levels of awareness, trial, and use for a particular brand.[13] The NEWS system of estimating would thus become part of a comprehensive media

---

[13] See Charnes, Cooper, Learner, De Voe, and Reinecke (1968) and Charnes, Cooper, Learner, De Voe, Reinecke, and Snow (1968) for an example application of goal programming to media scheduling with "inconsistent" requirements. See also Charnes and Cooper (1961, chap. X) for a more general discussion.

scheduling model. In the meantime it can serve as a guide for the data assembly that must first be undertaken if the relations between advertising and sales (and ultimately profits) are to form meaningful (rather than misleading) parts of such a model.

Leaving aside considerations such as promotion and distribution, which evidently also require treatment as part of a comprehensive model, we can direct attention to such psychological phenomena as forgetting, learning, and remembering. These will naturally bear consideration as part of a comprehensive media-mix system. Here too, a period of organized data assembly will be needed if systematic and continuing exploitation of these possibilities is to be secured.

Brand switching and related phenomena are also suggested for examination along the route to such extensions. Information on usage rate—to isolate the heavy, light, and average users—also requires attention. Attempts to further identify advertising as distinguished from product properties will make it necessary to replace some of the present NEWS relations with others that are more detailed.[14]

In the meantime, we can present the NEWS system as a possible contributor to progress in these directions. A comprehensive model will also point up the need for research on "wear-out" and related psychological phenomena.[15] The use of sensitivity and evaluator analysis routines can be coupled with models of the proposed types, which can then be used to determine the kinds of accuracy that will be needed for such "qualitative" data.[16] Thus it is proposed once more (Charnes and Cooper, 1965) to have a comprehensive model to tie estimation and prediction together with the evaluations and decisions, rather than treating these as separate functions, following current practice in marketing analysis, economic forecasting, and company decision making.

We have focused on NEWS as a recursive (causal) regression model. Extensions of the kind we have indicated will evidently require something more. Identification, simultaneous estimation (see,

---

[14] These distinctions are more difficult in relation to new products, where the marketing approach and the product (including the price, its physical properties, and other phenomena usually assumed as steady-state "givens" in, e.g., economic demand theory) are best regarded as a total package of information wherein alteration produces a new package of information for transmission to consumers.

[15] "Wear-out" refers to the supposed tendency of an advertising message to lose its power with continued use of the same copy.

[16] See Charnes and Cooper (1965) for a discussion of sensitivity analysis and evaluator routines in the context of a model for budgeting advertising.

e.g., Bass, 1967, and Farley, 1968) and related statistical models and methods will be needed even to accommodate promotion with distribution, sales effort, and advertising in a single system. Both stationary and nonstationary time series are also likely to be encountered en route to some of the other extensions. This approach in turn, will probably point toward additional research, some of it perhaps involving very fundamental inquiries into mathematics and statistics. This is to the good, of course, insofar as such efforts stimulate progress in these basic sciences and do not, at the same time, bring all progress in applications to a halt. It should be possible to avoid the latter alternative by recourse to suitably devised simulations and heuristics and, indeed, these may provide insight and guidance for the former as well.

C
EMPIRICAL TESTING

16

GROUP CHARACTERISTICS AND AGGREGATE INNOVATIVE BEHAVIOR: PRELIMINARY REPORT

THOMAS S. ROBERTSON
Associate Professor of Marketing
Wharton School
University of Pennsylvania

Although it has generally been recognized that the group affects the consumption behavior of its members, few studies have demonstrated this relationship (Arndt, 1967b; Bourne, 1957; V. J. Cook, 1967; J. G. Myers, 1966; Stafford, 1966; Venkatesan, 1966). Considerably more research has been conducted focusing on personal influence—that is, an encounter of persons resulting in changed behavior or attitudes of participants (Merton, 1957). However, "personal influence" should not be confounded with collective "group influence," which occurs over time and is a function of group characteristics.

The present research objective is to assess the effect of the group on the innovative behavior (new product adoption) of its members. The analysis is at a group rather than an individual level. The theoretical perspective taken and the resulting hypotheses drawn are based heavily on the works of Homans (1950, 1958) and Festinger (1950, 1954).

Research underlying this paper was carried out under the joint financial support of the Bureau of Business and Economic Research and the Division of Research, UCLA. Thanks is expressed to Jim Koch and Brian Horsfall for their roles in the completion of this research.

THEORETICAL FRAMEWORK
Homans's Conceptual Scheme

Innovative behavior is an "activity" engaged in by individuals and can be measured by observation, recorded data (e.g., doctors' prescriptions or retail sales receipts), peer report, or the individual's own report of new product purchases.

Within the context of society or a more narrowly defined social system such as a neighborhood, individuals meet, see, and talk with other individuals—that is, "interaction" occurs. The definition of a group requires such interaction among a set of people over time. Measurement of interaction is generally based on reported incidents of communication among group members and could also be based on observation, particularly participant observation.

Interaction over time leads to the formation of group norms governing expected activity patterns, if the activity is important to the group. "Sentiment" will exist in terms of differential liking among group members. It will be possible to evaluate the cohesiveness of the group using sociometric techniques whereby the members specify the attractiveness of the group for them. The research objective could now be reformulated in terms of Homans's conceptual scheme as the assessment of the effect of interaction and sentiment variables on the activity of new product adoption.

Relevant Concepts

Interaction affects activity. Homans (1950, p. 135) postulates: "Persons who interact with one another frequently are more like one another in their activities than they are like other persons with whom they interact less frequently." Coleman, Katz, and Menzel (1966) have documented the "interaction" or "snowball" effect in new product diffusion: the socially more integrated members of a social system adopt sooner than the socially less integrated members.

E. Katz and Lazarsfeld (1955) have found that gregariousness, or extent of interaction with others, is most often correlated with opinion leadership. Other researchers have viewed the opinion leader as central in the communication network (J. G. Myers, 1966; Stafford, 1966). Myers has discovered that the exercise of opinion leadership is reflected in likeness of innovative activity patterns among group members. Other research evidence (W. E. Bell, 1964; Coleman, Katz, and Menzel, 1966; E. Katz, 1961; Robertson, 1968; Rogers, 1962) indicates that the opinion leader is generally more innovative than the average group member.

Sentiment affects activity. It is quite basic to sociological theory that group norms affect member behavior. Rogers (1962) has used the ideal types of "modern" and "traditional" norms to account for high and low innovativeness in social systems. It has been proposed by Festinger (1950) that there will be high reliance on social reality when the physical reality is ambiguous or unstructured. Venkatesan (1966) has documented that in a consumer decision-making situation, where objective standards are lacking, individuals exposed to a group norm tend to conform to that norm.

Research by Festinger (1950) and Back (1951) revealed that the greater the attractiveness of the group to its members, the greater the amount of influence successfully exerted on the members, and the greater the resulting behavioral conformity. In terms of orientation beyond or to the local community or group, the cosmopolitan-local dichotomy proposed by Merton (1957), has been applied by several researchers, including Rogers (1962), with findings that innovators are considerably more cosmopolitan than later adopters.

Literature exploring the perceived-risk concept indicates that if an individual is experiencing risk, he will seek to reduce it by communication with relevant persons (Arndt, 1968b; Bauer and Wortzel, 1966). Communication tends to occur to the extent that the reward derived exceeds the cost incurred (Homans, 1958). Arndt (1967b) has also found that avoiding new products is a risk-handling tactic used by high-risk perceivers.

HYPOTHESES

A. Interaction

A-1. The more the interaction among group members,
   (a) the more alike the group in regard to innovative behavior, and
   (b) the more innovative the group as a whole.

A-2. The more the communication among group members about innovation,
   (a) the more alike the group in regard to innovative behavior, and
   (b) the more innovative the group as a whole.

A-3. The more prevalent the interaction among group members, the greater the occurrence of opinion leadership.

A-4. The greater the level of opinion leadership within the group,

(a) the more alike the group in regard to innovative behavior, and

(b) the more innovative the group as a whole.

B. Sentiment

B-1. The more favorable the group norm on innovation, the more innovative the group as a whole.

B-2. The more cohesive the group, the more alike is the group in regard to innovative behavior.

B-3. The more cosmopolitan the group, the more innovative the group as a whole.

B-4. The higher the perceived risk among group members, the greater the communication about innovation.

B-5. The lower the perceived risk, the more innovative the group as a whole.

B-6. The more cohesive the group, the greater the incidence of opinion leadership.

RESEARCH DESIGN

Research was conducted in the spring of 1967 in the Los Angeles suburb of Encino. A middle-class neighborhood was selected, where almost all heads of households held white-collar or professional positions. Most households were composed of families with children living at home. The research design involved the identification of small, informal neighborhood groups. These groups were preferred to formal groups, such as PTA or church groups, which carry out explicit functions and possess a specified organizational structure. Although working within the confines of a formal group would have simplified the research task (since the social system is defined, membership is known, and sociometric techniques can be more readily applied), it was felt that the formal group is not the relevant reference group for most consumption-related activities. Consumer information may be transferred within the formal group but it is incidental to the ongoing group purpose.

Another approach would have been to identify a defined social system in terms of a common attribute, such as residing in the same apartment complex. This would have again simplified the research design. However, a pilot venture along these lines in the Los Angeles area revealed that too little interaction occurred among residents to permit us to meaningfully identify groups. A married student housing project, where interaction is considerable, could have been used, as in other research (Arndt, 1967b; J. G.

Myers, 1966), but the range of consumption of concern to student wives is limited.

Sampling
Identification of informal neighborhood groups proceeded as follows:

1. One woman was randomly selected from each block within the 32-block area. She was interviewed, and the interview contained the question: "Could you name some woman within the neighborhood—say within a mile—that you see most often and with whom you are most friendly?" A minimum of three names was sought and these constituted the preliminary definition of the group.

2. Next the actual existence of groups was tested by interviewing each person mentioned and measuring the level of interaction among group members. Figures 16.1 and 16.2 are sociograms depicting the flow of interaction for two of the groups obtained.

3. As operationally defined, a group had to include at least three people, all of whom interacted with one another.

Nonresponse could not be tolerated under these conditions, since the existence of a group could not be determined nor could group characteristics be completely assessed. Therefore, we used an elaborate procedure to ensure response, consisting of an advance letter requesting cooperation, follow-up telephone calls to arrange appointments, and further letters and calls when necessary.

The final sample included 20 groups consisting of 85 members. Losses from the original 32 contacts occurred for the following reasons:

1. Six of the initial contacts refused to be interviewed, refused to identify their friends, or maintained that they did not have three friends in the neighborhood.
2. Three groups were eliminated because they did not include at least three members.
3. Three groups were eliminated because designated members refused to be interviewed.

Data Collection and Analysis
In-home personal interviews were conducted with the 85 group members. Interviews took approximately 90 minutes to complete. The group characteristics of concern and their forms of measure-

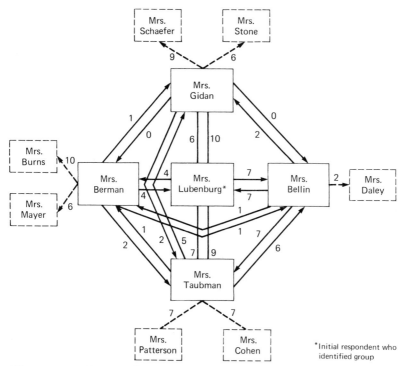

Figure 16.1 Reported Interaction, Group 6: Numbers Represent Total Reported Interactions by Telephone or in Person per Week: Solid Boxes—Specified Group; Dashed Boxes—Subsidiary Friendship Mentions

ment are given in Table 16.1. These characteristics were measured for each individual, and overall group means and standard deviations were computed. Basically, three types of measures are involved:

1. **Reported behavior measures**—innovativeness, cosmopolitanism, interaction, new product communication.
2. **Peer evaluations**—opinion leadership and group cohesion.
3. **Attitudinal measures**—norms on innovation and perceived risk.

When appropriate, data were secured for three product categories—food, clothing, and appliances—and a "total" score was generally based on these three component scores. Thus we can identify differences in findings depending on the product category

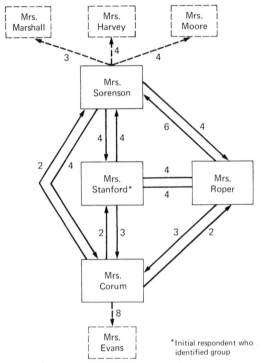

Figure 16.2 Reported Interaction, Group 11: Numbers Represent Total Reported Interactions by Telephone or in Person per Week: Solid Boxes—Specified Group; Dashed Boxes—Subsidiary Friendship Mentions

under consideration. Such differences can be noted initially in Table 16.2, which shows the total sample mean and standard deviation scores for each characteristic. Nonparametric techniques of hypothesis testing were used, and the Spearman (r_s) rank correlation coefficient was usually relied on.

FINDINGS

Rank correlation coefficients for each hypothesis are presented in Table 16.3. It can be concluded initially that the hypotheses relating to interaction are almost exclusively nonconfirmed, but the hypotheses relating to sentiment are generally confirmed.

Interaction

Extent of general group interaction in and of itself apparently does not lead to high innovativeness nor to similarity in innovative

TABLE 16.1
MEASUREMENT

CHARACTERISTIC	MEASURE
Innovativeness: food, clothing, appliances, total	Number of new products owned from a list of 42
Opinion leadership: product related	Peer evaluation of member's exercise of opinion leadership in food, clothing, and appliances
Opinion leadership: nonproduct related	Peer evaluation of member's "influence in general"
Norm on innovation	Attitude toward women who are first to buy new products
Group cohesion	Liking of group members for one another
Cosmopolitanism	Ratio of friends within the neighborhood to friends outside the neighborhood
Interaction	Telephone and in-person contacts per week
New product communication: food, clothing, appliances, total	Discussion with group members about new products
Perceived risk: food, clothing, appliances, total	Scale ranking of how "dangerous" or "safe" it is to buy new products

behavior patterns; neither, however, does new-product-related communication (A-1, A-2). This may be because both positive and negative information are transferred, and group agreement does not exist on the topic of new product adoption.

Arndt (1967b) has found that women who were exposed to positive word-of-mouth information about a new product were more likely to buy than women who were exposed to negative information. To the extent that a mixture of positive and negative information is relayed, a high level of innovative behavior would not be expected.

Festinger (1950) has found that group pressure to communicate concerning "item x" increases with perceived discrepancy in opinion among members of the group concerning that item. Thus higher communication about new products may relate less to consistency of innovative behavior than to perceived inconsistency.

This finding could also reflect the fact that members of a group do not have the same probability of buying new products —no matter how much communication occurs. Innovative behavior

TABLE 16.2
OVERALL MEANS AND STANDARD DEVIATIONS OF
CHARACTERISTICS

CHARACTERISTIC	MEAN/MAXIMUM	STANDARD DEVIATION
Activity		
Innovativeness:		
Food	8.7/14.0	2.6
Clothing	3.2/14.0	2.0
Appliances	4.2/14.0	1.8
Total	16.0/42.0	4.5
Interaction		
New product communication:		
Food	4.0/6.0	1.7
Clothing	4.2/6.0	1.5
Appliances	3.2/6.0	1.4
Total	3.8/6.0	1.3
Opinion leadership:		
Food	0.5[a]	0.6
Clothing	0.4[a]	0.7
Appliances	0.5[a]	0.8
Total	1.5[a]	1.1
Sentiment		
Norm on innovation		
Food	3.9	1.7
Clothing	3.1	1.4
Appliances	3.2	1.5
Total	4.1/6.0	0.9
Group cohesion	4.8/6.0	0.9
Social integration	3.4	1.7
Cosmopolitanism	2.7/6.0	1.1
Perceived risk:		
Food	2.4/6.0	1.2
Clothing	2.6/6.0	1.3
Appliances	2.7/6.0	1.3
Total	2.5/6.0	1.1

[a] Mean score is based on frequency of mentions without a specified range.

is very much related to certain predispositions of the person, and the innovator has indeed been found to be "different" from the later adopter. Within a group are individuals who may represent several adopter categories: innovators, early adopters, early majority, late majority, and laggards.

It would also seem desirable, in retrospect, to know the basis

TABLE 16.3
HYPOTHESIS TESTING: RANK CORRELATIONS

HYPOTHESIS	r_s
Interaction	
A-1. a) > interaction, > likeness	−.13
b) > interaction, > innovativeness	−.01
A-2. a) > innovation communication, > likeness	−.06
b) > innovation communication, > innovativeness	
total	−.19
food	−.10
clothing	.31
appliances	.00
A-3. > interaction, > opinion leadership	.38[b]
A-4. a) > opinion leadership, > likeness	−.03
b) > opinion leadership, > innovativeness	−.07
Sentiment	
B-1. > norm, > innovativeness	
total	.49[b]
food	.20
clothing	.53[a]
appliances	.34
B-2. > cohesiveness, > likeness	−.16
B-3. > cosmopolitanism, > innovativeness	
total	.48[b]
food	.15
clothing	.53[a]
appliances	.38[b]
B-4. > perceived risk, > communication	
total	.49[b]
food	.31
clothing	.35
appliances	.45[b]
B-5. < perceived risk, > innovativeness	
total	.56[a]
food	.53[a]
clothing	.00
appliances	.23
B-6. > cohesiveness, > opinion leadership	.56[a]

[a] r_s significant at .01 level.
[b] r_s significant at .05 level.

for the occurrence of communication. What percentage of communication is information seeking to arrive at a new product purchase decision? What percentage is related to a need for social support, given a state of cognitive dissonance? What percentage is related to attempts by group members to gain status in the group by novel or conspicuous consumption? Communication may serve a multiplicity of needs for group members and may not significantly alter an individual's propensity to innovate.

Degree of opinion leadership exercised by all group members is found to be significantly related to group interaction (A-3: $r_s = .38$, $< .05$ level). In framing this hypothesis, opinion leadership was not viewed as a discrete trait that either does or does not exist within the individual. Instead, opinion leadership is a matter of degree, and all persons can exercise a certain amount of influence. Also, opinion leadership was not viewed as a one-way occurrence—a dominant opinion leader influencing others—but, most often, as a two-way occurrence, whereby in the process of interaction, group members influence and are influenced.

The opinion leadership concept is misleading in many ways. One tends to think in terms of a dominant influential seeking out influencees who never influence the influential. Yet our research clearly shows that both source-initiated and recipient-initiated influences occur, influence often flows two ways, and influence is a matter of degree—no one person is exclusively influential. The idea of opinion transfer or *influence transfer* may more accurately reflect the underlying process.

The remaining interaction hypotheses, concerning posited relationships between opinion leadership and consistency and extent of innovative behavior, are not supported (A-4).[1] Again, it appears that both positive and negative influence transfer can occur; that the exercise of opinion leadership need not change a person's propensity to innovate; and that various underlying needs, which may not relate to consistency and extent of innovativeness, may prompt influence transfer.

Sentiment

Group innovativeness is significantly correlated with the favorability of the group norm on innovation (B-1: $r_s = .49$, $< .05$ level). The extent of this relationship, however, varies for the three product categories. Food ($r_s = .20$) and appliances ($r_s = .34$) innovativeness scores, although positively related to group norms, are not significantly related. Clothing innovativeness, on the other hand, is highly related to group norm ($r_s = .53$, $< .01$ level).

We would expect a greater relationship to exist between an activity (such as innovativeness) and the group norm on that

---

[1] C. W. King (1964) is one of the few researchers to report a similar "nonrelationship" between these variables.

activity to the degree that one or both of the following conditions are met: (1) the more important the activity to the group, the more binding the norm and the more severe the sanction for norm violation; (2) the more likely the observation of norm violation, the greater the risk in deviant behavior. In the present case, the norm-innovativeness correlation for clothing may be more significant because clothing activity is more meaningful than food and appliance activity, therefore a more rigidly defined norm is present. The higher correlation may also be due to the greater visibility of clothing, leading to greater norm adherence, since deviance is readily observable and punishable.

Results for hypothesis B-2 are not supported; indeed, a somewhat negative (although nonsignificant) relationship exists between group consistency on innovativeness and group cohesiveness. Greater attractiveness of the members for one another apparently does not mean that they will behave more alike in the purchase of new products. Again, the group seems to provide enough latitude for the performance of numerous innovativeness roles from innovator to laggard.

Group innovativeness is significantly related to cosmopolitanism (B-3: $r_s = .48$, $< .05$ level). Here we find that the more group members relate to people beyond the bounds of their group, the more innovative the group is likely to be. Cosmopolitanism is in some ways the inverse of cohesion or group interaction and communication; therefore, the positive findings here are consistent with findings for these other variables. Extragroup communication would seem to affect innovativeness more than intragroup communication, perhaps because the variety of outside contacts brings more new ideas for innovativeness to the group.

Variation in findings occurs for the cosmopolitanism-innovativeness relationship, by product category. A significant correlation is not achieved for food ($r_s = .15$), but the correlation coefficient for appliances is significant at the .05 level ($r_s = .38$), and the correlation coefficient for clothing is significant at the .01 level ($r_s = .53$). It can be argued that the woman does not have to be very cosmopolitan for food because mass media advertising emphatically promotes new food items. Somewhat more cosmopolitanism may be required for appliances, although this was not documented in an earlier study by Robertson (1968). Cosmopolitanism may well be necessary for the clothing area, since mass media cannot as clearly define new styles. There is considerable ambiguity about what is—or, especially, what will become—a new style, what is too new, what is appropriate to a given age group, and so on. The cosmopolitan (oriented beyond one's immediate group) quality itself may be accompanied by greater fashion consciousness due to more out-of-home, out-of-neighborhood visiting, requiring more dressing up.

Greater communication about new products is related to a higher level of perceived risk regarding new products (B-4: $r_s = .49, < .05$ level). This is most true for appliances. Communication as a risk-handling tactic is documented here much as in a number of other studies stemming from Bauer's (1960) original formulation of the perceived risk concept (Arndt, 1967b, 1968b; Bauer and Wortzel, 1966).

As a subsidiary issue, it was tested whether opinion leadership was associated with perceived risk. Cunningham (1967) found that high-risk perceivers exercise greater product-related influence, and Arndt (1968b) discovered that opinion leaders are lower on perceived risk. In the present analysis, groups high on opinion leadership are more likely to be high on perceived risk but not significantly ($r_s = .19$). Furthermore, this finding is fairly consistent across product categories (food: $r_s = .24$; clothing: $r_s = .25$; appliances: $r_s = .22$), which suggests that the Cunningham-Arndt difference is not due to differences in the products studied.

Innovativeness is associated with lower levels of perceived risk (B-5: $r_s = .56, < .01$ level). Despite the high association on a total basis, however, food is the only product category for which innovativeness is significantly correlated with perceived risk (food: $r_s = .53, < .01$ level; clothing: $r_s = .00$; appliances: $r_s = .23$). Yet less risk is perceived for food than for clothing or appliances, although the difference is not statistically meaningful (see Table 16.2).

A proposed explanation is, of course, appropriate although, unfortunately, beyond the data. It has been found previously that innovators are also risk takers (Robertson, 1968; Rogers, 1962). Perhaps women exhibit their capacity for daring activity in the clothing realm. If this is true, a certain amount of risk (e.g., in the purchase of a miniskirt or high boots) may be desirable and may yield the present finding. The appliance finding may have arisen partly because appliance purchases are most often joint husband-wife decisions, which spreads the risk and neutralizes the relationship with innovativeness.

Finally, it is found that greater opinion leadership is associated with greater group cohesiveness (B-6: $r_s = .56, < .01$ level). Therefore, group attractiveness, as well as group interaction, encourages influence transfer within the confines of the group.

TABLE 16.4
NORM-COMMUNICATION INTERRELATIONSHIP

NORM COMMUNICATION	HIGH		LOW		TOTAL FREQUENCY
	HIGH	LOW	HIGH	LOW	
Innovativeness					
High	2	4	2	1	9
Low	2	1	4	4	11
Total frequency	4	5	6	5	20
Percentage high					Expected
innovativeness	50	80	33	20	value[a] 45

[a] Expected value score is percentage of high innovativeness that would be obtained, assuming no relationship between variables.

Some Cross-Relationships

We now combine pairs of the more interesting variables and assess their associated values in terms of innovative behavior. Results here must be regarded as exploratory because of the small frequencies involved.

The first analysis (Table 16.4) concerns the interrelationship between norms and communication with innovativeness. The figures of most interest appear in percentage form at the bottom of the table. It is shown that a group has maximum probability of high innovativeness if it is high on norms and low on communication. This combination gives four times the chance of high innovativeness than low norm–low communication gives. It is further indicated that high communication lowers the probability of high innovativeness when the norm is high but increases it slightly when the norm is low.

Table 16.5 presents results quite similar to those of Table 16.4. Maximum probability of high innovativeness is under conditions of high norm and low cohesion. Other combinations give considerably lower and similar probabilities of high innovativeness. The norm-cosmopolitanism interrelation is explored in Table 16.6.

Table 16.7 gives results for the cohesion-cosmopolitanism Groups high on both variables or high on norm and low on cosmopolitanism are most likely to be high on innovativeness. coupling. As might be expected, low cohesion–high cosmopolitanism gives maximum probability of high innovativeness. The next best combination, however, is high cohesion–high cosmopolitanism,

TABLE 16.5
NORM-COHESION INTERRELATIONSHIP

	HIGH		LOW		TOTAL
NORM COHESION	HIGH	LOW	HIGH	LOW	FREQUENCY
Innovativeness					
High	1	5	2	1	9
Low	2	1	4	4	11
Total frequency	3	6	6	5	20
Percentage high					Expected
innovativeness	33	83	33	20	value[a] 45

[a] See note, Table 16.4.

indicating that these two factors can jointly contribute to innovativeness. The lowest incidence of high innovativeness is under conditions of high cohesion and low cosmopolitanism. A tightly knit group is less likely to be exposed to new ideas and (from Table 16.5) is less likely to be receptive to new ideas.

Table 16.8 gives some interesting results concerning the risk-communication interrelation. When risk is high, the probability of high innovativeness is very low. High risk–high communication actually results in less chance of high innovativeness than high risk–low communication. It would appear, therefore, that high-risk perceivers use both greater communication and less innovativeness as risk-handling tactics, and that high communication does not encourage them to engage in innovative behavior. This helps ex-

TABLE 16.6
NORM-COSMOPOLITANISM INTERRELATIONSHIP

NORM	HIGH		LOW		TOTAL
COSMOPOLITANISM	HIGH	LOW	HIGH	LOW	FREQUENCY
Innovativeness					
High	4	2	2	1	9
Low	2	1	2	6	11
Total frequency	6	3	4	7	20
Percentage high					Expected
innovativeness	67	67	50	14	value[a] 45

[a] See note, Table 16.4.

TABLE 16.7
COHESION-COSMOPOLITANISM INTERRELATIONSHIP

COHESION COSMOPOLITANISM	HIGH		LOW		TOTAL FREQUENCY
	HIGH	LOW	HIGH	LOW	
Innovativeness					
High	2	1	4	2	9
Low	2	4	2	3	11
Total frequency	4	5	6	5	20
Percentage high					Expected
innovativeness	50	20	67	40	value[a] 45

[a] See note, Table 16.4.

plain further why, in the earlier results, communication and innovativeness were not positively correlated. Under conditions of low risk and high communication, the probability of high innovativeness is at a maximum. Innovativeness and communication seem to bear a positive relationship, therefore, for low-risk perceivers.

Finally, Table 16.9 presents results relating norms and opinion leadership to innovativeness. Maximum probability of innovativeness occurs under conditions of high norm–low opinion leadership and minimum probability of innovativeness occurs under conditions of low norm–high opinion leadership. It has generally been held that the opinion leader is the most norm abiding, and we would expect that when norms are high, exercise of opinion leadership would result in highest innovativeness. This is apparently not the

TABLE 16.8
RISK-COMMUNICATION INTERRELATIONSHIP

RISK COMMUNICATION	HIGH		LOW		TOTAL FREQUENCY
	HIGH	LOW	HIGH	LOW	
Innovativeness					
High	1	1	4	4	10
Low	5	2	0	3	10
Total frequency	6	3	4	7	20
Percentage high					Expected
innovativeness	17	33	100	57	value[a] 50

[a] See note, Table 16.4.

TABLE 16.9
NORM-OPINION LEADERSHIP INTERRELATIONSHIP

NORM OPINION LEADERSHIP	HIGH		LOW		TOTAL FREQUENCY
	HIGH	LOW	HIGH	LOW	
Innovativeness					
High	2	4	1	2	9
Low	2	1	4	4	11
Total frequency	4	5	5	6	20
Percentage high					Expected
innovativeness	50	80	20	33	value[a] 45

[a] See note, Table 16.4.

case, and it appears that opinion leadership is operating in the service of conservatism rather than change.

CONCLUSION

Examination of small, informal neighborhood groups has revealed that certain group variables are strongly correlated with innovative behavior. Generally, group "sentiment" characteristics are more important than "interaction" characteristics in determining innovative "activity." Variables correlating most highly with innovativeness are group norm on innovation, cosmopolitanism, and level of perceived risk. Group interaction and cohesion are found to be related to opinion-leadership activity. Variables are found to have differential effects depending on the product category—food, clothing, or appliances. In predicting new product adoption, product-category characteristics should be systematically studied and related to group variables.

The group has been found to be a meaningful unit of analysis. Group study, in conjunction with individual consumer research, could well lead to improved predictions of the probability that an individual will adopt a new product in a given product category.

17

NEW PRODUCT DIFFUSION: THE INTERPLAY OF INNOVATIVENESS, OPINION LEADERSHIP, LEARNING, PERCEIVED RISK, AND PRODUCT ATTRIBUTES

JOHAN ARNDT
Research Director
Norwegian School of Business and Economics
Bergen

Since the turn of the century, researchers in a variety of behavioral science disciplines have studied the process of social contagion by which new ideas, practices, and products are spread through a society. Because marketing is concerned with the diffusion of products, such work ought to receive particular attention in marketing. However, in his review of research traditions in the diffusion of innovations, Rogers (1962) failed to include any marketing tradition. Moreover, C. W. King (1966, pp. 673–676), who surveyed 30 leading companies, concluded that industry expertise in adoption and diffusion research and theory was low.

But fortunately there are some encouraging signs. By 1967 more than 40 new product adoption studies were completed in marketing. Innovations investigated include coffee (Arndt, 1967a, 1968c; Frank, Massy, and Morrison, 1965), freeze-dried grocery

The author extends appreciation to the following Columbia graduate students who conducted the field work and participated in the design of the study and the data analysis: Laurence De France, Joseph F. Fennell, Wayne W. Rogers, Richard A. Temkin, and Angelo J. Trapasso.

products (J. G. Myers, 1966), frequently purchased household products (Haines, 1966), heavy-duty detergents (Pessemier, Burger, and Tigert, 1967), stainless steel razor blades (Sheth, 1968), dental products (Silk, 1966), new durable consumer goods (W. E. Bell, 1964), Touch-Tone telephones (Robertson, 1967), air conditioners (Whyte, 1954), fashions (C. W. King, 1964, 1965; Robertson and Rossiter, 1967), selection of physicians (S. P. Feldman, 1966), and patronage of new retail outlets (Kelly, 1967). The topics explored by marketing diffusion research includes characteristics of innovators (Arndt, 1968c; W. E. Bell, 1964; Frank et al., 1965; C. W. King, 1964, 1965; Opinion Research Corporation, 1959; Pessemier et al., 1967; Robertson, 1967), role and characteristics of opinion leaders (Arndt, 1967a; S. P. Feldman, 1966; C. W. King, 1964; Marcus and Bauer, 1964; J. G. Myers, 1966; Nicosia, 1965; Robertson and Rossiter, 1967; Silk, 1966), relative importance of personal and impersonal sources of information (W. E. Bell, 1964; S. P. Feldman, 1966; Haines, 1966), and the role of perceived risk (Arndt, 1967a, 1968c; Cunningham, 1965, 1967; Popielarz, 1967).

So far, most of the marketing diffusion studies have tended to focus on one or a few factors in the diffusion process, leaving out other variables of possible importance. Hence the studies have been somewhat narrow and have lacked sufficient theoretical bases. This has created a situation in which different research has frequently given conflicting results. For instance, some studies (Marcus and Bauer, 1964) have found overlap of opinion leadership across different areas, others (Silk, 1966) have found little overlap. Some clues to the reconciliation of such apparently discrepant findings may appear when we examine variables that may interact with degree of overlap. One such interacting variable may be the characteristics of the innovations.

The purpose of the exploratory study reported here was to throw more light on the dynamics of new product diffusion by investigating relationships among four key conceptual variables in three product classes. The products selected, which differed in complexity and unit price, were soft margarine, electric toothbrushes, and electric dishwashers.

The diffusion literature (Arndt, 1967c; Rogers, 1962) suggests that the following variables are particularly important elements in the diffusion process: innovativeness, opinion leadership, learning, and perceived risk.

The *innovators* and *opinion leaders* are *change agents* in the new product adoption process. The innovator or early buyer starts the diffusion process and gives new products "legitimacy." The opinion leader or influential is important because he or she occupies a central position in the word-of-mouth communication networks.

Learning and *perceived risk* are *informational* or "cognitive" variables. Learning refers to knowledge and experience relevant to the product category; perceived risk is the uncertainty discerned by consumers when confronted with new products. Since learning is expected to reduce uncertainty, these two variables would normally be inversely related.

How are these four conceptual variables related? The innovators are expected to be better informed. Hence they would be higher in learning and lower in perceived risk. Because of the competence and experience acquired, the innovators would be particularly likely to be sought for advice and to exert opinion leadership. Second, the competence and experience acquired for one product category may be transferred to other related product categories. Therefore, overlap of the conceptual variables across product categories may be expected when the product categories are similar in characteristics. The following two hypotheses were tested:

1. Within product classes, the four conceptual variables are interrelated. Specifically, positive relationships were expected among innovativeness, opinion leadership, and learning, but these three variables were expected to be negatively related to perceived risk.

2. The more similar the products, the more overlap of the conceptual variables across product classes. Specifically, overlap was expected between electric toothbrushes and electric dishwashers, but not between either of these products and soft margarine.

METHOD

The data reported were obtained from a telephone survey of 250 housewives selected by systematic sampling from the telephone directory of Queens, New York. The products chosen for study— soft margarine, electric toothbrushes, and electric dishwashers —differed in several characteristics, including perceived risk[1] and market saturation.

Table 17.1 shows the operational definitions and scoring ranges of the four conceptual variables: innovativeness, opinion leadership, learning, and perceived risk. As the table reveals, the

---

[1] Of the 250 wives in the sample, 15 percent reported they were "unsure" about picking the right brand of soft margarine, as compared with 22 percent for electric toothbrushes and 31 percent for electric dishwashers.

TABLE 17.1
OPERATIONAL DEFINITIONS AND SCORING RANGES OF FOUR
CONCEPTUAL VARIABLES IN THREE PRODUCT CLASSES

VARIABLE	SOFT MARGARINE
	MEASURE
Innovativeness	Time of first purchase of soft margarine
	1 (nonadopter)–6 (bought three years ago or before)
	MEASURE
Opinion leadership	"How often have friends sought your advice about soft margarine?
	1 (never)–5 (very often)
	MEASURE
Learning	Number of soft margarine brands recalled
	1 (none)–6 (five or more)
	MEASURE
Perceived risk	"How sure would you be of picking the best brand of soft margarine?"
	1 (very sure)–5 (unsure)

---

measure of *innovativeness* was time of first purchase. In all, 60 percent of the respondents had bought soft margarine, as compared
with 26 percent for electric toothbrushes and electric dishwashers.

For all three product classes, *opinion leadership* was measured by the self-designating technique. The question pertaining
to opinion leadership was: "How often have friends sought your
advice about (product class): never, seldom, sometimes, often, or
very often?"

In this study, the *learning* measure related to brand awareness (familiarity) and not to extent of brand loyalty. Learning
was operationally defined in terms of number of brands of the
product category the respondent could name by unaided recall.

Finally, *perceived risk* (uncertainty) was measured by the
responses to the following question: "How sure would you be of
picking the best brand of (product class): very sure, quite sure,
sure, not too sure, or unsure?"

ELECTRIC TOOTHBRUSH	ELECTRIC DISHWASHER
MEASURE Time of first purchase of electric toothbrush 1 (nonadopter)–7 (bought five years ago or before)	MEASURE Time of first purchase of electric dishwasher 1 (nonadopter)–7 (bought five years ago or before)
MEASURE "How often have friends sought your advice about electric toothbrushes?" 1 (never)–5 (very often)	MEASURE "How often have friends sought your advice about electric dishwashers?" 1 (never)–5 (very often)
MEASURE Number of electric toothbrush brands recalled 1 (none)–6 (five or more)	MEASURE Number of electric dishwasher brands recalled 1 (none)–6 (five or more)
MEASURE "How sure would you be of picking the best brand of electric toothbrush?" 1 (very sure)–5 (unsure)	MEASURE "How sure would you be of picking the best brand of electric dishwasher?" 1 (very sure)–5 (unsure)

FINDINGS

The findings are presented in two phases: (1) relationships among the four conceptual variables within product classes and (2) overlap of the variables across product classes.

Relationships Within Product Classes

As stated in the first hypothesis, innovativeness, opinion leadership, and learning were expected to be positively related, but these three variables were predicted to be negatively related to perceived risk. This hypothesis is strongly supported by the results in Table 17.2, which shows the intercorrelations among the four conceptual variables within the three product classes. All relationships were in the predicted direction, and all the correlation coefficients were significantly different from zero at the .01 level.

On the basis of diffusion theory (Arndt, 1967c, pp. 42–43;

TABLE 17.2
CORRELATIONS AMONG FOUR CONCEPTUAL VARIABLES
WITHIN THREE PRODUCT CLASSES[a]

(*Product-Moment Correlation Coefficients*)

VARIABLES CORRELATED	SOFT MARGARINE	ELECTRIC TOOTHBRUSH	ELECTRIC DISHWASHER
Innovativeness and opinion leadership	.40	.45	.70
Innovativeness and learning	.48	.44	.38
Innovativeness and perceived risk	−.43	−.42	−.33
Opinion leadership and learning	.30	.34	.31
Opinion leadership and perceived risk	−.36	−.39	−.40
Learning and perceived risk	−.35	−.41	−.43

[a] All the correlation coefficients are different from zero at the .01 level of significance.

Rogers, 1962, p. 184)[2] and previous work in marketing (Arndt, 1967a, 1968c; Nicosia, 1965; Pessemier et al., 1967; Robertson, 1967; Robertson and Rossiter, 1967),[3] it was predicted that the early buyers, having more experience and familiarity with the product, would be particularly likely to exert personal influence. The data in Table 17.2 give strong support to this hypothesis. For all the three products, innovativeness and opinion leadership were significantly correlated. Furthermore, the data suggest that the extent of overlap depends on the complexity and perceived risk of the product class. As complexity and risk increased from soft margarine to electric dishwashers, so did the overlap of innovativeness and opinion leadership. It was also expected that the prior experience of the early buyers would be reflected in a higher degree of learning and a lower perceived risk. The data support this prediction.

Since opinion leadership was found to be strongly related to

[2] According to Rogers (1962, pp. 233–236), overlap of innovativeness and opinion leadership is expected only when community norms are "modern"; that is, the norms favor innovativeness. In this case, it is believed that early purchase was compatible with the norms of the social systems.
[3] There are two notable exceptions. C. W. King (1965) and Pessemier et al. (1967) failed to find any positive relationship between innovativeness and opinion leadership.

innovativeness, it was expected that the profile of the opinion leaders would be similar to that of the early buyers. As seen in Table 17.2, this expectation is confirmed, as the leaders were higher in learning and lower in perceived risk. Thus the results corroborate previous findings reported by Arndt (1967a, 1968c) and Nicosia (1965). As predicted, perceived risk was inversely related to learning for all the three products.

Although the directions of the causal relationships cannot be established from correlational data such as these, it may be that before buying a new product, adopters try to reduce their perceived risk by seeking information. Once they have bought the product, the experience with the product, added to their already lower risk and higher learning, enables them to assume positions as opinion leaders. In the words of Elihu Katz (1957), their leadership roles rest on their competence ("what they know").

Overlap of the
Variables Across Product Classes

The published research on overlap of important diffusion variables across product classes is sparse. Moreover, some of the few studies reported have yielded conflicting results. Rogers (1962, p. 187) concludes that certain persons are consistently high in innovativeness in different areas. In marketing, Opinion Research Foundation (1959), Robertson (1967), and Whyte (1954) have reported findings that suggest a generalized tendency among certain individuals to be among the early buyers.

For opinion leadership, the picture is not clear. In the well-known Decatur study, E. Katz and Lazarsfeld (1955, pp. 332–334) concluded that there was little overlapping opinion leadership in fashion, marketing, and public affairs. Marcus and Bauer (1964) reanalyzed the Decatur data and claimed that there *were* generalized opinion leaders. However, in a study of leaders for five dental products and services, Silk (1966) found little overlapping.

Regarding perceived risk, Cunningham (1967), who studied risk for headache remedies, fabric softeners, and dry spaghetti, found that "some people have a generalized tendency to perceive either high or low risk across a range of products."

One clue to when to expect overlapping is provided by learning theory. A person's buying behavior regarding a new product is a function of prior experience or stored information ("what one knows"). The stored information relating to one product class may be generalized to other similar product classes. However, this information cannot be generalized to product classes that are very

TABLE 17.3
OVERLAP OF FOUR CONCEPTUAL VARIABLES
ACROSS PRODUCT CLASSES

(Product-Moment Correlation Coefficients)

PRODUCT CLASSES	INNOVA-TIVENESS	OPINION LEADER-SHIP	LEARN-ING	PER-CEIVED RISK
Soft margarine and electric toothbrush	−.01	.05	.20[a]	.07
Soft margarine and electric dishwasher	−.01	.06	.17[a]	−.04
Electric toothbrush and electric dishwasher	.06	.31[a]	.28[a]	.22[a]

[a] Significant at the .01 level.

different in characteristics. In this case, electric toothbrushes and electric dishwashers were thought to be fairly similar in the sense that both were complex appliances that were high in perceived risk. Soft margarine, on the other hand, being a low-price grocery product, would appear to be very different from the appliances. Therefore, it was expected that there would be overlap of the four conceptual variables for toothbrushes and dishwashers, but little overlapping was predicted between soft margarine and either of the appliances. The data in Table 17.3 bear out the expectations. For opinion leadership, learning, and perceived risk, but not for innovativeness, there were significant overlaps for toothbrushes and dishwashers. Between the two appliances and soft margarine, there was overlap only for learning.

In summary, the findings in this study lend little support to the notion that the four conceptual variables represent generalized personality tendencies. On the other hand, the variables are not completely specific to one product class only. The extent of overlap seems to depend on the similarity of the product classes and/or the extent to which prior learning may be generalized.

SUMMARY AND CONCLUSION

The results of this exploratory survey have given evidence that the early buyers of three new products differ systematically in characteristics from other adopter categories. The early buyers are consistently high in opinion leadership and learning and low in perceived risk. There is overlapping for these four conceptual variables for similar products. When the products differ in characteristics, there is less overlap.

In a correlational study such as this, the direction of causality is not clear. For instance, are the early buyers more responsive to new products because they are higher in learning and lower in risk? Or have they become higher in learning and lower in risk as a result of their experience with the product? Future research should aim at determining the temporal sequence of these conceptual variables by means of laboratory and field experimentation.

18

REPEAT BUYING OF A NEW BRAND:
A 10-POINT CASE HISTORY

A. S. C. EHRENBERG and G. J. GOODHARDT
Aske Research Ltd.
London, England

MEANINGLESS STATISTICS

It has long been recognized in the marketing of new products that
the repeat-buying rate is crucial to success or failure. Three things
are needed to make this notion operational: (1) repeat-buying
behavior has to be actually measured, (2) the data have to be
suitably tabulated, and (3) the tabulated figures have to be interpreted. We discuss these three stages in terms of a case history;
the first two are covered in the first part of this paper and the
interpretive one in the second part.

Data on Repeat-Buying Behavior

Repeat buying for many nondurable products is automatically
measured by continuous consumer panel operations. Vast amounts
of raw data are accumulated in the basic panel records. Such
measurements, however, have to be extracted (e.g., by way of a
buying pattern) and suitably tabulated. Little of this is done; apart

Based on a case study carried out for the Marketing Analysis and
Evaluation Group, Unilever Ltd. The data are from the Attwood Consumer
Panel and the Television Consumer Audit operated by Audits of Great Britain
Ltd.

TABLE 18.1
4-WEEKLY RATES OF BUYING THE BRAND N

(Large and Small Pack Sizes During First 18 Months)

	4-WEEK PERIODS DURING	
	FIRST HALF-YEAR	SECOND AND THIRD HALF-YEARS
PENETRATION AND BUYING ROLE	INCREASING FAST TO	DECREASING SLOWLY TO
Small Pack Size		
Percentage of households buying	1.5	1.2[a]
Average units per buyer in period	1.7	1.8[a]
Large Pack Size		
Percentage of households buying	1.5	1.1[a]
Average units per buyer in period	1.7	1.7[a]

[a] Irregular 4-weekly fluctuations average at about ±0.3.

from extracting simple brand-share and demographic breakdowns, most of the data collected are barely analyzed and studied.

One buying pattern that was recently examined covered the first 18 months of a certain new brand N. The basic rates of purchasing in successive 4-week periods can be summarized briefly for each pack size, as in Table 18.1.

The Small Pack Size. The penetration of the small pack size of brand N increased rapidly during the first half-year or so of the launch, to about 1.5 percent of the population buying per 4 weeks, as is summarized in Table 18.1. During the following year the percentage of 4-weekly buyers dropped slowly to about 1.2 percent.

The average amounts bought similarly rose at the start to a level of about 1.7 units per household buying in 4 weeks. Amounts then stayed at roughly this level for the rest of the study period.

The basic repeat-buying tabulations are summarized in Table 18.2. During the first half-year about 25 percent of buyers in one 4-week period bought again in the following 4 weeks. They bought at an average rate of just under 2 units per repeat buyer per 4 weeks. In the next year the percentage of such repeat buyers was higher at about 45 percent; these repeat buyers then bought just over 2 units per average repeat buyer.

TABLE 18.2
4-WEEKLY REPEAT BUYING OF BRAND N

(Large and Small Pack Sizes During First 18 Months)

	4-WEEK PERIODS DURING	
	FIRST HALF-YEAR	SECOND AND THIRD HALF-YEARS
REPEAT BUYING	AVERAGE LEVEL	AVERAGE LEVEL
Small Pack Size		
Percentage of buyers in one period who also bought in preceding period	25	45
Average units per repeat buyer	1.7	2.2
Large Pack Size		
Percentage of buyers in one period who also bought in preceding period	55	42
Average units per repeat-buyer	1.9	2.1

The Large Pack Size. The statistics for the large pack size of brand N were similar to those for the small size, except that in the initial launch months, the percentage of 4-weekly repeat buyers who bought again (55 percent) was higher than in the next year (40 percent), a reversal of the pattern for the small pack size.

High or Low: Good or Bad?

What do these data mean. Are the observed repeat-buying rates in Table 18.2 high or low? Do the figures imply future "success" or future "failure" of the brand in question? What marketing action do they indicate? Are the 4-weekly repeat-buying indices in Table 18.2 the correct ones to use? Do we know what quarterly repeat-buying figures, for example, would tell us? Would another kind of repeat-buying rate lead to radically different interpretation and decisions?

The notion that repeat-buying data are crucial in the assessment and prediction of the progress of a new product is often put forward when no repeat-buying data are available. When we actually have the data, their meaning seems less clear. We still need a framework of generalizable background knowledge to interpret the observed statistics.

AN INITIAL INTERPRETATION
Basic Requirements for Interpretation

The interpretation of repeat-buying data requires past experience of a wide range of cases. Without having studied past data, one cannot know anything. We are unaware that anyone has successfully studied many cases—certainly we have not done so. Despite this, we are constantly being asked whether we can predict the subsequent success or failure of a newly launched brand! Perhaps this is because some analysts have in fact put forward procedures for "predicting" the future success of new brands.

Some of them (e.g., Baum and Dennis, 1961; Fourt and Woodlock, 1960) describe predictors that appear to have "worked" in the two or three case histories in which they were developed. A development of some of this earlier work (e.g., Parfitt and Collins, 1968) involves the rejection of one of the radical assumptions in the earlier work (that the particular "repeat rate" in question was constant). Other work such as Massy's STEAM model (1966, 1968) is much more unambiguously nonempirical in its roots. This is not to say STEAM will not work, only that no one knew at the time of its conception whether it would, or how valid any "predictions" based on it might be.

In contrast, Davis (1964) described the simple up-and-down patterns of the aggregate sales curves of 44 newly launched brands. There was nothing explictly predictive about the main part of Davis's paper. It was an unpretentious attempt to distill a lot of explicit experience of one of the simpler aspects of what actually happens in a new product launch. By the same token, we do not aim to predict anything about new products in the present paper, which is limited to an examination of the repeat-buying statistics in the single case history of brand N, as described previously.

To understand these repeat-buying statistics, we need to refer to more general experience. This experience is indirect, since it concerns repeat-buying behavior for established brands and under stationary or "no-trend" conditions (Chatfield, Ehrenberg, and Goodhardt, 1966). We do not refer to any other kinds of generalizable background experience—concerning, for example, new products as such or nonstationary trend conditions in general —simply because we have no systematic generalizable knowledge and understanding of such other situations.

What Measures of Repeat Buying to Use?

Perhaps the first question to consider in analyzing repeat-buying behavior involves the measures or indices of repeat buying to be used. The measures that appear in Table 18.2 describe repeat buying in successive equal time periods. One alternative would be to analyze the observed buying records in terms of each consumer's successive purchases (e.g., Kuehn, 1962). Little seems to be known about this approach, aside from isolated case histories and speculative theory. The choice of any particular measure of repeat buying is not a matter of fundamental importance; the different measures must relate to one another. Suitably handled, they would all lead to the same conclusions. The choice at this stage must fall on the measures one can handle most efficiently, and they tend to be the ones that are already best understood.

Average Amount Bought per Buyer

We know that the repeat-buying characteristics of an established brand whose sales are stationary from one period to another are generally uniquely related to (or predictable from) a *single* aspect of purchasing. This is the average amount bought per buyer in just one period, which we usually denote by w.

Examples of such one-parameter relationships are that the number of packs bought by the average repeat buyer is about $1.2w$, and the number of repeat buyers as a proportion of all buyers in a single period is about $2(1 - w)/1 - 2.3w)$. These simple but approximate formulas hold for $w \geq 2$; for lower values of w, somewhat more complex formulas take over (Chatfield et al., 1966).

As an illustration, consider a stationary established brand whose 4-weekly buyers buy it at an average rate of 2 packs in the 4 weeks. One would then find that about 56 percent of its buyers in one 4-week period had bought it also in the previous equal period and that these repeat buyers would have bought the brand at an average rate of about $1.2 \times 2 = 2.4$ packs in each period.

Comparisons of Brand N with
the Stationary Repeat-Buying Norms

The observed repeat-buying statistics for the two pack sizes of brand N in Table 18.2 can now be compared with the repeat-buying patterns for an established brand with the same value of w. Such comparisons appear in Table 18.3, restricted for simplicity to the second and third half-years of the launch, when the overall

TABLE 18.3
4-WEEKLY REPEAT BUYING OF LARGE AND SMALL
SIZES OF BRAND N

**Comparisons with Stationary Norms for Established Brands Bought at
Same Average Rate Per Buyer During Second and Third Half-Years
(After Launch of Brand N)**

	SMALL PACK[a]		LARGE PACK[b]	
	OBSERVED	NORM	OBSERVED	NORM
Percentage of buyers who also bought in previous period	45	53	42	50
Average units per repeat-buyer	2.2	2.2	2.1	2.1

[a] Average amount bought per buyer: $w = 1.8$.
[b] Average amount bought per buyer: $w = 1.7$.

penetration and buying rates of brand N were already relatively
stable. The results are of two kinds.

First, the average amounts bought per repeat buyer were the
same as the stationary norms. Thus the observed values showed
little if any difference from what has been found in these respects
for established brands—the average repeat buyer buying about
2.2 or 2.1 units per 4 weeks.

In contrast, the observed incidence of repeat buyers was
some 8 percentage points lower than generally occurs for established brands bought at the same average rate $w = 1.7$ or 1.8. This
difference from the norm is in line with every day experience;
namely, that new brands tend to be tried out by a relatively large
number of new buyers, making the relative incidence of repeat
buyers somewhat low. The comparisons in Table 18.3 confirm this
effect and give a quantitative measure of it.

Nonstationarity

One feature of the brand N data is that although in the second
and third half-years the 4-weekly penetration and purchasing rates
stayed fairly steady at the levels summarized in Table 18.1, there
were quite a few short-term fluctuations from one 4-week period
to the next, as noted in the footnote to Table 18.1.

Little is known about repeat-buying patterns under such nonstationary conditions, even for established products. To explore
the situation, the observed repeat-buying patterns for brand N for

TABLE 18.4
4-WEEKLY REPEAT BUYING IN NONCONSECUTIVE PERIODS

Comparison with Stationary Norms (*Second and Third Half-Years*)

	SMALL PACK[a]		LARGE PACK[b]	
	OBSERVED	NORM	OBSERVED	NORM
Percentage of buyers who bought also in other period	36	53	40	50
Average units per repeat buyer	2.1	2.2	2.1	2.1

[a] Average amount bought per buyer: $w = 1.8$.
[b] Average amount bought per buyer: $w = 1.7$.

certain nonconsecutive pairs of time periods were tabulated. These periods were chosen to form pairs that had virtually no difference in sales or penetration levels. Comparisons between these observed patterns and those that would have occurred for a fully stationary established brand with the same values of w are summarized in Table 18.4. The average amounts bought per repeat buyer are again "normal" at about 2.1; but the incidence of repeat buyers differs from the normal stationary results by even more than the 8-point differences for consecutive periods shown in Table 18.2.

Some Follow-up Data

The comparisons in Tables 18.3 and 18.4 show that even 18 months after the launch, neither pack size of brand N had "settled down" to the normal repeat-buying pattern found for established brands. However, in the last pair of 4-weekly periods, the incidence of repeat buyers for the small pack size increased markedly to 56 percent, reaching in effect the "normal" repeat-buying percentage of 53 percent. However, for the large pack, the observed number of repeat buyers in the last two periods remained some 5 percentage points below the stationary norm. This is summarized in the first two lines of Table 18.5.

Although it looked as though at least the small pack size was beginning to "settle down" to the normal repeat-buying level, this effect was observed in only one pair of time periods, and there was some question of statistical significance. Thus no firm conclusion was possible.

Some time after this case history study had been completed, additional data for brand N became available covering most of

TABLE 18.5
4-WEEKLY REPEAT BUYING IN A FOURTH HALF-YEAR[a]

Comparison with Stationary Norms

	SMALL PACK (%)		LARGE PACK (%)	
	OBSERVED	NORM	OBSERVED	NORM
Second and Third Half-Year				
All periods (as in				
Table 18.2)	45	53	42	50
Last two 4-week periods	56	53	45	50
Fourth Half-Year	45	47	35	45

[a] Data from a different region and a different consumer panel.

the fourth half-year after its launch. The observed and estimated 4-weekly percentages of repeat buyers are given in the last line of Table 18.5. The data were for a different region of the country and came from a different consumer panel, operated in a somewhat different technical manner, but they confirm (*a*) that the incidence of repeat buyers for the small pack size had virtually settled down to the normal level for an established brand (45 vs. 47 percent); and (*b*) that the incidence of repeat buyers for the large pack size was still below the normal level, even two years after the launch (35 vs. 45 percent).

A Challenge and a Wager

The question remains whether any of the results reported here generalize to other new product launches, and if so, under what conditions, and how do such data relate to eventual success or failure. If we knew that we might be able to forecast successfully whether a new brand would succeed or fail!

The results summarized so far, together with one or two other fractional case histories, represent the sum total of our knowledge of repeat-buying patterns for new brands. We obviously know extraordinarily little. Even so; the foregoing results seem to represent more understanding about new brands than has otherwise been available. We are certainly prepared to challenge anyone who is examining a new brand to stop his speculative model building, and instead of merely thinking about the future of the new brand, let him state what he already knows and understands of its past.

Ultimately it is of course necessary to be able to use one's understanding for making improved forecasts and more successful marketing decisions—will the new brand succeed. And what marketing action should one take? At this stage there is virtually no basis for making such informed forecasts, because our organized understanding of the facts is so limited. We are, however, prepared to wager that by eschewing attempts to predict the future before we have generalizable understanding of the past, progress will be quicker.

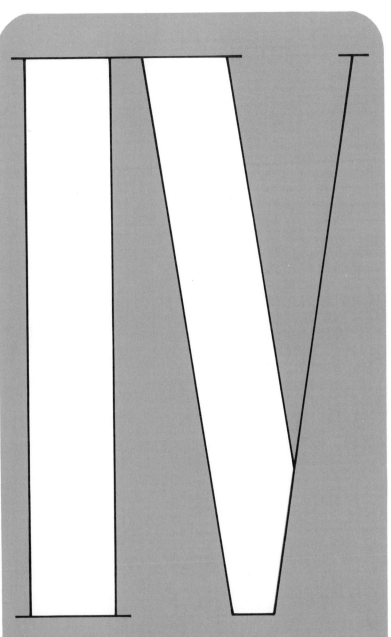

IV

MODELS OF
CONSUMER TYPOLOGY AND
MARKET SEGMENTATION

19

AN EMPIRICAL FRAMEWORK FOR PRODUCT CLASSIFICATION

CHARLES K. RAMOND
Adjunct Professor
Graduate School of Business Administration
New York University
and President, Marketing Control, Inc.
HENRY ASSAEL
Professor of Business
Graduate School of Business Administration
New York University

In this paper, we attempt to develop a framework for a product typology based on both consumer and distributive responses. The purpose is to suggest new ways of defining products and brands with a view toward simplifying and improving managerial and research decisions that must follow from the explicit or implicit definition used by the decision maker.

The development of a logical classification of products has appeal, the assumption being that similarly defined products can be priced, distributed, and promoted in a similar manner. The treatment of every product as unique does not serve the need to develop generalizations in conditions of uncertainty. Product classifications are useful as a comparative framework for evaluating current strategy and as a starting point for developing new product strategies. Valid product classification might assist the product manager in defining the arena in which he chooses to compete, the competition he will regard as important, and the denominator he generally uses as his personal and corporate score card: brand share. It might assist the market researcher in determining what he will investigate in his search for new product ideas and the techniques he will use in those investigations.

The best-known classification schemes—Copeland's (1923) early delineation of products as convenience, shopping and specialty goods, and Aspinwall's later (1962) characteristics of goods theory—could be rationalized on this basis. The recent emphasis on product taxonomy, especially cluster analysis, could be viewed as a more heuristic approach to the classification problem. Brands clustered together by consumer perceptions or similarity ratings can be assumed to be purchased on the same criteria. Promotional or pricing implications required for maintaining a brand in a given cluster or moving it to another position in perceptual space are then formed. This approach also has appeal because it moves away from classifications by product characteristics, which may not be relevant, to a classification by consumer perceptions and responses, which must be relevant.

The heuristic nature of these techniques poses problems for the marketing manager, however, for the relationships are not likely to remain constant and do not provide a basis for a system of classification.

Ideally, a classification scheme would represent a fixed scale of values on which a product could be positioned. Such a scale should be:

1. Measurable for the brand or product category
2. Independent of the characteristics by which the object's position is defined (i.e., not self-fulfilling)
3. Related to a number of relevant consumer, distributive and product characteristics
4. Continuous
5. Operationally meaningful to marketing management

Neither Copeland's nor Aspinwall's classifications clearly fit these criteria.

We would like to identify three approaches to product classification. All three find it necessary to define a product as a relation between two kinds of information. First, they must view the product as a relation between physical ingredients and psychological responses (a *psychophysical* definition). Here a measure of classification might be developed by clustering techniques. Second, they must define the product in terms of consumer actions and channel response (or what might be termed a *distributive velocity* definition). We later propose that such a measure might be the lag between factory shipments and retail sales. Third, they need a relation between awareness, attitude change or other communications effects, and purchase behavior (or what might be defined as a *mental velocity* measure).

Each definition naturally follows from the practical problem it addresses. The resulting taxonomies are rudimentary at best, and few data can be adduced to support any correlation between the product types thus defined. The psychophysical mechanism of classification is considered first. Then we describe a framework for classification centering on distributive velocity, but incorporating such consumer decision processes as mental velocity.

A PSYCHOPHYSICAL CLASSIFICATION

All students of buyer behavior at some time must have experienced the frustration caused by the inadequate taxonomies they have inherited from years of usage of traditional product categories. Perhaps the keenest frustrations are felt by those in search of new brands, for to them the right or wrong definition of a product can mean success or failure on a million-dollar scale.

A product is not a unitary or indivisible phenomenon. On the one hand, it has many physical attributes that together define it objectively. On the other hand, it gives rise to a number of consumer responses, most of them being hopefully of the pleasant or rewarding sort, and these psychological responses together define the product subjectively. Thus a product may be thought of as a vehicle or mediator of a bundle of physical attributes that produce a bundle of psychological or behavioral responses.

This definition is valuable because it permits us to classify products into logically different types, each of which can be associated with a kind of inferential research that ought to be uniquely appropriate in generating new ideas for products of that type. If a product is defined as a collection of physical attributes that produce a collection of psychological responses, we ought to be able to classify all products according to the *number* of rewarding responses they typically provide. An automobile provides more rewards than an aspirin, for example, and a cosmetic more rewards than a soft drink. This is an important dimension for determining what kind of idea-generating approach is most appropriate to each product class. Products that provide many rewards will require idea-generating techniques different from products that provide few.

The next dimension we must consider is that of *how well we know how to deliver whatever rewards the product provides.* In analytical terms this dimension is simply our degree of knowledge about how to generate the rewarding psychological responses from manipulation of the physical attributes of the product class. We may be sure, for example, that a great new product idea in analgesics would be one that provided faster pain relief. No further consumer research is needed to demonstrate this. Unfortunately, however, drug manufacturers apparently do not yet know how to change the physical attributes of analgesics to provide even faster pain relief than that now offered. In this product class, what is clearly needed is pharmacological research or physical research and development, not more consumer research to identify which of several possible rewards analgesics should try to provide.

A rough typology of product classes can be made from these two dimensions, the number of rewards the product class generates, and our knowledge of how to deliver these rewards. The four resulting types are presented in Table 19.1, along with examples of products that fall in each type, and the inferential research technique most appropriate to each type.

There are basically two messages in Table 19.1:

1. If the product class generates many rewards, we must first identify and put priorities on rewards that are most important to consumers; this requires *reductive* research (i.e., research designed to reduce the number of dimensions of preference for brands in this product class down to a manageable number, like three or four). For one of the earliest illustrations of such reductive research, see Stoetzel (1960).

2. If we do not know how physically to generate a high level of the most important rewards, we must do psychophysical research to learn "recipes" for producing them; in other words, it does us little good to learn the most important consumer benefits in a product class if we do not know how to manipulate the physical ingredients of the product to generate them.

Most of the fashionable techniques for generating new product ideas have concentrated on reductive research, to the virtual exclusion of psychophysical research or "recipe development." Market structure analysis and perceptual mapping are basically

TABLE 19.1
A WAY OF CLASSIFYING PRODUCTS TO SUGGEST
WHICH KINDS OF CONSUMER RESEARCH ARE NEEDED
TO GENERATE PROFITABLE NEW PROUCT IDEAS

	PRODUCT TYPE			
DATA	SIMPLE-PHYSICAL	COMPLEX-PHYSICAL	SIMPLE-PSYCHO-LOGICAL	COMPLEX-PSYCHO-LOGICAL
Number of rewards it provides	Few	Many	Few	Many
Our present knowledge of how to deliver those rewards	Good	Good	Poor	Poor
Products in this class	Metals, chemicals	Automobiles, cameras	Analgesics, air travel	Food, drugs, toiletries, clothing
Kind of consumer research needed	None	Reductive	Psycho-physical	Reductive and psycho-physical

techniques for learning how consumers perceive actual brands or verbal descriptions of possible new brands. Such knowledge should make it possible to identify "gaps in the preference structure" that could presumably be filled by a formulatable new product. This is not always the case, however, since technological feasibility and the relevance of consumer purchasing criteria are also significant.

THE DAY WE
REINVENTED CHOCOLATE MILK

Better than any single case with which we have been involved, the following story illustrates most of the logical and technical errors one can make in using research to generate new product ideas.

The object was to create the "better brownie." We knew, or thought we knew, the dimensions of preference for existing kinds of brownies; indeed, these dimensions had been so often spoken of around the client's office that "everybody knew" the factors determining consumers' preference for brownies. These were sweet-

ness, chocolatiness, and moistness. It seemed relatively straightforward to invite consumers to taste various existing brands of
brownies and rate them on each of these three dimensions as well
as on an overall preference scale. It was then a simple matter to
plot each brand in a three-dimensional space where the coordinates stood for sweet, chocolate, and moist, and to number each
brand according to its overall preference. Unlike some of our previous research, the results here were exceedingly clear. Consumer
preference for a brownie was clearly and positively related to how
sweet and moist they perceived it and not related to how choc-
laty they perceived it. Thus we concluded that the "better brownie"
should be sweeter and moister, and we said to the kitchen: "Make
us such a brownie."

"Congratulations," came back a memo. "You have just re-
invented chocolate milk."

The reader who has followed the argument thus far will
already have seen the four major errors in our approach:

1. *We made the mistake of assuming we knew the most
important dimensions of preference.* Instead of taking for granted
the traditional assumptions that the most important independent
dimensions of preference for brownies were sweetness, chocolatiness, and moistness, we should have analyzed simple preference
ratings of existing brands of brownies, probably by factor analysis,
to see (as Stoetzel did for the liquor preferences of French consumers) whether we could identify or infer the consumers' real
dimensions of preference without putting words in their mouths.
To many consumers, the sweetness, chocolatiness, or moistness of
a brownie might have made no difference at all. Every consumer,
however, could rank a series of brownies in order of preference.
The moral here is that only by examining the rearrangement of
brands evaluated according to their loadings on the factors that
underlie the simple preference ratings can one avoid the trap of
having the consumer merely repeat back ratings on possibly irrelevant dimensions.

2. *Since we did not actually undertake reductive research,
we were led to assume that these dimensions were independent.*
It is not surprising that having merely assumed the dimensions of
preference, these turned out not to be independent. Chocolatiness,
for example, is highly correlated with sweetness, not only in the
consumer's mind but in the ingredient formulation as well. To
make a brownie more chocolaty, after a certain point one adds
not more chocolate but more sugar. Again factor analysis would
have saved us from this error, since whatever dimensions it may

unearth are by definition as independent of each other as the data will permit.

3. *We failed to identify the boundary conditions of even the fallacious relationships we observed.* Instead of producing a moister brownie, our results called for what the kitchen could only call "lumpy chocolate milk." Clearly one cannot follow even the best inferences from consumer ratings too far from the values on which they rest.

4. *As a result, we failed to examine the psychophysical relationships between the consumers' perceptions of brownies and the physical ingredients of brownies.* Had we done this, or even talked to the knowledgeable cooks in the kitchen, we would have needed no factor analysis to show that sweet and chocolate were not independent dimensions. Nor would we have needed anything more than a good cook's advice to tell us that the boundaries of the relationships we had observed were very near at hand—that the moistest of the brownie brands evaluated was about as moist as it could get, and to add any more fluid to the recipe would leave us with a soggy mess. In summary, therefore, this fourth error of ignoring the psychophysical relationships subsumes two of the three previous errors; to know the psychophysical relationships for existing brands at the outset can guide the planner in his choice of the most appropriate analytic techniques.

But even when we know the necessary psychophysical relationships to reproduce existing brands, we must avoid the first error listed—assuming that we know the dimensions of preference. These must be inferred from the best data available, and these data are almost never consumer ratings of brands on arbitrary ratings scales. The reader may wonder if our error in the brownie example was simply that of assuming too few ratings scales. After all, brownies have more characteristics than sweetness, chocolatiness, and moisture. Perhaps this trap can be avoided by using a much larger number of rating scales. This is also a snare and delusion, as the following case indicates.

THE DAY THEY FOUND
THAT COFFEE WAS REALLY COFFEE

A major food manufacturer once hired an Indian Ph.D. candidate to design and analyze a study of consumer preferences for coffee brands in hopes of developing a superior new brand for certain market segments (Mukherjee, 1965). The study was done in the classic fashion. Each consumer rated the brand on a number of scales and then gave it an overall preference rating. The scaled ratings were correlated with the preference scores and factor analyzed in the hope of isolating the underyling dimensions of preference.

What makes this study interesting is that unlike the brownie example, several dozen attributes of coffee were examined. Indeed, it seemed that the analyst had gone to great pains to include every word in the English language that might conceivably describe coffee (e.g., smooth, aromatic, bitter, pleasant, acid). Surely, one would argue, with such a massive list of possible attributes the investigator could hardly be accused of overlooking anything that might be part of a major dimension of preference.

The results of the factor analysis were not too enlightening. The first factor to be extracted had high loadings on perhaps 20 or 30 of the attributes scaled, most of them relating to the consumer perceptions one might reasonably expect to differentiate coffee from other beverages (coffee taste, Colombian flavor, coffee aroma, etc.). To name this factor, one would be obliged to choose "coffeeness" as the best possible name; that is, the major dimension of preference for coffee is that it taste like coffee. There was no other dimension of preference anywhere near it in explanatory power.

So we see that merely to use a large dictionary of product attributes is no guarantee that we will find the "underlying dimensions of preference." The reason for this is not hard to find. By now the reader has probably begun to suspect that there are distinct perils in using verbal descriptions of products or brands as the basic data from which to start. The consumer may understand, or think she understands, the brands to be evaluated, and she may also think she understands the words by which she is invited to evaluate them. The trouble is that each consumer may find it more or less difficult to express her true preference for the *brands* in terms of the *descriptors* provided, no matter how many of them there are.

For the word is not the thing. Each of us has learned habitual responses to familiar brands and habitual ways of using the English language. But our habits of language are much better learned than our habits of response to such trivial objects in our total experience as brands of consumer products. When we consider all the habits and preferences an individual has acquired in his lifetime, it becomes clear that those relating to brand choice are among the most trivial. In some product classes, for example, it can be shown that brand-switching behavior is essentially random, with a few constraints related to such obvious factors as price, store loyalty, and demographic characteristics. The various brands of the product are so alike that almost any brand can provide the real and learned satisfactions inherent in the product class—and this is often true no matter how staunchly advertising has struggled to create or teach perceived differences among the brands. To test this assertion, let the reader ask himself how he would rate Maxim versus Taster's Choice on aroma, using a seven-point hedonic scale or any other rating system, or how he would rate Budweiser versus Schlitz in "real beer taste."

Even when brands in a product class can be shown to differ in certain perceptible attributes, the average consumer is in deep trouble when asked to express her personal preferences for brands on these attributes in terms of the blunt instrument we call the English language. It is hardly surprising that not many such verbal responses can be replicated. The few tests of the reliability of verbal ratings scales have not been favorable. If a new product planner is determined to use such scales to generate new product ideas, he owes it to his firm to check their reliability before recommending new formulations on the basis of their results.

But there is a better way out of the tempting verbal trap: use only nonverbal ratings. Stoetzel recognized this as early as 1960 when he determined the dimensions of preference for liquors from no other data than respondents' numerical rankings of nine brands of liquor. He put no words in the respondents' mouths; he made no assumptions about which attributes should be rated; he merely asked respondents to arrange the nine brands in order of preference. If the respondent protested or asked "preference for what?" the interviewer would simply say, "your overall preference" or something equally nondescriptive. In effect, the interviewer was saying: You tell me.

To develop new product ideas one may ask the consumer to evaluate a sample of a universe of words or a sample of a universe of things; clearly the rule should be: *evaluate things, not words*. This is probably the most violated rule in research to generate new product ideas today. Almost all such studies have used verbal rating scales of one kind or another. Indeed, the establishment of a word-thing dictionary has often become an end in itself, to the exclusion of learning the logically prior relationships between a brand's physical ingredients and the consumer's preference for it. Yet there is no compelling reason why this should be. Methods of nonverbal evaluation have been with us for ages, and worked examples of the analytic procedures have been in print since the mid-1950s.

In any case, the moral is simply that to define products in terms of how well we understand their psychophysical relationships aids our search for new brand ideas.

DISTRIBUTIVE VELOCITY
AS A CLASSIFICATION SCHEME

In a similar fashion, defining products in terms of consumer and distributive input/output relationships can also assist in developing the marketing mix. In fact, the earliest product classifications were based on consumer response in terms of frequency of purchase and search time. We propose to revert to these considerations by offering a related basis for classification—distributive velocity—and extending it more fully to consumer decision processes. *Distributive velocity* is the speed with which a brand reaches the consumer's shelf, or alternately, the amount of lag between factory shipments and retail sales. This classification is somewhat similar to those of Copeland (1923) and Aspinwall (1962). Goods with a high velocity are likely to be convenience goods, or "red" goods to use Aspinwall's terms; those with a low velocity are likely to be specialty or "yellow" goods.

Yet classification by distributive velocity has several important advantages related to the criteria mentioned at the beginning of the paper. First, it is an empirical basis for classification. Second, it can be measured independent of the categories by which it is defined. Copeland and Aspinwall provide no such independent check of the validity of their classification. Convenience versus specialty, or red versus yellow goods, must be preclassified, then related to the definitional characteristics.

Third, as a result, the relationships between distributive velocity and a number of behavioral and product attributes can be tested. This represents an advance in classification, since the validity of the scheme can be established through tests on a large number of product categories. Fourth, distributive velocity is a continuous measure. Fifth, the classification scheme has operational meaning, since distributive velocity reflects demand and distributive patterns.

The classification scheme is predicated on the assumption that a functional relationship exists between factory shipments and retail sales, identifying a pattern of distributive velocity. If this is true, not only will a scale for classification be established, but a predictive model would be determined to forecast retail sales.

Three steps are required: (1) developing hypotheses, (2) determining distributive velocity, (3) equating distributive velocity to the relevant product and behavioral characteristics. We concentrate on the first point.

Table 19.2 represents an amalgam of hypotheses from past research and writings. In some cases, the hypotheses represent recent extensions of classification of good's theories to include consumer decision processes. In others, behavioral concepts have been applied to distributive velocity primarily by inference. Most of the relationships are assumed to be linear, from high to low distributive velocity. There are four classes of characteristics: consumer, product, market, and distributive. The consumer characteristics are divided into stimulus, intervening variables, and response. The classification schemes are listed on the top.

The first set of hypotheses deals with the relations between communications effects and distributive velocity. A.1. states that immediate advertising effects on purchase will be related to quick channel responses. On the other hand, when promotional effects may be delayed because of environmental or personal constraints, channel response will reflect the lag.

A.2. and A.3. state that when distributive velocity is high, the level of reinforcement is also likely to be high due to frequency of purchase (C.1.). Therefore, there is little search for additional information. As Howard (1963) suggests, this would also tend to describe buyer passivity and a lack of stimulus ambiguity. Thus the distributive velocity of goods and the mental velocity of ideas required to generate these goods are inversely related.

Yet reinforcement can also produce extinction. As Grass (1968) points out, a stimulus satiation effect occurs when attitudes are not strong (B.2). Putting it differently, when there is a lack of stimulus ambiguity, a consumer may search for ambiguity. There is a wear-out of cognitive content for decision making requiring a reordering of information. Under such a condition, high distributive velocity could also produce periodic extinction and search behavior.

The relationship between intervening variables and distributive velocity is hypothesized to reflect Howard's (1963) definition of limited and extensive decision making. A high frequency of purchase and reinforcement suggest that the consumer will restrict the range of considerations involved in choice under conditions of moderate to low uncertainty and ambiguity. Given a high distributive velocity, product cues will dominate over informational or symbolic cues (resulting in an emphasis on sampling and dealing —F.1.). The evoked set of alternatives will be limited, cues will be readily discriminated, and environmental constraints on pur-

TABLE 19.2
HYPOTHESES

SOURCES	TYPE OF CLASSIFICATION SCHEME		
Ramond and Assael	High distributive velocity	Medium distributive velocity	Low distributive velocity
Copeland-Holton	Convenience goods	Shopping goods	Specialty goods
Aspinwall-Miracle	Red goods	Orange goods	Yellow goods
Ramond	Complex psychological	Simple psychological	Complex physical

RELATIONSHIPS

A. Stimulus

Ramond and Assael	1. Having direct promotional effects	Cumulative
Ramond and Assael	2. Very high level of reinforcement (extinction)	Moderate
Howard; Holton	3. Limited cognitive search	Extensive
Howard	(a) Passive buyer	Active
Howard	(b) Lack of stimulus ambiguity	Ambiguous

B. Intervening Variables

Howard	1. Limited decision making	Complex decision making
Howard	(a) Product cues dominate	Informational cues
Howard; Holton	(b) Limited evoked set	Extensive
Howard	(c) Cue discrimination	Generalization
Howard	(d) Limited environmental constraints	Extensive
Ramond and Assael	(e) Low psychological risks	High
Ramond and Assael	2. Limited effect of intervening variables	Extensive

C. Response

Copeland-Holton/ Aspinwall	1. High frequency of purchase	Low
Howard	2. High probability of repurchase	Low
Holton; Dommermuth	3. Limited physical search	Extensive
Kaish	4. Low level of cognitive dissonance	High

RELATIONSHIPS

D. Product Characteristics

Miracle	1. Low unit value	High
Miracle	2. Low technical change	High
Miracle	3. Wide variety of uses	Limited
Ramond and Assael	4. Low level of financial and technological risk	High

E. Marketing Characteristics

Aspinwall	1. Intensive distribution	Selective
Aspinwall; Ramond and Assael	2. High advertising-to-sales ratio	Low
Miracle	3. Little product variety	Greater variety
Miracle	4. Little control of retail price	Greater control

F. Distributive Characteristics

Ramond and Assael	1. Heavy sales promotion	Light
Ramond and Assael	2. High transactional costs	High carrying costs
Alderson	3. Routinized transactions	Personal selling and negotiation
Assael; Ridgeway; Palamountain	4. Little interdependence between consumers, retailers, and manufacturers	Greater interdependence
Palamountain	5. Low level of vertical channel conflict	High
Palamountain	6. High level of intertype conflict	Low

chasing will be few. Holton (1958), in his clarification of the convenience-specialty good typology, also equates convenience goods to a limited number of alternative sellers, thus suggesting that both the evoked set of sellers and brands are restricted.

Under such conditions, brand attitudes are likely to have less effect on behavior. Support for this position on the aggregate level is found in a study by Assael and Day (1968). In studying 13 analgesic, deodorant, and instant coffee brands, it was found that attitudes explained the most variance in market share (relative to trend effects) for two analgesic brands. Analgesics have the lowest repurchase rate and would be assumed to have the lowest distributive velocity.

Moving to consumer response, both Aspinwall and Copeland centered their classification scheme on frequency of purchase. It is here assumed that a high frequency of purchase will require a greater frequency of retail orders and will permit more precise adjustments of factory shipments to patterns of demand. Given a condition of limited decision making and reinforcement, it is hypothesized that distributive velocity will be related to a higher probability of repurchase. Brand loyalty would impart greater certainty in the pattern of retail inventory and orders, permitting a shorter lag between factory shipments and retail sales.

As with cognitive search, physical search will be limited. Holton implies that physical search is limited because of a low unit price compared with search costs. Yet it may be more likely that the consumer is constrained by a fixed set of brand and store alternatives. Moreover, as Kaish (1967) recognized, cognitive dissonance is unlikely to occur with a small evoked set of alternatives. Since dissonance is not anticipated, search behavior is not stimulated.

The product and market characteristics are derived from Aspinwall's characteristics of goods theory and Miracle's (1965) elaboration of the theory. Aspinwall classified high- and low-frequency items by distribution and promotional policy. Miracle equated a high frequency of purchase to a low unit value, a low level of technical change, and a wide variety of product uses. By inference, these characteristics could also be equated to a high distributive velocity. One might also add a low level of technological and financial risk, since a high consumption rate would mean the purchase of a smaller stock of utility at one time. Aspinwall also hypothesized that such "red" items are likely to be in the mature stage of their life cycle and relatively undifferentiated compared with "yellow" or potentially low-velocity items.

In relating product to market characteristics, Aspinwall classified high-frequency goods as those characterized by intensive distribution and heavy advertising expenditures. A high advertising-to-sales ratio, rather than heavy advertising expenditures, would probably be more accurate for "yellow" goods and for items with a high distributive velocity.

Since intensive distribution can be equated to low search time, low unit value, and high frequency of purchase, it is consistent to hypothesize that products with a high distributive velocity are fairly ubiquitous. Miracle (1965) extends these concepts to product and price policies. He postulates that few variations will be offered when the significance of an individual purchase and the effort in the purchasing process are low. Moreover, the degree of control over retail price will be low. Again, these relationships can be applied to the concept of distributive velocity.

The distributive characteristics center on the hypothesis that high-velocity items are intensively distributed. F.1. states that high-velocity items are more likely to apply couponing, deals, and cents-off promotions. Because of the frequency of reorders, trans-actional costs are likely to outweigh carrying costs. As Alderson (1957b) points out, given a high rate of purchase frequency, transactions become more routinized in an attempt to reduce transactional costs.

One could also equate distributive flow to channel relations. A high level of distributive velocity is likely to induce little inter-dependence between manufacturer, retailer, and consumer. Since an item distributed intensively cannot represent a significant pro-portion of total sales, little leverage can be generated (Assael, 1968; Ridgeway, 1957). Vertical channel pressures are unlikely, resulting in a minimum of conflict yet also a minimum of coopera-tion. Applying Palamountain's (1955) distinction between vertical and intertype channel conflict, intertype conflicts are likely to dominate because of greater price control by retailers and the application of different concepts of retailing the same local areas.

The foregoing hypotheses are diverse, yet internally con-sistent. As such, they could constitute a theory of classification. The essential point is that they can be tested against a framework of which they are independent.

Their validation could lead to some interesting interrelation-ships. For instance, consider the following:

1. Brands characterized by direct advertising effects are more likely to be dealed.
2. A dominance of product over symbolic cues is related to a low level of product differentiation.
3. Cognitive dissonance is most likely when interdependence between consumer and retailer is high.
4. Limited evoked sets of alternatives are most likely for ubiquitous products.
5. Limited physical and cognitive search is related to a high advertising-to-sales ratio.

6. A low level of control over retail price is related to
   a low level of vertical channel conflict and a high level
   of intertype conflict.

These relationships demonstrate the value of a measurable product classification scheme. Given a positioning of products, we can begin to discern broad interrelationships between environment and strategy, and ultimately these will assist the manager in formulating a marketing mix.

We have little progress to report in the testing of these hypotheses. At present we have data for four product categories and are only beginning to establish the functional relationships between factory shipments and retail sales to develop a measure of distributive velocity. Progress promises to be slow because of the large number of product categories that will have to be examined. But we have hopes that a valid and reliable classification scheme will emerge.

20

AN OPERATIONAL FRAMEWORK
FOR THE STUDY OF CONSUMER
TYPOLOGY AND PROCESS

JOHN G. MYERS
Associate Professor
School of Business
University of California
Berkeley

The several anomalies of consumer literature are well represented in reviews by Glock and Nicosia (1967) and Perloff (1968). Each provided a synopsis of work done in the area in the past few years, the first from a sociological and the second from a psychological viewpoint. One overriding conclusion of each is that neither sociologists nor psychologists have supplied a satisfactory theory or theoretical foundation for the study of consumer and consumption behavior.

Glock and Nicosia recognize the development of descriptive, predictive, and explanatory traditions in the field. The predictive tradition, or perhaps a more useful term—the prescriptive tradition —has grown out of and has been shaped by the interests of client groups such as marketers, advertising agencies, and mass media. It can be differentiated from the explanatory tradition for what it does not do—"investigate the cognitive mechanism or mechanisms

I wish to acknowledge the financial support of the Institute of Business and Economic Research through the Ford Foundation Research Program in Marketing, and the Survey Research Center, University of California, Berkeley.

which transform a stimulus into a response, nor does it specify the contextual conditions which make one mechanism rather than another operative" [Glock and Nicosia, 1967, p. 362]. The authors appeal explicitly for more attention to the area by sociologists, recognizing that "relatively speaking, sociology has given substantially less attention to consumer and consumption behavior than have psychology and economics" [p. 381].[1]

Even though psychologists have made a considerable contribution to the development of consumer literature, there is general agreement that the contributions have been more methodological than theoretical. In the explanatory tradition deriving from clinical paradigms, for example, Glock and Nicosia suggest that there is not "a single clinical paradigm akin to Lazarsfeld's or Katona's which would comprehend the varied conceptualizations sometimes explicit, but more often implicit, in motivation research" [p. 367].

Similar reactions to the contributions of psychology are reflected in Perloff's review. The rationale for the author's decision to focus on methodological studies (covering the consumer psychology literature published between July 1964 and June 1967) derives from "the paucity, and quite possibly the absence, of any theoretical underpinnings which could give direction, meaning, and permanence to substantive investigations" [Perloff, 1968, p. 437]. Some writers have concluded that it may be more profitable for marketing management purposes to concentrate on group theory than on individual theory, and one study concluded:

> Much of the confusion about market segmentation, we
> believe, stems from the failure to recognize . . . [that]
> the absence of a satisfactory theory of individual behavior
> does not imply the absence of valid propositions about
> the behavior of groups. For purposes of marketing strategy,
> it is the behavior of groups, not individuals, which is
> of primary importance. [Bass, Tigert, and Lonsdale, 1967]

Although one might conclude that neither theoretical psychologists nor theoretical sociologists have found it profitable to

---

[1] The authors note that the literature in the field is virtually dominated by the other two disciplines. Sociological contributions have been impeded by "(1) historical factors which have made psychology and economics more visible than sociology to the business community; (2) the prevailing perception in the business community of its needs for research on the consumer; (3) differences in how the three disciplines relate to these perceived needs; and (4) differences in prevailing attitudes among sociologists, economists, and psychologists about engaging in consumer research."

develop a theory of consumer behavior from the perspective of their own disciplines, it is difficult to argue that the consumer area lacks for theory development. The two most extensive works in the field (Nicosia, 1966, and Howard and Sheth, 1969) can hardly be considered insignificant theoretical contributions. What characterizes these theories, however, is their interdisciplinary nature—their comprehension of the consumer from a global, integrating, and systemic perspective that crosses basic disciplinary bounds.

Among the many difficulties of constructing an interdisciplinary global theory of a behavioral unit like the consumer, we have the task of translating a profusion of conceptual material and the associated theoretical schemes into meaningful and relevant questions for client groups such as marketing management. The favored analytical unit has been the individual, and the principal process to be understood, individual decision making. These perspectives seem to run directly contrary to the conclusion of Bass et al. (1967) that "it is the behavior of groups, not individuals, which is of primary importance."

This paper develops an argument that both individual *and* group perspectives are important—that the advance of explanatory consumer theory should rest on *inter*disciplinary perspectives, both individual and group, and on the several disciplines that they imply.[2]

A better representation of the present state of the consumer field might emphasize not a lack of theory development but a lack of an understanding of the prerequisites necessary for its test, verification, and application. Students of the consumer are faced with the traditional scientific problems of identifying the operational or epistemic relations between construct and observed phenomenon. These problems are compounded by the complexities of an interdisciplinary perspective. One need only consider the forest of conceptual material in the basic social sciences to appreciate the complexity of anything purporting to transcend those sciences.

[2] The call for a theory of consumer behavior in the basic disciplines is to some degree a contradiction in terms. Presumably it is the study of behavior alone that makes these disciplines basic—qualifications of the term such as consumer behavior, political behavior, and religious behavior, suggest application. Although applied theories should search for fundamental principles in the basic disciplines, they should not depend solely on developments within those disciplines. As Gouldner (1956, p. 9) has stated: "The applied social scientist cannot assume that theoretical guidance and aid will always derive from the efforts of the pure social scientist; he must be trained and prepared to make his own theoretical innovations."

Although such complexity often appears to generate more heat than light, there are strong reasons to argue for an interdisciplinary approach. Consumer activities are essentially economic, but at the same time, and particularly in an affluent society, they are heavily influenced by social and psychological considerations.

PURPOSE AND ORGANIZATION

This paper develops an operational framework or paradigm for use in translating complex interdisciplinary conceptual material into empirically testable and significant questions. It is argued that both individual and group perspectives have an important place in the development of consumer knowledge, neither being necessarily more important than the other. Group perspectives are generally referred to as the study of "typology" and individual perspectives as the study of "process." Each has a set of different objectives, goals, and operational procedures. The framework is designed to provide a foundation for work in either direction.

THEORIES AND PARADIGMS

Theory development in the behavioral sciences often begins with an attempt to locate fundamental axes or dimensions as the basis for a framework for the representation of the behavioral unit. The procedure is particularly used in those global or general theories of individual, society, or group that attempt to capture the totality of the unit and in doing so inevitably cross basic disciplinary bounds. The paradigms that derive from such coordinate axes cannot be considered to be theories of the behavioral unit if they do not proceed to a discussion of process or function. Thus a paradigm may provide an insightful guide to the functioning of a system, but it is classificatory only. Questions of process must be seen as derivatives or functions of its structural frame.

It might be said that client management interests are generally in structural rather than in process questions—the identification of particular object or person states on some set of classifying criteria. The developing typological tradition in consumer research has been stimulated by the "prescriptive" needs of management for meaningful representations of consumer types, brand types, product types, and so on. For example, appeal of Bass et al. (1967) for a study of consumer groups rather than individuals reflects a sense of the greater utility of group rather than individual representations for management's strategy and planning purposes.

In recent years, consumer theoreticians have tended to stress the need for the study of process—the function and flow of a consumer structure or system. Attention is directed to how and why a particular system operates—its physiology and dynamics. Fundamental processes of a human system—learning, decision making, communication, persuasion, influence—are studied in the context of a consumer unit. These process principles have done much to add to our knowledge of how and why a consumer system operates.

A framework that might serve as an operational guide to either of these two research directions is relatively easily generated by the simple intersection of two or more coordinate axes that reflect relevant characteristics of the behavioral unit. Evaluative criteria are needed as guides to the relative utilities of such frameworks. For purposes of this paper, these have been chosen to be (1) simplicity, (2) flexibility, and (3) quantifiability.

Simplicity is an important criterion because of the various interests to be served in studies of the consumer—in both its cross-disciplinary and applied qualities—and because operational mechanics requires relatively simple statements of the basic relations to be tested. The framework should be easily interpretable and should identify meaningful components of the behavioral unit. This criterion, for example, suggests that a two-dimensional framework may be superior to a three-or-more dimensional framework if such structure will make the various questions of typology and process that relate to it more readily understood.

By *flexibility* is meant the capacity to incorporate a wide variety of theoretical and operational positions relating to the study of typology and process. The framework should be capable of generating or structuring significant questions for interests of many researchers. Here again, the significance of the criterion of flexibility stems directly from the interdisciplinary and applied nature of the subject.

Quantifiability concerns the quantification, mathematical analysis, or other means used to formally specify and clarify construct and relationship. For example, Berger, Cohen, Snell, and Zelditch (1962) illustrate three types of formalized models: explicational, representational, and theoretical construct. Explicational models are designed to render one or more basic concepts more precise as, for example, in the authors' extension of Heider's balance theory. Representational models attempt to indicate in a precise and formally simple manner a specific type of observed phenomenon. (The Asch conformity experiments are used as illustrative examples.) Theoretical-construct models attempt to provide a formal treatment of a general explanatory theory. (The Estes-Burke learning experiments are used to develop these principles.)

A formalized approach to typology construction is given in Barton's (1955) notion of "property space." As in any coordinate system in which points are identified with reference to some axes, people can be classified according to various degrees of the property or attribute held. The classifications that are generated can be a breaking down of an existing typology into its fundamental parts; a building up, for a given set of types, the property space in which they are located; or a transforming of a system of types from one property space into another. These so-called typological operations are referred to as reduction, substruction, and transformation, respectively. The notion of classifying coordinates or criteria as sets of reference axes is fundamental to them all.

Many other evaluative criteria could be derived to judge operational frameworks of the type developed in this paper. For example, if it is to serve as an interdisciplinary guide to research studies in the explanatory tradition, particularly where the study of cognitive-internal mechanisms and contextual-external conditions are to be explicitly included, it should postulate a set of internal and external actor conditions. Such paradigms, and of course theory itself, can be evaluated on the degree to which they generate significant empirical research. Initially, at least, the three criteria of simplicity, flexibility, and quantifiability provide useful guides to judging the utility of the scheme.

THE I/E PARADIGM

The paradigm to be developed is referred to as the I/E paradigm as a means of identification and to emphasize the choice of the principal defining axes—internal and external. This is a common means of dividing actor space in behavioral science and it immediately suggests two important implications. First, the paradigm is to be interdisciplinary—some disciplines deal with internal, and others with external, actor considerations. Second, it suggests that internal questions are to be explicitly treated. The study of cognitive, motivational, and attitudinal mechanisms is believed to be a prerequisite to any comprehensive theoretical position that deals with consumer process or classification.

One additional axis completes the basic paradigm—an axis that will divide the internal and external spaces into meaningful components of a consumer actor system. The partition of the internal space should suggest the possible division of that space

	Personal	Nonpersonal
Internal	I-P	I-NP
External	E-P	E-NP

Figure 20.1 Basic Framework of the I/E Paradigm

into relevant systems where one may be considered an environment of the other even though both are fully interactive. Similarly, the external space needs a partition that leads to the identification of meaningful differences in contextual situations. This axis is defined as personal-nonpersonal. The guiding principle both in the construction of the paradigm itself and in all the questions of typology and process that can be generated from it is one of intersection or interaction.

Figure 20.1 shows the basic skeletal framework for the paradigm—the intersection of the two dimensions of internal-external and personal-nonpersonal that generate four cells or components of consumer actor space, I–P, I–NP, E–P, and E–NP, respectively.

Identification of Space Components

Perhaps the more difficult conceptual task to be faced in assigning some means of identifying the various spaces is a nonobvious distinction in the internal-personal and internal-nonpersonal components. It would seem that something internal should also be personal, if by definition only. The decision to retain the axes and the paradigm itself was made because the two components can be shown to represent important conceptual distinctions in the analysis of mental or psychological "intervening mechanisms." Thus the internal-personal space is considered to be the seat of motivation of the actor where personality theory and clinical notions of drives, needs, values, and so on, relate to it. The internal-nonpersonal space represents the cognitive, affective, and intellectual structure that surrounds it. Clinicians, for example, usually premise their speculations about personality on some notion of "self" or "ego" made up of a bundle of conscious and subconscious needs, whereas cognitive and attitudinal theorists are more likely to concentrate on perceptual, cognitive, and affective mechanisms. From either perspective, both positions may be represented as in Sarnoff's psychoanalytic theory of attitude change (Sarnoff, 1960), or in Rokeach's (1968) value-belief-attitude theory.

The two space components, internal-personal and internal-nonpersonal, are considered to be internal systems referred to as "needs" and "meanings." Although the choice of these terms is somewhat arbitrary, they are intended to convey the possibilities of at least two principal areas of interest in the internal aspects of a consumer system. The structure and process of each is discussed in later sections of the paper.

The remaining two spaces are intuitively more tractable. The external environment is divided quite simply into contextual situations made up of people and objects, or in another sense, into a social context and an object context. The spaces are referred to as "social" and "object." Here again, it is useful to consider them as systems, where this implies some notion of structure and function (or process). Each space is thus given a system definition as follows:

Space	System
I–P	Need
I–NP	Meaning
E–P	Social
E–NP	Object

Identification of System Structure

Each space is considered to represent parts of the total system and is itself a system with its own structure and function. Attention is now directed to the structure of each.[3] The objective is to identify fundamental dimensions of each space system that provide guides to its nature and content. The key to an understanding of its function or process lies in knowing the kinds of interactions among these space components.

Need System. As suggested earlier, the structure of the need system is psychoanalytical; more generally, it deals with notions of needs, drives, values, wishes, goals, and the like. Many personality theories could be brought to bear to speculate on and reason through, its content. It provides the source of criterion variables for studies of

---

[3] Readers are referred to J. G. Myers (1968) for a detailed discussion of the structure and function of each component. This work contains the supporting literature that has been drawn on to provide the specification of the content and physiology of each system that is excluded here. Much more fully developed illustrations of formal typology and process operations and their relations to measurement questions can also be found.

motivation research in marketing, much of which is premised on a notion of "self" and an implicit mechanism of self–object matching. As a foundation for consumer theory, self–object matching has been criticized for the assumption that needs are a necessary *and* sufficient condition for purchasing rather than being necessary only. Focusing on this system alone ignores the complexity of cognitive, attitudinal, behavioral, and social processes that may intervene to distort message flow or the intended content of a stimulus. As one possible structure for this space, we could recognize a distinction between conscious and unconscious needs. It is more useful to recognize the conscious-unconscious dimension, however, as overt and covert qualities of sets of *primary* or physiological and *secondary* or learned (social-psychogenic) needs. Primary needs are those stemming from the organism's requirements for survival or physical well-being—hunger, thirst, elimination, pain-avoidance, mating, and so on. Secondary needs are those not in the direct service of physical requirements—to strive for social acceptance or status, to work, to write a book, to explore, etc.[4]

Meaning System. The general structure of the meaning system encompasses a vast quantity of social-psychological theory and reasoning. Much of the attitude change literature deals with this space. (See, e.g., the recent review of empirically based theories of Insko, 1967.) Theories of cognitive functioning in psychology (the developmental processes of Piaget and Tolman, or the representational mediation theories of Osgood and Tannenbaum) and in sociology (the tradition of symbolic interactionism initiated by Mead and developed in a sociological context by Rose) are directly applicable. One very general division of the space in theoretical terms is the distinction between theories that rest on a conflict-consistency notion and those that rest on a complexity notion. Some writers have chosen to call the system attitudinal with cognitive, affective, and conative components; others have tended to label it cognitive, where affective states can be represented as some function of the interconnections in the cognitive structure.

In marketing, the space generally encompasses the so-called hierarchy of effect models such as the original Lavidge and Steiner

---

[4] It is interesting to reflect here on the degree to which advertising appeals are directed to the secondary group with the objective of stimulating purchases (say of foods and beverages) that logically should satisfy only needs in the primary. For good discussion of this point, see Rokeach (1968, pp. 179–188).

scheme of Awareness → Knowledge → Liking → Preference →
Conviction → Purchase, or the so-called AIDA advertising model
of Attention → Interest → Desire → Action. Views on the possible
structure and functioning of this system comprise much of the
content of recent comprehensive consumer models.

At the most primitive conceptual level, D. T. Campbell (1963)
has pointed out that such a system-space should contain as a
minimum a notion of cognition and response tendency—"hopes
for integration would seem more likely to lie in the utilization
of acquired behavioral dispositional terms that have explicitly
both connotations, are both response tendencies and views of the
world . . ." [p. 134]. The conceptual components have thus been
chosen as *image* and *attitude*. These terms have taken on special
significance in the consumer literature and are developed much
more fully in J. G. Myers (1968).

Social System. It is tempting to refer the reader to theoretical works
in sociology such as the global theories of Parsons or the antholo-
gies of Martindale or Coser and Rosenberg. Indeed, these theoretical positions can add much to the perspectives on structure
that are intended as representations of this space. It is interesting
to note, however, that theorizing in a much narrower range has
caught the imagination of consumer specialists, particularly those
dealing explicitly with diffusion as in the E. Katz-Lazarsfeld (1955)
two-step flow model and in Everett Rogers's (1962) development
of a theory of the diffusion of innovations.

The distinguishing feature of this space is a notion of group
or group process on which the study of sociology rests. The unify-
ing thread that might serve as the basis for understanding its structure and function is the sociologist's notion of "influence." The
extensive discussions of this concept in sociological literature suggest its complexity. Analysts dealing with social or personal influence should, as a minimum, recognize what might be called
"explicit" and "implicit" social influence. The former refers to
attempts of one individual or group purposively and explicitly to
persuade or influence another individual or group in a specific
and prescribed direction. The latter refers to nonpurposive individual or group effects in which notions of purposiveness and
explicitness play no part. Implicit social influence operates as a
function of contextual situation or social position and is best
represented in the extensive writings on role theory. Explicit social
influence derives from social interaction processes, even though
such interactions contain implicit influences as well. Interaction

may be a necessary and sufficient condition for explicit influence but not a necessary condition for implicit influence.[5]

To describe the simple structure of this space, terms have been chosen that convey alternative levels of social aggregation: *individual, group, subculture,* and *culture.* Here again, the choice has been guided by the utility of these dimensions as reference points in studies of social influence in current consumer literature. For example, dyadic relationships such as salesman-customer, small and large group relationships such as the family unit, social class, and socioeconomic status groupings, and subcultural (ethnic) and cultural (international) dimensions, have all provided meaningful units for consumer analysis.

Object System. The structure of the object system is not well developed in any behavioral science theory. It should contain all object stimuli relevant to the behavioral unit. Stimuli tend not to be specified in basic disciplines, however, and one reason for this is our ability to generalize them as stimuli with little relevance for an understanding of basic psychological or sociological mechanisms. Indeed, even specifying the space raises classic philosophic debates on whether "objects" can exist without people, and/or whether objects carry any meaning independent of specific person referents.

There are good reasons to argue, however, that the contents of this space should be explicitly identified if the paradigm is to be used in applied research contexts. It is largely the content of this space that distinguishes one applied science (from a behavioral, interdisciplinary perspective) from another. All applied behavioral sciences might be said to have in common a concern with the preceding three systems, although they differ in their concern with what we refer to here as "objects." Thus political science is involved with politicians and political parties, religion with churches and ministers, and so on. Consumer "science" should concern itself with a similar array of objects.

The choice of these objects and the structure of the consumer object system is derived from three criteria. First, they should be nonpersonal or "inanimate" to distinguish them from the points of

---

[5] As an interesting derivative of a recognition of these distinctions, we can note the degree to which diffusion models in marketing are based on axioms of explicit, rather than implicit, social influence. The two-step flow models of E. Katz and Lazarsfeld and the Rogers schemes depend heavily on notions of overt, verbal, and persuasive behavior in the personal influence process, rather than on the more covert possibilities contained in a type theory such as Kelman's notions of compliance, identification, and internalization.

		Personal		Nonpersonal	
	System	Dimension	System	System	Dimension
Internal	Need	Primary Secondary	Meaning		Image Attitude
External	Social	Individual Group Subculture Culture	Object		Brand Product Retailer Manufacturer

Figure 20.2 The I/E Paradigm

reference in the social system. Second, they should be cognitively relevant to the consumer—should contain some significant meaning in a purchase situation (e.g., wholesaler would not logically fall into this class). Third, they should be purposively conditioned or manipulated by some management agency because of the particular relevance of these considerations in studies of consumer and consumption behavior. The management agency is the complement of the consumer-buyer—namely, the seller. These three criteria suggest the choice of *brand, product, retailer,* and *manufacturer* as structural components of a consumer object system.

Figure 20.2 shows the completed paradigm, identifying the various systems and components. The following sections suggest operational procedures that might be followed in using it as a guide to the study of consumer typology and process.

THE PARADIGM AND
STUDIES OF CONSUMER TYPOLOGY

As explained by Barton (1955), a typology is essentially a classification of persons (or objects) into various types or classes based on a set of criteria or coordinate axes. The analogous problem in psychology is to identify people or objects, usually in a multi-dimensional space in which the dimensions serve as the reference axes and a scaling procedure is used. The principles of classification, although not the operations themselves, are similar whether the set of criteria is psychological, sociological, or demographic. It is not often recognized that typology is an implicit goal of many marketing research and consumer studies, even though highly complex multivariate statistical procedures may be used in the analysis. Classic questions of product differentiation and market segmentation (Smith, 1956) can be cast in operational terms as questions of object and person typologies (J. G. Myers, 1968). A great deal of marketing literature is devoted to the task of identifying such person and object differences because they provide the manager with useful guides for planning and strategy.

To begin the examination of the utility of the paradigm for the study of consumer typology, each of the system spaces is first defined as containing a universal set of points, objects, or bits, not necessarily those specified as space components. Using set theory notation, U for the universal set, the sets analogous to each system space are the following:

System	Space	Universal Set
Need	I–P	U_N
Meaning	I–NP	U_X
Social	E–P	U_L
Object	E–NP	U_O

Potential classifiers or criteria that could enter into typology construction are derivable from any and all of these universal sets. The obvious question is whether they should be drawn entirely *within* (intrasystem) each universal or should cross system boundaries (intersystem) and center on *between*-set criteria. Each approach has some interesting implications, and each is developed in the following sections.

Intrasystem Analysis:
A Differentiation Question

A major question of image research in marketing is the difference (differentiation) in a manufacturer's and a competitor's brand. Image research generally considers psychological and perceptual variables when one brand, for example, is examined for its trustworthiness, quality, value, and so on, relative to another. Advertising can add appreciably to the formation of these impressions to the point where consumer opinion may be far removed from "objective" reality. We can demonstrate through intrasystem and intersystem analysis the difference between subjective impression and objective characteristic rather simply, in the process revealing a fundamental distinction between economic-rationalistic and behavioral-cognitive approaches to the problem.

Focusing on the Object system $(E–NP; U_O)$, define the four objects given in the I/E paradigm as subsets of the universal set U_O,

$\mathcal{B}$ = a set of brands such that $\mathcal{B} \subset U_O$
$\mathcal{P}$ = a set of products such that $\mathcal{P} \subset U_O$

U_0 (E-NP)

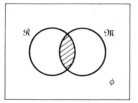

Figure 20.3 Venn Diagram of Retailers and Manufacturers in Object Space (E–NP)

$\mathcal{R}$ = a set of retailers such that $\mathcal{R} \subset U_0$
$\mathcal{M}$ = a set of manufacturers such that $\mathcal{M} \subset U_0$

In general, let B be a set of B brands such that $B \epsilon B$, and so on, so that the elements of each set are defined as follows:

$\mathcal{B}$ = $\{B | B \epsilon \mathcal{B}\}$
$\mathcal{P}$ = $\{P | P \epsilon \mathcal{P}\}$
$\mathcal{R}$ = $\{R | R \epsilon \mathcal{R}\}$
$\mathcal{M}$ = $\{M | M \epsilon \mathcal{M}\}$

A fundamental principle of typology construction can now be stated as the classificatory value of set-component interactions—to what degree does interset mapping generate meaningful differences in the objects being classified?[6] Consider the interaction possibilities of just two of the sets, $R \cap M$. It is obvious that such interactions (or intersections) give some typological meaning to each set component. For example, in the Venn diagram in Figure 20.3, manufacturers and retailers in the intersection $R \cap M$ differ somewhat from manufacturers and retailers not in the intersection $R \cap \overline{M}$, $\overline{R} \cap M$, and ϕ, simply because they have something (perhaps products and brands) in common. This principle can be generalized to complete set interaction analysis, and differentiation can be defined as any difference in a contributing element of the set of classifying criteria that results from mapping one set into another. For example, if brand differences are defined on the basis of associational qualities only and B_1 was associated with M_1, R_1, and P_1, but was also associated with M_1, R_2, and P_1 then technically the first B_1 is not the same as the second B_1. Different retailers are involved in each case.

[6] This principle might also be stated in other terms as the informational content of differences generated at various levels of set specification within or between space systems.

As a formal definition of differentiation, or as a basis for differentiating object types, interaction analysis at this level is not very useful—its informational content is very low. Even though one object may provide some basis for classifying another, little is known about the characteristics of either.

Here we can see a fundamental principle of measurement long recognized by psychometricians—classificatory criteria should include some measure of the kind, characteristic, or nature of the object to be classified, and some notion of the amount, quantity, or magnitude of the characteristic held. Any person or object type is fundamentally derived from a characterization of differences in magnitude or degree on a set of classifying criteria. For purposes of the paradigm, the members of the set of classifiers are called *attributes*, and differences in magnitude or degree of the attribute held are called differences of *condition* on those attributes. The problem can be handled notationally to extend the informational content of a classification by considering the attribute and condition possibilities on each object in the object system. Attributes and conditions can differ. Conditions can be expressed in categorical (qualitative) or continuous (quantitative) form and attributes can be either "objective" or "subjective"—either denotative and named or connotative and implied. If a denotative assumption is made (or at least no specific reference is given to particular individuals who are assigning meanings), the assigned attributes are considered to be completely contained within the object system (i.e., the attribute set conveys a denotative meaning only; a brand is a certain price, quality, package color, etc.). If a connotative assumption is contained in the chosen perspective and a specific person reference is identified, the analysis would imply a person-object interaction—for example, an intersection of object and meaning systems. To a considerable degree, this distinction contributes to an understanding of rationalist and cognitive approaches to the differentiation question, for the rationalist tends to deal with the object system and denotative meaning only, whereas the cognitive theorist tends to deal with the intersection of object and meaning systems and connotative meaning.[7]

---

[7] It is interesting to note in this connection Simon's (1963) views in reference to the question of broadening the definition of rationality in economics. We need, he states, "a distinction between the objective environment in which the economic actor 'really' lives and the subjective environment that he perceives and to which he responds. When this distinction is made, we can no longer predict his behavior—even if he behaves rationally—from the characteristics of his objective environment; we also need to know something about his perceptual and cognitive processes" [p. 710].

To provide a formal approach to typology construction, subscripts on the universal set can be included to refer to specific sets, elements, attributes, and conditions, and the resulting person or object type represented as an index. For example, O_{ijkl} would refer to the ith object in the object space, partitioned at the jth element, on which a kth attribute and a lth condition were being considered.[8] Thus the ith object in this set could be a brand B_{jkl} and all subscript sets be considered closed, such that $j = 1, 2, 3, \ldots, m$; $k = 1, 2, 3, \ldots, p$; and $l = 1, 2, 3, \ldots, q$. Differentiation then becomes the degree of difference in various attribute-condition possibilities, each mutually exclusive k attribute and l condition representing a j brand.[9] By the simple counting rule of numbers of mutually exclusive and exhaustive events, the number of j brand possibilities (m) is the pth (number of attribute possibilities) power of q (number of condition possibilities), $m = q^p$, if each attribute has the same number of conditions.

The interesting question now arises as to whether intrasystem analysis (between-object interactions) provides a useful approach to the differentiation question. There is no doubt that some $\mathcal{B} \cap \mathcal{P} \cap \mathcal{R} \cap \mathcal{M}$ object does exist that is represented by O_{ijkl}. Can attribute and condition possibilities on one set of objects contribute to differentiation in another? Two approaches suggest themselves: (1) attributes of one object could be interpreted as attributes of another, or (2) each object could be assigned a distinctive set of attributes, and the results of their contribution to the differentiation in any one set could be examined. J. G. Myers (1968) provides extended examples of the procedures involved in the second ap-

[8] For example, one could characterize brand differences on the basis of objective price and advertising policies of a variety of manufacturers. If, however, the same information was sought by obtaining consumer reactions, even though the attributes were the same, the conditions reported might vary widely according to various perceptual and cognitive considerations, degree of respondent knowledge, and so on. The blossoming of image research in marketing has occurred partly because the latter may be a more important consideration in consumer purchase and an understanding of sales patterns than the former.

[9] Contrast this with the traditional definition of product differentiation in economics—the degree to which a stimulus (say, advertising) results in a change in the price elasticity of demand for the product (Telser, 1964). In our terms, a change in a product attribute (advertising) condition results in a change in a person attribute (buying) condition under similar product attribute (price) conditions. The economic principle is potentially generalizable to other objects. Thus if a store has a certain location (L) which is associated with a certain level of sales $(Q) = f(L)$, better service could result in an increase in Q at the same level of L. In other terms, the store is differentiated by a change in an attribute (service) condition.

proach for object and person typologies. The number of possible differentiated objects can be readily found by the counting rule as long as a record is kept of the number of attributes and conditions on each. In general, $m = q_1^{p1} \cdot q_2^{p2} \cdot q_3^{p3} \cdots q_n^{pn}$, where 1, 2, 3, . . . , n refer to mutually exclusive attribute and condition possibilities.

Intersystem Analysis:
A Segmentation Question

Intraobject system analysis implies, among other things, that typologies can be constructed from purely objective characteristics—an object type does not imply a reciprocal person type, nor does a person type imply an object type. Thus a brand might have a certain price condition independent of the person who made the assignment. It is interesting to note, however, that almost all questions of typology of causal relation in consumer work contain implicitly or explicitly both a person and object reference. In the economist's definition of elasticity, then, market response (the person attribute of buying) is the reference for the definition of a product difference.

In marketing research, questions of brand or object image are determined on the basis of person impressions and opinions. By far the largest number of real-world questions deal with typologies derived from data that provide the potential for classifying persons in terms of object referents, and vice versa. In formal terms, these data deal with intersystem or cross-boundary analysis in which a two-, three- (or more) space consideration is the focus of attention —for example, $U_O \cap U_X$, $U_O \cap U_X \cap U_N$, $U_O \cap U_X \cap U_N \cap U_L$. If the person reference is "internal," the intersection crosses the internal-external axis; otherwise it does not. The effects of contextual situation, age, income, social class, and so on, on tendencies to be associated with certain brands could thus be considered a $U_L \cap U_O$ question as long as the person variables used involved no internal indicator of attitude, opinion, beliefs, need, and so on.[10]

Intersystem analysis raises an important consideration, not heretofore made explicit, that highlights the full complexity of a consumer system. What is needed is a fifth system to represent the various behaviors of the consumer (purchasing, shopping, convers-

[10] It has long been recognized that social class, for example, can be measured by either objective or subjective indicators as demonstrated in the works of Lloyd Warner—in our terms, either by focusing on internal or external environments.

ing, etc.) that are only implied in the I/E framework. This system, now defined as a universal set of behaviors U_H, provides the criterion variables for most consumer research of the panel and econometric type and for all implicitly or explicitly simple or reduced-form models in which behavior is the response criterion of interest.

Work reported in J. G. Myers and Nicosia (1968a, 1968b), using cluster and latent structure analysis, can illustrate intersystem analysis and questions of market segmentation. The data in these studies came from a semantic differential in which respondents gave their impressions of a supermarket on nine defining supermarket characteristics. In terms of the I/E paradigm, the data represent an interaction between the U_X meaning system and the U_O object system, or possible $X_{ijkl} \cap O_{ijkl}$ intersections. The X_{ijkl} could be represented as measures of awareness, preference, affect, or some other psychological dimension used to classify persons. The X_i components of the meaning system have been purposely left nonspecific and are given no aggregate representation as sets of persons analogous to the brand, product, retailer, and manufacturer sets in object space. It is possible to carry the attribute-condition principles of classification into the meaning system, however, by letting X_i refer to a general person class and defined by appropriate j, k, and l notation. For example, $M°$ might represent a set of males and $F°$ a set of females, and analysis might be confined to the construction of a typology based on appropriate attribute and condition characteristics within each.

In the data presented in Myers and Nicosia, for example, the subjects were female; thus the data are described by certain $F°_{jkl} \cap R_{jkl}$ intersections. It is important here to see that the k and l attribute-condition possibilities are the same for each set, whether the typological interest is in person types (F_j) or object types (R_j). The number of possible types in either case is l^k if each of the attributes (in this case nine store characteristics) and conditions (a six-point semantic scale was used) are considered to generate a type, regardless of the number of stores or persons in the sample—that is, 6^9 possibilities. This large number of types is not likely to exist (few samples are of this size); nor would it be particularly useful for any interpretive purpose to identify them. Thus the objectives of the analyst become a type of clustering operation, as represented in the cluster analytic procedures of the BC TRY system, in which the type becomes not the individual but a group of individuals whose conditions on the defining attributes are similar even though not the same. A wide variety of alternative multivariate statistical procedures can be used in the reduction and classifying operations such as the latent class model described in J. G. Myers and Nicosia (1968a).[11]

THE PARADIGM AND
STUDIES OF CONSUMER PROCESS

Empirical studies of consumer process differ in fundamental ways from studies of consumer typology. From the conceptually simple stimulus-response predictive models to the complex S–O–R explanatory models, the process analyst is fundamentally interested in testing relationships, flows, functions, or physiology, rather than in classifying types, structures, or points. A process perspective generally considers an explicit reference to time and an explicit notion of the process operating to convert one state into another. Thus learning theory might be used as a foundation for studies of behavior change, cognitive search to explain decision making, affective response to explain communication effects, and so on. The extensive work on consumer panel studies, for example, in which some probabilistic or Markov process model has been the basis for attempts to represent aggregate patterns of consumer brand choice, could be considered to be a process-oriented perspective in which time and behavior are the relevant considerations.

More conceptually complex views of consumer-buyer process are represented in the works of Nicosia (1966), Howard and Sheth (1969), and Amstutz (1967). Each involves a conceptual consideration of all parts of the I/E paradigm, theorizing about the whole and the dynamics and interrelationships of its many parts. Feedbacks and loops from one component to the next are explicitly considered, and various processes might be brought to bear to explain the functioning of the total system.

The I/E paradigm is easily adjusted to a process perspective by the simple expedient of considering the direction and content of subsystem interactions. For the general scheme, these inter-

---

[11] Green, Halbert, and Robinson (1967) have suggested that the advent of the computer has done much to mechanize the implementation of these procedures, but has not been a necessary condition to their development. Nonmetric scaling, now being introduced into marketing studies, is "no less interesting than more 'traditional' techniques—e.g., factor and discriminant analysis —which have been embraced by researchers with a zeal almost bordering on evangelism" [p. 129]. It is interesting to note that where the data are of the $X_{ijkl} \cap O_{ijkl}$ form, the procedures generally might be referred to as psychometrics, and in the $H_{ijkl} \cap O_{ijkl}$ form, as econometrics.

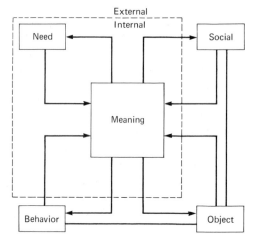

Figure 20.4 System Interactions of the I/E Paradigm

actions are taken to be completely looped with the meaning system, for it is here that the perceptual, cognitive, affective, and all filtering-mediating and intellectual processes are considered to operate. Determining how this system functions is, of course, a principal goal of much psychological and social-psychological theorizing.

Figure 20.4 shows the meaning system as the center of a closed, global, interconnected supersystem of inputs and outputs to each of the other parts of the paradigm and the added fifth system of behavior. Behavior includes verbal and motor responses of all kinds. The I/E distinction is retained by a dotted box that encloses the two internal systems and separates them from the three external systems. Meaning is considered to be a function of its interaction with all other systems. For example, consider the relation between meaning and behavior. Behavior is perhaps the single most influential determinant of image and attitude formation. Much theory suggests the reciprocal notion that behavior is the result of some type of cognitive process or, in our terms, some condition of the meaning system. Meaning, however, is affected by other system interactions as well. An illustration of one possible interactive sequence that involves all systems follows.

The Process of Communication

A significant marketing question concerns the process whereby advertising does or does not result in purchase. This deceptively simple matter involves the full complexity of the interdisciplinary perspective represented in the I/E paradigm. The question might be thought of as one kind of communication process, the communicator-sender being the manufacturer and the receiver being the consumer. The following illustration is not a fully elaborated description of the process of communication and is intended only as a vehicle to demonstrate the flexibility of the paradigm for studies of consumer process. A variety of other theoretical positions might be called on to explain the specifics of an advertising process or the generalities of a communication process.

Advertisers often attempt to arouse their audiences emotionally. Although the primary purpose may be to gain attention or respondent involvement, one type of advertising purposively attempts to create tension or fear and then tries to alleviate it by offering the advertised product or service as the means to reduce the emotion created.[12] The sequence of events can be formalized as general principles of communication and influence by considering various interactions among systems in the I/E paradigm. We are specifically concerned with how tension is aroused and reduced. Figure 20.5 represents the process.

Tension Arousal. What conditions in the object system might affect the degree of tension aroused in the meaning system? Communications research suggests they may be considered to be (1) the characteristics of the communication—whether the argument is one or two sided, whether the conclusion is stated, the order of the presentation, the nature of the appeal, and (2) the characteristics of the communicator—his credibility, the amount of change he advocates, and so on. These characteristics can be seen in an objective sense as existing in the environment, independent of the meaning system of the individual. They are susceptible to perceptual distortion, however, and the effects of all such distortions of stimulus attributes are summarized in the notion of stimulus *relevance.* Thus the message may be considered to have a certain degree of arousal potential that stems either from its content or from the vehicle through which it is delivered, which has some actor relevance. The message has a certain discrepancy-creating power that is recognized objectively and publicly, and this power

---

[12] This principle, widely used in deodorant, life insurance, and drug advertising, is now the main strategy of campaigns sponsored by the American Medical Association designed to reduce the incidence of smoking.

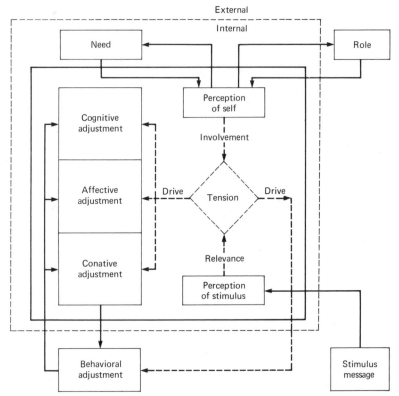

Figure 20.5 Explanation of the Communication Process Based on System Interactions of the I/E Paradigm

is perceptually distorted by the individual in question. It is a function of what the communication theorist refers to as "message conditions."

The degree of tension aroused is also a function of other internal and external characteristics and conditions of the individual —the so-called audience conditions in communications theory. In that literature, these are often considered to be various degrees of "persuasibility," "cognitive styles or needs," or related concepts. In the Festinger scheme, they are expressed as the "importance" of the cognition to the individual and the one with which it is dissonant. The degree of arousal can be expressed as the ratio of the number of dissonant to consonant elements, where each element is weighted for its importance. Each message is made up of many attributes, and the interrelationships among them are important. The notion of a resolution of these several characteristics of the receiver in relation to the message is contained in the concept of *involvement*. The summary effects of message relevance and subject involvement determine the degree of tension aroused.

Notice in the model that involvement is taken to be a function of self-perception. The "self" is equated with the need system and has a perceptual environment. Thus the individual perceives not only the stimuli in his external environment but also himself. An arrow from the social system feeds into self-perception to suggest the social forces that operate to condition it. The social effect can derive from either implicit or explicit forces of social influence. It can stem implicitly from the role of the individual at a specific moment in time and from the roles he has played over time. Role, in some senses, summarizes all such social influences, and here it is used as the primary social determinant of self-perception. These effects could be extended to other aggregation levels and other forms of implicit and explicit social influence, as well.

Tension Reduction. In the Festinger (1957) scheme, dissonance is reduced by decreasing the number or importance of dissonant elements and/or by reducing the importance of all relevant elements together. Which alternative is chosen depends on (1) the resistance to change of relative cognitive elements (cognitions with low resistance to change will change first), (2) the extent to which the change would produce new dissonance, and (3) the responsiveness of the cognitions to reality (in purchasing situations where reality is ambiguous, studies have shown that cognitive elements can be changed relatively easily).

These reactions in the model appear as various types of *adjustments* to the meaning and behavior systems. The meaning system is divided into the familiar cognitive, affective, and conative parts. Various theories (congruity, balance, and dissonance) suggest that adjustments will take place in *each* part. Thus aroused tension creates a *drive* that may or may not result in cognitive-affective activity and/or behavior. It need not affect behavior— the resolution of tension can take place entirely within the intellect, as opposed to resolving itself in some behavioral response. It has long been recognized that dissonance can be reduced by selective exposure, perception, retention, or action.

Krugman (1965) has suggested explanations of television advertising and other effects that do not depend on high degrees of relevancy or involvement.[13] We stress once again that *many* types of process explanations may be incorporated into the basic scheme as some interaction within or between systems. Notice that the scheme could also be used in studies of dyads, triads, or higher-order social interactions of either a "vertical" or "horizontal" hierarchy type. Consider two persons, one I/E paradigm for each. It can be reasoned that an advertising stimulus so affects the meaning system of an "opinion leader" that he makes a resulting purchase. Either implicitly or explicitly, this activity can provide a cue to the social system of the second person—the follower—who enters the meaning system through this route and undergoes the same kind of mediating process.

Another example demonstrates the flexibility of the paradigm for studies of consumer process. A great deal of theoretical conjecture concerns which of two models—an attitude → behavior sequence (the so-called communication model) or a behavior → attitude sequence (the so-called dissonance model)—is a better representation of the dynamics of the process. Much has been made of this debate in the advertising literature, for the former model tends to treat advertising as the initiator and stimulator of an attitude-to-behavior chain and the latter as a post hoc reinforcement of a behavior-to-attitude chain.

The model in Figure 20.5 suggests a third possibility and incorporates all three. For example, the typical attitude-to-behavior sequence is suggested by the loop through tension arousal and cognitive, affective, and conative adjustments to behavior. This could represent a communication in which some cognitive activity or intelligence was involved. Notice, however, that tension arousal is shown as working on behavior directly, without passing through the attitude system. This effect could occur if the stimulus message and the tension aroused were cues to a behavioral response, with no associated cognitive activity. The first situation could represent

---

[13] Krugman (1965, p. 355) also makes some interesting comments on the relevance of particular theoretical positions for explaining these effects:

"The distinction between the commercial and the noncommercial use of the mass media, as well as the distinction between "commercial" and "academic" research, has blinded us to the existence of two entirely different ways of experiencing and being influenced by mass media. One is characterized by lack of personal involvement. . . . The second is characterized by a high degree of personal involvement. . . . The significance of conditions of low or high involvement is not that one is better than the other, but that the processes of communication impact are different."

an early stage of learning and the second a more advanced stage. The subject in the second would be "conditioned" in the learning theory sense and would exhibit behavior patterns affected only by the stimulus message.

The dissonance model suggests a reverse process. Behavior itself is the most significant cue. Assuming, for example, that the stimulus in the object system is a brand, behavior with the brand (purchasing and using it) would feed back into the meaning system. Satisfaction with it would introduce positive feelings and beliefs that could be reinforced from information introduced from the social system (a friend's opinion) or the object system (an advertisement).

The efficiency of each model may be related more to the roles played by each subject than to the fact that one is a better representation of psychological functioning than the other. Consider, for example, the roles of opinion leader and follower and the two-step flow process alluded to earlier. Assuming that the leader is the principal advertising message receiver and that his actions are the primary cues governing the behavior of the follower, the communication model may be a more accurate description of the leader's process, and the dissonance model a more accurate description of the follower's. In the first, advertising serves as a primary source of information and influence on behavior; in the second, it reinforces behavior that has already taken place. Common to all these theoretical positions, of course, is the mental or meaning system of the individuals involved.

CONCLUSION

On the basis of the volume of research done and the amount of research funds expended, the consumer is one of the most intensively studied behavioral units in the social sciences. The intensity of this effort is not reflected in the basic disciplines, however, and it suggests more the prescriptive direction of management interests than the explanatory needs of a developing science. The situation leads to the conclusions of several writers that the subject is essentially atheoretical, or at least barren of widely accepted theoretical foundation. The case has been made in this paper that individual basic social science disciplines should not be expected to provide the integrating perspectives for theoretical development in the consumer area, even though the call for more attention to the consumer in the basic sciences seems to be highly justified. The peculiar nature of the consumer—the highly economic and social-psychological characteristics of consumption—suggests the need for an integrative, interdisciplinary, and essentially applied science viewpoint.

Much theoretical work, resting on conceptual ideas of typology and process borrowed from basic disciplines, is under way and is available in published form. There now seems to be a need not for more theory but for an understanding of how theory might best be subjected to verification and test. In another sense, concern must be with "connections"—those between conceptual materials in basic disciplines, and those between the theoretical positions generated and the methodological requirements that their testing implies.

The solution offered in this paper is the potential utility of frameworks such as the I/E paradigm, which should be simple, flexible, and readily adaptable to formalization and quantification. The I/E paradigm meets each of these evaluative criteria with varying degrees of success. As a framework, it is certainly simple —perhaps too simple, considering the complexity of cross-disciplinary work. Its flexibility is demonstrated by the relative ease with which it can be used to study questions of consumer typology and process. Formalization in typology construction indicates the need for a recognition of fundamental classificatory principles such as the attribute and condition concepts discussed in this paper. The set theoretic principles on which these foundations are laid can be extended to questions of consumer process as well, with the potential advantages of rigorous specification of construct and relationship.

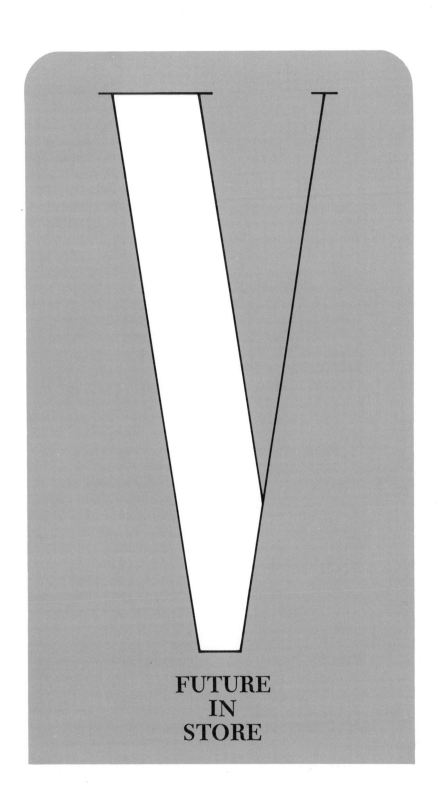

FUTURE
IN
STORE

21

THE NEXT DECADE OF BUYER BEHAVIOR THEORY AND RESEARCH

JAGDISH N. SHETH
Professor of Business
Department of Business Administration
University of Illinois at Urbana-Champaign

Predictions typically entail the Bayes theorem in some way because prognosis implies revising the prior probability on the basis of the assessment of symptoms currently manifested in the phenomenon whose direction is to be forecast. Predictions are also hazardous to one's welfare in any discipline, since due to the relatively short histories of the disciplines, the prior probabilities are often no better than random probabilities; moreover, the assessment of contemporary symptoms is made very difficult by the rapid and complex changes a discipline may be undergoing. Buyer behavior theory and research seem to present these problems.

Accordingly, my objective in this paper is to estimate the prior probability by briefly reviewing the historical perspective of the buyer behavior discipline and then to deal with a number of current events that are likely to determine both the velocity and the direction of buyer behavior theory. I shall focus on changes in the structure and content of buyer behavior theory and research that are likely to arise during the current decade, going out on a limb in my speculative tree, so to speak.

A BRIEF HISTORICAL PERSPECTIVE
ON THE BUYER BEHAVIOR DISCIPLINE

I believe that in the last quarter-century we have come a long
way from the dark ages of sporadic and random research in buyer
behavior. That the cumulative research effort in buyer behavior
—academic and professional, theoretical and empirical, published
and unpublished—is indeed impressive can be gauged from several
recent reviews (Burk, 1967; Guest, 1962; Howard, 1965; Perloff,
1968; Sheth, 1967; and Twedt, 1965a). A closer examination of
these reviews clearly indicates that we can identify four distinct
phases of differential thought and emphasis in the discipline.

The Empirical-Inductive Phase

The decades between 1930 and 1950 seemed to be dominated by
empirical research, mostly conducted by industry's marketing
people to determine the impact of their own decisions in the
marketplace. Furthermore, the major emphasis was on gauging the
effects of distribution, advertising, and promotion decisions.

Among the several distinct characteristics of this phase, we
may list (1) the dominance of economic theory of the firm and
especially the concepts of monopolistic competition, marginal
utility analysis, and welfare economics; (2) macro-market analysis
at the aggregate level or at best at some predefined segmented
level; and (3) emphasis on the market's behavior responses as
opposed to psychological responses.

The only exception to the above characterization of this phase
of the buyer behavior discipline seemed to be the acceptance of
motivation research in which both the concepts and the methods
of clinical psychology were widely applied to the understanding of
buyer behavior.

The Formative Phase

The 1950s must be regarded as the formative years of the buyer
behavior discipline, for during this decade several major elements
cemented the foundation of buyer behavior theory. First we saw
the shift from measuring aggregate buyer behavior to measuring
individual behavior. Two different groups of scholars simultaneously contributed to bringing about this change. One the Lazarsfeld
school of sociologists, whose interest in measuring total change in
voting behavior based on longitudinal panels led to the establishment of household consumer panels in buyer behavior. The second
was the Katona school of economic psychologists, who were interested in building better indicators of economic growth based on

the micro data of household acquisitions and inventories of durable appliances. The availability of data on household purchase behavior eventually led to interest in developing quantitative measures of brand or store loyalty and switching behaviors, which in turn brought the utilization of stochastic processes such as Markov chains.

A second major element of the 1950s was a growing interest in providing explanations for buyer behavior differences based on the *social* environment of the consumer. This led to the borrowing of the concepts of social stratification, reference groups, role orientations, and opinion leadership. Therefore, the major disciplines relied on tended to be sociology and economic anthropology. Even though these theorizing attempts were unsystematic and less refined, they were pioneering efforts in the search for causal explanations from disciplines other than economic theory.

The third distinct element was the introduction to formal model building of buyer responses to marketing stimuli that were based on the optimization theory of operations research and econometrics (see Bass et al., 1961, for examples). Simultaneously, the utility theorists in economics were formalizing Samuelson's revealed preference theory of consumption. The combined effect was the birth of deductive formal model building based on normative axioms and assumptions. This development was further facilitated by the feasibility of using the computer to build complex simulation models. Thus it is quite surprising to observe that management science was adopted in the infancy of buyer behavior theory. But it is therefore not at all surprising that most efforts at normative-deductive model building met with failures and premature rejection. As we shall see later, this negative circumstance has had tremendous implications for the future of buyer behavior theory.

It must be pointed out that all through these formative years the empirical research on buyer behavior continued to accelerate independently, thanks to the availability of micro data and the computer facilities to analyze them.

The Middle-Range-Theory Phase

The first half of the 1960s can best be described as the identification stage. Buyer behavior began to be understood for its own sake rather than from the point of view of the marketer, the government, or some other entity with vested interests. In my opinion, this is directly attributable to the intensive borrowing of theories and concepts from the branches of the behavioral sciences that had emerged as "pure" disciplines. These included experimental psychology with emphasis on learning and perception, social psychology with emphasis on cognitive consistency, and rural sociology with emphasis on adoption processes of innovative products, practices, and services. For further discussion, see the excellent review provided by Burk (1967).

The intensive borrowing from the behavioral sciences by numerous researchers, each one interested in some aspect of buyer behavior and predisposed or trained in some branch of the behavioral sciences, resulted in the development of well-identified middle-range theories of buyer behavior. Any examples must include Howard's learning theory, Bauer's perceived-risk theory, and several researchers' development of theories based on Festinger's cognitive dissonance, Lewin's field theory, opinion leadership, innovativeness, and even several personality theories. As I have pointed out elsewhere (Sheth, 1967), the outstanding characteristic of this borrowing phase was the *partial explanations* that each theory provided to the otherwise complex phenomena of buyer behavior, especially those related to the problem-solving and habitual buying decisions. Not very surprisingly, these middle-range theories neglected other types of buyer behaviors, including unplanned impulsive behavior, novelty seeking, and situationally anchored behaviors, because very little theorizing was offered by the behavioral sciences in these areas.

Even though most efforts in this era concentrated on building middle-range theories, the attempts to build formal models based on optimization theory (including linear programming), stochastic processes (including Bernoulli and Markovian processes), and heuristics and other Monte Carlo techniques continued. In fact, the early 1960s can be regarded as the golden era of management science in buyer behavior, as evidenced in Massy, Montgomery, and Morrison (1970).

The Integrative-Comprehensive-Theory Phase
The years between 1965 and the present are best identified with the emergence of comprehensive theories of buyer behavior. This basically entailed integrating several middle-range theories that had come to be accepted, as well as putting together empirical research not identified with any theory in buyer behavior (Andreasen, 1965; Engel, Blackwell, and Kollat, 1968; Howard and Sheth, 1969; Nicosia, 1966; Sheth, 1972, and chap. 2 of this volume). In my opinion, integrative-comprehensive theory building introduced three factors in the development of the discipline. First, it emphasized the limitations of directly borrowing theories from the

behavioral sciences without first adapting them to the complexity of buyer behavior. Furthermore, it established a precedent in reversing the process of borrowing by first conceptualizing the buyer behavior phenomenon and then searching for as many constructs as could logically be found in the behavioral and social sciences.

Second, and perhaps most important, the integrative-comprehensive theories brought to bear the self-confidence of independently building theories of buyer behavior in place of simply applying a social science theory to the buyer behavior area, with or without modifications. This must be regarded as the genesis of buyer behavior as a discipline in itself rather than simply a problem area that could be explained by some social science discipline. Finally, the theories provided insights into building complex, but realistic, formal models of buyer behavior. This may have contributed to changing the traditional course of model building in terms of starting with simple, unrealistic assumptions and relaxing them to make them realistic (e.g., as in utility theory, Katona, 1953).

Two other developments in buyer behavior theory during this phase are worth noting. The first was the discarding of deductive-normative model building based on operations research methods in favor of statistical inductive model building with the use of multivariate analysis of large-scale survey data. The second development was the broadening of marketing and buyer behavior horizons to nontraditional areas such as population control, nutrition, and public service delivery systems under the pioneering efforts of Kotler and Zaltman.

Assessment of History
and Contemporary Signals

The brief historical review just presented indicates that buyer behavior theory is a far cry from random thinking. Within a very short period of time, we seem to have laid a firm foundation for building a distinct discipline of buyer behavior that will not be a subsystem of marketing nor of any of the other, older social sciences. An even more pleasant observation is that we seem to have achieved greater progress with respect to richness of thinking, comprehensiveness of theorizing, and testing of theories in naturalistic and realistic settings than many of the older behavioral science disciplines have in their comparative periods of development. And why should it not be that way? Unless the newer disciplines can begin to avoid the trial-and-error learning of other disciplines, how can we progress from being strict problem solvers for the government or industry?

However, an assessment of a number of contemporary events also indicates that the velocity of growth will not only be more rapid and diffused but will likely change significantly the course of the growth curve. Rather than evaluating these events and then forecasting the future directions of buyer behavior theory, I am devoting the rest of this paper to detailing the major dimensions of the future direction of the theory and linking them to my assessment of contemporary events. The future developments are described below in terms of the following categories: (1) structural changes in buyer behavior theory, (2) broadening of the horizons of relevance and applications of buyer behavior principles, and (3) active interest of other disciplines in borrowing from buyer behavior theory.

STRUCTURAL CHANGES
IN BUYER BEHAVIOR THEORY

In the Bayesian crystal urn, I foresee four types of structural changes in the development of buyer behavior theory during the 1970s. They are (1) the establishment of criteria to evaluate the relevance of different theories of buyer behavior; (2) the construction of tests and scales to measure widely accepted hypothetical constructs in buyer behavior theory; (3) the building of complex, formal, but highly realistic and inductive models based on comprehensive theories of buyer behavior; and (4) theoretical and empirical research on nonpurposeful buyer behavior, hopefully leading to a comprehensive theory.

Criteria for Evaluating
Theories of Buyer Behavior

Although we have developed several theories of buyer behavior in both middle-range and comprehensive categories, we have so far failed to develop widely accepted criteria with which to evaluate their usefulness or even their relevance to buyer behavior. To be sure, existing theories are differentially accepted and diffused, but this condition seems based on tenuous factors such as the degree of face validity or predictive validity, the reputation of an author, the prestige of an institution, and the ability to generate more research funds and, commensurately, more publicity about the theory. Since an even greater number of researchers are likely to contribute in the coming years, I think the discipline will experience personal rivalries and showmanship among competing authors unless some evaluative criteria are developed and accepted. Within the next five years, I foresee three different types of criteria emerging to minimize rivalry and showmanship.

The first type of criterion seems to be already visible in the form of the development of a metatheory of buyer behavior (Zaltman, Pinson, and Angelmar, 1973). In other words, theories of buyer behavior are likely to be critically examined, compared, and contrasted on the basis of fundamental judgments from the philosophy of science. This type of criterion is strictly discipline oriented and tends to emphasize the evaluation of the *process* of theorizing.

The second type of criterion is likely to be pragmatic, being based on the usefulness of a theory of buyer behavior in solving specific problems. This type of evaluation will probably emphasize the capability of a theory in enabling the problem solver to achieve his own goals. What entities are likely to increasingly utilize buyer behavior theories to help solve their problems? The public policy makers, the business managers, and the consumer advocates seem to be the most probable candidates. To the extent that each entity differs in its perspectives and activities, we are likely to see for each entity very different ways of putting buyer behavior theories to use. For example, the research of consumer advocates that is based on buyer behavior theories is likely to be very specific, ad hoc, and symptomatic, since such workers have tended to be issue oriented. The public policy makers, on the other hand, are more likely to utilize comprehensive theories to conduct exhaustive and systematic research to find the root causes of problematic symptoms pointed out by the consumer advocates. At least this is my hope. Finally, the marketing management is certainly likely to favor comprehensive theories of buyer behavior to understand and monitor market behavior simply because past experience has proved that middle-range theories are not satisfactory.

The final type of criterion is likely to stem from efforts to generalize a theory to diverse and nontraditional areas of buyer behavior. The greater the ability of a theory to extend itself with a minimum number of modifications to unexplored areas of buyer behavior, such as the search for information process, or to nontraditional areas, such as product utility and value formation, the greater the likelihood of its popularity and diffusion. However, the diffusion of the theory is likely to be evaluated in terms of specific criteria similar to the criteria in statistics for parameter estimation procedures.

It is my hope that with the development of agreed criteria

in buyer behavior, we shall see greater rigor and deductive logic in theories of buyer behavior.

Standardized Measurement of Buyer Behavior Constructs

Even though we are still striving to develop better theories of buyer behavior, I think we have a consensus on several hypothetical constructs. These include the constructs of brand and store loyalty, behavioral intentions or buyer plans, predispositions toward choice alternatives, and perceptual biases in selective exposure and processing of information. In addition, there seems to be a basic understanding that individual differences in buyer behavior are likely to be determined by constructs such as life cycle, life style, socioeconomic status, and role orientation among consumers. We have also tended recently to follow the psychometric tradition of data analysis, especially with the use of multivariate methods. This has brought to our attention the need for better and isomorphic measures of the above-mentioned constructs, which we strive to relate to one another to describe and explain buyer behavior.

I therefore foresee major research effort in buyer behavior channeled toward the development of standardized scales for many of the constructs in buyer behavior mentioned previously. I also think that this research effort will probably be heavily influenced by the psychometric theories of scaling. This forecast yields several important implications. First, we are likely to become more skeptical of the *direct use* of standardized scales and tests developed for comparable constructs in the behavioral sciences. In the area of attitudes, for example, it is more probable that we will question the measurement procedures proposed in expectancy-value models in social psychology. Thus we are likely to separate theories from measurement as we continue to borrow from the behavioral and social sciences. Second, it is very probable that buyer behavior theory will become more mathematical and formal, due to the research thrust in measurement and development of tests for the constructs. Finally, the development of standardized tests is likely to augment empirical research in the unexplored areas of buyer behavior because research efforts will tend to be routinized, as they are today in some branches of psychology.

Quantitative Modeling of Buyer Behavior

In the distant future, I foresee reemergence of quantitative model building in buyer behavior. In other words, it will be quite some time before good mathematical models of buyer behavior appear. Furthermore, the model-building effort is likely to be distinctly different from what has been historically attempted in marketing. First, the models are likely to be problem oriented instead of technique oriented. Thus by definition they will be empirical, summarizing the efforts to research a problem area with the use of existing theories of buyer behavior. For example, a number of researchers are currently applying various theories of buyer behavior to understand how advertising works, how public delivery systems can be made more efficient in health, education, and welfare, and how future transportation and communication needs can be fully met without endangering the environment.

Second, the models are likely to utilize several statistical techniques in a sequential multistage process rather than to try fitting the empirical problem into a single technique such as mathematical programming or multidimensional scaling. Finally, the quantitative models of buyer behavior will be more positive than normative. In other words, we are more likely to see predictive models of buyer behavior and less likely to see control models. Accordingly, the model-building effort will coincide with testing and continuous updating. Furthermore, the adaptive control concepts are likely to be at the core of the updating process. In short, Bayesian philosophy is likely to dominate the model-building effort, replacing the search for optimality.

I also think that a number of researchers will attempt to decompose agreed comprehensive theories of buyer behavior into smaller theories and to develop models for them. We have already seen some efforts in this direction in the information-processing and attitude-structure subsystems of buyer behavior.

Research on Nonpurposeful Behavior

Based on the historical review, it is fair to state that we have so far concentrated on habitual, purposeful, and problem-solving buyer behavior. Furthermore, we have developed several quite comprehensive theories to explain it. However, nonpurposeful behavior has received relatively little attention in the past, and it is therefore likely to become the major substantive area of empirical research and theory building. By nonpurposeful behavior, I am primarily referring to curiosity, novelty seeking, and exploratory behavior, as well as cue-triggered impulsive buyer behavior. Some theorizing on this aspect of buyer behavior based on Berlyne's theory has been recently developed by several researchers (Hansen, 1972; Howard and Sheth, 1969; and Venkatesan, 1972). However, considerable work remains to be done, especially in terms of gathering empirical data, before a good systematic theory of non-purposeful behavior can be developed.

It seems inevitable to speculate that any comprehensive theory of nonpurposeful behavior will be extremely difficult to build, and when built, it will depend more heavily on the typology of situational influences surrounding the nonpurposeful behavior than on the personal attributes of the buyer.

BROADENING THE HORIZONS
OF BUYER BEHAVIOR PRINCIPLES

Simultaneous with the structural changes in buyer behavior theory, I foresee rapid applications of buyer behavior concepts to three broadly defined substantive problem areas. These are (1) cross-cultural buyer behavior research demanded by the needs of multinational corporations, (2) public policy research on marketing institutions and practices required by increased concern in consumer welfare on the part of regulatory agencies, and (3) extension of buyer behavior to nontraditional areas of societal problems directly attributable to our mass-consumption society. I expect that the bulk of applied research in buyer behavior will be limited to these problem areas in the coming decade.

Cross-Cultural Buyer Behavior Research

I foresee extensive applied research in buyer behavior across different cultures simply because of the increased multinational character of most large business corporations. With the maturity of many foreign markets, the multinational corporations have become sensitive to marketing orientation in their efforts to diffuse products and services throughout the world. The need to understand the impact of cultures on buyer behavior is obvious. In fact, surprisingly little attention has been paid to assessing cultural influences on buyer behavior, even though the United States is recognized as the melting pot of diverse ethnic groups.

I think research on cross-cultural buyer behavior is likely to go through the same stage through which buyer behavior theory itself has passed. First, there will be clusterings of studies, mostly localized to some industries and some countries. Given the pattern of multinational business expansion, it is logical to presume that cross-cultural studies will be concentrated in European markets and will be concerned with nondurable consumer goods. Second, we should expect the development of several middle-range theories of cross-cultural buyer behavior based on the research in the first stage. Furthermore, because of the substantial costs involved in cross-cultural research, the middle-range theories will be generated by the marketing practitioners and not by the academicians. Of course the scholars are likely to be instrumental in guiding the marketing practice's efforts to build middle-range theories. Finally, I foresee the eventual emergence of several comprehensive theories of buyer behavior. These will mostly constitute efforts to integrate both diverse middle-range theories and existing empirical research in cross-cultural buyer behavior. Furthermore, I think that there will be virtually no differences in structure between cross-cultural and domestic theories of buyer behavior.

Public Policy Research

Inevitably, there will be rapid applications of buyer behavior theories for the purpose of better regulating marketing practices and institutions. Perhaps the most important factor contributing to this observation is the singular inadequacy of the traditional concepts of microeconomic theories to properly guide the function of regulation. A related reason is the divorce of marketing from economics during the past two decades. A second major factor is the increased pragmatism recently exhibited by regulatory agencies such as the Federal Trade Commission and the Food and Drug Administration. This has brought home the need for empirical research on buyer behavior at the micro level both before and after major regulatory decisions (e.g., the policy of corrective advertising) to ensure that desired consequences follow from them. Finally, the recent spread of consumerism is likely to encourage public policy makers to conduct fundamental research on buyer behavior in the hope of producing good legislative policies.

The bulk of research in buyer behavior for public policy is likely to be problem oriented, and most of the problems are likely to come from the negative side effects of mass marketing and mass consumption—for example, mass media effects on citizens' values.

Buyer Behavior Research on
Social and Environmental Problems

Perhaps the most critical applications of buyer behavior theories will arise from research on social and environmental problems. We have already witnessed some application of marketing and buyer behavior concepts to the social problems of less-developed economies—for example, population explosion and malnutrition. However, the societal and environmental problems directly related to mass consumption and mass production are more relevant to most people working in consumer behavior. These problem areas include environmental and social pollution, welfare of minorities, and delivery of public services such as education and health care. The greater social consciousness in solving these problems fortunately seems to be transcending the vested interests of the components of our mass production and mass consumption system, and research in these areas thus should tend to be nonpartisan.

In addition to the broadening of the horizons of buyer behavior, I foresee two subtle and indirect benefits of research on social and environmental problems. The first is the separation of buyer behavior theory from marketing theory. In other words, I foresee greater respectability for buyer behavior theory by its extension to socially relevant issues. It is surprising, on reflection, to see how much psychology has suffered from the crisis of relevance because it emerged as a discipline in areas of research that were not considered to be relevant or essential to mass consumption societies.

The second benefit is the rapid cross-fertilization of philosophy, theory, and methodology between the natural sciences and buyer behavior theory. I think it is simply inevitable that we will be working together with researchers from the hard sciences, such as physics, mechanics, and biochemistry, in the search for solutions to social and environmental problems. Thus, rather than borrowing from the other social sciences, it is likely that we will be borrowing philosophy and methodology from the hard sciences. To me, this appears to be a unique opportunity for buyer behavior theory to elevate itself to a more mature level.

BORROWING FROM
BUYER BEHAVIOR THEORY

Historically, we have borrowed a great deal from other disciplines to build buyer behavior theory. Within a decade, however, I think it very likely that other disciplines will be actively interested in buyer behavior and consequently will borrow a set of concepts and research tools from it. Implicit in this prediction is my conviction that we either already have or will very soon have achieved richness of thinking, variety of methodology, and respectability of the discipline to motivate other disciplines to search buyer behavior theory for relevant concepts and methods. It is interesting, therefore, to speculate on which disciplines are likely to borrow what from buyer behavior theory. I describe below three types of borrowing activities: (1) the less mature social science disciplines borrowing the research methodology of buyer behavior, (2) the older social sciences borrowing the concepts and theories of buyer behavior, and (3) the hard sciences borrowing both the theories and methodology of the buyer behavior discipline.

Less Mature Social Sciences
Compared to some mature social sciences such as macroeconomics and experimental psychology, the buyer behavior discipline looks less mature. By the same token, many other social sciences are even less mature than buyer behavior. I include political science, parts of sociology, history, religion, home economics, law, and public health in the category of less mature social science disciplines. Just as we have borrowed from psychology and economics, I believe the disciplines named are likely to borrow from us. In fact, this is already evident from the recent trend of these disciplines to cite marketing and buyer behavior references.

The less mature social sciences are likely to borrow the research methods identified and routinely utilized in buyer behavior. These include longitudinal panels, cost-oriented sampling procedures, the survey methods of data collection, and the use of multivariate methods. In addition, there is always the possibility of employing marketing strategies and tactics to diffuse radical innovations in each of those disciplines.

Mature Social Sciences
Although some of my colleagues may not agree, I think that many of the traditional social sciences to which we owe so much are likely first to participate in understanding buyer behavior and eventually to borrow from it. My prediction is based on two facts. First, these traditional disciplines are currently facing the crisis of relevance because the foundations of their theory and research have been based on less critical areas of human behavior. I include experimental psychology, social psychology, and small group theory among the fields that have encountered this crisis in recent years. Second, many of the traditional disciplines have built formal models of behavior that have tended to be unrealistic or have become obsolete because of unprecedented technological changes in our society in the last 30 years. Utility theory, micro theory of the firm, and allied areas of economics and decision making are illustrative of this type of social science. As these disciplines search for socially relevant and useful problem areas, and as they begin to build realistic theories, the probability is extremely high that

buyer behavior will become the center of attention, because it tends to directly reflect the social problems of a mass-consumption society.

Owing to the problem-solving interests of the traditional social sciences, I believe that these disciplines are likely to be more interested in the theoretical concepts and substantive findings than in the research methodology of buyer behavior. This also seems plausible because the traditional disciplines are often rich in methodology. I think that buyer behavior has much to offer to the utility theory in economics from its thinking on choice behavior anchored to cognitive-evaluative structures. Similarly, I think that we have much to offer to social psychology both in theory and research methodology in terms of conducting complex longitudinal studies of attitude change and brand choice behavior in naturalistic settings. Furthermore, the growing literature and theory on diffusion of innovations in buyer behavior may enable rural sociology to rethink diffusion theory. Finally, recent efforts of buyer behavior researchers to build test batteries to measure life styles are likely to alter significantly the thrust of personality tests in clinical psychology.

Although most of the borrowing from buyer behavior by the traditional social sciences is likely to involve concepts and substantive findings, there are certain areas of research methodology that may also be useful to them. These include the survey research aspects entailed in the design and execution of large-scale studies in naturalistic settings.

Hard Sciences

By hard sciences I mean the natural sciences and engineering based on physics, mechanics, chemistry, and biochemistry. The hard sciences have reached such a level of maturity in their own disciplines that they will inevitably broaden their horizons. I expect them, therefore, to become concerned with the *social consequences* of expanded technology and depletion of natural resources. This includes the areas of pollution of resources, urban planning, and the like. Recently we have witnessed research undertakings by the hard sciences in areas of social concern that typically have been the domain of social scientists. It seems certain, therefore, that sooner or later the hard sciences will become exposed to and interested in buyer behavior. When that happens, it is equally certain that they will borrow extensively both the substantive findings and research methodology, because the newer research areas will force them to examine alternative theories and methodology. For it is generally conceded that the concepts of hard sciences may only be analogously related to social problems.

SUMMARY

In this attempt to speculate on the future of buyer behavior theory, I limited myself to forecasting the major directions that are likely to be taken in the next decade. These predictions were based on a review of the historical perspective of buyer behavior theory, taking into account contemporary events. First, I suggested that four major changes are likely to occur in the structure of buyer behavior theory. They are (1) development of criteria to evaluate theories of buyer behavior, (2) construction of standardized tests and scales to measure buyer behavior constructs, (3) complex model building in an inductive manner with the use of several statistical procedures, and (4) research emphasis on nonpurposeful buyer behavior.

Second, I suggested three major ways by which buyer behavior theory is likely to broaden its horizons—namely, (1) development of cross-cultural theories of buyer behavior, (2) research and theories of buyer behavior for public policy purposes, and (3) research on social and environmental problems created by mass consumption societies.

Third, I predicted that a number of other disciplines will become actively interested in buyer behavior and will therefore borrow research methodology and theory typically identified with buyer behavior theory. Specifically, I have suggested that (1) less mature social sciences such as political science, law, education, and public health will probably borrow research methodology, (2) more mature and older social sciences are likely to borrow concepts and theories from buyer behavior in their efforts to become more relevant and realistic disciplines, and (3) some natural sciences will borrow both methodology and theory from buyer behavior in the process of broadening their horizons to understand the social consequences of technology.

Despite the bright predictions for the future of buyer behavior theory, I think that certain identifiable ailments in today's theories may impede the achievement of these predictions. First, most theories look on buyer behavior as the consequence of some form of the decision-making process, thus they implicitly concede that buyer behavior consists of only goal-directed behavior. This may well restrict the horizons of buyer behavior theory. Second, a large number of theories of buyer behavior often examine the buyer decision process from the point of view of marketing. Although marketing management has made the greatest use of the findings and concepts of buyer behavior, there is no reason why others from different viewpoints cannot utilize the same concepts and findings. Not only has this tendency made buyer behavior theory somewhat myopic, it has produced a terminology and vocabulary for buyer behavior that impedes its extension to nontraditional areas. Third, it seems that most theories of buyer behavior tend to overemphasize the process leading to behavior, while underemphasizing the buying behavior or the antecedent and subsequent events surrounding the behavior. Unless we consciously strive to remove these ailments, buyer behavior theory may take longer than necessary to gain respectability across disciplines.

REFERENCE BIBLIOGRAPHY

Adorno, T. W., et al., *The Authoritarian Personality.* New York: Harper & Row, 1950.

Alderson, Wroe, *Basic Research Report on Consumer Behavior.* Philadelphia: Alderson and Sessions Associates, April 1957. (a)

Alderson, Wroe, *Marketing Behavior and Executive Action.* Homewood, Ill.: Irwin, 1957. (b)

Alexander, R., "Some Aspects of Sex Differences in Relation to Marketing." *Journal of Marketing,* 12 (October 1947), 158–72.

Alexis, Marcus, "Pathways to the Negro Market." *Journal of Negro Education,* 28 (Spring 1959), 114–27. (a)

Alexis, Marcus, "Racial Differences in Consumption and Automobile Ownership." Ph.D. dissertation, University of Minnesota, 1959. (b)

Alexis, Marcus, "Racial Differences in Consumption Patterns." *Business News Notes,* No. 50. Minneapolis: School of Business Administration, University of Minnesota, September 1960.

Alexis, Marcus, "Some Negro-White Differences in Consumption." *American Journal of Economics and Sociology,* 21 (January 1962), 11–28.

Alexis, Marcus, George Haines, Jr., and Leonard S. Simon, "Consumer Information Processing: The Case of Women's Clothing." In Robert L. King (ed.), *Marketing and the New Science of Planning.* Proceedings of the Fall Conference of the

American Marketing Association, August 1968. Chicago: American Marketing Association, 1968, pp. 197–205.

Alexis, Marcus, and Leonard S. Simon, "The Food Marketing Commision and Food Prices by Income Groups." *Journal of Farm Economics,* 49 (May 1967), 436–446.

Alexis, Marcus, and Kenneth M. Smith, "Some Determinants of Food Buying Behavior." In Marcus Alexis, Robert J. Holloway, and Robert S. Hancock (eds.), *Empirical Foundations of Marketing: Research Findings in the Behavioral and Applied Sciences.* Chicago: Markham, 1969, pp. 20–32.

Amstutz, Arnold E., *Computer Simulation of Competitive Market Response.* Cambridge, Mass.: M.I.T. Press, 1967.

Andreasen, Alan R., "Attitudes and Customer Behavior: A Decision Model." In Lee E. Preston (ed.), *New Research in Marketing.* Berkeley: Institute of Business and Economic Research, University of California, 1965, pp. 1–16.

Armstrong, J. Scott, "Long-range Forecasting for a Consumer Durable in an International Market." Ph.D. dissertation, Massachusetts Institute of Technology, 1968.

Arndt, Johan, "Word of Mouth Advertising: The Role of Product-Related Conversations in the Diffusion of a New Food Product." Ph.D. dissertation, Graduate School of Business, Harvard University, 1966.

Arndt, Johan, "Perceived Risk, Sociometric Integration, and Word of Mouth in the Adoption of a New Food Product." In Donald F. Cox (ed.), *Risk Taking and Information Handling in Consumer Behavior.* Cambridge, Mass.: Division of Research, Graduate School of Business Administration, Harvard University, 1967, pp. 289–316. (a)

Arndt, Johan, "Role of Product-Related Conversations in the Diffusion of a New Product." *Journal of Marketing Research,* 4 (August 1967), 291–295. (b)

Arndt, Johan, *Word of Mouth Advertising.* New York: Advertising Research Foundation, 1967. (c)

Arndt, Johan, *Insights into Consumer Behavior.* Boston: Allyn & Bacon, 1968. (a)

Arndt, Johan, "Perceived Risk and Word of Mouth Advertising." In Harold H. Kassarjian and Thomas S. Robertson (eds.), *Perspectives in Consumer Behavior.* Glenview, Ill.: Scott, Foresman, 1968, pp. 330–337. (b)

Arndt, Johan, "Profiling Consumer Innovators." In Johan Arndt

(ed.), *Insights into Consumer Behavior.* Boston: Allyn
& Bacon, 1968, pp. 71–83. (c)

Arndt, Johan, "Testing the 'Two-Step Flow of Communication
Hypothesis.'" In Johan Arndt (ed.), *Insights into Consumer
Behavior.* Boston: Allyn & Bacon, 1968, pp. 189–202. (d)

Aspinwall, Leo V., "The Characteristics of Goods Theory."
In William Lazer and Eugene J. Kelley (eds.), *Managerial
Marketing: Perspectives and Viewpoints* (rev. ed.).
Homewood, Ill.: Irwin, 1962, pp. 633–643.

Assael, Henry, "The Political Role of Trade Associations in
Distributive Conflict Resolution." *Journal of Marketing*, 32
(April 1968), 21–28.

Assael, Henry, and George S. Day, "Attitudes and Awareness
as Predictions of Market Share." *Journal of Advertising
Research*, 8 (December 1968), 3–10.

Atkinson, John W., *An Introduction to Motivation.* New York: Van
Nostrand Reinhold, 1964.

Atkinson, Richard C., Gordon H. Bower, and Edward J. Crothers,
An Introduction to Mathematical Learning Theory.
New York: Wiley, 1965.

Averink, G. J. Aeyelts, "Marketing Models for Consumer Durable
Products." *Esomar Congress Papers* (1970), 155–180.

Back, Kurt W., "Influence Through Social Communication."
Journal of Abnormal and Social Psychology, 46 (1951), 9–23.

Bailey, Norman T. J., *The Mathematical Theory of Epidemics.*
New York: Hafner, 1957.

Barton, Allen H., "The Concept of Property-Space in Social
Research." In Paul F. Lazarsfeld and Morris Rosenberg
(eds.), *The Language of Social Research.* New York: Free
Press, 1955, pp. 40–53.

Bass, Frank M., "A Simultaneous-Equation Regression Study
of Advertising and Sales—Analysis of Cigarette Data."
Institute Paper No. 176. Lafayette, Ind.: Krannert Graduate
School of Industrial Administration, Purdue University, 1967.

Bass, Frank, et al. (eds.), *Mathematical Models and Methods
in Marketing.* Homewood, Ill.: Irwin, 1961.

Bass, Frank, Douglas J. Tigert, and Ronald T. Lonsdale, "An
Analysis of Socio-Economic-Related Market Segments for
Grocery Products." Working paper. Lafayette, Ind.: Krannert
Graduate School of Industrial Administration, Purdue
University, 1967.

Bass, Frank, Douglas J. Tigert, and Ronald T. Lonsdale, "Market

Segmentation: Group vs. Individual Behavior." *Journal of Marketing Research*, 5 (August 1969), 264–270.

Batten, Barton, Durstine & Osborn, Inc., *One Hundred Media Terms Defined.* New York: BBD&O, 1966.

Bauer, Raymond A., "Consumer Behavior as Risk Taking." In Robert S. Hancock (ed.), *Dynamic Marketing for a Changing World.* Proceedings of the 43rd National Conference of the American Marketing Association, June 1960. Chicago: American Marketing Association, 1960, pp. 389–398.

Bauer, Raymond A., "The Obstinate Audience: The Influence Process from the Point of View of Social Communication." *American Psychologist*, 19 (May 1964), 319–328.

Bauer, Raymond A., "Attitudes, Verbal Behavior, and Other Behavior." Paper presented at the Bermuda Attitude Research Conference, American Marketing Association, January 1966.

Bauer, Raymond A., "Source Effect and Persuasibility: A New Look." In Donald F. Cox (ed.), *Risk Taking and Information Handling in Consumer Behavior.* Cambridge, Mass: Division of Research, Graduate School of Business Administration, Harvard University, 1967, pp. 559–578.

Bauer, Raymond A., and Lawrence H. Wortzel, "Doctor's Choice: The Physician and his Sources of Information About Drugs." *Journal of Marketing Research*, 3 (February 1966), 40–47.

Baum, J., and K. E. R. Dennis, "The Estimation of the Expected Brand Share of a New Product." Paper presented at the Esomar Congress, Baden-Baden, September 1961.

Beale, E. M. L., et al., "A Computer Assessment of Media Schedules." *Operations Research Quarterly*, 17 (December 1966), 381–411.

Bell, Wendell, "Social Choice, Life Styles, and Suburban Residence." In William Dobriner (ed.), *The Suburban Community.* New York: Putnam, 1958, pp. 276–283.

Bell, William E., "Consumer Innovators: A Unique Market for Newness." In Stephen A. Greyser (ed.), *Toward Scientific Marketing.* Proceedings of the Winter Conference of the American Marketing Association, December 1963. Chicago: American Marketing Association, 1964, pp. 85–95.

Berger, Joseph, Bernard P. Cohen, J. Laurie Snell, and Morris Zelditch, Jr., *Types of Formalization in Small Group Research.* Boston: Houghton Mifflin, 1962.

Berlyne, D. E., "Motivational Problems Raised by Exploratory and Epistemic Behavior." In Sigmund Koch (ed.),

Psychology: The Study of a Science. New York: McGraw-Hill, 1963, vol. 5, pp. 284–364.

Berlyne, D. E., "Curiosity and Exploration." *Science*, 153 (July 1, 1966), 25–33.

Berry, L. A., and R. W. Pollay, "The Influencing Role of the Child in Family Decision Making." *Journal of Marketing Research*, 5 (February 1968), 70–72.

Bird, M., and A. S. C. Ehrenberg, "Consumer Attitudes and Brand Usage." *Journal of the Market Research Society*, 12 (October 1970), 233–247.

Blood, Robert O., "The Effects of the Wife's Employment on Family Power Structure." *Social Forces*, 36 (1958), 347–352.

Blood, Robert O., and D. M. Wolfe, *Husbands and Wives: The Dynamics of Married Living*. New York: Free Press, 1960.

Bortel, Dorothy G., and Irma H. Gross, *A Comparison of Home Management in Two Socioeconomic Groups*. Technical Bulletin No. 240. East Lansing, Mich.: State Agricultural Experiment Station, 1954.

Bott, Elizabeth, *Family and Social Network*. London: Tavistock, 1957, pp. 59–60.

Bourne, Francis S., "Group Influence in Marketing and Public Relations." In Rensis Likert and Samuel P. Hayes, Jr. (eds.), *Some Applications of Behavioral Research*. Paris: UNESCO, 1957, chap. 6.

Boyd, Harper, Jr., and Ronald E. Frank, "The Importance of Private Labels in Food Retailing." *Business Horizons*, 9 (Summer 1966), 81–90.

Brehm, Jack W., "Post-Decision Changes in the Desirability of Alternatives." *Journal of Abnormal and Social Psychology*, 52 (July 1956), 384–389.

Brehm, Jack W., and A. R. Cohen, *Explorations in Cognitive Dissonance*. New York: Wiley, 1962.

Bridgman, P. W., *The Logic of Modern Physics*. New York: Macmillan, 1927.

Brown, George H., "The Automobile Buying Decision Within the Family." In Nelson N. Foote (ed.), *Household Decision-Making*. New York: New York University Press, 1961, pp. 963–999.

Brown, R. W., *Social Psychology*. New York: Collier-Macmillan, 1965.

Bucklin, Louis B., and James M. Carman, *The Design of Consumer Research Panels: Conception and Administration of the*

Berkeley Food Panel. Berkeley: Institute of Business and Economic Research, University of California, 1967.

Burchinal, Lee G., and Ward W. Bauder, "Decision-Making and Role Patterns Among Iowa Farm and Nonfarm Families." *Journal of Marriage and the Family,* 27 (November 1965), 525–530.

Burk, M. C., "Survey of Interpretations of Consumer Behavior by Social Scientists in the Postwar Period." *Journal of Farm Economics,* 49 (1967), 1–31.

Buzzell, Robert D., *Mathematical Models and Marketing Management.* Cambridge, Mass.: Division of Research, Graduate School of Business Administration, Harvard University, 1964.

Campbell, Brian M., "The Existence and Determinants of Evoked Set in Brand Choice Behavior." Ph.D. dissertation, Columbia University, 1968.

Campbell, Donald T., "Social Attitudes and Other Acquired Behavioral Dispositions." In Sigmund Koch (ed.), *Psychology: A Study of Science.* New York: McGraw-Hill, 1963, vol. 6, pp. 94–172.

Campbell, Donald T., and Donald W. Fiske, "Convergent and Discriminant Validation by the Multitrait-Multimethod Matrix." *Psychological Bulletin,* 56 (March 1959), 81–105.

Campbell, Donald T., and Julian C. Stanley, *Experimental and Quasi-Experimental Designs for Research.* Skokie, Ill.: Rand McNally, 1966.

Campbell, Rex, "A Suggested Paradigm of the Individual Adoption Process." *Rural Sociology,* 31 (December 1966), 458–466.

Carman, James M., "Brand Switching and Linear Learning Models." *Journal of Advertising Research,* 6 (June 1966), 23–31.

Carman, James M., "Correlates of Brand Loyalty: Some Positive Results." *Journal of Marketing Research,* 7 (February 1970), 67–76.

Carment, D. W., C. G. Miles, and V. B. Cervin, "Persuasiveness and Persuadability as Related to Intelligence and Extraversion." *British Journal of Social and Clinical Psychology,* 4 (1965), 1–7.

Carroll, John B., "Words, Meanings and Concepts." In J. A. Emig, James T. Fleming, and Helen M. Popp (eds.), *Language and Learning.* New York: Harcourt Brace Jovanovich, 1964, pp. 73–101.

Carter, L. F., "Recording and Evaluating the Performance of Individuals as Members of Small Groups." *Personnel Psychology*, 7 (1954), 477–484.

Cerha, Jarko, *Selective Mass Communication*. Stockholm: Norstedt, 1967.

Chapple, Eliot D., and Gordon Donald, Jr., "An Evaluation of Department Store Salespeople by the Interaction Chronograph." *Journal of Marketing*, 12 (October 1947), 173–185.

Charnes, Abraham, and William W. Cooper, *Management Models and Industrial Applications of Linear Programming*. New York: Wiley, 1961.

Charnes, Abraham, and William W. Cooper, "Data Decision and Model Evaluations." In Frederick E. Webster, Jr. (ed.), *New Directions in Marketing*. Proceedings of the 48th National Conference of the American Marketing Association, June 1965. Chicago: American Marketing Association, 1965, pp. 505–517.

Charnes, Abraham, William W. Cooper, J. K. De Voe, and David B. Learner, "DEMON: A Management Model for Marketing New Products." *California Management Review*, 11 (Fall 1968), 31–46.

Charnes, Abraham, William W. Cooper, David B. Learner, J. K. De Voe, and W. Reinecke, "A Goal Programming Model for Media Planning." *Management Science, Applications Series*, 14 (April 1968), B423–B430.

Charnes, Abraham, William W. Cooper, David B. Learner, J. K. De Voe, W. Reinecke, and E. F. Snow, "Note on an Application of a Goal Programming Model for Media Planning." *Management Science, Applications Series*, 14 (April 1968), B431–B436.

Chatfield, C., A. S. C. Ehrenberg, and G. J. Goodhardt, "Progress on a Simplified Model of Stationary Purchasing Behavior." *Journal of the Royal Statistical Society, Series A*, 129 (1966), 317–360.

Chein, I., "Behavior Theory and the Behavior of Attitudes: Some Critical Comments." *Psychological Review*, 55 (May 1948), 175–188.

Cherry, Colin, *On Human Communication*. Cambridge, Mass.: M.I.T. Press, 1957.

Christopher, Martin, "2001—the Existential Consumer." *British Journal of Marketing*, 4 (Autumn 1970), 160–164.

Clawson, C. Joseph, "Family Composition, Motivation, and Buying

Decisions." In Nelson N. Foote (ed.), *Household Decision-Making*. New York: New York University Press, 1961, pp. 200–217.

Cofer, C. N., and M. H. Appley, *Motivation: Theory and Research*. New York: Wiley, 1964.

Cohen, Arthur R., *Attitude Change and Social Influence*. New York: Basic Books, 1964.

Coleman, James S., *Introduction to Mathematical Sociology*. New York: Free Press, 1964.

Coleman, James S., Elihu Katz, and Herbert Menzel, *Medical Innovation: A Diffusion Study*. Indianapolis: Bobbs-Merrill, 1966.

Converse, Paul, and Crawford, Merle, "Buying Habits in the Home." *Advertising Age* (February 1950), 46–47, 144–150.

Cook, Stuart W., and Claire Selltiz, "A Multiple Indicator Approach to Attitude Measurement." *Psychological Bulletin*, 62 (1964), 36–56.

Cook, Victor J., "Group Decision, Social Comparison, and Persuasion in Changing Attitudes." *Journal of Advertising Research*, 7 (March 1967), 31–37.

Cooper, Peter, "Insights from Psychology." Paper presented at a seminar on Strategic Analysis of Customer Behavior, University of Bradford, Harrogate, December 1969.

Copeland, Melvin T., "Relation of Consumers' Buying Habits to Marketing Methods." *Harvard Business Review*, 1 (April 1923), 282–289.

Coulson, John S., "Buying Decisions Within the Family and the Consumer-Brand Relationship." In Joseph Newman (ed.), *On Knowing the Consumer*. New York: Wiley, 1966, pp. 59–66.

Cox, Donald F. (ed.), *Risk Taking and Information Handling in Consumer Behavior*. Cambridge, Mass.: Division of Research, Graduate School of Business Administration, Harvard University, 1967.

Cronbach, Lee J., and P. E. Meehl, "Construct Validity in Psychological Tests." *Psychological Bulletin*, 52 (July 1955), 281–302.

Crowne, D. P., and D. Marlowe, *The Approval Motive*. New York: Wiley, 1965.

Cunningham, Scott M., "Perceived Risk as a Factor in Product-Oriented Word-of-Mouth Behavior: A First Step." In L. George Smith (ed.), *Reflections on Progress in Marketing*. Proceedings of the Educators' Conference of the American

Marketing Association, December 1964. Chicago: American
Marketing Association, 1965, pp. 229–238.

Cunningham, Scott M., "Perceived Risk as a Factor in the
Diffusion of New Product Information." In Raymond M. Haas
(ed.), *Science, Technology and Marketing.* Proceedings
of the Fall Conference of the American Marketing Association, August–September 1966. Chicago: American
Marketing Association, 1966, pp. 698–721.

Cunningham, Scott M., "The Major Dimensions of Perceived Risk."
In Donald F. Cox (ed.), *Risk Taking and Information
Handling in Consumer Behavior.* Cambridge, Mass.: Divi-
sion of Research, Graduate School of Business Administration,
Harvard University, 1967, pp. 82–108.

Curtis, Richard F., and Elton F. Jackson, "Multiple Indicators
in Survey Research." *American Journal of Sociology,*
68 (September 1962), 195–204.

David, Martin H., *Family Composition and Consumption.*
Amsterdam: North Holland Publishing, 1962.

Davis, E. J., "Test Marketing: An Examination of Sales Patterns
Found During Forty-Four Recent Tests." In *Research
in Marketing.* London: The Market Research Society and
Oakwood Press, 1964.

Day, George S., *Buyer Attitudes and Brand Choice Behavior.*
New York: Free Press, 1970. (a)

Day, George S., "Changes in Attitudes and Intentions as Predictors
of New Product Acceptance." Paper presented to the
Third Annual Attitude Research Conference of the American
Marketing Association, Mexico, March 1970. (b)

de Grazia, Alfred, et al. (eds.), *The Velikovsky Affair.* New York:
University Books, 1966.

de Jong, P. L. F., "Market Forecast Models for Consumer
Durables." *Esomar Congress Papers* (1970), 125–153.

De Voe, J. K., "Plans, Profits and the Marketing Program." In
Frederick E. Webster (ed.), *New Directions in Marketing.*
Proceedings of the 48th National Conference of the
American Marketing Association, June 1965. Chicago:
American Marketing Association, 1965, pp. 473–478.

Dommermuth, William P., "The Shopping Matrix and Marketing
Strategy." *Journal of Marketing Research,* 2 (May 1965),
128–132.

Doob, L. W., "The Behavior of Attitudes." *Psychological Review,*
54 (May 1947), 135–156.

Dulany, Don E., "Awareness, Rules, and Propositional Control:

A Confrontation with S-R Behavior Theory." In T. R. Dixon and D. L. Horton (eds.), *Verbal Behavior and General Behavior Theory*. Englewood Cliffs, N.J.: Prentice-Hall, 1968, pp. 340–387.

Ehrenberg, A. S. C., "Review of *Consumer Decision Processes,* by Francesco M. Nicosia." *Journal of Marketing Research*, 5 (August 1968), 334.

Ehrenberg, A. S. C., "Towards an Integrated Theory of Consumer Behaviour." *Journal of the Market Research Society,* 11 (October 1969), 305–337.

Engel, James F., David T. Kollat, and Roger D. Blackwell, *Consumer Behavior*. New York: Holt, Rinehart & Winston, 1968.

Etzioni, Amitai, *A Comparative Analysis of Organizations*. New York: Free Press, 1961.

Evans, Franklin, B., "Selling as a Dyadic Relationship—A New Approach." *American Behavioral Scientist*, 6 (May 1963), 76–79.

Farley, John U., " 'Brand Loyalty' and the Economics of Information." *Journal of Business*, 37 (October 1964), 370–382.

Farley, John U., "Estimating Structural Parameters in Marketing Systems: Theory and Applications." In Reed Moyer (ed.), *Changing Marketing Systems: Consumer, Corporate, and Government Interfaces*. Proceedings of the Winter Conference of the American Marketing Association, December 1967. Chicago: American Marketing Association, 1968, pp. 316–321.

Farley, John U., and L. Winston Ring, "An Empirical Test of the Howard-Sheth Model of Buyer Behavior." *Journal of Marketing Research*, 7 (November 1970), 427–438.

Feldman, Shel (ed.), *Cognitive Consistency: Motivational Antecedents and Behavioral Consequences*. New York: Academic Press, 1966.

Feldman, Sidney P., "Some Dyadic Relationships Associated with Consumer Choice." In Raymond M. Haas (ed.), *Science, Technology, and Marketing*. Proceedings of the Fall Conference of the American Marketing Association, August–September 1966. Chicago: American Marketing Association, 1966, pp. 758–775.

Fendrick, Harry, "The Structure of Retail Markets." Unpublished manuscript, School of Business Administration at Los Angeles, May 1965.

Ferber, Robert, "The Role of Planning in Consumer Purchases
of Durable Goods." *American Economic Review,* 44 (December 1954), 854–874.

Ferber, Robert, "Research on Household Behavior." *American
Economic Review,* 52 (March 1962), 19–63.

Ferreira, Antonio J., and William D. Winter, "Family Interaction
and Decision-Making." *Archives of General Psychiatry,*
13 (1965), 214–223.

Ferreira, Antonio J., and William D. Winter, "Stability of Interactional Variables in Family Decision Making." *Archives
of General Psychiatry,* 14 (1966), 352–355.

Festinger, Leon, "Informal Social Communication." *Psychological
Review,* 57 (September 1950), 271–282.

Festinger, Leon, "A Theory of Social Comparison Processes."
Human Relations, 7 (May 1954), 117–140.

Festinger, Leon, *A Theory of Cognitive Dissonance.* Stanford,
Calif.: Stanford University Press, 1957.

Festinger, Leon, "Behavioral Support for Opinion Change." *Public
Opinion Quarterly,* 28 (Fall 1964), 404–417.

Festinger, Leon, and James M. Carlsmith, "Cognitive Consequences
of Forced Compliance." *Journal of Abnormal and Social
Psychology,* 58 (March 1959), 203–210.

Fishbein, Martin, "The Relationship Between Beliefs, Attitudes,
and Behavior." In Shel Feldman (ed.), *Cognitive Consistency.*
New York: Academic Press, 1966, pp. 200–223.

Fishbein, Martin (ed.), *Readings in Attitude Theory and Measurement.* New York: Wiley, 1967.

Fishbein, Martin, "The Search for an Attitudinal-Behavior Consistency." In Joel B. Cohen (ed.), *Behavioral Science
Foundations of Consumer Behavior.* New York: Free Press,
1972.

Fisk, George, "Media Influence Reconsidered." *Public Opinion
Quarterly,* 23 (Spring 1959), 83–91.

Fliegel, Frederick, Joseph Kivlin, and G. S. Sekhon, "A Cross-National Comparison of Farmers' Perceptions of Innovations
as Related to Adoption Behavior." Paper presented at
the meetings of the Rural Sociological Society, Boston,
August 1968.

Fontela, E., "Forecasting with Mathematical Models. *Esomar
Congress Papers* (1970), 117–124.

Foote, Nelson N. (ed.), *Household Decision-Making.* New York:
New York University Press, 1961.

Foote, Nelson N., and Leonard Cottrell, *Identity and Interpersonal*

Competence: A New Direction in Family Research.
Chicago: University of Chicago Press, 1955.

Fothergill, Jack E., "Do Attitudes Change Before Behavior?"
Esomar Congress Papers (1968), 875–900.

Fourt, L. A., and J. W. Woodlock, "Early Prediction of Market
Success for New Grocery Products." *Journal of Marketing,* 25
(October 1960), 31–38.

Frank, Ronald E., William F. Massy, and Donald G. Morrison,
"The Determinants of Innovative Behavior with Respect to a
Branded, Frequently Purchased Food Product." In
L. George Smith (ed.), *Reflections on Progress in Marketing.*
Proceedings of the Educators' Conference of the American
Marketing Association, December 1964. Chicago: American
Marketing Association, 1965, pp. 312–323.

Friedman, Milton, *A Theory of the Consumption Function.*
Princeton, N.J.: Princeton University Press, 1957.

Fry, Joseph N., "Family Branding and Consumer Brand Choice."
Journal of Marketing Research, 4 (August 1967), 237–247.

Garner, Wendell R., *Uncertainty and Structure as Psychological
Concepts.* New York: Wiley, 1962.

Garner, Wendell R., and Harold W. Hake, "The Amount of
Information in Absolute Judgments." *Psychological Review,*
58 (November 1951), 446–459.

Gensch, Dennis H., "A Computer Simulation Model for Selecting
Advertising Schedules." *Journal of Marketing Research,*
6 (May 1969), 203–214.

Gilbert, Eugene, *Advertising and Marketing to Young People.*
Pleasantville, N.Y.: Printers' Ink Books, 1957.

Gisler, C. R., "Is the Buying Influence of Men Underestimated?"
Printer's Ink, 224 (September 24, 1948), 38 ff.

Glick, Paul, "The Family Cycle." *American Sociological Review,* 12
(April 1947), 164–174.

Glock, Charles Y., and Francesco M. Nicosia, "Sociology and
the Study of Consumers." *Journal of Advertising Research,* 3
(September 1963), 21–37.

Glock, Charles Y., and Francesco M. Nicosia, "Uses of Sociology
in Studying 'Consumption' Behavior." *Journal of Marketing,*
28 (July 1964), 51–54.

Glock, Charles Y., and Francesco M. Nicosia, "The Consumer."
In Paul F. Lazarsfeld, William H. Sewell, and Harold L.
Wilensky (eds.), *The Uses of Sociology.* New York: Basic
Books, 1967, pp. 359–390.

Gouldner, Alvin W., "Explorations in Applied Social Science." *Social Problems,* 3 (January 1956), 169–181.

Graf, Franklin H., *New Items: Problems and Opportunities.* New York: Nielsen, 1967.

Granbois, Donald H., "The Role of Communication in the Family Decision-Making Process." In Stephen A. Greyser (ed.), *Toward Scientific Marketing.* Proceedings of the Winter Conference of the American Marketing Association, December 1963. Chicago: American Marketing Association, 1964, pp. 44–58.

Grass, Robert C., "Satiation Effects of Advertising." *Proceedings of the 14th Annual Conference,* Advertising Research Foundation, New York, 1968.

Green, Paul E., "Uncertainty, Information, and Marketing Decisions." In Reavis Cox, Wroe Alderson, and Stanley J. Shapiro (eds.), *Theory in Marketing.* Homewood, Ill.: Irwin, 1964, pp. 333–354.

Green, Paul E., Michael H. Halbert, and Patrick J. Robinson, "Perception and Preference Mapping in the Analysis of Marketing Behavior." *Proceedings of the American Statistical Association,* Business and Economic Section (1967), 129–143.

Guest, Lester, "Consumer Analysis." *Annual Review of Psychology,* 13 (1962), 315–344.

Haines, George H., Jr., "A Theory of Market Behavior After Innovation." *Management Science,* 10 (July 1964), 634–658.

Haines, George H., Jr., "A Study of Why People Purchase New Products." In Raymond M. Haas (ed.), *Science, Technology, and Marketing.* Proceedings of the Fall Conference of the American Marketing Association, August–September 1966. Chicago: American Marketing Association, 1966, pp. 685–697.

Haines, George H., Jr., *Consumer Behavior: Learning Models of Purchasing.* New York: Free Press, 1969.

Halbert, Michael H., "Discussion." In Montrose S. Sommers and Jerome B. Kernan (eds.), *Explorations in Consumer Behavior.* Austin: Bureau of Business Research, University of Texas, 1968, pp. 30–45.

Hansen, Flemming, "An Attitude Model for Analyzing Consumer Behavior." In Lee Adler and Irving Crespi (eds.), *Attitude Research on the Rocks.* Chicago: American Marketing Association, 1968, pp. 139–159.

Hansen, Fleming, *A Cognitive Model of Consumer Choice Behavior.* New York: Free Press, 1970. (a)

Hansen, Fleming, "The Role of Beliefs and Values in Prediction of Consumer Choices." *Esomar Congress Papers* (1970), 13–33, (b)

Hansen, Fleming, *Consumer Choice Behavior.* New York: Free Press, 1972.

Haskins, J. B., *How to Evaluate Mass Communications: The Controlled Field Experiment.* New York: Advertising Research Foundation, 1968.

Heer, David M., "Dominance and the Working Wife." *Social Forces,* 36 (1958), 341–347.

Heer, David M., "The Measurement and Bases of Family Power: An Overview." *Marriage and Family Living,* 25 (May 1963), 133–139.

Hendrickson, A. E., "Choice Behavior and Advertising." Paper presented at Admap World Advertising Workshop, New York, October 1967.

Herbst, P. G., "The Measurement of Family Relationships." *Human Relations,* 5 (February 1952), 3–36.

Herbst, P. G., "Conceptual Framework for Studying the Family." In O. A. Oeser and S. B. Hammond (eds.), *Social Structure and Personality in a City.* London: Routledge & Kegan Paul, 1954.

Hilgard, Ernest R., *Introduction to Psychology,* 2nd ed. New York: Harcout Brace Jovanovich, 1957.

Hill, Reuben, "Marriage and Family Research." *Eugenics Quarterly,* 1 (March 1954), 58–63.

Hill, Reuben, "Family Buying Decisions: Who Makes Them, Who Influences Them?" *Printers' Ink,* 264 (September 19, 1958), 21–23.

Hoffman, Lois W., "Effects of the Employment of Mothers on Parental Power Relations and the Division of Household Tasks." *Marriage and Family Living,* 22 (February 1960), 27–35.

Holdren, Bob R., *The Structure of a Retail Market and the Market Behavior of Retail Units.* Englewood Cliffs, N.J.: Prentice-Hall, 1960.

Holton, Richard H., "The Distinction between Convenience Goods, Shopping Goods, and Specialty Goods." *Journal of Marketing,* 23 (July 1958), 53–56.

Homans, George C., *The Human Group.* New York: Harcourt Brace Jovanovich, 1950.

Homans, George C., "Social Behavior as Exchange." *American Journal of Sociology,* 62 (May 1958), 597–606.

Hovland, Carl I., "Reconciling Conflicting Results Derived from Experimental and Survey Studies of Attitude Change." *American Psychologist,* 14 (January 1959), 8–17.

Hovland, Carl I., Irving L. Janis, and Harold H. Kelley, *Communication and Persuasion.* New Haven, Conn.: Yale University Press, 1953.

Hovland, Carl I., Arthur A. Lumsdaine, and Fred D. Sheffield, *Experiments on Mass Communication and Persuasion.* New Haven, Conn.: Yale University Press, 1953.

Howard, John A., *Marketing Management, Analysis and Planning.* Homewood, Ill.: Irwin, 1963.

Howard, John A., *Marketing Theory.* Boston: Allyn & Bacon, 1965.

Howard, John A., and Jagdish N. Sheth, "A Theory of Buyer Behavior." In Harold H. Kassarjian and Thomas S. Robertson (eds.), *Perspectives in Consumer Behavior.* Glenview, Ill.: Scott, Foresman, 1968, pp. 467–487.

Howard, John A., and Jagdish N. Sheth, *The Theory of Buyer Behavior.* New York: Wiley, 1969.

Hudson, Liam, *Contrary Imaginations.* London: Methuen, 1966.

Hudson, Liam, *Frames of Mind.* London: Methuen, 1968.

Hughes, G. David, and P. A. Naert, "A Computer-Controlled Experiment in Consumer Behavior." *Journal of Business,* 43 (July 1970), 354–372.

Ingersoll, Hazel L., "Transmission of Authority Patterns in the Family." *Marriage and Family Living,* 10 (Spring 1948), 36.

Insko, Chester A., *Theories of Attitude Change.* New York: Appleton-Century-Crofts, 1967.

Johnson, Robert P., "Study of Intentions vs. Behavior." Unpublished manuscript, Graduate School of Business, Columbia University, 1968.

Johnston, J., *Econometric Methods.* New York: McGraw-Hill, 1963.

Joyce, T., "What Do We Know About How Advertising Works?" *Proceedings of the Esomar Seminar on Advertising Research,* 1967.

Juster, F. T., *Anticipations and Purchases: An Analysis of Consumer Behavior.* Princeton, N.J.: Princeton University Press, 1964.

Kaish, Stanley, "Cognitive Dissonance and the Classification of Consumer Goods." *Journal of Marketing,* 31 (October 1967), 28–31.

Katona, George C., "Rational Behavior and Economic Behavior." *Psychological Review,* 60 (September 1953), 307–318.

Katz, Daniel, "The Functional Approach to the Study of Attitudes." *Public Opinion Quarterly,* 24 (Summer 1960), 163–204.

Katz, Daniel, and E. Stotland, "A Preliminary Statement to a Theory Attitude Structure and Change." In Sigmund Koch (ed.), *Psychology: A Study of a Science.* New York: McGraw-Hill, 1959, vol. 3, pp. 423–475.

Katz, Elihu, "The Two-Step Flow of Communication: An Up-to-Date Report on an Hypothesis." *Public Opinion Quarterly,* 21 (Spring 1957), 61–78.

Katz, Elihu, "The Social Itinerary of Technical Change: Two Studies on the Diffusion of Innovation." *Human Organization,* 20 (Summer 1961), 70–82.

Katz, Elihu, and Paul F. Lazarsfeld, *Personal Influence: The Part Played by People in the Flow of Mass Communications.* New York: Free Press, 1955.

Kelly, Robert F., "Estimating Ultimate Performance Levels of New Retail Outlets." *Journal of Marketing Research,* 4 (February 1967), 13–19.

Kelman, Herbert C., "Processes of Opinion Change." *Public Opinion Quarterly,* 25 (Spring 1961), 57–78.

Kempthorne, Oscar, *The Design and Analysis of Experiments.* New York: Wiley, 1952.

Kenkel, William F., "Influence Differentiation in Family Decision Making." *Sociology and Social Research,* 42 (September–October 1957), 18–25.

Kenkel, William F., "Decision Making and the Life Cycle: Husband-Wife Interaction in Decision Making and Decision Choices." *Journal of Social Psychology,* 54 (August 1961), 255–262, 349–358.

Kenkel, William F., *The Family in Perspective.* New York: Appleton-Century-Crofts, 1966.

Kenkel, William F., and Dean K. Hoffman, "Real and Conceived Roles in Family Decision Making." *Marriage and the Family,* 17 (November 1956), 311–316.

Kernan, Jerome B., "Choice Criteria, Decision Behavior, and Personality." *Journal of Marketing Research,* 5 (May 1968), 155–164.

King, Charles W., "Fashion Adoption: A Rebuttal to the 'Trickle Down' Theory." In Stephen A. Greyser (ed.), *Toward Scientific Marketing.* Proceedings of the Winter Conference of the American Marketing Association, December 1963. Chicago: American Marketing Association, 1964, pp. 108–125.

King, Charles W., "The Innovator in the Fashion Adoption Process." In L. George Smith (ed.), *Reflections on Progress in Marketing.* Proceedings of the Educators' Conference of the American Marketing Association, December 1964. Chicago: American Marketing Association, 1965, pp. 324–339.

King, Charles W., "Adoption and Diffusion Research in Marketing: An Overview." In Raymond M. Haas (ed.), *Science, Technology, and Marketing.* Proceedings of the Fall Conference of the American Marketing Association, August–September 1966. Chicago: American Marketing Association, 1966, pp. 665–684.

King, Karl, "A Comparison of the Negro and White Family Power Structure in Low Income Families." *Child and Family,* 6 (1967), 65–74.

Kirkpatrick, C., *The Family as Process and Institution.* New York: Ronald Press, 1963.

Klonglan, Gerald E., Walter Coward, Jr., and George M. Beal, "Conceptualizing and Measuring Extent of Diffusion: The Concept of Adoption Progress." Paper presented at the meetings of the Rural Sociological Society, Boston, August 1968.

Kollat, David T., James F. Engel, and Roger D. Blackwell, "Current Problems in Consumer Behavior Research." *Journal of Marketing Research,* 7 (August 1970), 327–332.

Komarovsky, Mirra, "Cultural Contradictions and Sex Roles." *American Journal of Sociology,* 52 (November 1946), 184–189.

Komarovsky, Mirra, "Class Differences in Family Decision-Making on Expenditures." In Nelson N. Foote (ed.), *Household Decision-Making.* New York: New York University Press, 1961, pp. 255–265.

Krech, David, Richard S. Crutchfield, and Egerton L. Ballachey, *The Individual in Society.* New York: McGraw-Hill, 1962.

Krugman, Herbert E., "The Impact of Television Advertising: Learning Without Involvement." *Public Opinion Quarterly,* 29 (Fall 1965), 349–356.

Kruskal, William H., and Lester G. Telser, "Food Prices and the Bureau of Labor Statistics." *Journal of Business,* 33 (July 1960), 258–279.

Kuehn, Alfred A., "Consumer Brand Choice as a Learning

Process." *Journal of Advertising Research,* 2 (December 1962), 10–17.

Lambin, J. J., "Black-Box Simulation Models of Market Behavior: A Case Study." In Paul A. Pellemans (ed.), *Insights in Consumer and Market Behavior.* Namur, Belgium: Publications Universitaires, Namur University, 1971, pp. 165–185.

Lampert, Shlomo, *Word-of-Mouth Activity During the Introduction of a New Product.* Ph.D. dissertation, Graduate School of Business, Columbia University, 1969.

Lancaster, Kevin J., "A New Approach to Consumer Theory." *Journal of Political Economy,* 74 (April 1968), 132–157.

Lanzetta, John T., "Uncertainty as a Motivating Variable." Conference on Experimental Social Psychology, Vienna, Austria, 1967.

Lanzetta, John T., and Vera T. Kanareff, "Information Cost, Amount of Payoff, and Level of Aspiration as Determinants of Information Seeking in Decision Making." *Behavioral Science,* 7 (October 1962), 459–473.

Lavidge, Robert J., and Gary A. Steiner, "A Model for Predictive Measurements of Advertising Effectiveness." *Journal of Marketing,* 25 (October 1961), 59–62.

Lawrence, R. J., "Models of Consumer Purchasing Behavior." *Applied Statistics,* 45 (1966), 216–233.

Learner, David B., "Profit Maximization Through New-Product Marketing and Planning." In Frank M. Bass, Charles W. King, and Edgar A. Pessemier (eds.), *Applications of the Sciences in Marketing Management.* New York: Wiley, 1968, pp. 151–167.

Lewin, Kurt, "Group Decision and Social Change." In Eleanor E. Maccoby, Theodore M. Newcomb, and E. L. Hartley (eds.), *Readings in Social Psychology.* New York: Holt, Rinehart & Winston, 1952, pp. 197–211.

Life, "Family Participation and Influence in Shopping and Brand Selection." 1964 Study, pts. 1–2.

Life, "A Pilot Study of the Roles of Husbands and Wives in Purchasing Decisions." 1965 Study, pts. 1–10.

LoSciuto, Leonard A., and Robert Perloff, "Influence of Product Preference on Dissonance Reduction." *Journal of Marketing Research,* 4 (August 1967), 286–290.

Lu, Yi-Chuang, "Predicting Roles in Marriage." *American Journal of Sociology,* 58 (July 1952), 51–55.

Luce, R. Duncan, and Howard Raiffa, *Games and Decisions.*
New York: Wiley, 1957.

Lunn, J. A., "New Techniques in Consumer Research." In Denis
Pym (ed.), *Industrial Society: Social Sciences in Management.*
Harmondsworth, England: Penguin, 1968, pp. 401–425.

Lunn, J. A., "Buyer Behavior Theory in Practice." Paper presented
at the Third Conference of Buyer Behavior Theory,
Columbia University, New York, May 1969. (a)

Lunn, J. A., "Perspectives in Attitude Research: Methods and
Applications." *Journal of the Market Research Society,*
11 (July 1969), 201–213. (b)

Lunn, J. A., "Attitudes and Behavior in Consumer Research—
A Reappraisal." *Proceedings of the Esomar Seminar on
Attitude and Motivation Research,* Helsingor, 1970, pp. 1–16.

Lunn, J. A., "Market Segmentation—An Overview." In Johan
Aucamp (ed.), *The Effective Use of Market Research.*
London: Staples, 1971. (a)

Lunn, J. A., "Segmenting and Constructing Markets." In
R. M. Worcester (ed.), *Handbook of Consumer Marketing.*
New York: McGraw-Hill, 1971. (b)

Mansfield, Edwin, *Industrial Research and Technological
Innovation.* New York: Norton, 1968.

March, James G., and Herbert A. Simon, *Organizations.* New York:
Wiley, 1958.

Marcus, Alan S., and Raymond A. Bauer, "Yes: There Are
Generalized Opinion Leaders." *Public Opinion Quarterly,*
28 (Winter 1964), 628–632.

Mason, Robert, "The Use of Information Sources by Influentials in
the Adoption Process." *Public Opinion Quarterly,* 27 (Fall
1963), 455–466.

Massy, William F., "A Dynamic Model for Monitoring New
Product Adoption." Working Paper No. 95. Stanford, Calif.:
Graduate School of Business, Stanford University, March
1966.

Massy, William F., "Stochastic Models for Monitoring New-Product
Introductions." In Frank M. Bass, Charles W. King, and
Edgar A. Pessemier (eds.), *Applications of the Sciences in
Marketing Management.* New York: Wiley, 1968, pp. 85–111.

Massy, William F., David B. Montgomery, and Donald G.
Morrison, *Stochastic Models of Buying Behavior.* Cambridge,
Mass.: M.I.T. Press, 1970.

Mayer, Charles S., and Rex V. Brown, "A Search for the

Rationale of Non-Probability Sample Designs." In Peter D. Bennett (ed.), *Marketing and Economic Development.* Proceedings of the Fall Conference of the American Marketing Association, September 1965. Chicago: American Marketing Association, 1965, pp. 295–308.

McGuire, William J., "An Information Processing Model of Advertising Effectiveness." Paper presented at the Symposium on Behavioral Sciences and Management Sciences in Marketing, Chicago, 1969. (a)

McGuire, William J., "The Nature of Attitudes and Attitude Change." In Gardner Lindzey and Elliot Aronson (eds.), *The Handbook of Social Psychology,* 2nd ed. Reading, Mass.: Addison-Wesley, 1969, vol. 3, pp. 136–314. (b)

McGuire, William J., "The Guiding Theories behind Attitude Change Research." Paper presented at the Third Annual Attitude Research Conference of the American Marketing Association, Mexico, March 1970.

Media/Scope, "Working Women: Why They Do What They Do." 12 (July–December 1968), 9–28.

Merton, Robert K., *Social Theory and Social Structure.* New York: Free Press, 1957.

Meyer, Harold D., "The Adult Cycle." *Annals of the American Academy of Political and Social Science,* 313 (September 1957), 58–67.

Meyer, John Robert, and Edwin Kuh, "How Extraneous are Extraneous Estimators?" *Review of Economics and Statistics,* 39 (November 1957), 380–392.

Miller, David W., and Martin K. Starr, *Executive Decisions and Operations Research.* Englewood Cliffs, N.J.: Prentice-Hall, 1960.

Miller, George A., "What is Information Measurement?" *American Psychologist,* 8 (January 1953), 3–11.

Miller, George A., "The Magical Number Seven, Plus or Minus Two: Some Limits on Our Capacity for Processing Information." *Psychological Review,* 63 (March 1956), 81–97.

Miller, George A., Eugene Galanter, and Karl H. Pribram, *Plans and the Structure of Behavior.* New York: Holt, Rinehart & Winston, 1960.

Miller, Neal E., "Liberalization of Basic S-R Concepts: Extensions to Conflict, Behavior, Motivation, and Social Learning." In Sigmund Koch (ed.), *Psychology: A Study of a Science.* New York: McGraw-Hill, 1959, vol. 2, pp. 196–292.

Mincer, Jacob, "Market Prices, Opportunity Costs and Income

Effects." In D. Patinkin (ed.), *Measurement in Economics.* Stanford, Calif.: Stanford University Press, 1964, pp. 67–82.

Miracle, Gordon E., "Product Characteristics and Marketing Strategy." *Journal of Marketing,* 29 (January 1965), 18–24.

Morgan, J. N., "Household Decision-Making." In Nelson W. Foote (ed.), *Household Decision-Making.* New York: New York University Press, 1961, pp. 81–102.

Morganstern, Oskar, *On the Accuracy of Economic Observations.* Princeton, N.J.: Princeton University Press, 1963.

Moscovici, Serge, "Attitudes and Opinions." *Annual Review of Psychology,* 14 (1963), 231–260.

Motz, Annabelle Bender, "Conceptions of Marital Roles by Status Groups." *Marriage and Family Living,* 12 (Fall 1950), 136, 162.

Mukherjee, Bishwa Nath, "A Factor Analysis of Some Qualitative Attributes of Coffee." *Journal of Advertising Research,* 5 (March 1965), 35–38.

Murphy, Gardner, "New Knowledge About Family Dynamics." *Pastoral Psychology,* 2 (1960), 39–47.

Myers, James H., and Mark I. Alpert, "Determinant Buying Attitudes: Meaning and Measurement." *Journal of Marketing,* 32 (October 1968), 13–20.

Myers, John G., "Patterns of Interpersonal Influence in the Adoption of New Products." In Raymond M. Haas (ed.), *Science, Technology, and Marketing.* Proceedings of the Fall Conference of the American Marketing Association, August–September 1966. Chicago: American Marketing Association, 1966, pp. 750–757.

Myers, John G., *Consumer Image and Attitude.* Berkeley: Institute of Business and Economic Research, University of California, 1968.

Myers, John G., and Francesco M. Nicosia, "New Empirical Directions in Market Segmentation: Latent Structure Models." In Reed Moyer (ed.), *Changing Marketing Systems: Consumer, Corporate, and Government Interfaces.* Proceedings of the Winter Conference of the American Marketing Association, December 1967. Chicago: American Marketing Association, 1968, pp. 247–252. (a)

Myers, John G., and Francesco M. Nicosia, "On the Study of Consumer Typologies." *Journal of Marketing Research,* 5 (May 1968), 182–193. (b)

Nakanishi, Masao, "A Model of Market Reactions to New Products."

Doctoral dissertation, Graduate School of Business Administration, University of California, Los Angeles, 1968.

Naylor, T. H., and T. M. Finger, "Verification of Computer Simulation Models." *Management Science*, 14 (October 1967), 92–101.

Neiman, L. J., "The Influence of Peer Groups upon Attitudes Toward the Female Role." *Social Problems*, 2 (October 1954), 104–111.

Newell, Allen, J. C. Shaw, and Herbert A. Simon, "Chess-Playing Programs and the Problem of Complexity." *IBM Journal of Research and Development*, 2 (October 1958), 320–335.

Nicosia, Francesco M., "Opinion Leadership and the Flow of Communication: Some Problems and Prospects." In L. George Smith (ed.), *Reflections on Progress in Marketing*. Proceedings of the Educators' Conference of the American Marketing Association, December 1964. Chicago: American Marketing Association, 1965, pp. 340–358.

Nicosia, Francesco M., *Consumer Decision Processes: Marketing and Advertising Implications*. Englewood Cliffs, N.J.: Prentice-Hall, 1966.

Nicosia, Francesco M., "Advertising Management, Consumer Behavior, and Simulation." *Journal of Advertising Research*, 8 (March 1968), 29–37.

Nicosia, Francesco M., "Brand Choice: Toward Behavior-Behavioristic Models." Paper presented at the Symposium on Behavioral Sciences and Management Sciences in Marketing, University of Chicago, June 1969.

O'Brien, Terrence V., "Information Sensitivity and the Sequence of Psychological States in the Brand Choice Process." Doctoral dissertation, Graduate School of Business, Columbia University, 1969.

Oeser, O. A., and F. E. Emery, *Social Structure and Personality in a Rural Community*. New York: Macmillan, 1954.

Olsen, Marvin E., *Distribution of Responsibility Within the Family as Related to Social Stratification*. Grinnell, Iowa: Grinnell College Press, 1956–1957.

Opinion Research Corporation, *America's Tastemakers*, vols. I and II. Princeton, N.J.: Opinion Research Corporation, April and June, 1959.

O'Rourke, John F., "Field and Laboratory: The Decision-Making Behavior of Family Groups in Two Experimental Conditions." *Sociometry*, 26 (1963), 422–435.

Osgood, Charles E., "A Behavioristic Analysis of Perception and

Language as Cognitive Phenomena." *Contemporary Approaches to Cognition: A Symposium Held at the University of Colorado.* Cambridge, Mass.: Harvard University Press, ,1957, pp. 75–118. (a)

Osgood, Charles E., "Motivational Dynamics of Language Behavior." In Marshall R. Jones (ed.), *Nebraska Symposium on Motivation.* Lincoln: University of Nebraska Press, 1957, pp. 348–424. (b)

Osgood, Charles E., "Studies in the Generality of Affective Meaning Systems." *American Psychologist,* 17 (January 1962), 10–28.

Osgood, Charles E., G. J. Suci, and P. H. Tannenbaum, *The Measurement of Meaning.* Urbana: University of Illinois Press, 1957.

Oxenfeldt, Alfred R., *Executive Marketing in Action.* Belmont, Calif.: Wadsworth, 1966.

Palamountain, Joseph C., Jr., *The Politics of Distribution.* Cambridge, Mass.: Harvard University Press, 1955.

Palda, Kristian S., "The Hypothesis of a Hierarchy of Effects: A Partial Evaluation." *Journal of Marketing Research,* 3 (February 1966), 13–24.

Parfitt, J. H., and B. J. K. Collins, "Use of Consumer Panels for Brand-Share Prediction." *Journal of Marketing Research,* 5 (May 1968), 131–145.

Parsons, Talcott, and Robert F. Bales, *Family, Socialization and Interaction Process.* New York: Free Press, 1955.

Payne, Stanley L., *The Art of Asking Questions.* Princeton, N.J.: Princeton University Press, 1951.

Pellemans, Paul A., "The Consumer Decision-Making Process." In Paul A. Pellemans (ed.), *Insights in Consumer and Market Behavior.* Namur, Belgium: Publications Universitaires, Namur University, 1971, pp. 5–31.

Perloff, Robert, "Consumer Analysis." *Annual Review of Psychology,* 19 (1968), 437–466.

Pessemier, Edgar A., Philip C. Burger, and Douglas J. Tigert, "Can New Product Buyers Be Identified?" *Journal of Marketing Research,* 4 (November 1967), 349–354.

Pollay, Richard W., "A Model of Family Decision Making." *British Journal of Marketing,* 33 (Autumn 1968), 206–216.

Popielarz, Donald T., "An Exploration of Perceived Risk and Willingness to Try New Products." *Journal of Marketing Research,* 4 (November 1967), 368–372.

Reitman, Walter R., *Cognition and Thought: An Information Processing Approach.* New York: Wiley, 1965.

Rhine, R. J., "A Concept-Formation Approach to Attitude Acquisition." *Psychological Review,* 65 (1958), 362–370.

Ridgeway, Valentine F., "Administration of Manufacturer-Dealer Systems." *Administrative Science Quarterly,* 1 (March 1957), 464–483.

Riesman, David, *The Lonely Crowd.* New Haven, Conn.: Yale University Press, 1961.

Robertson, Thomas S., "Consumer Innovators: The Key to New Product Success." *California Management Review,* 10 (Winter 1967), 23–30.

Robertson, Thomas S., "Determinants of Innovative Behavior." In Reed Moyer (ed.), *Changing Marketing Systems: Consumer, Corporate, and Government Interfaces.* Proceedings of the Winter Conference of the American Marketing Association, December 1967. Chicago: American Marketing Association, 1968, pp. 382–332.

Robertson, Thomas S., and John R. Rossiter, "Fashion Diffusion: The Interplay of Innovator and Opinion Leader Roles in College Social Systems." Unpublished paper, Graduate School of Business Administration, University of California, Los Angeles, 1967.

Rogers, Everett M., *Diffusion of Innovations.* New York: Free Press, 1962.

Rogers, Everett M., and G. M. Beal, "The Importance of Personal Influence in the Adoption of Technological Changes." *Social Forces,* 36 (May 1958), 329–335.

Rokeach, Milton, "Attitude Change and Behavioral Change." *Public Opinion Quarterly,* 30 (Winter 1966), 529–550.

Rokeach, Milton, *Beliefs, Attitudes and Values: A Theory of Organization and Change.* San Francisco: Jossey-Bass, 1968.

Rosenberg, Milton J., "Cognitive Structure and Attitudinal Affect." *Journal of Abnormal and Social Psychology,* 53 (November 1956), 367–372.

Rosenberg, Milton J., "An Analysis of Affective-Cognitive Consistency." In Carl I. Hovland and M. J. Rosenberg (eds.), *Attitude Organization and Change.* New Haven, Conn.: Yale University Press, 1960, pp. 15–64.

Russell, Robert R., "The Empirical Evaluation of some Theoretically Plausible Demand Functions." Working paper, Department of Economics, Harvard University, 1966.

Sampson, P., "Attitude Measurement and Behavior Prediction in Market Research Using A Priori Psychological Models of Consumer Behavior: A Review of the Supporting Evidence for the Value of Such Models." *Esomar-Wapor Congress Papers* (1971), 45–75.

Sarnoff, I., "Psychoanalytic Theory and Social Attitudes." *Public Opinion Quarterly*, 24 (Summer 1960), 251–279.

Scheibe, K. E., *Beliefs and Values*. New York: Holt, Rinehart & Winston, 1970.

Schroder, Harold M., Michael J. Driver, and Siegfried Streufert, *Human Information Processing*. New York: Holt, Rinehart & Winston, 1967.

Selltiz, Claire, Marie Jahoda, Morton Deutsch, and Stuart W. Cook, *Research Methods in Social Relations*. New York: Holt, Rinehart & Winston, 1959.

Sexton, D. E., Jr., "The Construction of a Market Simulation." *Computer Operations*, 2 (January–February 1968), 53–55.

Shaffer, H. J., *Household Consumption Management*. New York: Forbes Research, 1963.

Shannon, Claude E., and Warren Weaver, *The Mathematical Theory of Communication*. Urbana: University of Illinois Press, 1949.

Sharp, Harry, and Paul Mott, "Consumer Decisions in the Metropolitan Family." *Journal of Marketing*, 21 (October 1956), 149–156.

Sherif, Carolyn W., Muzafar Sherif, and Roger E. Nebergall, *Attitude and Attitude Change: The Social Judgment-Involvement Approach*. Philadelphia: Saunders, 1965.

Sheth, Jagdish N., "A Review of Buyer Behavior." *Management Science*, 13 (August 1967), B718–B756.

Sheth, Jagdish N., "Perceived Risk and Diffusion of Innovations." In Johan Arndt (ed.), *Insights into Consumer Behavior*. Boston: Allyn & Bacon, 1968, pp. 173–188.

Sheth, Jagdish N., "Attitude as a Function of Evaluative Beliefs." Paper presented at the American Marketing Association Workshop on Consumer Behavior, Columbus, Ohio, August 1969. (a)

Sheth, Jagdish N., "How Advertising Works." *IAA–ARF Joint Publication on Multiple Measures of Advertising*, 1969. (b)

Sheth, Jagdish N., "Importance of Word-of-Mouth in the Diffusion of Low Risk and Highly Advantageous Innovations." Working paper No. 16. Graduate School of Business, Columbia University, 1969. (c)

Sheth, Jagdish N., "Affect, Behavioral Intention and Buying

Behavior as a Function of Evaluative Beliefs." In Paul A.
Pellemans (ed.), *Insights in Consumer and Market Behavior.*
Namur, Belgium: Publications Universitaires, Namur
University, 1971, pp. 98–124.

Sheth, Jagdish N., "A Theory of Industrial Decision Buying."
Faculty Working Paper No. 61. Urbana: College of
Commerce, University of Illinois, 1972.

Sheth, Jagdish N., "Brand Profiles from Beliefs and Importances."
Journal of Advertising Research, 13 (February 1973), 37–42.

Silk, Alvin J., "Overlap Among Self-Designated Opinion
Leaders: A Study of Selected Dental Products and Services."
Journal of Marketing Research, 3 (August 1966), 255–259.

Simon, Herbert A., "Economics and Psychology." In Sigmund
Koch (ed.), *Psychology: A Study of Science.* New York:
McGraw-Hill, 1963, vol. 6, pp. 685–723.

Smith, Wendell R., "Product Differentiation and Market Segmentation as Alternative Marketing Strategies." *Journal of
Marketing,* 21 (July 1956), 3–8.

Staats, A. W., "An Outline of an Integrated Learning Theory of
Attitude Formation and Function." In Martin Fishbein
(ed.), *Readings in Attitude Theory and Measurement.* New
York: Wiley, 1967, pp. 373–376.

Stafford, James E., "Effects of Group Influences on Consumer
Brand Preferences." *Journal of Marketing Research,*
3 (February 1966), 68–75.

Steward, John B., *Repetitive Advertising in Newspapers: A Study
of Two New Products.* Cambridge, Mass.: Division of
Research, Graduate School of Business Administration,
Harvard University, 1964.

Stigler, G., "The Economics of Information." *Journal of Political
Economy,* 59 (June 1961), 213–225.

Stoetzel, Jean, "A Factor Analysis of the Liquor Preferences of
French Consumers." *Journal of Advertising Research,*
(December 1960), 7–11.

Strodtbeck, Fred L., "The Family as a Three-Person Group."
American Sociological Review, 19 (February 1954), 23–29.

Strotz, Robert H., "The Empirical Implications of a Utility Tree."
Econometrica, 25 (April 1957), 269–280.

Suppes, Patrick, and Richard C. Atkinson, *Markov Learning
Models for Multiperson Interactions.* Stanford, Calif.: Stanford
University Press, 1960.

Telser, Lester G., "Advertising and Competition." *Journal of
Political Economy,* 72 (December 1964), 537–562.

Thurstone, L. L., *The Reliability and Validity of Tests*. Ann Arbor, Mich.: Edwards Brothers, 1937.

Tinbergen, J., *On the Theory of Economic Policy*. Amsterdam: North Holland Publishing, 1952.

Tosdal, Harry, *Principles of Personal Selling*. Chicago: Shaw, 1925.

Triandis, Harry C., *Attitude and Attitude Change*. New York: Wiley, 1971.

Tuck, M. and E. H. Nelson, "The Relationship Between Attitudes and Behavior." *Proceedings of the Esomar Annual Congress*, 1969.

Tukey, J. W., "The Future of Data Analysis." *Annals of Mathematical Statistics*, 33 (1962), 1–67.

Twedt, Dik Warren, "Consumer Psychology." *Annual Review of Psychology*, 16 (1965), 265–294. (a)

Twedt, Dik Warren, "How Can the Advertising Dollar Work Harder?" *Journal of Marketing*, 29 (April 1965), 60–62. (b)

Twyman, W. A., "The Structure of the Advertising Process." Unpublished report, Research Bureau Ltd., London, 1969.

Twyman, W. A., "The Pre-Testing of T.V. Commercials." Unpublished report, Research Bureau Ltd., London, 1970.

Velikovsky, Immanuel, *Worlds in Collision*. New York: Macmillan, 1950.

Velikovsky, Immanuel, *Earth in Upheaval*. Garden City, N.Y.: Doubleday, 1955.

Venkatesan, M., "Experimental Study of Consumer Behavior Conformity and Independence." *Journal of Marketing Research*, 3 (November 1966), 384–387.

Venkatesan, M., "Novelty Seeking." Working paper. Iowa City: University of Iowa, 1972.

Warr, P. B., "Proximity as a Determinant of Positive and Negative Sociometric Choice." *British Journal of Social and Clinical Psychology*, 4 (1965), 104–109.

Watkins, J. W. N., "Ideal Types and Historical Explanation." In Herbert Feigl and May Brodbeck (eds.), *Readings in the Philosophy of Science*. New York: Appleton-Century-Crofts, 1953, pp. 723–743.

Webb, E. J., et al., *Unobtrusive Measures: Non-reactive Research in the Social Sciences*. Skokie, Ill.: Rand McNally, 1966.

Weller, Robert H., "The Employment of Wives, Dominance, and Fertility." *Journal of Marriage and the Family*, 30 (1968), 437–442.

Wells, William D., "Children as Consumers." In Joseph W.

Newman (ed.), *On Knowing the Consumer.* New York: Wiley, 1966, pp. 138–145.

White, Irving S., "The Perception of Value in Products." In Joseph W. Newman (ed.), *On Knowing the Consumer.* New York: Wiley, 1966, pp. 90–106.

Whyte, William H., Jr., "The Web of Word of Mouth." *Fortune,* 50 (November 1954), 140 ff.

Wicker, A. W., "Attitudes Versus Actions: The Relationship of Verbal and Overt Behavioral Responses to Attitude Objects." *Journal of Social Issues,* 25 (1969), 41–78.

Wiener, Norbert, *Cybernetics.* Cambridge, Mass.: M.I.T. Press, 1948.

Wilkening, Eugene A., "Change in Farm Technology as Related to Familism, Family Decision Making, and Family Integration." *American Sociological Review,* 19 (February 1954), 29–37.

Wilkening, Eugene A., "Joint Decision-Making in Farm Families as a Function of Status and Role." *American Sociological Review,* 23 (April 1958), 187–192.

Wilkening, Eugene A., and Lakshmi K. Bharadwaj, "Dimensions of Aspirations, Work Roles, and Decision-Making of Farm Husbands and Wives in Wisconsin." *Journal of Marriage and the Family,* 29 (November 1967), 703–711.

Wold, Herman O. A., *Econometric Model Building.* Amsterdam: North Holland Publishing, 1964.

Wold, Herman O. A., and Lars Jureen, *Demand Analysis: A Study in Econometrics.* New York: Wiley, 1953.

Wolgast, Elizabeth, *Economic Decisions in the Family.* Ann Arbor: Survey Research Center, Institute for Social Research, University of Michigan, 1957.

Wolgast, Elizabeth, "Do Husbands or Wives Make the Purchasing Decisions?" *Journal of Marketing,* 23 (October 1958), 151–158.

Young, Michael, "Distribution of Income Within the Family." *British Journal of Sociology,* 3 (December 1952), 305–321.

Young, Michael, and Peter Willmott, *Family and Kinship in East London.* New York: Free Press, 1957.

Zaltman, Gerald, Christian Pinson, and Reinhard Angelmar, *Metatheory and Consumer Behavior Research.* New York: Holt, Rinehart & Winston, 1973.

Zimmerman, Carle C., *Family and Civilization.* New York: Harper & Row, 1947.

Zober, Martin, *Marketing Management.* New York: Wiley, 1964.

Index

Page numbers in italics indicate figures or tables.

74 75 76 7 6 5 4 3 2 1